Greg Meetham

THE END TIME

The Bible Study Textbook Series

NEW TESTAMENT

New Testament & History By W. Wartick & W. Fields Vol. I - The Intertestament Period and The Gospels	The Gospel of Matthew In Four Volumes By Harold Fowler	The Gospel of Mark By B. W. Johnson and Don DeWelt
The Gospel of Luke By T. R. Applebury	The Gospel of John By Paul T. Butler	Acts Made Actual By Don DeWelt
Romans Realized By Don DeWelt	Studies in Corinthians By T. R. Applebury	Guidance From Galatians By Don Earl Boatman
The Glorious Church (Ephesians) By Wilbur Fields	Philippians - Colossians Philemon By Wilbur Fields	Thinking Through Thessalonians By Wilbur Fields
Paul's Letters To Timothy & Titus By Don DeWelt	Helps From Hebrews By Don Earl Boatman	James & Jude By Don Fream
Letters From Peter By Bruce Oberst	Hereby We Know (I-II-III John) By Clinton Gill	The Seer, The Saviour, and The Saved (Revelation) By James Strauss

OLD TESTAMENT

O.T. & History By William Smith and Wilbur Fields	Genesis In Four Volumes By C. C. Crawford	Exploring Exodus By Wilbur Fields	Leviticus By Don DeWelt
Numbers By Brant Lee Doty	Deuteronomy By Bruce Oberst	Joshua - Judges Ruth By W. W. Winter	I & II Samuel By W. W. Winter
I & II Kings By James E. Smith	I & II Chronicles By Robert E. Black	Ezra, Nehemiah & Esther By Ruben Ratzlaff & Paul T. Butler	The Shattering of Silence (Job) By James Strauss
Psalms In Two Volumes By J. B. Rotherham	Proverbs By Donald Hunt		Ecclesiastes and Song of Solomon — By R. J. Kidwell and Don DeWelt
Isaiah In Three Volumes By Paul T. Butler	Jeremiah and Lamentations By James E. Smith		Ezekiel By James E. Smith
Daniel By Paul T. Butler	Hosea - Joel - Amos Obadiah - Jonah By Paul T. Butler		Micah - Nahum - Habakkuk Zephaniah - Haggai - Zechariah Malachi — By Clinton Gill

DOCTRINE

The Church In The Bible By Don DeWelt	The Eternal Spirit Two Volumes By C. C. Crawford	New Testament Evidences By Wallace Wartick	Survey Course In Christian Doctrine Two Bks. of Four Vols. By C. C. Crawford
New Testament History—Acts By Gareth Reese	Learning From Jesus By Seth Wilson		You Can Understand The Bible By Grayson H. Ensign

WHAT THE BIBLE SAYS SERIES

*From The Library of
Greg Cheatham*

WHAT THE BIBLE SAYS ABOUT
THE END TIME

By
Russell Boatman

College Press Publishing Company, Joplin, Missouri

Copyright © 1980
College Press Publishing Company

Printed and bound in the
United States of America
All Rights Reserved

Library of Congress Catalog Card Number: 79-56542
International Standard Book Number: 0-89900-075-4

Scripture quotations, unless otherwise noted, are from the American Standard Version, 1901. New York: Thomas Nelson and Sons.

Topical Index from *Topical Index and Digest of The Bible* edited by Harold E. Monser. Reprinted 1960 by Baker Book House and used by permission.

Dedication

This book is lovingly dedicated to my parents who taught me the ABC's of the spiritual life—A. An abiding adherence to "the faith once and for all delivered to the saints," B. Basic values, including a work ethic, stewardship and life style based on the Biblical revelation of God's will for man, and C. Commitment to Christian service where ever and in whatsoever way God's will should be sensed or made manifest.

Richard Andrew and Verba Melissa (Shaddy), "Andy and Verbie," Boatman began their migration from the Missouri Ozarks near the close of World War I. After a brief sojourn in southern Idaho they settled in the San Bernardino Valley of southern California. Through the instrumentality of Evangelist Clayton C. Root, and mother's prayers, Father was converted at the age of 36. Though I was but a lad of ten I remember the day vividly, and with reverence. His conversion was all that the Biblical word implies—a *turning point* that changed not only his life but the whole family. Only God knows how many more. Mother renewed her covenant with Christ and became a tower of strength in her husband's resolve to live for Christ.

Dad and Mom soon became modern counterparts of Aquila and Priscilla. Though denied the advantage of formal education beyond grade school years they soon became apt students of "the wisdom that is from above." The Scriptures were discussed in our evenings at home. Dad pressed upon me the importance of memorizing the Scriptures, and inculcated in his children a reverence for the authority of the Word.

Early in their Christian life my parents became deeply interested in Biblical prophecies concerning the end time, through the exciting lectures on Revelation by the inimitable

WHAT THE BIBLE SAYS ABOUT THE END TIME

Evangelist John W. Tyndal. It may well be said this book began in our family living room half a century ago. With profound and deep appreciation I hereby solemnly dedicate this book to my aging parents as they prepare for their next migration — to "the land that is fairer than day," graced by "the city which hath the foundations, whose builder and maker is God."

Table of Contents

Dedication v

Introduction 1

Chapter		Page
One	De-Escalating, Defining and Demythologizing Eschatology	7
	Eschatology Defined 8	
	Scope of the Subject 12	
	Pedigree of Millennialism 15	
Two	History of Millennialism in the Christian Era	23
Three	Outline of Millennial Theories	38
	General Theory 38	
	Simple Historical Premillennialism 40	
	Tribulational Premillennialism 42	
	Ultradispensationalism 45	
	Postmillennialism 48	
	Amillennialism 53	
Four	What the Bible Says About the Millennium: Revelation Twenty	61
	What John Said He Saw 75	
	Binding and Loosing of Satan 77	
	First and Second Resurrections 85	
	What About the Thousand Years? 89	
Five	The Kingdom of the Messiah	95
	The Church in Prophecy 103	
	Two Significant Visions 109	
Six	Signs of the Times	119
	History of Sign-seeing Soothsayers 124	
	Jesus' Olivet Discourse 134	

WHAT THE BIBLE SAYS ABOUT THE END TIME

Chapter		Page
Seven	The Appearing of the Antichrist and the Man of Sin	154
	John's Doctrine of the Antichrist 155	
	Paul's Doctrine of the Man of Sin 169	
Eight	The Rupture of the Doctrine of the Rapture	180
Nine	When He Cometh	202
Ten	Significant and Not So Significant End-time Topics	224
	Regathering of Israel (Zionism) 225	
	Belated Salvation of Israel 233	
	Fig Tree Figments 254	
	Agog over Gog and Magog 261	
Eleven	Concerning Death and Dying	266
Twelve	The Interim State of the Dead	291
	Nihilism (Annihilationism) 291	
	Innate Immortality Views Reviewed 296	
	Conditional Immortality Theory 321	
Appendix — The Big Lie		330
Appendix — The Nature of Man		351
Bibliography		373
Topical Index		379
Index of Scriptures		409
Index of Subjects		420

Introduction

WHAT THE BIBLE SAYS ABOUT THE END-TIME

What would it take to set forth what the Bible says about the end-time? Actually not much, in terms of time and space. The Bible does not have a great deal to say about it. Its purpose is to teach us how to live in order that we may face the future unafraid — able to say with the apostle Paul, "For me to live is Christ, and to die is gain." (Philippians 1:21) The focus of the Scripture is upon the life we now live in the flesh. Due attention to the will of God in this present world is the best way, indeed the only means, of being prepared for the world that is to come.

What would it take to set forth what people have been led to believe the Bible has to say about the end-time? Ah, that is another question. That would require volumes. One book would not suffice.

To know the difference between the two — what the Bible says and what the populace has been led to believe it says — and to prefer the one to the other, what an assignment that is. Is not "what the people want, the people should have" the first law in marketing? Indeed. But is it not written: "God forbid Yea, let God be found true and every man a liar . . . that thou mayest be justified in thy words and mightest prevail when thou comest into judgment" (Romans 3:4).

We suspect this book will prove disappointing to some who will be attracted by the title, simple and non-sensational though the title be. It will lack many things some expect to find discussed under the title, *What the Bible Says About the End-Time*.

On every hand there are those who would have us believe almost every seemingly significant happening of these times is the fulfillment of some specific end-time prophecy. Over and over we are told that from one fourth to one half of the Bible is prophecy. It could be. In a sense it all is.

The words "prophecy" and "prophet" are derived from the Greek preposition "pro" (for) and the verb "phe-té-o" (to speak). Hence to prophesy is to speak for someone, in his behalf. You may recall that when Moses sought to beg off when God called him to speak for Him, God suggested that Moses could put into Aaron's mouth the words Jehovah would put in Moses' mouth, Thus "Aaron thy brother shall be thy prophet." (See context of Exodus 7:1.) As it turned out, this was not necessary.

A prophet is a spokesman, a forth-teller, not necessarily a foreteller. An anecdote of early American history comes to mind. Miles Standish loved dearly Priscilla Alden but got tongue-tied when he tried to tell her so. Therefore he asked his friend John Smith to propose to her for him. Her answer was, "Why don't you speak for yourself, John?" Thus ended Smith's role as the prophet of Miles Standish. The story recalls the case of the soldier boy who wrote his girl friend every day while he was in his country's service. She married the postman.

Since it is written, "no prophecy of Scripture is of private interpretation. For no prophecy ever came by the will of man, but men spake for God, being moved by the Holy Spirit" (II Peter 1:20, 21), all the Bible is prophecy, but it is not all predictive prophecy. The greater part of the books of the Old Testament which we refer to as the books of History the Jews called "the Early Prophets." And the later books which we call the books of Prophecy were for the most part commentaries on the times in which they lived, and likewise are books of history. But all the divisions of Old

INTRODUCTION

Testament literature contain predictive prophecy: the Law, the books of History, the books of Poetry and the ones we call Prophecy. But the portion devoted to predictive prophecy does not measure up to the ratio cited by prophecy "experts."

So too with the New Testament. The prophecies written by men who "spake from God, being moved by the Holy Spirit" seldom compare in either volume or detail with the pronouncements which come "by the will of man." History repeats itself. Ezekiel pronounced a woe upon "the foolish prophets" of his day who, said he, "follow their own spirits, and have seen nothing" (Ezek. 13:2, 3).

Before laying this book aside, if you fail to find some things you expected, ask yourself some questions. Does the Bible actually say what some have said that it does? Is the Bible as explicit about signs and events of the end-time as some would have us believe? Is the Bible really so interlaced with eschatalogical revelation as to provide answers to all our curious questions? In all the days of our Lord's sojourn among men, how much did He see fit to tell His disciples about what it is like to die? and what happens then? and what heaven is like? Where was He when His body was in the sepulchre? And what did He do? How explicit was He about the time of His return and the succession of events which would immediately precede and follow? Did He voice any warnings with regard to some who would profess to have some secret information about His coming?

Would you believe it, most of the end-time events one hears about are subjects about which the Bible says very little (in some cases next to nothing). Consider a few examples.

First, the rapture. Are you aware that the word (as such)

WHAT THE BIBLE SAYS ABOUT THE END TIME

is not in our Bible, much less the greater part of what is currently taught on the subject? Only one passage of Scripture describes an event which could be properly called the rapture of the saints (I Thessalonians 4:13-17). But the familiar rapture rhetoric is almost wholly lacking.

Secondly, the battle of Armageddon. Are you aware this term is not found in the Bible? Again there is but one passage of Scripture from which such an expression may be adduced (Revelation 16:13-16). But the details of the battle so widely touted are not included.

Thirdly, the millennium. Again the question is the same and the facts as well. Only one passage of Scripture provides any basis for the term (Revelation 20:1-10). But the widely proclaimed succession of events is scarcely to be found there.

Such considerations take me back a half century or so. As a teen age boy I was greatly impressed by an evangelist whose lectures on Revelation drew capacity crowds. He was reputed to know the Bible by memory. Such Scriptures as he had occasion to refer to he certainly knew well enough to give credence to the report. Vividly do we recall how he used the apocalyptic Scriptures to show that all the wonders of the day, automobiles, airplanes, submarines, electricity, telephones, etc. were seen aforetime by the Biblical prophets, and described in their use, particularly in the warfare of the end-time predicted in Revelation.

Years passed and the teen age boy had become a preacher. My preaching did not pack the house, particularly on Sunday night. What could I do about it? I could preach a series of sermons on the book of Revelation. This intent was announced, and to spark interest a preview was given of the wonders that would be disclosed.

INTRODUCTION

The experience which ensued was traumatic. I couldn't find all those clear depictions of wonders and happenings! I frantically besought my father to send posthaste the four volume set, *Revelation Revealed* authored by the aforementioned evangelist. The books arrived but still the goodies could not be found. The claims were there in a muted form, but the presence of the authority figure, his charismatic smile, the aura of being in the know, these were required to bring to light the things he had found "uncovered" by the book of Revelation.

From the experience three lessons were learned which are worth citing. They bear on the text of that which is to follow.

Lesson One. Do the research first. Advertise only what one is definitely able to deliver and substantiate.

Lesson Two. While a childlike faith has somewhat to commend it, still it is "more noble" to examine the Scriptures daily to see whether the things we are taught are so.

Lesson Three. It is easier to persuade an audience in public address than through the printed page. The latter setting allows the recipient time to think things through, check them out, and consult with others. Unfortunately, even the printed page can be persuasive, however much the truth is stretched or voided, if one remembers the first law of marketing, "what the people want, the people should get." Many live by that law, and live high. But it is not the law of God.

The foregoing observations dictate the format of this book. Were we simply to set forth what the Bible says about the end-time, this book would end much sooner than we anticipate that it will. But one thing the Bible says (or to be more precise, it is said of the Bible and recorded therein) is:

WHAT THE BIBLE SAYS ABOUT THE END TIME

"Every Scripture inspired of God is profitable for teaching, for reproof, for correction and for instruction which is in righteousness" (II Timothy 3:16).

In the writing of this book that text will be constantly kept in mind, and reflected in what is written. Readers may at times become a bit impatient that so much time, especially in the opening chapters, is spent clearing the air — in "correction" and at times in "reproof." The truth of the Scripture is all important, but sometimes one has to unswath it of the wrappings of the words of men before it can be seen and set free to complete us for every good work.

Chapter One

DE-ESCALATING, DEFINING AND DEMYTHOLOGIZING ESCHATOLOGY

In generation after generation a time of crisis or the portent of impending peril has triggered the doomsday syndrome. This is unfortunate, if for no other reason than that eschatology, the doctrine of the end time, has come to be equated with a general worsening of affairs—both human and divine. Consequently interests in the subject tend to wane in times of social and spiritual progress. The hope or expectation of Christ's return is put on lay-by until the next decline in morals or threat of world carnage seems to be looming on the horizon. Christ is thereby come to be regarded as a kind of Superman who normally and presently exists as a relatively quiescent Clark Kent type of person. His alter ego will be evoked only by a super world crisis.

One is caused to wonder how many crises can be heralded as the onset of the apocalyptical "battle of Armageddon," the beginning of "the great tribulation," the sign of "the Antichrist," etc. before the "wolf, wolf" cry of the promoters of end-time prophecy shall cease to gain attention.

Is the study of the consummation of the present order a subject of no relevance except as it relates to doomsday speculation? Is there no eschatology of victory in Christ? Or is such victory as we are given Scriptural warrant to hope for to be realized only after the direst of peril and the sorest of tribulation has come once again, "as in the days of Noah," upon the earth in cataclysmic proportions? Unless current eschatalogical speculations can be de-escalated and the subject viewed in Biblical perspective, "things are going to get a lot worse before they can get any better" insofar as our understanding of this important subject is concerned. We will have more to say about this later, particularly as we examine the pedigree and mythological basis of the greater part of current millennial hypotheses.

In calling for a de-escalation and defusing of eschatalogical study we have no intention of playing down the relevancy of the subject to Biblical prophecy, and to our generation, else this book would never have been attempted. We simply want to call attention to the obvious fact that clear thinking is quite impossible in an atmosphere of emotionalism and contrived panic.

The warnings of the Scriptures which, incidentally, have been relevant in every generation are of themselves sufficiently ominous and solemn to stand on their own merit. And the sober fact that death is only a heart beat removed from any one of us at any time ought to be sufficient to draw our attention to the solemn dictum of Hebrews 9:27, to wit: "It is appointed unto men once to die, and after this cometh the judgment."

ESCHATOLOGY DEFINED

The word "eschatology" is not found in the Scriptures. Nonetheless eschatology is a legitimate field of Biblical study. When it is stripped of various and sundry sensational speculations the topics normally included under the caption are definitely included in the scope of Biblical prophecy.

Eschatology is a compound word, comprised of two

DE-ESCALATING, DEFINING, DEMYTHOLOGIZING ESCHATOLOGY

somewhat familiar Greek words—*eschatos* and *logos*. *Logos*, the more familiar of the two, appears in the Greek text of the New Testament over three hundred times.[1] It is most commonly translated *word* or *saying*. In technical usage, in combination form, in such words as archeology, biology, Christology, demonology, eschatology, etc., *logos* signifies "the doctrine of" or "the study of" that area of knowledge or inquiry designated by the noun to which it is suffixed.

Eschatos is a term of somewhat general application, but nonetheless a word of no uncertain meaning. It is used fifty-four (54) times in the Greek text of the New Testament.[2]

1. It is used with reference to place four times.
    a. Lk. 14:9, 10 speak of "the *lowest* place."
    b. Acts 1:8, 13:47 speak of "the *uttermost* parts of the earth."
2. It is used with reference to rank twenty times. For example:
    a. Mt. 19:30 warns that "many shall be *last* that are first," cp. Mk. 9:35.
    b. Jn. 8:9 speaks of the "eldest even unto the *last*."
3. It is used with reference to time thirty times.
    a. Of time, as it relates to persons. For example:
        1) Mt. 12:45, "the *last* state of that man becometh worse than the first," cp. II Peter 2:20.
        2) I Cor. 15:8, "*last* of all as to a child untimely born he appeared unto me also."
        3) I Cor. 15:26, "the *last* enemy that shall be abolished is death."

---

1. See the Index-Lexicon of *Young's Analytical Concordance of the Bible* (hereafter referred to as YAC), p. 79.
2. YAC, Index-Lexicon, p. 70.

b. Of time, as it relates to things. For example:
1) Mt. 5:26, "the *last* farthing."
2) Mt. 27:64, "the *last* error shall be worse than the first."
3) I Cor. 15:22, "at the *last* trump."
4) Jn. 6:39, 40, 44, 54; 7:37; 11:24; 12:48; Acts 2:17; II Tim. 3:1; Heb. 1, 2; Jas. 5:3; I Pet. 1:5; II Pet. 3:3; I Jn. 2:18; Jude 18, "the *last* day(s), time, hour, etc."

Eschatology therefore is defined as 1) the study of last things, or 2) the doctrine of the end-time, or more properly the doctrine and study of both the last things and the end-time.

ESCHATOLOGY VS. TELEOLOGY

The Greek text of the New Testament contains another somewhat relevant word to which some attention needs to be called — *teleios* (te-lei-os). From this word comes such familiar terms as telescope, telegraph, telephone and television. In its two principal forms, nominative and verbal, the term appears well over one hundred times in the Greek text of the New Testament. It is commonly translated "perfect" (in the sense of maturation, maturity). It is also rendered "finish, fulfill, accomplish, complete, make an end of," etc.

The study of eschatology might properly have been called teleology except for the fact that the latter term has come to signify the study of design, or purpose; that is, the *end* towards which a process is designed, or the purpose an inherent factor is designed to serve. The term,

DE-ESCALATING, DEFINING, DEMYTHOLOGIZING ESCHATOLOGY

teleology, therefore has long since been taken over by philosophers, and more recently by scientists who attribute to nature inherent processes (evolutionary in nature, generally) designed to lead to a certain end result. Thus teleology is ordinarily stripped of its relevance to the causative and purposive action of God, and is used of that study of nature which seeks to find in the natural order of things an explanation of observed phenomena.

A parallel is to be found in the terms "astrology" and "astronomy." Centuries before the Christian era, Babylonian star-gazers developed a system of "star study" overlaid with mythology and polytheism. Thus scientists, in quest of a name for their naturalistic study of the heavens (as opposed to a supernatural, theistic viewpoint) found the term "astrology" bearing a connotation which was not to their liking. They coined therefore the term "astronomy," (the law of the stars) to designate their study of the universe.

Teleology likewise has come to be associated with a thought system foreign to the Scriptures. Thus eschatology has been chosen by Biblically oriented scholars to designate the study of the end-time, the doctrine of the last things.

Actually, eschatology is a term which may very well be applied much more broadly. It applies in a sense to the whole of the Christian era as well as to the consummation of the ages and the order that shall supersede the present cosmos. The term "the latter days" or "the last days" (depending on the translation one prefers) is used in both Testaments to designate the whole Christian dispensation, as distinguished from "the former days" — the days preceding the coming of Christ and His church. Cp. Joel 2:28 ff. and Acts 2:16, 17 ff., Jer. 31:31 ff. and Heb. 8:8 ff. Note also the implications of such passages as Acts 3:24, Heb. 1:1, 2, and other pertinent references.

WHAT THE BIBLE SAYS ABOUT THE END TIME

Currently, eschatology is ordinarily applied only to the end-time of the present dispensation. Since we are concerned about what the Bible has to say concerning "the last days" we will not use the term so restrictively.

THE SCOPE OF THE SUBJECT

The scope of the subject is twofold. Included, necessarily, is the study of:

1. The end(?) of you (and of mankind generally), as such an inquiry relates to the end of life we "now live in the flesh" (Gal. 2:20), and the nature of that state (or states) into which both the redeemed and the unredeemed enter in consequence of physical death.

2. The end(?) of the universe, that is, of the present cosmic order (including the fate of the human race and of Satan and his angels). What will supersede the end of the present cosmic and spiritual order?

A vast range of sub-topics, some theoretic, speculative, and many subjects directly dealt with in the Holy Scriptures, belong to the area of inquiry commonly called eschatology.

Unless the second coming of Christ is very near (which indeed it may be), for most of us our personal involvement in events related to the end-time will begin with the experience of physical death. Part One of this study might have been directed therefore to a study of the Biblical revelation concerning death and its aftermath — both immediate and ultimate. But in view of the fact the Scriptures teach a resurrection of both the just and the unjust, and the redeemed are promised a future life with God beyond the

DE-ESCALATING, DEFINING, DEMYTHOLGIZING ESCHATOLOGY

present order, chapters 11 and 12 will touch upon the state of the dead twixt death and the resurrection. The Biblical doctrine of the ultimate state of the saved and lost will be dealt with in a later publication projected for this series.

DEMYTHOLOGIZING ESCHATOLOGY

Deeply imbedded in the sub-conscious mind of Bible believers, is a world-view which is now surfacing. We have reference to a chronological system developed by Bishop Usher which was superimposed upon the King James Version of the Bible, and continues to be included in many reference editions thereof.

Archbishop James Usher published in 1650-54 his most celebrated work, *Anneles Viteris et Novi Testamenti*. Therein he fixed the date of creation precisely 4000 years before the birth of Christ. The adoption of the Gregorian calendar soon afterwards necessitated a four year shift of the two most important dates—the birth of Christ, and hence of the creation. This moved the latter back to 4004 B.C. and the birth of Christ to 4 B.C., giving rise to the incongruity of the birth of Christ being dated four years "before Christ."

Bishop Lightfoot (1828-91), following slavishly Usher's computations, pinpointed the creation week October 18-24, 4004 B.C. (of the Gregorian calendar) and the creation of Adam, Friday, October 23, 9:00 A.M., 45th meridian time. Such implausible dogmatism prompted one, E. T. Brewster, to remark, wryly: "closer than this, as a cautious scholar, the vice chancellor of Cambridge University did not venture to commit himself."

What has this to do with demythologizing eschatalogy?

13

WHAT THE BIBLE SAYS ABOUT THE END TIME

If Usher's chronology has any credibility, we crossed the threshold (as of 1971) of the fourth and final quarter of the twentieth century A.D., and we are fast approaching the end of the world's third bi-millennium — the end of six thousand years of human history. This of itself would not be so significant were it not for the fact that Usher's chronology in turn was strongly influenced by a millennial world-view which hypothesized the end of the present order and the ushering in of a seventh-day world-sabbath utopian millennium at the close of the present century (actually, at the end of 1996 in the light of the Gregorian revision). Of this we will have more to say later.

In view of these things we are destined in the years ahead to witness a spate of eschatological speculations rivaling and perhaps surpassing anything the world has known since the fall of Jerusalem, AD 70. Already end-time speculations have upstaged the so-called "charismatic revival" which has enjoyed the spot-light in Christendom since the middle of the present century. What we are witnessing may be only the tip of the iceberg. Sheer economics, to say nothing of human vanity, would dictate this. Charlatans and sensationalists are hardly going to sit idly by and watch such men as Hal Lindsay, Salem Kirban and their like grow rich and famous catering to a mind-set probably more disposed to believe the end of the age is at hand than any generation living since the fall of Jerusalem some 1900 years ago.

As a people, our brethren have generally been "johnny-come-latelies" in the realm of religious faddism. This is to our credit. But on the other hand we have all too often waited until perverted emphases have snowballed, making inroads into our own constituency, before rising to the challenge. Thus we have been cast in the role of killjoys, or at best as brakemen, or firemen. If we are not to be viewed as spoil-sports in the burgeoning eschatological binge which is upon us we need to enunciate positively, loudly and clearly some basic exegetical and hermeneutical principles on which a sane and Scriptural view of the end-time can be constructed.

Unfortunately the doctrine of the end-time has become so embellished and perverted by millennial hypotheses as to virtually obscure the Biblical revelation. An examination of the origin of popular millennial hypotheses is long overdue.

THE PEDIGREE OF MILLENNIALISM

The roots of millennialism extend well into antiquity, antedating the Christian era by at least three thousand years. The oldest known form, possibly the paternity thereof, is found in the zodiac world-view of the primitive astrologers of the ancient Near East. The zodiac was supposed to represent the zone of the heavens in which lie the paths of the sun, moon and principal stars. Each day Marduk, the sun God, the chief deity of the Babylonians, was believed to race across "the Dominion of the Zodiac" in his golden chariot. At night, his dazzling brilliance having now passed by, the astrologers were able to make out the dim outline of the symbols of the twelve supporting deities in their pantheon of gods.

As early as 3000 B.C. various configurations of the fixed stars were grouped into constellations supposedly conforming to the outline of certain animals or objects. The Babylonians fixed their number at twelve to conform to

WHAT THE BIBLE SAYS ABOUT THE END TIME

the supporting cast in their house of gods. If you have wondered how the ancient astrologers could see in the stellar configurations a lion, a bear, a hunter, the scales of the balance, etc., you have your introduction to the high degree of imagination that has been the hallmark of millennial hypothesis from its inception until now.

The original application of astrology to a millennial worldview took this form: The twelve divisions of the zodiac were assigned time values of one thousand years. (See Fig. 1.)

Fig. 1						THE DOMINION OF THE ZODIAC					
Formation of the World						Duration of Mankind					
1	2	3	4	5	6	1	2	3	4	5	6
6000 Years						6000 Years					

The twelve thousand year time span thusly envisioned was called *The Dominion of the Zodiac.* The dominion was divided into two six thousand year eras. The first era was allotted to the formation of the world and the latter to the duration of mankind.

With the rise of the Persian empire, which supplanted Babylonia, a series of modifications ensued. These were probably suited to the Persian emphasis upon the weekly cycle.

An important step toward modern millennial theory is represented by *The Persian Magi Modification.* (See Fig. 2.)

Fig. 2						THE PERSIAN MAGI MODIFICATION
This Present World						Happiness — Age to Come
1	2	3	4	5	6	7th unit (Indefinite)

16

DE-ESCALATING, DEFINING, DEMYTHOLOGIZING ESCHATOLOGY

The magi were apparently quite indifferent toward the time involved in the formation of the world. Their concern focused on the future. To the six one-thousand year units representing the duration of this present world they added a seventh unit of indefinite duration, a time of happiness in an age to come. Thus we have the beginning of the popular concept of an utopian age at the end of the present world order.

More relevant still is the revision which bears the title, *The Rule of Hushedar Mah*. See Fig. 3. This important

Fig. 3.						THE RULE OF HUSHEDAR MAH	
Conflict: Good Vs. Evil						C R I S I S	1000 Years of Peace
1	2	3	4	5	6		7th Day World Sabbath
This Present World							The Age to Come

revision contains several ingredients of popular millennial theory. For example, the scheme envisions a messianic coup ushering in a thousand year reign of peace. The coup is precipitated by a crisis of universal proportions. As in the Persian Magi Modification the present order is again considered to overshadow any consideration of the past. The focus is on the future state. The six one-thousand year units assigned to this present world are described as a time of conflict between good and evil. This is to climax in a world crisis ending in the appearance of one, Hushedar Mah, who will inaugurate a world-sabbath — a millennium of messianic peace.

The foregoing scheme forms the basic outline of popular millennial systems of Biblical chronology and eschatology. But the prophets thereof are pagan star gazers. This should disturb us. Do the surmisings of pagan astrologers provide a much better perspective for understanding the end-time than do the Holy Scriptures? Should mythology shape our views of the consummation of the ages? No wonder astrology is again having a heyday.

Some years ago we engaged in a public forum in which the significance of the one thousand years spoken of in Revelation chapter twenty was the topic of dialogue. The foregoing data was presented in somewhat greater detail. My respondent, an able champion of pre-millennialism, acknowledged he was familiar with the information presented but countered that this could have been the working of Divine providence to facilitate the understanding and acceptance of a doctrine to be later revealed in the Scriptures. In support of that rationale he called attention to the fact that the concept of a virgin born deity is found in pagan mythology antedating the Christian era. That, he suggested, may have providentially predisposed the Roman world to accept the miracle of the virgin birth of Jesus Christ.

There is a vast vital difference between the absurdities of mythology and the birth narratives of Matthew and Luke. Consider the case of Mithra. Mithra was a god whom the Romans borrowed from the Persians. His Persian name was Ahura Mazdas — the sun God, the god of light. Now the birth of Mithra (according to mythology) was on this wise: His mother, while eating a pomegranate, inadvertently dropped one of the seed kernels into the cleft of her bosom. Whereupon she conceived and brought forth a son, the god of light. There is but little similarity between the two "virgin birth" accounts. The father of Mithra would have to be a pomegranate tree. And the site and manner of conception is ridiculous beyond degree. But modern millennial theories parallel at almost every salient point the millennial

DE-ESCALATING, DEFINING, DEMYTHOLOGIZING ESCHATOLOGY

world-view of pagan mythology. Proponents thereof are hard pressed to find in the Scriptures aught to support their millennial schemes comparable to the specifics detailed by Matthew and Luke in their accounts of the birth of Jesus.

Others who are aware of the pagan pedigree of the utopian millennium concept have countered that if a doctrine is to be questioned because of some affinity to pagan mythology, one would have to reject the Genesis account of the Noachial flood and even the Biblical account of the giving of the Law of Moses. Our response is that we do not reject a doctrine (in the context of this discussion, the utopian millennial dogma) because it has some affinity to pagan mythology. We reject it because it has no solid basis in the Scriptures. Of that we shall have more to say in our discussion of the twentieth chapter of the book of Revelation.

Millennialism was introduced into rabbinical Jewish theology during the inter-testamental period. The voices of the prophets of Jehovah were stilled in the land for some four hundred years. Impatient men looked elsewhere for a word from heaven. Astrologers were at hand. In *The Tradition of the House of Elias* (See Fig. 4.) we find a world-view that makes our present date, according to the Usher chronology, one of unusual interest to proponents of millennial theories.

Fig. 4 THE TRADITION OF THE HOUSE OF ELIAS					
This Present World					The Renewed World
Void of Law		Under the Law		Under Messiah	7th "Day" World Sabbath
1	2	3	4	5	6	7th Unit
2000		2000		2000	1000 Years

WHAT THE BIBLE SAYS ABOUT THE END TIME

In this scheme the present world order is divided into three "bi-millenniums" — two thousand years void of the law, two thousand years under the law, and two thousand years under the Messiah — followed by a seventh-day world-sabbath millennium. The latter time segment is now conceived to be the long awaited "restoration of the kingdom of Israel" at the *second* coming of Christ. And the time is at hand! It is less than a score years removed, according to the Gregorian revision of the Usher chronology. The fact is the time has already come according to the Watchtower revision of said calendar. But we will discuss that later. The year 1975 did not culminate as the Jehovah's Witnesses had predicted.

The foregoing concept represents a wedding of pagan mythology with the creation-week account of Genesis. It is the prototype of the age-day creation-week hypothesis which underlies much of the sub-conscious thinking of Bible readers generally, and many fundamentalist teachers in particular. The non-canonical *Epistle of Barnabas* introduced the concept into Christian theology. Briefly stated, it is conjectured that the six "days" of creation were actually periods of one thousand years, and are prophetic of a six thousand year time span for this present world order, and a thousand year world-sabbath.

This takes us back to *the Dominion of the Zodiac* scheme of the Babylonians (Fig. 1) and the Persian *Rule of Hushedar Mah* revision (Fig. 3). The Babylonian captivity and the Persian takeover of the Jewish exiles obviously had their effect upon Jewish thinking. It is worthy of note, however, that we read nothing of this in the canonical books of the post-exilic period, nor in the New Testament.

DE-ESCALATING, DEFINING, DEMYTHOLOGIZING ESCHATOLOGY

In a work published only in German, *Geschichte des Juedischen Volkes im Zeitakter Jesu Christi, II.*, Emil Scherer traces the development of millennial thought in Judaism in both the pre-Christian and early Christian eras. D. H. Kromminga in *The Millennium in the Church*, p. 25. condenses Scherer's systematic representation of Jewish messianic dogma in the manner suggested by the noncanonical *Apocalypse of Baruch* and the *Fourth Book of Esdras*. The following distinct teachings are cited.

1. A last period of tribulation and confusion.
2. The appearance of Elijah as a forerunner of the Messiah.
3. The appearance of the Messiah for the overthrow of hostile powers.
4. A final attack made by those powers upon the Messiah, at His appearance.
5. The destruction of those powers in a mighty Divine judgment.
6. The restoration of Jerusalem after the manner of the apocalyptical predictions of Ezek. chs. 40-48, and other Old Testament predictions.
7. The return of the dispersed Israelites.
8. The kingdom in glory, with Palestine as its center, reaching out over the whole world. In that kingdom the former generations of Israel will share via a resurrection.
9. The renewal of the world.
10. A general resurrection and final judgment.

It is noteworthy that many of the features of the foregoing scheme have been carried over into current extra-biblical eschatology. Modern interpreters simply assume that although things did not go as prophesied they will do so eventually. The Messiah will come again, this time in heavenly power and glory, flanked with angels, to complete the task He failed to accomplish at the first try. Except for some accommodation to include the New Testament saints in "the first resurrection" the eschatological outline of inter-testamental, non-canonical Judaism differs little from the expectations and schemes of current millennial writers.

The imposition of the Usher chronology upon the text of the Scriptures throughout the greater part of the past three hundred years has subtly predisposed Bible readers to a ready acceptance of millennialism. Thus the study of the end-time is generally so overlaid with millennial predicates that the Biblical revelation is interpreted in the light of millennial theory rather than millennial theories being interpreted in the light of the Scriptures.

A world-view conceived and developed in strangely familiar detail by pre-Christian era astrologers and non-canonical Jewish literature provides the framework into which the Biblical doctrine of the second coming of Christ, His kingdom and the consummation of the ages is, unfortunately, most frequently fitted.

Chapter Two

HISTORY OF MILLENNIALISM IN THE CHRISTIAN ERA

For the uninitiated, the term "millennial" is derived from an anglicized Latin word, "millennium." Millennium is made up of the Latin word for thousand (*mille*) and the Latin for year (*annus*). The term "millennial" means simply, "pertaining to a thousand years." Millennialism refers to a doctrine pertaining to a thousand years. A millennialist is one who accepts or teaches a doctrine pertaining to a thousand years. The terms curently are used principally in the context of eschatology. Millenarian is another form of reference to a millennialist.

Historically, millennialism has polarized around two rival systems, pre- and post-millennialism. The two systems of interpretation receive their names from the supposed relationship of Christ's second coming to an assumed one thousand year golden age, postulated at the end-time.

If the second coming of Christ is reckoned as an event that shall occur *prior* to the millennium that view is called premillennialism. If His coming is reckoned as *posterior* to the millennium, that view is called postmillennialism. In the premillennial systems Christ's coming is supposed to usher in the millennium. In the postmillennial system His coming is thought to climax the millennium.

In the premillennial systems Christ is generally believed to have failed to establish His kingdom at His first coming, due to the rejection of the Jews. His return therefore is to complete the task He failed to accomplish at His first coming. His return engagement will be augmented by angelic hosts who will assure the success of the kingdom venture on the second try.

WHAT THE BIBLE SAYS ABOUT THE END TIME

In the postmillennial system Christ's kingdom is viewed as a spiritual kingdom of which the church is the visible manifestation. In this system His coming is not to set up a kingdom but to receive His kingdom subjects. His coming will consummate this present world.

Lately a growing array of Bible scholars have converged on an escape route from the horns of the traditional millennial dilemma. Finding both pre- and post-millennial systems preposterous a fresh approach to end-time study has provided a viable alternative. The key that has been found is in the rejection of one of the few points that pre- and post-millennialism share in common — the non-biblical dogma of a literal one thousand year utopian era (millennium) at the end of the present world order. The demythologizing of millennialism has long been overdue.

The alternate to pre- and post-millennialism is commonly called a-millennialism. In a sense the term is a misnomer. Amillennialists do not teach that the Bible provides no basis for a millennial view of any kind, else Revelation, chapter twenty, would have to be ignored. To the contrary amillennialists (more aptly called "church-age millennialists") devote much attention to the exegesis of that key chapter of Scripture. What amillennialists reject is the dogma of a literal one thousand calendar year utopian era. It is *millennialism,* in its two traditional forms, which they negate, and for which negation they are saddled with the misnomer, amillennialists. Our use of the term in this study will be in the context just mentioned.

Amillennialism is somewhat of a mediating position. The view shares with postmillennialism the persuasion that the church is the visible manifestation of Christ's kingdom on earth. It differs with postmillennialism chiefly in two particulars. The "thousand years" mentioned five times in

HISTORY OF MILLENNIALISM IN THE CHRISTIAN ERA

Revelation, chapter twenty, is viewed as a symbolic number embracing the whole church age, not a number to be taken literally any more than anything else described in the chapter is to be taken literally. The second main difference is the rejection of the utopian age dogma. It is no more believed that the wheat will choke out the tares, insomuch as there shall virtually be no tares in the world for a thousand years, than it is to be believed that the tares shall virtually choke out the wheat. According to Jesus' parable of the tares "both grew together until the harvest" (Mt. 13:30). Incidentally the angels are to do the harvesting, the harvest time is the end of the world, and it is the tares that are taken first. (See vs. 30, 39-42.)

Amillennialism shares with premillennialism the hope and expectancy that Christ may come in our lifetime, and even that He may come soon. The fact is amillennialists have an even more "lively hope" in this regard. They are not caught up in fanciful identifications of apocalyptic sayings with current events and anticipated political coalitions which must first come to pass before Christ can come again. Thus the proverbial "carrot on the stick" syndrome which characterizes premillennial expectations rarely infects amillennialists. The second coming of Christ is not therefore ever "just around the corner," then the next corner, and then the next, and the next, etc., etc. ad infinitum.

A personal example of the foregoing may be cited appropriately at this point. The writer was brought up, and once caught up, in the post millennial tradition. Later study convinced me that the position was seriously flawed. If for no other reason, it was defective in that one so minded could hardly expect Christ's return in our lifetime if the church must first effectively evangelize the world and enjoy a millennium of dominion over the forces of evil. Yet the New Testament exhorts us to be looking for and anxiously desiring His coming. Since the only known alternative was premillennialism an open-minded study of that option seemed in order, with the hope that one of the varieties of premillennial interpretation might prove acceptable. Simple historical premillennialism, of which further mention and evaluation will be made later, came the closest to being found compatible with the Scriptures. But the offspring it has spawned through the centuries betrays the fact that the system is flawed genetically.

Meanwhile another student of the Word, drilled and dedicated in premillennialism, found his searching of the Scriptures moving him in the opposite direction — away from premillennialism and towards postmillennialism. But the latter he too found flawed. The two of us came to be associated for more than a decade in the administration and classroom responsibilities of St. Louis Christian College. In the assignment of course offerings it was his lot to teach the book of Revelation. It was my lot to teach a course in eschatology. At times outside engagements interfered with our classroom schedule. On occasion we filled in for one another. Though we had not "compared notes" the students did. They found our views compatible.

In our sojourning through the melange and morass of millennialism, coming from opposite positions, and each surveying the encampment the other had long occupied, we met and found common ground in the position commonly called amillennialism.

One swallow of course does not make a summer. There are those who may counter the foregoing experience with their own testimony. We recall the case of a school mate, a

HISTORY OF MILLENNIALISM IN THE CHRISTIAN ERA

strong contender for the postmillennial position. Upon graduation he entered the general evangelistic field. Some time later his sermons were definitely oriented to the premillennial system in vogue at the time. Mussolini, and then Hitler, and the impending onset of World War II provided the grist for the doomsday syndrome.

As a close acquaintance and a concerned Christian I interrogated him as to the reason for the change. "What insight have you gained from the Scriptures," he was asked, "that you should now espouse a doctrine you once opposed?" He was evasive. Upon further prodding he confided that he had not actually changed his mind, only his methods. He explained one can convert more people by preaching premillennialism. Reasoning that conversion is the name of the game in evangelism, he had concluded that the end justifies the means.

The evangelist was half right. One can indeed "convert" (or at least appear to convert) more people through premillennial scare tactics. The Jehovah's Witnesses bear witness to that. Conversions to the Watchtower Society had plateaued at slightly over 60,000 annually at the midcentury mark. In 1966 the number of baptisms dwindled to 59,000. Whereupon the astute chronologers of the Watchtower hierarcy came up with a computation fixing 1975 as the end of the world. The next year (1967), following the *Awake* announcement, baptisms jumped to 75,000 and in 1974, with "the end of the world just around the corner," the number soared to nearly 300,000.

Obviously scare tactics work. With "the word of prophecy (Watchtower predictions in this case) made the more sure" by the exercise of the dictum that any lie can be made to appear to be the truth if repeated often enough, the Jehovah's

Witnesses regained the dubious honor of being one of the fastest growing cults of our time.

Some one once quipped, "the coat and pants do all the work but the vest gets all the gravy." The atoning death of Christ on Calvary and the preaching of the Word of the Cross are the power of God unto salvation but the promoters of fear and fantasy get the drippings, or should one say, "the dippings." The Christ of Gospel history is being eclipsed by the Christ of futuristic fancy. The popular mind, nourished by the news media on sensationalism and violence, is geared to excitement and suspense. The purveyors of apocalyptic apprehension are therefore having a hey day. The more bizarre the interpretations the greater their popular appeal. Whereunto will it grow?

The situation will scarcely improve. The impending approach of the date 2000 A.D., with minor calendar revisions forward and backwards, will be played for all it is supposed to be worth. The Watchtower chronologists revised the date of creation back to 4025 B.C. to arrive at the year 1975 A.D. as the end of the present world and the ushering in of the (fabled) millennium. Now that the end of the world (first announced for 1914 by the predecessors of the Watchtower empire) has been postponed again, watch for the Watchtower brain trust to come up with some towering explanation to cover their latest boo-boo. Fortunately for them they are living in the dispensation of grace, rather than the Law of Moses, else they would be stoned as false prophets (see Deut. 13:1-5).

CONCERNING MILLENNIAL CONCEPTS

We find ourselves somewhat impatient at this point. Rather than extending an analysis and history of millennial theory, we would be pleased to get on with the subject matter suggested by the title of this text — *What the Bible Says About the End-Time*. But millennialism, particularly premillennialism, has for so long heavily overlaid the study of the end-time that the Biblical doctrine has been all but obscured. It is therefore imperative that the origin, nature and history of millennialism be understood in order that the study of the end-time can be stripped of the shrouds of fanciful speculations.

In Chapter One we took occasion to expose the pagan origin of millennialism and its infusion into Jewish eschatology in the inter-testamental period. The latter was inevitable considering the "close encounter" of the Jews with the Babylonians and Persians in the time of the exile.

In the present chapter we will attempt an overview of the history of millennialism in the Christian era. A number of exhaustive studies in this regard are available for those who wish to pursue the matter further. It would not serve the purpose of a work proposing to set forth what the Bible says to repeat the voluminous data available in other sources. In his book *The Millennium in the Church* (Eerdman's Publ. Co.), D. H. Krominga has provided a concise analysis of the history of millennialism in the church from its earliest appearance.

It is worthy of notice that despite the infusion of Babylonian and Persian mythology into the theology of inter-testamental Judaism, the New Testament is untainted thereby. Neither the teachings of Jesus, nor the sermons and history of Acts, nor the twenty-one epistles make any allusion to a millennial period to be anticipated at the end-time.

Only one short chapter (ch. 20) of the book of Revelation says anything which of itself could be so interpreted. And a study of that chapter in the perspective of the whole of the book will reveal that the millennium mentioned there is not that of popular theory. The fact that the concept is only mentioned in an apocalyptical setting ought of itself to establish the fact that a literal thousand year era is not to be understood.

Researchers have determined that millenialism was first introduced into the early church subsequent to the death of the apostles, in the period called the sub-apostolic era. Contrary to the claims of ardent millennialists the doctrine was not by any means held with practical unanimity by the churches of the first few centuries.

The name of one called Barnabas is often included in the list of early millennialists. *The Epistle of Barnabus* is one of the earliest Christian writings outside of the New Testament to be preserved. It is commonly dated between 96 and 131 A.D., although Lightfoot attempted to date it shortly after 70 A.D. The epistle comments on several Scriptures which have come to be the stock-in-trade of millennialists, but what he said scarcely squares with modern interpretations. He would appear to be a millennialist only in the fact that he accepted the symbolic equation of the days of creation with the millennia of history. But his comments on the Danielic visions and other salient Scriptures would seem to certainly preclude postmillennialism and are difficult to reconcile with premillennial theory.

The main thrust of the epistle is decidedly anti-judaistic in the sense that he is obviously resisting the notion that the messianic age will climax with the Jewish nation front and center in the kingdom of the Messiah — a feature that pervades almost all premillennial systems. Krominga concluded that Barnabas at best should be regarded as an

HISTORY OF MILLENNIALISM IN THE CHRISTIAN ERA

amillennialist, hence not a millenarian at all in the popular sense of the term.

For example, in Ch. Xl of his epistle Barnabas unhesitantly interprets Zeph. 3:19 and Ezek. 47:12 as fulfilled in the believers in Christ, through the impartation of the Holy Spirit, and cleansing from sin through baptism and the promise of everlasting life in Christ Jesus. So too with other glowing kingdom prophecies. Barnabas clearly did not believe in a literal, materialistic Jewish dominated Messianic kingdom.

In the August and September, 1938 issues of the *Calvin Forum*, Dr. Albertus Pieters, Emeritus professor of Western Seminary, published a two part landmark article entitled *Chiliasm in the Writings of the Apostolic Fathers*. Chiliasm is the anglicized Greek equivalent of the more familiar anglicized Latin term millennium. Pieters carefully reviewed the literature of the sub-apostolic period, consisting of fifteen documents representing nine authors. His purpose was to test the claim that the early church was almost wholly premillennial. He found that references to the second advent of Christ are few and references to a millennium *very rare*. Moreover, what little millennial references were found were traceable very definitely to Judaistic influences. He concluded that only Barnabas and Papias could be considered chiliasts. Krominga's review of the Pieter's survey reduces the number to one in that Barnabas was hardly a millennialist in the popular sense of the term. (See "The Millennium in the Church," p. 41ff.)

It does not serve our purpose to detail and extend a review of the history of the millennium in the Christian era. The most that can be said of it is that Christian(?) millennialism is grounded in the socio-historical perspective rather than in Biblical exegesis.

WHAT THE BIBLE SAYS ABOUT THE END TIME

Due to the socio-historical perspective in which millennial theories have flourished and waned, the history of millennial controversy is reminiscent of the Punch and Judy puppet shows of yesteryear. The checkered history of the human race, with ever recurring wars tending to become more massive and bloody, interspersed with respite from armed conflict in which the sinews of war are transformed into peacetime pursuits (some of which actually contribute to the progress of the Gospel) constitutes a kind of Punch and Judy show favoring first one and then the other classical theory.

Premillennialism depends on an ensuing or eminent world crisis for its credence and popular appeal. Postmillennialism requires an extended period of peace and progress for its credibility. If the signs of Christ's coming are "wars and rumors of war" with "wicked men waxing worse and worse," premillennialists will find it easy to shout, "We told you so!" every time a new world crisis, real or imaginary, moral or military, looms on the horizon or breaks out in full force. But let the crisis pass and a new era of peace and righteousness appear to be dawning; the prophets of doom are muted and the postmillennialists are able to again articulate their hopeful expectations.

Suppose that you, as a committed millenarian, were living at almost any other time in history. Which theory would you find most credible? And for how long might you do so?

Suppose you were living in the days of Nero, or Trajan or Diocletian. You would hardly believe the millennium had dawned and the golden age of the church was at hand. You could more readily believe that Satan had been loosed and only the second coming of Christ could spare the elect. You would likely be a teary-eyed premillennialist.

HISTORY OF MILLENNIALISM IN THE CHRISTIAN ERA

But suppose you were living instead in the time of Constantine, following his professed conversion to Christ. As you witnessed the transformation of the Christian faith from a persecuted cause to the role of the official religion of the Roman empire you might well recall that the book of Revelation predicts a time when "the kingdom of this world is become the kingdom of our Lord and His Christ" (Rev. 11:15). You could very well believe you were standing on the threshold of the long awaited millennial kingdom of Christ. You might very well be a starry-eyed postmillennialist.

But let it be supposed you were living instead a millennium later, when the so-called "Holy Roman Empire" was now seen to be only about 1% holy and 99% Roman. Were you living in the dark ages, amid the terrors of the inquisition, with an apostate church drunk with power and the blood of the martyrs wallowing in wantonness and cruelty, you might well identify the then reigning pope with the man of sin predicted by Paul in II Thess. 2:1-11, and conclude you were living in the time of the end and cry out for a premillennial and soon second coming of Christ.

But let it be supposed you were living rather in the aftermath of the reformation, perhaps in America, in the days of Alexander Campbell. As you witnessed a turning away from the authority of creedal systems and power-ridden ecclesiastical establishments to the simplicity of apostolic Christianity, if you were a writer and publisher, and Alexander Campbell had not already beat you to it, you might entitle your journal *The Millennial Harbinger*.

Viewing the matter at shorter range, there are some of us who can remember that World War I was hailed as the beginning of the end by the vanguard of premillennialist then gaining the ascendancy — the Seventh Day Adventists

33

and Millennial Dawnites (the Russellites, today known as the Watchtower Society or Jehovah's Witnesses). Surely, we were told, a war of such magnitude and awesomeness, with planes carrying the warfare into the heavens (a la pictorial visions in the Apocalypse) and poisonous gas introducing another dread weapon of terror — surely this had to be the onset of the long feared battle of Armageddon. But the war ended without the second coming of Christ (despite the fact that JW's would have us believe He actually did come, but secretly. After all they had predicted 1914 would be the year of His return). Moreover, the sinews of that awesome war were transformed into instruments of peace and social progress. The League of Nations was formed to assure that the war just ended would be the war to end all war and make the world safe for democracy. Thus men began to assure themselves that war had now become too horrible, too costly for all concerned for any nation ever again to resort to war as a means to an end — lest it be just that, the end of mankind. At this juncture the postmillennialists came out of hiding and announced the beginning of a millennium of peace and righteousness was at hand.

It was at this point the writer was introduced into the thought world of millennialism. Being thoroughly indoctrinated in the certitude of the postmillennial system, the writer proclaimed his faith in that context. But World War II shattered the dream. World War II was even more worldwide and horrendous. My principal mentor undertook to cover his mistake by insisting that World War I had not actually ended. Only an armistice had been signed and World War II was simply the second act of the same power play. With the ending of the second act in the drama of

HISTORY OF MILLENNIALISM IN THE CHRISTIAN ERA

the battle of Armageddon the millennium would surely begin. I could no longer believe it without reservations. But once again the sinews of war and the inventions and innovations and advanced technology which wars inevitably stimulate began to serve the public good. Moreover, hundreds of GI's returned from the battlefields of the world to prepare for the Christian ministry. Many returned to the areas of conflict to become missionaries. The post World War II era has witnessed one of the greatest strides forward in missionary expansion in the history of the church.

Such is the Punch and Judy aspect of millennial controversy. Current events, the socio-historical perspective, and the foreboding fears of the future are not the proper perspective for the understanding of the Biblical doctrine of the end-time. For those who have books to sell to the popular audience and radio and TV programs to pay for and promote, the socio-historical phenomena may be so interpreted as to persuade the gullible to part with their cash before they are parted from it. But the truth of the matter is, there are no signs cited in the Scriptures whereby one can know whether or not the beginning of the end-time is at hand. That runs counter to what we are generally told, but when we come to an analysis of Christ's Olivet Discourse, (Mt. 24, Mk. 13, Lk. 21) we shall speak to that point with proof.

Amillennialists, better called "church-age millennialists" avoid speculative systems. They recognize that evil men indeed "wax worse and worse" (II Tim. 3:13) unless brought under the power of the Gospel, as millions have been. But it is not said that the number of them, nor their ratio to the total population, will become ever greater. Furthermore, the specific "signs" Jesus cited in comparing the end-time of the present dispensation and/or the Jewish age to the antedeluvian age hardly squares with the exegesis of the prophets of gloom and doom. After all, eating and drinking, marrying and giving in marriage, working in fields and at mills, and sleeping — these are hardly monstrous forms of evil. The specific point Jesus seems to have had in mind is that life will be going on quite as usual right up to the time of His coming. It was so in the days of Noah.

If the ratio of wicked to the righteous in the total population and the extent of human violence and wickedness were the points of comparison Jesus meant to make, He somehow failed to mention them. He stressed instead the suddenness of the day the flood came, despite the preaching of Noah. Had Noah been given a "sign" to proclaim, signaling the day and the hour, such as a certain cloud formation arising at a given point on the horizon, or a series of striking phenomena or events, Noah might have gotten some "eleventh hour" converts into the ark when that sign (or signs) appeared. As it was, "they knew not until the flood came and took them," Jesus informs us, adding: "And so shall be the coming of the Son of Man" (Mt. 24:39).

The parable of the tares indicates that good men and evil men will be living together right up till the moment Christ comes. The parable says nothing of the tares all but choking out the wheat (or vice versa). The two grow together till the time of harvest. The Olivet discourse suggests a very similar social situation. "Two men shall be in the field . . . two women shall be grinding at the mill; one is taken, one is left" (Mt. 24:40, 41). Note he did not say "a thousand shall be in the fields, in the factories; one shall be taken and nine hundred and ninety nine left," a la popular rapture rhetoric.

HISTORY OF MILLENNIALISM IN THE CHRISTIAN ERA

On the other side of the coin, such parables as the parable of the leaven and of the dragnet (Mt. 13:33, 47-50) and the glowing predictions enunciated by Isaiah in his predictions of the Messiah's birth and kingdom (for example, 9:6-8) are not to be construed as teaching that the leavened lump (or lumps) would have no impurities, or portions less thoroughly leavened, or that the Kingdom of the Messiah would have no recalitrant subjects or sojourners, or not leave room for such in the great sea of humanity. Mt. 13:41 certainly affirms the contrary. The assumption that at the time of Christ's coming it shall be all one or the other or even chiefly so is the brain-child of millenarians.

It has well been said, "the only thing we learn from history is that we don't learn anything from history." Biblical prophecy, in a sense, is history written beforehand. The history of ages past should tell us something, particularly in view of the fact that Paul says of it, "these things happened unto them (those who lived aforetime) by way of example (Gr. *tupoi*, v. 6, *tupikos*, v. 11) and are written for our admonition upon whom the ends of the ages are come" (I Cor. 10:6, 11). From that is to be concluded that the history of those who have gone before us is quite typical of the present, and shall be right down to the end-time. It behooves us therefore to become so mature in our knowledge of Christ that we be no longer children, tossed to and fro by every wind of doctrine — cast up first on the horn of doom and gloom and then upon the "all is well" horn of millennial theory and dilemma.

The Bible treats the subject of the end-time, as it does all subjects, in a frank and objective manner, having little to say about matters which cater to our curiosity, but much to say about matters which should make us wise unto salvation.

Chapter Three

OUTLINE OF MILLENNIAL THEORIES

PREMILLENNIALISM

The General Theory

Premillennial views of the end-time are normally lumped together under the general title of premillennialism, simply and properly because they share in common the view that Christ's second coming will be prior to the millennium. The millennium means a literal one thousand year reign of Christ upon earth at the end of the church age, supposedly the thousand years referred to in Revelation, chapter twenty.

Several other features are also common to premillennial views although a few shades of difference may be found. The various forms normally proceed along these lines:

1. Upon His descent from heaven Christ will bind Satan and confine him to the abyss for a thousand years, depriving him of his power to deceive the nations.

2. While yet in the clouds above the earth He will rapture the righteous saints then living and resurrect the righteous dead to meet Him in the air.

3. The Jews will look upon Him whom they have pierced and be converted, and the lost tribes of Israel dispersed among the nations shall be regathered and "so shall all Israel be saved."

4. Christ will set up His throne in Jerusalem, restoring thus the throne of David and the kingdom to Israel.

5. Certain classes of believers, generally from among the raptured and resurrected saints, will reign with Him over the nations.

6. The nations shall be brought in subjection under His

feet, but in a rebellious and unconverted state; thus He shall rule them with a rod of iron.

7. Despite their seething rebellion they shall be kept under control by Christ's awesome power and stern rule; thus the time will be an age of peace and righteousness.

8. At the end of the millennium Satan will be loosed for a little while and shall gather the nations to make war against Christ and His saints.

9. Fire shall destroy Satan's hosts and he shall be cast into the lake of fire, alongside the beast and the false prophet.

10. The wicked dead shall then be resurrected to appear before the great white throne in final judgment, and thence cast into the lake of fire.

11. The heavens and the earth shall be set afire. The consensus is they will not actually be destroyed, only purged.

12. All this will consummate in the renovation of the heavens and the earth, a new (renewed) heaven and earth wherein dwelleth righteousness.

While the above outline is the basic structure of pre-millennialism there are some important differences to be noted in several of the varieties.

1. While insisting upon a literal interpretation of the Scriptures "wherever possible" most premillennialists hold that the new heavens and earth will be our present solar system, the earth included, only purged by fire to prepare for a new cycle of life upon earth.

2. Some who teach this believe there was a pre-Adamic race that went astray and were destroyed in pre-history destruction of the earth antedating the Noachial flood. It is conjectured the devil and his angels are surviving "spirits" of that race. The regeneration therefore will mark God's fourth effort to colonize the earth with people to His liking. This serves to call attention to the fact that pre-millennialism

is highly speculative. That, and the inability to establish consistent ground rules on what is to be taken literally, accounts for the endless variety of sub-theories of premillennialism.

Despite the marked differences between various theories which share a common core, sub-theories may be classified as follows: 1. Simple historical, 2. Tribulational and 3. Ultra-dispensational. In view of the fact that there are many variations within each sub-group the attempted analysis and summary must be accepted as a generalization.

1. *Simple Historical Premillenialism*

Through the centuries an imposing list of scholars has subscribed to what is called simple historical premillennialism, structured along the lines of the general theory as outlined above. The title is somewhat of a misnomer in that the theory is only relatively simple, and it is not as deeply rooted in theological history as its proponents would have us believe. We have already touched upon the latter point.

In addition to the general outline the following features are included in the development of the system.

1. A great falling away will precede the second coming of Christ.

2. The Antichrist will appear and sieze this opportune time for a major assault upon the church.

3. The Great Tribulation shall then ensue, from which the church barely survives. God's intervention, shortening the days for the elect's sake spares a faithful remnant.

4. The appearing of Christ in the clouds brings an end to the tribulation, snatching victory from Satan.

5. At Christ's appearing a) the dead in Christ arise,

OUTLINE OF MILLENNIAL THEORIES

b) the living elect are raptured, c) Israel looks upon Him whom they have pierced, repenting and are saved thereby.

6. At the end of the rapture, 3-1/2 or 7 years in duration, Christ descends to earth to set up His millennial kingdom, destroying the Antichrist by the breath of His coming and summoning the nations before Him for the sheep and goat judgment scene.

7. Christ now imprisons Satan and proceeds to rule the nations with a rod of iron, extending thereby the throne of His father David to hold sway over all the earth.

8. At the close of the millennium Satan is loosed for a little while. He gathers the nations together to make war against Christ and His saints, He is defeated in the battle of Armageddon as fire from heaven destroys his hosts and Satan is cast into the lake of fire.

9. The wicked dead are now raised to stand in the final judgment after which they are cast into the lake of fire.

10. The renovation of the heavens and the earth is climaxed by the setting up of the eternal kingdom of God and His Christ.

Among the variants of the theory are disputations as to relative roles of the Jews and the resurrected Christian saints in the millennial kingdom. Some hold that only the martyrs and those who worshipped not the beast are given rule. Much confusion exists as to the role of the temple and its rites. There is also much confusion as to the problem of transfigured saints with spiritual bodies as contemporaries on earth with newly converted fleshly earthlings and unbelieving nations, wholly carnal, ruled with a rod of iron. Such problems have spawned countless varieties of the physical kingdom theory from its inception until now.

2. Tribulational Premillennialism

A little over a century ago J. N. Darby, founder of "the Brethren" (Plymouth Brethren) introduced a greatly modified version of the theory. C. I. Schofield, author of the built-in commentary published under the title of the *Schofield Reference Bible,* has perpetuated Darbyism. The theory is popularly known as Pre-tribulationalism because of its emphatic insistence that the rapture precedes the tribulation.

Disputants of the Darby-Schofield scheme are divided into two camps, the mid-tribulationalists and the post-tribulationalists. The terms are self-explanatory.

We take the time to present an outline of the Darby-Schofield hypothesis because it differs in a number of important features from the general theory as modified in various forms of so-called simple historical premillennialism.

1. Instead of one "second coming" there are really two: one "for" the saints, (the rapture) and the other "with" the saints. The latter is called the "revelation." Today this concept has spread into virtually all premillennialism.

2. His coming in the rapture will be secret. Some hold that only those "looking for and earnestly desiring the coming of the Lord" will be raptured. The rest will be left to pass through the great tribulation. Others include the righteous dead of the Old Testament dispensation. Others include all Christians.

3. During the rapture (fixed at seven years to accompany the gap hypothesis version of the Danielic seventy-weeks vision) the saints receive rewards at the marriage feast of the lamb.

4. On earth below the Antichrist sets up his kingdom and inaugurates the great tribulation.

OUTLINE OF MILLENNIAL THEORIES

5. The Holy Spirit is removed from the world as the rapture begins. The Jews regather in Palestine, mostly in unbelief. However, a small remnant of Jews faithful to God, though they do not accept Christ, preach the gospel of the kingdom, traveling far and wide to announce the time is at hand. An immense number of the earth's inhabitants believe the Gospel of the kingdom and pass through the great tribulation though they are not yet believers in Christ.

6. At the close of the rapture interval there will be a second "first resurrection." The martyred saints of the tribulation will be raised up to join those previously raised, although they are not a part of the church.

7. At the same time the Antichrist gathers his hosts against the faithful Jewish remnant and Gentile believers who escaped martyrdom in the great tribulation and against the raptured and resurrected saints in the battle of Armageddon.

8. Now Christ comes "with the saints" in His "revelation" or "appearing" (recall that his first second coming is supposedly secret). He now comes in glory, with His holy angels in flaming fire and destroys the armies of the Antichrist.

9. Christ now conducts the "sheep and goat" judgment of the nations, based on the manner in which they have treated His brethren, the Jews. The "sheep" nations and the living remnant of the Jews are invited to reign with Christ in His millennial kingdom which He now sets up in Jerusalem. These will still have natural bodies while the resurrected and raptured saints will have glorified bodies.

10. At His second "second coming," His "appearing," the "revelation," the Jews who have remained in unbelief will look on Him whom they have pierced and believe.

Though the Holy Spirit is absent from the world, and therefore these latecomers are not regenerated by the Holy Spirit, they nonetheless join with the others in Christ's millennial kingdom, also without glorified bodies.

11. The millennial kingdom is now readied to hold sway over all the world with the Jews in the chief places of authority; the temple and its rites are again established in Jerusalem. Even Christ will be obliged to submit Himself to the re-instituted scacrificial system.

12. As in other varieties of the theory, the nations over which Christ rules are rebellious at heart, but Christ's stern rod of iron rule keeps them in forced subjection, thus peace and righteousness prevail in the Messiah's kingdom — a kingdom of this world rather than a kingdom that is within men.

13. Satan is bound at the same time Christ sets up His kingdom. But at the close of the millennium he is set loose. The rebellious nations now revolt and gather to war against Christ under Satan's leadership. Fire from heaven destroys the nations and Satan is cast into the lake of fire to be tormented forevermore.

14. Satan's hosts just slain are then resurrected, along with the rest of the wicked dead of the ages past, and appear before the great white throne in final judgment. They too are cast into the lake of fire.

15. Christ now sets up his eternal kingdom, on earth — the earth and the heavens meanwhile, apparently in a flash, having been purged by fire, and as suddenly renovated for reoccupancy.

There are many incongruities in this popular premillennial system. Not the least of these is the assumption that a Jewish remnant, despite the total absence of the Holy Spirit, will be more effective evangelists of the Gospel of the kingdom than was the church with the help of the Holy Spirit. It is also an incongruity that "believers" unregenerated by the Holy Spirit are citizens of the same kingdom as Spirit-begotten Christians and particularly that Jewish representatives of that strange order, the johnny-come-latelies, should have the chief seats in the kingdom. Moreover the "gospel" they supposedly proclaim is "another Gospel," not the gospel of the death, burial and resurrection of Christ.

3. *Ultra-dispensationalism*

This far-out version of pre-tribulational premillennialism could well be called premillennialism gone to seed. The distinguishing mark of the system is the dividing of the time into a number (generally seven) of dispensations to accommodate the theories. The Darby-Schofield system represents the flowering stage. Schofield postulated seven dispensations in his widely used commentary, the *Schofield Reference Bible*(?).

1. Innocency - from the creation of Adam to the fall
2. Conscience - from the fall of man to the covenant with Noah
3. Human government - from the deluge to the call of Abraham
4. Promise - from the call of Abraham to the giving of the law of Moses
5. Law - from Mt. Sinai to Calvary
6. Grace - from Calvary through the church age
7. Kingdom - the millennial age

The Jehovah's Witnesses press the principles of ultra-dispensationalism to their advantage. They have devised an eschatological and soteriological system in which they make up their rules as they go along. Several schools among those who style themselves as "fundamentalists" also use the ultra-dispensational system to annul the Biblical doctrine of baptism for remission of sins. By extending the Jewish dispensation past Pentecost and by reckoning "the time of the Gentiles" as the church age, they allow that baptism for remission of sins was indeed preached and practiced during the first generation of the Gospel proclamation when the church was predominately Jewish. But after Acts 18:6, the beginning of the time of the Gentiles, baptism for remission of sins was soon phased out and salvation by grace alone (through faith alone) ensued. Thus baptism for remission of sins, if practiced today, would be a violation and denial of the all-sufficiency of God's grace and Christ's finished work on Calvary. Why it was not so from Acts chapter two to eighteen is not made clear, except that it was a carry over from the Jewish age being temporarily phased out. But then why was Cornelius called upon to submit to water baptism? To placate the Jews? They would rather he had been circumcised.

The appeal of the premillennial system is threefold. 1. It avows to take the Word of God literally. "God says what He means and means what He says." This is extended into the realm of figurative language and even into apocalyptic symbolism. Premillenarians indeed do take the Bible literally, *when* their theories demand it. Otherwise they too make allowances for figurative expressions, or else break prophetic utterances into widely separated time segments through the invention of "gap" hypotheses (Nebuchadnezzar's image-vision, Dan. 2, and Daniel's seventy-week vision, Dan. 9, are normally treated in that manner.). 2. The system is exciting. Apocalyptic language is exciting of itself. It is the more so when applied literally to anticipated impending events — the sun turned into darkness and the moon into blood, a third of the stars of the heavens and a third of about everything in the earth and the sea stricken, blood as deep as horses' bridles (the battle literally being fought by cavalry troops, with Christ and His saints likewise so mounted), every island of the sea inundated ("fled away") and every mountain leveled ("not found"), etc. Such a depiction of Divine Judgment is sensational to say the least.

Pre-millenarians do not say the least. They make the most of these and other apocalyptic symbols. They are the stock-in-trade that sell their line, particularly to a generation fed on horror movies, TV spectaculars and other forms of catastrophic reporting and/or imaginings by the communication media of our time. World-wide television and news gathering services provide an awareness of wars and rumors of war, earthquakes, violence, and so forth. Such reporting helps to give credence to premillennial end-time catastrophism.

3. The prophets of the system allege they are "looking for and earnestly desiring the coming of the Lord" and are fulfilling the solemn and divinely ordained task of being faithful watchmen warning a "Laodicean" church and an unbelieving world of the sure signs of Christ's coming.

The weaknesses of the premillennial system are many. For example: 1. Eisegesis supplants exegesis. Many points of the theory are read into the Scriptures rather than being drawn from them. The basic concept, as we have already noted, is drawn from pagan concepts developed outside the Biblical revelation. 2. The computations, calculations and sure identifications have so often turned out to be wrong that the repeated "wolf! wolf!" cry may actually cause the populace to be "turned off" and rendered the less ready for Christ's coming. 3. Though sharing a common core of teaching the varieties of millennial theory are so conflicting and in some cases implausible as to attract only those who, like the ancient Athenians, "come together only to hear something new." 4. The basis and the appeal of all current forms of the theory are grossly materialistic and are promoted in disdain of Christ's announcement that the kingdom of God is within us (Lk. 17:21, Jn. 18:36). 5. The devotees of current premillennial theories would have us believe that at Christ's second coming He shall proceed to do what the Jews expected Him to do at His first coming — deliver His people (the Jews primarily, and also the whole of dispersed Israel) and gather them in Palestine. There He will set up a world empire with the Jews front and center. Were that what He had in mind at His first coming the Jews would not have rejected Him. Rather, when they thought that He might do that they were about to "take Him by force and make Him king" (Jn. 6:14, 15). Only when He made it clear His was not to be that kind of kingdom did they reject Him (Jn. 6:66). This will be discussed in detail in a later chapter, "Concerning the Kingdom of the Messiah."

POSTMILLENNIALISM

The theory that Christ will return to earth after, posterior to, the millennium is called postmillennialism. Generally speaking, it is an optimistic theory of eschatology which envisions a general triumph of Christ through the Gospel and His church. The theory is much less speculative than premillennialism and differs otherwise in many details.

Postmillennialism shares the basic concept of a golden age but views Christ's return as the climax rather than the

OUTLINE OF MILLENNIAL THEORIES

inauguration thereof. Moreover, the figure one thousand is not taken so literally. In most varieties of the theory the number signifies an extensive period in which the church gains the ascendancy over infidelity, paganism, carnal warfare, immorality and other forms of unrighteousness. A few cling to the ancient seven-millennium concept of human history with a golden age reckoned as climaxing the seven. But the number one thousand is normally viewed as a round number. The beginning date will not be known at the time. Only God, the great Timekeeper, will know the time when the general triumph of the church, which shall prevail until near the very end of end-time, has begun.

The basic beliefs which distinguish postmillennialism may be outlined as follows:

1. The church will be glorious and triumphant in the end. The millennial era will begin imperceptibly, the beginning being the time when the church has gained an ascendancy which shall inaugurate an extended period of peace and righteousness.

2. The millennium will be ushered in by the worldwide proclamation and general acceptance of the Gospel. a) The gospel, not the second coming of Christ, is the power of God unto salvation. b) The church, not the Jewish nation is the evangelizing agency which shall usher in an age of peace and righteousness.

3. For all practical purposes the church and the kingdom of Christ (and of heaven, and of God) are the same. Hence, if His kingdom is to come on earth as it is in heaven the church must triumph.

4. The church is the true Israel of God and therefore the subjects of Christ's kingdom. Only as the Jews believe the Gospel and become a part of the church, as when the

church began, do they become a part of His kingdom (Rom. 2:28-29, 4:11, 9:6-8, Eph. 2:11-22, Gal. 3:7-9, 26-29, 6:14-16, Phil. 3:3).

5. Christ was inaugurated the King of Kings, seated on David's throne (Acts 2:29-37) the day the church began. Like David, His kingdom shall increase and extend itself until the full dominion promised Him (in Christ's case "the uttermost parts of the earth," Ps. 2:8, Acts 1:8) becomes His possession. Since the Jews are a part of the whole of the earth over which He is promised dominion, the Jews necessarily shall be evangelized and brought in subjection under His feet.

6. The millennial era of the church will be an era of universal justice and righteousness. Nations shall cease to make war and the knowledge of God shall cover the earth as the waters cover the sea.

7. The glowing messianic and kingdom prophecies of the Old Testament are to be interpreted figuratively, as fulfilled in a victorious church and consummated in heaven. The Jews shall not be dealt with as a nation, but individually, as gentiles are dealt with individually, and not as so many nations. Hence, Israel will not supplant the church in the end-time.

8. Concerning the "millennial" chapter, Revelation twenty: a) The binding of Satan refers to the limiting of Satan's power through the progress of the Gospel. b) The "first resurrection" is from the death of sin (Eph. 2:1-9, Rom. 6:1-11, Col. 2:12, 13). c) The loosing of Satan "for a little time" is possibly to permit millions who have not known Satan's diabolic cunning to see him as he is, the arch-foe of God, of Christ and of the saints. d) The battle that would seem to be shaping up but is cut short by fire

from heaven is a spiritual battle (Eph. 6:10-18). Some identify the impending battle with the "battle of Armageddon" (Rev. 16:16).

9. Christ's second coming will immediately accomplish the following: a) The righteous dead shall be raptured, caught up in the clouds. b) The saints in Christ which remain alive unto His coming shall together with them be caught up in the clouds. c) The wicked dead shall be raised at the same hour (Jn. 5:28, 29) and transported to the great white throne judgment (Rev. 20:11-15). d) The hosts of Satan, the apostates (of "the great falling away") and unbelievers who remain alive at Christ's coming shall be devoured by fire from heaven. e) These too shall then be raised from the dead, having not even been buried, and will be transported to the judgment seat along with the rest of the wicked dead who have been raised from the grave, whether on land or in the sea, to be judged according to their works. f) The saints likewise shall appear in the judgment, however for commendation, not for condenmation, and rewarded according to their works (Rev. 20:11-15). Postmillennialists equate the sheep/goat judgment of Mt. 25 with the great white throne judgment of Rev. 20, believing the two accounts refer only to different facets of the final judgment.

10. Following the judgment the wicked are cast into hell, and the saved ascend into heaven. A few postmillennialists ascribe to the theory that paradise will be restored to earth and the redeemed shall dwell together with God on a purged and refurbished earth. Most postmillenarians believe that only a vision of the new heavens and the earth came down to John. Since the heavenly state is to be spiritual, and the saints are raised with spiritual bodies,

it is incongruous they would spend eternity in a material place such as a fire-charred, renovated, refurbished earth. It needs to be noted here all who hold that this earth will constitute our eternal home uniformly believe the present cosmic order will not be "burned up" nor "dissolved with fervent heat," but only purged by fire. Most postmillenialists, however, take 2 Peter 3:5-13 literally and it is the premillennialists who take the passage figuratively.

11. The dissolution of the present cosmic order prepares the way for the new heavens and the new earth wherein there dwelleth righteousness.

12. Christ, having accomplished His mission, delivers up his kingdom, the saints of earth, to God and now subjects himself to Him who did subject all things unto Him, (1 Cor. 15:27, 28).

The strength of the postmillennial conception of Christ coming and His kingdom is that 1. It much more readily fits Daniel's interpretation of the image-vision of Nebuchadnezzar (Dan. 2), and Daniel's own seventy-week vision (Dan. 9). 2. The theory harmonizes readily with such parables as the parable of the leaven (Mt. 13:33) and of the nobleman who "went into a far country to receive a kingdom," and upon his return "having received the kingdom" (not to establish one) He called His kingdom subjects in for a reckoning (Lk. 19:11-27). 3. The theory harmonizes also with the New Testament writers' own interpretation of the great Messianic kingdom psalm, Psalms two. (See Acts 4:23-28, 13:33. Both passages equate the Psalm with the church age then begun.)

The weaknesses of the theory are that: 1. It weakens hope and expectancy of a soon coming of Christ, unless one is convinced the church has gained such sway that

OUTLINE OF MILLENNIAL THEORIES

the millennial era has long since begun. 2. The proponents of the theory are embarrassed by the outbreak of each new war and/or general decline in public and private morals. 3. While generally optimistic about the future of the church the theory does not reflect the hope and expectancy of the return of Christ which was manifested by the apostolic church and encouraged by apostolic writings. 4. The theory shares with premillennialism the fault that it contradicts, at least to a degree, Jesus' statements to the effect His coming would be at a time least expected, and hence it could be any time. Both pre- and post-millennialists take refuge from this charge by taking literally the words of Christ, "ye know not the *day* nor the *hour*." Whereupon the premillennialists proceed to predict the time or the season — the time (some times) right down to the year, and a few to the very day, and the postmillennialists conclude just as dogmatically that his coming could *not* be at this time in history. 5. The theory shares somewhat the error of subscribing to the pagan pedigreed seven-millennium time-slot for the whole course of human history. 6. Extremists of the position are obliged to play down the inference of the parable of the tares, and presume that the parable of the sower describes only the results of the preaching of the Gospel prior to the onset of the millennium.

AMILLENNIALISM

That view of the end-time which does not envision a thousand year reign of Christ on earth at the end of the church age is commonly called amillennialism. The term is apropos only if the millennium is equated with the popular conception that the thousand years John speaks of in

WHAT THE BIBLE SAYS ABOUT THE END TIME

Revelation, chapter twenty, is a literal one thousand calendar year utopian era following or climaxing the church age. The prefix "a" is a negative prefix. It is affixed to the terms "millennial," "millennialist," "millennialism" to communicate the fact amillennialists reject the popular theory, as stated above. The term is a misnomer, however, if one supposes that its use signifies those so called do not believe in any kind of millennium whatsoever. The fact is they have a great deal of positive things to say concerning John's use of the term. Far from passing lightly over Revelation, chapter twenty, amillennialism is deeply rooted in the chapter. This will be detailed in chapter four of this discussion of the end-time.

The general features of the amillennial view may be outlined as follows:

1. The term "one thousand" as used in Revelation, chapter twenty, is a symbolic number symbolizing completeness, in the sense of fullness (as the number seven symbolizes completeness in the sense of perfection). One thousand is the cube of ten, the basis of the digital system. As an apocalyptical symbol, and when it is used as a generalization or figuratively, the term is to be taken as an expression of largeness or fullness. For example: "A thousand years in thy sight are but a day" (Ps. 90:4, cp. II Pet. 3:8), and "every beast of the forest is mine, and the cattle on a thousand hills" (Ps. 50:10). As used in Rev. 20 the term is to be understood as a number expressing not only largeness and fullness, but more specifically it is a term embracing the whole time in which the events in John's apocalyptic vision ensue.

2. The church age is the last age of man upon the earth. At the consummation of the church age, Christ will

return to claim His own and bring the wicked unto judgment. The saints, His "kingdom," He will deliver up to God who shall then give them entrance into His eternal kingdom in heavenly glory.

3. The church constitutes Christ's earthly kingdom. His is a non-political, spiritual kingdom, a kingdom that is "within you" and "not of this world."

4. There will be a contemporary development of both good and evil. The "tares and the wheat" will "grow together unto the harvest." Neither will crowd out the other.

5. The first resurrection refers to our spiritual resurrection from the death unto sin, described in Romans 6, Ephesians 2 and Colossians 3, rather than the bodily resurrection of the righteous dead antedating the resurrection of the wicked by one thousand years. The second resurrection is the general resurrection of the bodies of the just and the unjust the same hour (Jn. 5:28, 29). Those who have part in the first resurrection have no part in the second death, the lake of fire.

6. At Christ's coming the living saints are raptured and those dead in Christ are to be raised to join the raptured saints in the clouds, to be received thence into heaven as He was at His ascension. "And so shall we ever be with the Lord" (I Thess. 4:17). The rapture is by no means a secret, seven-year episode. Where He is, there we shall be also when we too are taken up into the clouds.

The kingdom prophecies of the Old Testament are not to be interpreted literally, nor be applied primarily to fleshly Israel. They are to be interpreted in the manner that Jesus and His apostles, as recorded in the New Testament, interpreted them. For example, note the following:

1. Joel 2:28-32 as interpreted by Peter, Acts 2:16-36.

Peter is most specific. *"This,"* said he, "which ye see and hear" (see v. 33) "is *that* which was spoken by the prophet Joel" (see v. 16).

2. Ps. 16:8-11, Ps. 110:1, as interpreted by Peter, Acts 2:22-32, 30-36. Again Peter is most specific in announcing the predictions as fulfilled, yet at least the latter prophecy was by no stretch of the imagination fulfilled literally.

3. Psalms 2 as interpreted by the prayers of the church, recorded in Acts 4:24-31, and alluded to also by Paul in 13:13. The church is definitely set forth as the kingdom of the Messiah.

4. Deut. 18:15-19 as interpreted by Acts 3:19-24. Note that Peter not only identifies Christ as "that prophet" of whom Moses spake, but affirms "all the prophets from Samuel onward, as many as have spoken, spake of *these* days (v. 24). This scarcely squares with the stop-gap role hypothesized by dispensationalists as the unexpected role of the church.

5. Amos 9:11-14 as interpreted by Acts 15:14-18. James affirms the conversion of the Gentiles and their admission to the church fulfills the prophecy of Amos, rather than a regathering of fleshly Israel in some far off millennium.

6. Gen. 12:1-3, as interpreted by Paul in Romans 2:28, 29, 4:11, 12, 9:6-8, Eph. 2:11-22, Gal. 3:6-9, 26-29, 6:16, Phil. 3:3, Col. 3:11, etc. There can be no doubt about it. Paul viewed the church as the true seed of Abraham, and hence as the means to the fulfillment of the promises of God to Abraham.

7. Isa. 2:2, 3, Micah 4:1, 2 as interpreted by Heb. 12:22-24, and Isa. 28:16, 17 as interpreted by I Pet.

2:1-6. The author of Hebrews and the apostle Peter concur that the church, not a restored fleshly Israel, is the true Zion, the city of God.

The words of Jesus in announcing the establishment of the church, Mt. 16:13-28, and His reply to Pontius Pilate's questioning concerning His kingship, John 19:33-37, are in harmony with the foregoing interpretations of kingdom prophecies.

Premillennialists who follow their literalistic interpretations of kingdom prophecies to their logical conclusion not only have to explain away the foregoing sacred Scripture identifications, but further set the New Testament writers at variance with their own interpretations in other important respects. For example: If the Levitical priesthood is to be restored, literally, as they infer from Ezek. 44:15-31, then Heb. 7:11-17, 26-28, 8:4, etc. and I Pet. 2:9 must be rescinded. Again, if the temple and its ancient sacrificial system is to be restored, as per a literal interpretation of Ezekiel 46:2 ff., then Christ will have to wait at the temple gate while a mere priest of the Aaronic order presents a burnt and a peace offering on his behalf. Heb. chapter 7, 9:24-28, 10:19-22 are thusly rescinded. Literalists such as Schofield have suggested the revival of the sacrificial system and priesthood will serve as reverse types in the millennium, supplementing if not supplanting the Lord's supper.

In appraisal of amillennialism we suggest the following considerations be weighed.

1. Unlike the postmillennial position with which it shares much in common, amillennialism: a) does not have the effect of weakening the hope and expenctancy of our Lord's return in our own lifetime, even a soon coming.

It is a very present hope of amillennialists. b) It does not presuppose a complete or nearly complete triumph of the church. It sees in the Biblical warnings concerning man's perversity and Satan's cunning relevance throughout the whole course of the present age.

2. Unlike the premillennial systems, a) It is not wildly speculative. b) It is not materialistic, geocentric, even Palestine oriented as were the Jews, Christ's "own" at His first coming, and the premillennialists who profess to be above all other Christ's "own" today. c) It is not pessimistic nor depreciatory of the role of the church and the power of the Gospel. d) It is not subject to the gross absurdities that a literal interpretation of kingdom and apocalyptic prophecies entails. e) It does not envision a return to what Paul calls the "beggarly elements of the law," of which Christ "made an end," "nailing such to the cross." f) It does not have to resort to multiple comings of Christ, secret and visible, multiple bodily resurrections, a thousand years apart. g) It is not committed to a theology that perpetuates the role of the Jews as a separate and favored convenant people contrary to Eph. 2:14-18, Heb. 8:8-11, Gal. 3:28, 29, etc. h) And it does not make our returned Lord an unwanted despot, seated on an uncertain throne, as it were a "powder keg," ruling over subjects who are waiting for the day when they can revolt against Him.

3. It is a mediating position, bridging the gulf between the pre- and post-millennial systems. It embraces the best features of each, and avoids the worst features of each. It compares somewhat with the least speculative of the premillennial theories with regard to the events preceding Christ's return, and with the postmillennial views with regard to the events upon and subsequent to His return.

OUTLINE OF MILLENNIAL THEORIES

5. It accepts Christ's own appraisal of the accomplishments of His first coming, as expressed in His intercessory prayer: "I have glorified Thee (Father) on earth, having accomplished the work thou gavest me to do" (Jn. 17:4). He is recognized as king here and now. He is not represented as having failed a major part of His mission and is still away biding His time awaiting a more convenient season to return and finish the task of setting Himself up on David's throne in Jerusalem. His saints are now reigning with Him, having through Him gained the victory over sin and death, and are anticipating the full flowering of His kingdom in that "better country" where they shall be gathered when He comes again.

6. It provides a spiritual (not merely a spiritualistic) interpretation of the "millennial" chapter of the Bible, Revelation twenty, which can be harmonized with relevant Scriptures without resorting to forced and fanciful interpretations, and without being obliged to come up with "up-dated" interpretations as one by one former identifications prove unfounded.

7. It calls to mind that it is written of Christ's disciples who shared in the exultation of His triumphal entry only to share too in the despair of His crucifixion — "these things understood not His disciples at the first, but when Jesus was glorified, then remembered they that these things were written of him and they had done these things unto him" (Jn. 12:16). So too when Christ comes in His glory it is then we will fully understand many of the things we now see as in a glass darkly. Amillennialists do not pretend to be able to answer every curious question about things we have not yet seen.

Readers who may want to further pursue the variant

millennial views will find available a plethora of literature on the subject. The shelves of Bible bookstores abound with such, many in the more economical paper back edition. Premillennial oriented publications of course predominate for that is what sells. But postmillennial and amillennial sources are not lacking. The latter is enjoying growing popularity.

Several authors have attempted to set forth evaluations and comparisons of the principle forms of millennial theories. The foregoing outline constitutes my own personal appraisal. An extensive analysis may be found in the classic work of Loraine Boettner, *The Millennium* (Presbyterian and Reformed Publication Co.). Boettner attempts to provide not only a digest of the principal variants but also to cite the key Scriptures each uses as proof-texts, and an analysis of the same. Boettner is a postmillennialist but has sought to be objective in setting forth the case for the various schools of thought.

Those who prefer to gain their information directly from leading exponents who espouse the various interpretations will do well to consult a recent Inter-Varsity Press publication, *The Meaning of the Millennium: Four Views*. Robert G. Clouse brings together champions of four principle schools of thought. Historical and dispensational premillennialism are sufficiently divergent as to justify this. By the same token postmillennialism and amillennialism have long been recognized as two different schools of thought though they share in common the view that the second coming of Christ will be posterior to whatever the "millennium" is considered to consist of. The four author's Clouse has called upon are: George Eldon Ladd, stating the case for historical premillennialism, Herman A. Hoyt, dispensational premillennialism, Loraine Boettner, postmillennialism and Anthony G. Hoekema contending for amillennialism.

Chapter Four

WHAT THE BIBLE SAYS ABOUT THE MILLENNIUM: REVELATION TWENTY

To understand the twentieth chapter of Revelation, or any chapter of the Apocalypse, one needs to be aware of 1) the format, 2) the outline, 3) the schema (plot plan) and 4) the nature and purpose of apocalyptic language.

OVERVIEW OF THE BOOK OF REVELATION

1. *The Format*

The book of Revelation, much like John's first epistle, is written in cyclical fashion. It does not move in a straight line, progressively, chapter by chapter from the first century of the Christian era to the consummation of the ages.

To read the book is somewhat comparable to entering a lofty tower so situated that one has a panoramic view of the things close by on every side, and then finds a spiral staircase beckoning. As he ascends he comes at three successive levels to a series of seven encircling window openings through which one may look out upon vistas of more distant things breathtaking to behold, and from thence a view from the top that is "out of this world."

The revelation thus provided, to some degree, keeps in view the same points of interest on the horizon of "the things which must come to pass," but with each cycle the view is from a higher perspective. This is not to say the revelation contained in the vision of the seven seals is simply repeated in a different mode of expression in the vision of the seven trumpets and then again in the vision of the seven angels with the seven bowls of wrath. Neither do we mean to imply that the three cycles of seven visions contain the whole description of all that John saw. It is not that simple.

On the other hand there is a core of similarity which prevails in the three cycles. As one viewing a scene below will see some things not visible, or at least not so clearly so, from a lower or a higher vista point, so the three cycles of visions in Revelation are not repetitious reporting couched only in different words. Yet there are a number of parallels, not the least of which is the fact that each of the three cycles closes in much the same way — with a vision of Christ and His saints having gained the final victory.

There is also another pattern discernible. An interlude, an extended description, is inserted between the sixth and the seventh visions. The seventh vision of the series is then described and used to introduce the next cycle of visions.

2. The Outline

Prologue, Ch. 1

John introduces 1) the Revelator, Jesus Christ, 2) the heavenly messenger (angel) who was appointed to escort him as it were into "the projection room" where John was privileged to preview the drama of redemption right down to the end of time, and into eternity's dawn. 3) John himself, his credentials and his then present circumstances. 4) That accomplished, John states the purpose of the book he was called upon to write. The same serves also as one of the keys to the interpretation thereof: "Write therefore the things thou sawest: a) the things which *are*, and b) the things which shall come to pass hereafter" v. 19.

THE MILLENNIUM: REVELATION TWENTY

Section I., "The Things Which Are," Chs. 2, 3.

Chapters two and three describe the things which then were. The letters to the seven churches of Asia provide the vehicle of revelation. Contrary to popular theory, these letters do not represent seven successive periods of church history. Virtually every one who has ever entertained that motion, from its earliest conception, has thought himself and his contemporaries to be living in the worst of all times, in the last period — the Laodicean period. Such a view has been popular with crepe hanging premillenarians through the centuries. It is much more likely that the letters represent seven facets of the church in John's own time — constituting the things which "are," (which then were). If not, what in the book of Revelation does fulfill that first section of John's assignment? Since history has a way of repeating itself, the letters may describe seven facets of the church in every age. There are churches today comparable to each of the seven. And there are elements of the seven in virtually every congregation.

Section II., "The Things Which Shall Come to Pass Hereafter," Chs. 4-22.

Cycle One, Chs. 4-7

Chapters 4-7 comprise the first of the three cycles of predictive visions. The scene opens in the courts of heaven. The vehicle of revelation is a book with seven seals, and a quest for some one deemed worthy to open them. Round about the throne of God are seen 1) four and twenty elders, arrayed in white robes and with gold crowns on their heads. 2) He saw also four six-winged "living creatures." 3) He saw "the seven spirits of God," which some take to be the Holy Spirit, Who otherwise is not so much as mentioned in the book. The term Holy Spirit nowhere appears. None of these were worthy. 4) But in the midst of the throne John saw the Lamb of God. As He came forward and took the book out of the right hand of God the four and twenty elders and the four living creatures fell down before him saying:

> Worthy art thou to take the book, and to open the seals, for thou wast slain, and didst purchase unto God with thy blood men of every tribe and tongue and nation and people, and madest them to be a kingdom and priests, and they reign upon the earth. (5:9, 10)

Mark what has just been said. Those who were purchased by the blood of Christ are said, this early in the book of Revelation, to reign upon the earth. And they are said to do so as "a kingdom of priests"; if you please, "a royal priesthood — one of Peter's apt descriptions of the church. This bears heavily on the interpretation of the millennial reign of the saints described in chapter twenty. Reigning with Christ as priests of God and of Christ is not reserved for some distant millennium.

As the Lamb of God opened one after another the seven seals, seven tabloid views depicting the whole course of the Christian era passed before John's eyes. With the opening of the seventh seal John says:

> After these things I saw, and behold, a great multitude, which no man could number, out of every nation, and of all tribes, and peoples and tongues, standing before the throne and before the lamb, arrayed in white robes, and palms in their hands. And they cry with a great voice, saying: "Salvation unto our God who sitteth on the throne, and unto the Lamb" (7:9, 10).

THE MILLENNIUM: REVELATION TWENTY

At that, all the angels who were standing around the throne fell on their faces before the throne and worshipped God, saying:

> Amen: Blessing, and glory, and wisdom, and thanksgiving, and honor, and power, and might, be unto our God for ever, Amen. (v. 12).

One of the elders then addressed John, saying: "These that are arrayed in white robes, who are they and whence came they?" (v. 13). John played it safe, saying: "My Lord, thou knowest." And indeed he did, for he answered John, saying:

> These are they that have come up out of the great tribulation, and they washed their robes, and made them white in the blood of the Lamb. Therefore are they before the throne of God, and they serve him day and night in his temple; and he that sitteth on the throne shall spread his tabernacle over them. They shall hunger no more, neither thirst anymore, neither shall the sun strike upon them, nor any heat; for the Lamb that is in the midst of the throne shall be their shepherd, and he shall guide them unto fountains of waters of life; and God shall wipe away every tear from their eyes (7:14-17).

This sounds like chapters 21 and 22 already, does it not? And for good reason. This first cycle of visions, as with the two that shall follow and the grand finale (Chs. 20-22) covers the whole course of the Christian era and climaxes as the book itself does with a depiction of the glorious victory of Christ and His church.

Cycle Two, Chs. 8-11

In cycle two the vehicle of revelation is that of the sounding of seven trumpets. Again the whole course of the Christian era is depicted in seven tabloid visions. With the sounding of the seventh trumpet John hears the tumultuous sound of "a great voice in the heaven" saying:

> The kingdom of this world is become the kingdom of our Lord, and of His Christ: and He shall reign for ever and ever (11:15).

Thus a second time, we who ordinarily can not see the end from the beginning are caused to see the ultimate triumph and glorious victory of Christ and His church.

Cycle Three, Chs. 12-19

In cylce three the vehicle of revelation is again changed but the sweep of events brings us to the same point of time. The cycle gets off to a slower start by virtue of the fact it opens with a flashback to the birth of Christ. Seven angels, each with a bowl, laden with the seven last plagues, provide the principal imagery.

The scene opens with the birth of Christ depicted in apocalyptic symbols. Satan, the dragon, pursues the woman with the man-child to destroy Him. That failing, the revelation subtly shifts from Satan's assault against the physical body of Christ to his assault against His spiritual body, the church. Two awesome beasts appear, one out of the earth, the other out of the seas. Seven warnings and seven assurances are given as the vision of the seven angels with their seven bowls of wrath unfolds.

The cycle closes as did the first two, with the victory of Christ over His foes. This time the spotlight is focused more directly, more personally upon His second coming. John writes:

> And I saw the heaven opened: and behold, a white horse, and he sat thereon, called Faithful and True; and in righteousness he doth judge and make war. And his eyes are

THE MILLENNIUM: REVELATION TWENTY

a flame of fire, and upon his head are many diadems; and he hath a name which no man knoweth but himself.

And he is arrayed in a garment sprinkled with blood; and His name is called the Word of God. And the armies which are in heaven followed him upon white horses, clothed in linen, white and pure.

And out of his mouth proceedeth a sharp sword, that with it he should smite the nations: and he shall rule them with a rod of iron: and he treadeth the winepress of the fierceness of the wrath of God, the Almighty. And he hath on his garment and on his thigh a name written, KING OF KINGS AND LORD OF LORDS (19:11-15).

The Grand Finale, Chs. 20-22

Chapters 20-22 comprise the grand finale. Chapter twenty epitomizes the warfare of Satan versus the saints, the theme of the three foregoing cycles. Chapters twenty-one and twenty-two elaborate upon the victory and glorious rewards of Christ and His ransomed saints. This was only briefly touched upon in the closing paragraphs of the three cycles which make up the bulk of the revelation. The grand finale includes three different views of the eternal home of the saints, and a final certification of the authenticity of the visions.

The book closes with a prayer that ought to be on every tongue: "Amen, Come, Lord Jesus." (22:20)

3. *The Schema*

Having noted the format and outline John used in writing the Apocalypse, let us now consider the schema — the plot-plan, the threefold theme that runs throughout the book.

WHAT THE BIBLE SAYS ABOUT THE END TIME

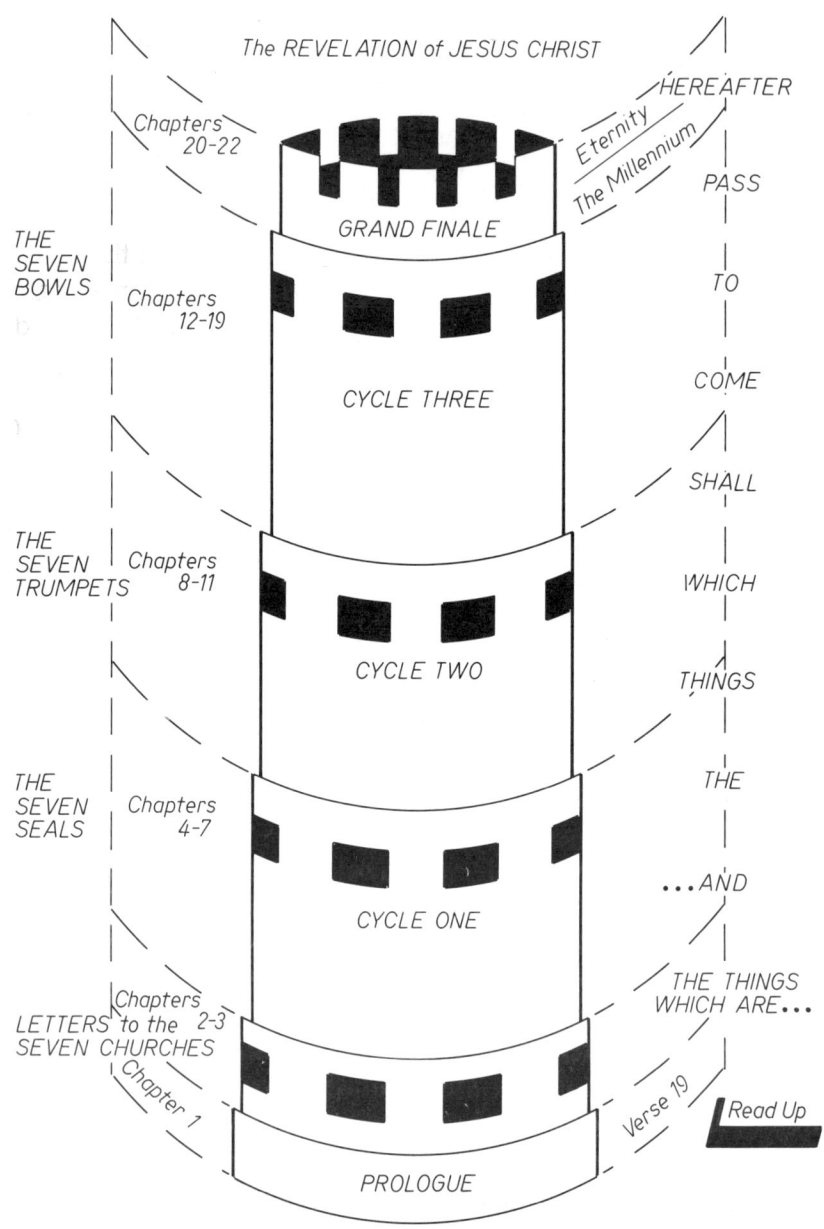

THE MILLENNIUM: REVELATION TWENTY

The book of Revelation is a pictorial enlargement, a "blow-up" of the key verse of the Bible — Gen. 3:15. This is true, of course, of the whole Bible, else Gen. 3:15 would not be the key verse thereof. However, it is not so dramatically set forth, nor so pictorially presented as it is in the book of Revelation.

Recall that subsequent to Adam's transgression the voice of God was heard in the garden of Eden. In the encounter which ensued God pronounced judgment upon Adam and Eve, the earth and the serpent. In the midst of those pronouncements, in veiled apocalyptic language, we find the first messianic promise. Included in His pronouncement of judgment upon "the serpent" (Satan, see Rev. 20:2) God said:

> I will put enmity between thee and the woman, and between thy seed and her seed. He shall bruise thy head and thou shalt bruise his heel (Gen. 3:15).

Gen. 3:15 contains in capsule form, the scheme — the plot-plan, the three-fold theme of the entire Bible: 1) the age-long struggle between God and Satan, the saints and sinners. 2) Suffering and travail for the saints, symbolized by the bruised heel — a painful, semi-crippling but not deadly injury. 3) Victory over Satan, symbolized by the bruising (not crushing) of the serpent's head. The Bible is the unfolding drama of that struggle, with its attendant tribulations and triumphs. The book of Revelation is the epitome of that struggle as it ensues in the Christian era, and a pictorial enlargement, or blow-up of Genesis 3:15.

1. *The Conflict — the Battle of Armageddon(?)*

The battle of Armageddon, of which the prophets of doom and gloom have so much to say, could very well be but an apocalyptical symbol for the age-old struggle introduced in Gen. 3:15, as it is consummated in Rev. 20:9, 10. Only in the fertile imaginations of end-time promoters is the battle some future spectacular, an eminent show-down between the good guys and the bad guys, several million strong, crowded into the narrow confines of the valley of Esdraelon. Lately, the battle is being projected as a final showdown of the East versus the West, with hordes of Africans arrayed on the side of the communist Sino-Russian alliance. The mention of Cush (originally a son of Ham) in Ezek. 38:5 among the participants in a great battle predicted in that chapter serves as the basis for the latter conjecture. Incidentally, Ezekiel does not specify the actual locale, except to say the military alliance described in the opening verses of the chapter (1-6) shall come against Israel "my people," saith the Lord Jehovah when they "dwell securely in the land."

The chapter contains the gist of the end-time catastrophic militarism. Viewed literally, and accepting the assumption that fleshly Israel, rather than the church, "the Israel of God" (Gal. 6:16), remains in God's sight and plan as His chosen people, even exclusively so right down to the time of the end, the chapter lends itself very well to currently popular interpretations. But interpreted apocalyptically, the real warfare is that which Paul speaks of in Ephesians 6:12ff.

> We wrestle not against flesh and blood, but against the principalities, against the powers, against the world rulers of this darkness, against the *spiritual hosts* of wickedness in heavenly places. (Italics are author's.)

Therefore, Paul exhorts his readers to arm and armor themselves spiritually that they may withstand the onslaughts of Satan and be overcomers in Christ.

THE MILLENNIUM: REVELATION TWENTY

In the Apocalypse John may well be seizing upon his readers familiarity with the military history and importance of the battlefield overlooked by the Hill of Megiddo, and may be using the term Armageddon (in Hebrew, Harmageddon) as a symbol for the spiritual warfare in which the saints of God are engaged. Remember the Alamo!, Remember the Maine!, Remember Pearl Harbor! These were rallying cries for Americans in the course of three wars. Armageddon is a term which would effectively serve as a synonym for warfare per se in the Biblical world of the first century.

2. The Bruised Heel — the Great Tribulation (?)

The Great Tribulation is not a single episode awaiting the church somewhere down toward the end of time. Already the church has passed through many great tribulations. At the time John was writing, great tribulations had already come upon the church in tidal wave proportion. He himself was exiled on Patmos by one of them, while many of his spiritual compatriots had already been martyred for the testimony of Jesus and the Word of God. He introduces himself as "I, John, your brother and partaker with you in *the tribulation and kingdom* (Note those terms.) and patience which are in Jesus" (Rev. 1:9). The great tribulation is a synonym for the rough and rocky road which the saints of God, with bruised heel, have ever trod as we journey through this vale of tears. Jesus said to His disciples, "In the world ye have tribulation, but be of good cheer, I have overcome the world" (Jn. 16:33).

3. The Bruised Head — the Binding of Satan, and Millennium (?)

The bruising of the head of Satan to effectuate a millennial kingdom for Christ and His saints is the other side of the coin, so to speak: the binding — not the crushing. Satan is to be cast alive into the lake of fire, as is the case with his arch collaborators, the beast and the false prophet. The binding of Satan and enthronement with Christ in His millennial kingdom are not future events. In his discussion of this subject Jay Adams speaks of *The Millennium Realized*. He so titles his book. The church is the earthly facet of Christ's millennial kingdom.

4. *The Nature and Purpose of Apocalyptic Language*

The angel who showed John the things which He was then commanded to write in a book said: "Blessed is he that readeth, and they that hear . . . and keep the things that are written therein" (1:3). It is not necessary to understand the book to be blessed by it. Probably no one will fully understand it this side of heaven. But even those with little or no knowledge of the nature and purpose of apocalyptic language can scarcely peruse the book without learning some things which bring blessing. If nothing else, this comes through loud and clear — for those who wash their robes and make them white in the blood of the Lamb (an apocalyptic expression that is generally understood) and remain faithful to the end (a literal statement, of which the book is not lacking), everything is going to come out all right. Gloriously, wondrously it shall be so, and shall remain so throughout all eternity.

A knowledge of the nature and purpose of apocalyptical language will add to our understanding as we read the book and guard us against many superficial errors.

The term, "apocrypha," is compounded from the Greek preposition, *apo* (from) and the verb, *kalupto* (to cover), hence "to take the cover from," "to unveil," "to reveal."

THE MILLENNIUM: REVELATION TWENTY

Thus the book is called "the Apocalypse," "Revelation." The book opens with the words, *Apokalupsis Iesou Christou*, "the *Revelation* of Jesus Christ."

The foregoing definition does not at all seem to describe the text of the book of Revelation, nor of apocalyptic literature in general. It isn't all that revealing, especially when studied piecemeal, line by line, phrase by phrase. Apocalyptic language is used when information is disclosed that is not intended to be taken literally, or when it is not intended to be understood should it fall into the wrong hands. Through such a device things are concealed and revealed at the same time, "hidden to the wise and revealed unto babes," to recall a saying of Jesus as he explained the reason for His use of parables (Mt. 11:25).

Apocalyptic language is parabolic; but more than that, it is highly dramatic and supra-symbolic. It is a rhetorical style employed by several of the Old Testament prophets, notably Ezekiel and Daniel, but including also Isaiah (in several sections of his book) and several of the minor prophets.

Apocalyptic language is sometimes described as oriental hyperbole. The trite saying, "God says what He means and means what He says," is to be applied advisedly in interpreting apocalyptic language. He obviously means what He says for His warnings and promises are always fulfilled, but not "to the letter," that is, not literally.

A classic example is to be found in Isaiah's prediction to the fall of Edom. The words are echoed by John in describing the punishment of those who worship the beast and his image (Rev. 14:9-11). Isaiah writes as follows:

> The streams of Edom shall be turned into pitch, and the dust thereof into brimstone, and the land thereof shall become burning pitch. It shall not be quenched night nor day; the

smoke thereof shall go up forever: from generation to generation it shall lie waste: none shall pass through it for ever and ever (Isa. 34:9, 10).

Is this to be taken literally? Hardly, otherwise tourists in the area today could not bring back on-the-spot photos of the land. There are no rivers of pitch, nor burning landscape, no smoke ascending endlessly, no terrain no longer trod by the foot of man. Then God did not say what He meant, or else changed His mind? Far from it. As a nation Edom was absolutely destroyed and the land devastated thoroughly as was prophesied. Edom remains a non-nation to this day, and her land desolated.

THE APOCALYPTIC MILLENNIUM OF REVELATION TWENTY

It is high time the Bible be permitted to speak for itself on the widely disputed subject of the millennium. Surprisingly, it says very little. Chapter twenty of Revelation contains the sole mention of a "thousand year" reign of Christ. Elsewhere in the scriptures the term "a thousand years" appears but three times, once in Ps. 90:4 and twice in II Pet. 3:8. The usage there in no sense compares to what we find in Rev. 20:2, 3, 4, 5, 6, and 7. These verses contain the sole mention of a thousand year time segment in which a reign is said to take place. Revelation 20:4-6 speaks of saints "living and reigning with Christ, as priests of God and of Christ" between a binding and a loosing of Satan.

The passage is as remarkable for what John is not reported as seeing (though currently credited with having done so) as it is for what he actually said that he saw. It

THE MILLENNIUM: REVELATION TWENTY

would do well to go over the text lightly at first to see what John actually said and with that perspective proceed with an analysis of the chapter.

It must be kept in mind what book the chapter is a part of, and the nature of the language in which the greater part of the book is couched. Unless one believes there are horses in heaven and Jesus will return to earth mounted on one, with the hilt of a sword clenched between His teeth, and His angels likewise descending from heaven on horseback, and the devil, a spirit being, can be bound with a chain, and locked up in a deep hole somewhere, some alternate to a crassly literal interpretation of the chapter must at least be allowed as a viable option.

Note What John Said That He Saw

v. 1 An angel, (lit., a messenger) descend from heaven, having a great chain in his hand and a key to the abyss (lit., a bottomless pit).

v. 2 The angel lays hold on Satan, and binds him for a thousand years.

v. 3 The angel casts Satan into the abyss and shuts and seals it over him. Presumably the key in the angel's hand is used in securing the abyss. The purpose of Satan's incarceration is said to deprive him of the freedom to deceive the nations.

v. 4 Thrones (pl.), occupied. Judgment (Gr., *krima*) was given to the occupants. The preposition suggests the right or power to exercise judgment was given to them. Souls, presumably those occupying the thrones, are seen — souls of decapitated Christian martyrs *and* of those who received not the mark of the beast on forehead or hand. These live and reign with Christ a thousand years.

v. 5 The first resurrection. The scene that has just been described is now called the first resurrection. Note that at this point John makes no mention of bodies being raised, unless the term "soul" is used in verse 4 in a synecdochal sense (in which a part stands for the whole).

v. 6 No new sighting is reported in this verse, but the first resurrection is further explained. Those having part in it are: a) pronounced "blessed and holy," b) the second death has no power over them, and c) they are now described as "priests of God and of Christ," and as such they are said to reign with Him a thousand years.

v. 7 Satan is loosed out of his prison.

v. 8 Satan now comes forth a) to deceive the nations which are in the four corners of the earth, Gog and Magog. (Note that Gog and Magog are not identified as the kings of the East, but as the nations of the entire earth.) b) to gather them (the nations) to the war. (What war? The battle of Armageddon? Or but an intended war that was cut short?) The number of the troops is said to be as the sand of the sea.

v. 9 The war, or near war. Satan's international army is said to go up over the breadth of the earth and to encompass the camp of the saints, and the beloved city. Zap! Fire descends from heaven and devours them.

v. 10 The devil that deceived them is cast into the lake of fire and brimstone, where the beast and the false prophet are. That great triumvirate of evil is sentenced to be tormented there day and night for ever and ever (lit., unto the ages of the ages).

vs. 11-15 focus on the aftermath of the millennium and the scene just described. John beholds the great white throne judgment, and describes the scenario as follows:

> And I saw a great white throne, and him that sat upon it, from whose face the earth and heaven fled away; and there

THE MILLENNIUM: REVELATION TWENTY

was found no place for them. And I saw the dead, the great and the small, standing before the throne; and the books were opened: and another book was opened, which is the book of life: and the dead were judged out of the things which were written in the books, according to their works. And the sea gave up the dead that were in it; and death and Hades gave up the dead that were in them: and they were judged every man according to their works. And death and Hades were cast into the lake of fire. This is the second death, even the lake of fire. And if any was not found written in the book of life, he was cast into the lake of fire.

Now back to vs. 1-10, the millennial sector of the chapter. How shall we interpret what John said that he saw? With caution and with candor. We are dealing with apocalyptic language, not crass literalism. Several live issues of end-time controversy are dealt with in these verses.

The Binding and Loosing of Satan

Revelation, chapter twenty, is the primary source of information concerning the binding and loosing of Satan, particularly so in a millennial context. Five questions are in order. By whom? Why? How? To what degree? and when?

In attempting to answer such questions it should be noted that the binding and the loosing of Satan are not only figurative expressions; they are relative terms also. By virtue of the fact that Jehovah God is "the Lord God Almighty" (See Rev. 1:8, 4:8, 11:17, 15:3, 16:7, 16:14, 19:6, 15, 21:22, and Old Testament references too numerous to be listed.), Satan therefore is always "bound." Conversely, inasmuch as Satan exists contemporaneously with God, the Almighty, he is also to some degree free. Such freedom as Satan has is by God's permission, or else Jehovah God is not omnipotent, almighty, all powerful. To overlook this is to overlook one of the keys to the interpretation of the binding and loosing of Satan in Revelation twenty. Since Satan is always bound, to some degree, and likewise always free, these figures of speech must be taken in a relative sense. Whatever freedom he has or has ever had or ever shall have is by God's permission; it is relative, not absolute.

The book of Job bears on this observation. God turned Satan loose on Job, so to speak, but not absolutely. He allowed him, for a time, more than ordinary freedom to afflict and test Job. Mark what we have just said. Satan did not have the freedom to do so himself, nor did he wrest it from God. Jehovah permitted Satan to put Job through the wringer, so to speak. But even then, Satan was bound. He could not take Job's life (Job 1:12, 2:6).

The book of Job has some bearing also on another question pertaining to the binding and loosing of Satan. By whom was he bound? John informs us he saw an angel descend from heaven with the obvious intent of curtailing Satan's activities, for he came carrying a great chain in his hand and a key to the abyss. Who is that angel? (Gr. *angelon,* "messenger")

Is Jesus that angel? He could be; however, that interpretation does not seem to rise naturally from the text before us, nor from the name(s) or terms John ordinarily uses to refer to Jesus.

Various individual angels, and several groups of angels are referred to in the book. The term appears sixty-eight times — frequently in groups of seven, sometimes in the aggregate and approximately a dozen times with references to individual angels apart from the individualizing of the groups of seven. Besides such angels as the angel of the church at Ephesus, and the angel of the church at Sardis,

THE MILLENNIUM: REVELATION TWENTY

etc., there are references to certain even more select individual angels, some of whom are described as "strong" (5:2), "mighty" (10:1), "having the seal of God" (7:2), "having great authority" (18:1).

One angel is spoken of as "the angel of the abyss" (9:11), but since this name is called Abaddon (in Hebr.) and Apollyon (in Gr.), that is "Destroyer," he can hardly be identified with one whose name means "Saviour." The angel of the abyss could more readily be identified as Satan, or one of the chief angels in his hierarchy. Be that as it may, the angel who came down from heaven obviously had power over his domain, and over him, for he certainly had power over Satan.

Returning to the binding of Satan, Jesus certainly has implied that He has done just that. In the context of His warning concerning the blasphemy against the Holy Spirit (See Mt. 12:22-32, Mk. 3:23-30, Lk. 11:14-23, 12:10) Jesus asked the question: "How can one enter into the house of the strong man and spoil his goods, except he first bind the strong man?" (Mt. 12:29).

Jesus had just healed a man that was "possessed with a demon, blind and dumb" (v. 22). The multitudes were amazed and said, "Can this be the son of David?" (v. 23). The Pharisees did not dispute that a miracle had taken place, but they charged that Jesus had accomplished the feat "by Beelzebub, the prince of demons" (v. 24). In answering them Jesus' logic was devastating. "How can Satan cast out Satan? If a kingdom (or house) be divided against itself it cannot stand. If Satan has risen up against himself, and is thus divided, he cannot stand, but hath an end" (Mk. 3:23-30).

There are but two power sources sufficient to account for

the miracle — the power of God and the power of Satan. Having effectively exploded the Pharisees' charge that He had the power of Satan, that left only the power of God to account for it. It was in this context Jesus warned against blasphemy against the Holy Spirit. And it is in this same context that Jesus asked how the house occupied by a strong man can be entered and his goods destroyed unless first of all the strong man is bound.

The implication of all this is too obvious to be gainsayed. Jesus declares he has bound Satan. The fact is, He said He had "put the finger" on him, so to speak. "If I by the finger of God cast out demons, then is the kingdom of God come upon you" (Lk. 11:20). This saying bears remembering. It relates to other questions concerning the binding and loosing of Satan and the beginning of the reign of saints with Christ.

In the previous chapter of Luke is found the account of the mission of the seventy. Upon their return they exulted, "Lord, even the demons are subject unto us in thy name." He replied, "I beheld Satan falling as lightning from heaven. Behold, I have given you authority to tread upon serpents and scorpions, and over all the power of the enemy" (Lk. 10:17-19). Granted Jesus' reply is couched in apocalyptic language, the thrust of His words still comes through. Luke has previously reported that following Jesus' baptism (at which time he was anointed with the Holy Spirit and power, Acts 10:37, 38), Jesus returned in the power of the Spirit into Galilee (Lk. 4:14) and came to Nazareth where he had been brought up. "And he entered into the synagogue on the Sabbath day and stood up to read. And they delivered unto him the book of Isaiah, and he found the place where it is written:

THE MILLENNIUM: REVELATION TWENTY

> The Spirit of the Lord is upon me, because he anointed me to preach good tidings to the poor: He hath sent me to proclaim release to the captives, and recovering of sight to the blind, to set at liberty them that are bruised, and to proclaim the acceptable year of the Lord (Lk. 4:18, 19).

"Then began he to say unto them, 'Today hath this scripture been fulfilled in your ears' " (v. 21).

There can be no doubt about it. The binding of Satan was initiated at the onset of Jesus' ministry. This conclusion, admittedly, leaves unsettled the precise identity of the angel of Rev. 20:1. But that is no great matter. The whole episode in which the binding and loosing of Satan is described is couched in apocalyptic language. Perhaps the angel can no more be indisputably identified than the precise nature of the chain and the key that was used, or the location of the abyss into which Satan was cast. Note that it is only sealed "over" him, though the Greek word *abusmos* means literally "bottomless." As a figure of speech it means "very deep" or "of immeasurable depth."

Premillennialists of every stripe and segment uniformly ridicule the suggestion that Satan has already been bound. "If Satan is bound," they scoff, "he must have a long tether." That could be. Job could well have so complained. But Satan was bound nonetheless.

Others scornfully ask, "If Satan is bound and imprisoned, how do you account for the array of wickedness that is in the world?" It is a good question. But let it be recalled that Jimmy Hoffa continued to operate through a gangster-ridden labor union from a cell in a federal prison. Does someone say, "But God can build a better prison." True. But Satan is by far a more wily and formidable adversary than Hoffa. For the record. Jimmy Hoffa, though "loosed for a little while," has now been wiped out, insofar as this earth is concerned. And so shall it be with Satan (Rev. 20:10).

If Satan were not bound, limited, in some way restrained, one should tremble to think what life might be like on earth today. In the days of Noah "every thought and imagination of man's heart was only evil continually (Gen. 6:5). Thus the record reads, "and the earth was filled with violence" (v. 11). Can you imagine what it would be like today with the horrendous powers of destruction presently in human hands if Satan were not held in check to some degree?

It has been suggested that the binding of Satan might be compared to a vicious dog chained to a stake enclosed by a chain link fence. Those who would be foolish or unfortunate enough to enter the enclosure and come within the tether of the beast would find him as vicious and potent as though he were unleashed, perhaps more so by reason of his infuriation at being bound.

It is to be granted that the text does not readily suggest such an analogy. However we have already demonstrated the binding and the loosing of Satan, by the very nature of God's sovereignty, are relative terms. Perhaps the words "no more" (Rev. 20:3) may be taken to mean that Satan shall not be permitted to extend his power beyond the measure Christ allowed him to exercise during the days of His ministry. This has deprived him of the opportunities he would otherwise surely seize by reason of the advanced technology, communication media, and population. My conclusion is, Satan is bound. I wish he were bound more. I wish he had never been turned loose in the garden of Eden. Is it not striking that he is identified in Rev. 20:2 in the same symbolical characterization? However, an all-wise God has seen fit to permit Satan to live and strive against

THE MILLENNIUM: REVELATION TWENTY

Him, and to do so through mankind, and throughout the whole mundane world order.

If the problem of the extent of evil in the world today is an obstacle to the thesis that Satan is now bound, I can offer two or three more. 1. How does one account for the continuance of Satan's power during our Lord's lifetime, in view of the fact Jesus affirmed He had to bind Satan in order to cast out demons? 2. How does one account for the continuation of evil in the world into the apostolic age despite the fact Paul declares in Eph. 1:20-22 that "when God raised Christ from the dead He made Him to sit at his right hand in heavenly places far above all rule, and authority, and power, and dominion, and every name that is named, not only in this world, but also in that which is to come, and He put all things in subjection under his feet." 3. If the binding of Satan is to be interpreted in an absolute sense, and to be relegated to the "millennium" hypothecized following Christ's return, how does one explain the fact that when Satan is suddenly loosed for a little while he immediately enjoys such abounding success, deceiving the nations in the four corners of the earth, gathering them together to war against the saints, in numbers like the sands of the sea? And how is it that throughout the "fabled" millennium of popular theory Christ must rule with a rod of iron? Who is accomplishing Satan's work in the hearts of men if for a thousand calendar years He has been absolutely bound and out of circulation?

A question remains: Why is Satan loosed at the end of the thousand years, even for a little while? If God is indeed omniscient, if the Bible is His inspired Word, including the book of Revelation, God surely knows what Satan will do the moment his restraints are removed. Once bound, even if not absolutely, but more so than normally, why loosen him?

WHAT THE BIBLE SAYS ABOUT THE END TIME

There comes to mind one good reason, and at least a few illustrations to support it. Recall that Israel showed no disposition whatsoever to return to Canaan when the famine which drove them into Egypt had passed. Not until God permitted the Egyptians to heap great burdens and afflictions upon them did they want out. While dwelling in the region of Goshen, enjoying the richness of the Nile delta and the military protectorate of one of the great super powers of the ancient world, Israel "never had it so good." They were not about to give up a good thing until it soured on them.

So too with the apostolic church. Not even the apostles of Christ showed any disposition to preach the Gospel outside of the environs of Jerusalem until persecution drove them out. They were so ethnically oriented and so caught up in the nostalgia of the temple and of Jerusalem, they might very well have spent their lives in Jerusalem, waiting for the annual pilgrimages to bring their countrymen to their doorstep.

For a more current example there comes to mind a large assembly of men seated in a lecture hall at one of the St. Louis meetings of the North American Christian Covention. The song leader had led the men in spirited singing of a couple of stanzas of the song, "When We All Get to Heaven." Before the singing of the last verse he asked: "How many of you want to go to heaven?" It appeared as though every hand shot up. Whereupon the song leader lowered the boom. "How many of you," he asked, "want to go *right now?*" What a let down. There was scarcely a raised hand in the place. "Great was the fall thereof."

Might it not be that at the consummation of the end-time, God who knows our hearts may open "the snake pit" and

THE MILLENNIUM: REVELATION TWENTY

permit Satan, "the old serpent," to make one last menacing gesture? Or perhaps He will permit the viability of this planet to sink so low as to threaten the survival of the human race, before we really come to think seriously of the fact of which we sometimes sing: "This world is not my home, I'm just a-passing through."

> Our citizenship is in heaven: whence also we wait for a Saviour, the Lord Jesus Christ: who shall fashion anew this body of our humiliation, that it might be conformed to the body of his glory, according to the working whereby he is able to subject all things unto himself (Philippians 3:20, 21).

The First and Second Resurrections

Another towering question has to do with the first and second resurrections. Fortunately, John supplies us with some helpful keys. In verse 4 he tells us what the first resurrection is, or should we say, is not. It is the resurrection of souls who are then to live and reign with Christ as priests of God and of Christ for a thousand years (vs. 4, 6) and afterwards to reign with Him forever and ever (22:5). He does not speak at this point (20:4) of the resurrection of bodies. That comes later in the chapter. (See vs. 12, 13.)

It must be granted that the word "soul" is occasionally used in a synecdochal sense (in which a part stands for the whole). For example, "all the souls that came with Jacob into Egypt, which came out of his loins . . . all the souls were threescore and six" (Gen. 46:27). However, when John details the second resurrection (vs. 12, 13), he does not use the term soul. It is obvious that he is talking of the resurrection from the grave, whether of land or sea. It is the general resurrection set forth by Jesus in John 5:28, 29, an "hour that cometh in which all that are in the tombs shall come forth, they that have done good to the resurrection of life, and they that have done evil unto the resurrection of judgment."

As the first resurrection focuses on the new life that is enjoyed by those raised up to be priests of God and of Christ, so the second resurrection focus on the judgment of the wicked, but not exclusively so. Note that "the Book of Life" is opened, as well as the books containing the work record of all mankind. It is written, "they were judged *every man* out of the things which were written in the books, according to their works" (v. 12). Those not found written in the Book of Life were cast into the lake of fire, defined as the second death (v. 14).

The specific identification of the second death is a further clue to the nature of the first resurrection. Is it not logical that the first resurrection would be the resurrection of that which needs to be raised first? This brings us to the question, what is the first death? That fixed we should be able to fix the certainty of the phrase, the first resurrection.

To find the answer to the question of the nature of the first death, we need simply to go back to Genesis, chapter three, wherein is recorded the entry of death into the world. Note that the first death was not the death of the body. Physical death was only a side effect. God had warned Adam and Eve concerning the forbidden tree: "In the day thou eatest thereof thou shalt surely die" (Gen. 2:17). Did He mean it? Adam and Eve certainly did not die physically that day, else the human race would had died at the stem. Adam at least lived some eight hundred years after he and Eve were banished from the garden of Eden (Gen.5:4,5). But the day they sinned they died spiritually. That very day they forfeited rapport with God. And as we follow in his footsteps, as we become sinners, we too die, spiritually.

THE MILLENNIUM: REVELATION TWENTY

It is from this first death that we die, spiritual death, that we must first be raised if we are to live and reign with Christ and escape the power of the second death. This is the thrust of such a passage as Ephesians 2:1ff.

> And you did he make alive, when you were dead through your trespasses and sins, wherein ye once walked according to the course of this world, according to the prince of the powers of the air, of the spirit that now worketh in the sons of disobedience, among whom we also once walked in the lusts of our flesh, doing the desires of the flesh and of the mind, and were by nature children of wrath, even as the rest (vs. 1-3).

There can be no doubt about it. The first death we experience, as did Adam, is spiritual death. That being so, God through Christ has initiated a redemptive process whereby the first resurrection shall redeem us from the first death. Hear it, as Paul continues to say:

> But God, being rich in mercy, for his great love wherewith he loved us even when we were dead through our trespasses, *made us alive together with Christ* (by grace have ye been saved) *and raised us up with him,* and *made us to sit with him in heavenly places in Christ Jesus* (vs. 4-6).

Do we not have here a perfect parallel to what John speaks of in Rev. 20:4-6? However, Ephesians 2:1ff. is not Paul's only witness to this fact. Paul's extended baptism discourse, Romans, chapter six, affirms the same thing, as does also the condensed statement of the same doctrine in Col. 2:12, 13.

Reigning with Christ in His kingdom is not something denied us in this life, to be postponed unto some future time, Christ having failed to establish His kingdom at His first coming. "The kingdom of God is within you" (Lk. 17:21). Having been given the victory over the world, the flesh and the devil, and having been made an elect race, a holy nation, a royal priesthood, a people for God's own possession, the light of the world, the salt of the earth, the pillar and ground of the truth, even temples of the Holy Spirit and a habitation of God in the Spirit, we are here and now reigning with Christ in his true millennial kingdom.

And if we can believe what Paul has to say, as he continues in Ephesians, chapter two, we shall reign with Him the more gloriously and triumphantly, even everlastingly, in the consummation of the ages. Hear it from him. Having just said that God has raised us up with Christ and made us to sit with Him in heavenly places in Christ Jesus, he adds:

> That in the ages to come he might show the exceeding riches of his grace in kindness toward us in Christ Jesus. For by grace have ye been saved, through faith; and that [grace, salvation — gracious salvation] is not of yourselves, it is the gift of God (vs. 7, 8).

Hallelujah! The Lord God omnipotent reigneth. And we are living and reigning with Christ as priests of God and of Christ. Moreover, the best is yet to come.

A problem remains. If the millennial kingdom of Christ is His present spiritual kingdom, His church, how can it be said of those whose span of threescore years and ten, perhaps a little more but often less, that they live and reign with him throughout the course of the church age? Is this really a problem? Is not "to be absent from the body to be at home with the Lord" (II Cor. 5:8)? This is not necessarily to say that the dead in Christ are actually with Him in glory, seated at the right hand of God, any more than Paul in Ephesians, chapter two, is trying to tell us that as we now live and reign with Christ "in heavenly places" (no less) we are actually with Him in glory. But assuredly the "blessed dead," those

THE MILLENNIUM: REVELATION TWENTY

who die in the Lord, do indeed henceforth rest from their labors, their toils and their cares, and their works do follow them (Rev. 14:13). They are still, yea now more so, more than conquerors in Christ. For neither death nor anything else, present or yet to come, can separate them (Rom. 8:35-39). The dead in Christ join that "great cloud of witnesses" of whom Hebrews 12:1 speaks. "God is not the God of the dead, but of the living" (Mt. 22:32). The dead in Christ are still living and reigning with Christ. John saw their souls beneath the altar (Rev. 6:9) and their concerns were noted and received due attention, vs. 10, 11. They are no longer exercising their priestly function, for they are said to "rest from their labors," but they are alive and well.

What About the Thousand Years

We have already touched upon the nature of the thousand years, but as the term is used in each of six consecutive verses (Rev. 20:2, 3, 4, 5, 6, and 7) the picture becomes clearer as other facets of John's vision are recorded. The number, "a thousand," as with other elements of the vision, is symbolic.

In Hebrew, particularly in poetical and apocalyptical usage, the number communicates fullness or largeness. It is the cube of the digits which are the root of mathematics. $10 \times 10 \times 10 = 1000$. If God had created man with a different number of digits, the digital system would have been different. But He did not.

We think of the circle as a symbol of perfection. This is a point of emphasis in the ring facet of the wedding ceremony. But the word does not even appear in the Hebrew text of the Old Testament. It appears but once even in translation, and not at all in the New Testament. Isa. 40:22 speaks of Jehovah as "he that sitteth above the circle (Hebr. *chug* — lit., vault, arch) of the earth." The text is viewed today in the light of relative modern disclosure of the sphericity of the earth. But the Hebrew text, while not contradictory thereto, nonetheless is not a revelatory anticipation of advanced scientific knowledge. Its purpose is to tell us something about God, not to inform us of the shape of the earth. God is enthroned far above the vaulted sky which extends to the limits of earth's horizon in every direction.

To the Hebrews it was the cube that symbolized fullness, completeness, perfection. Thus the Holy of Holies, the throne room of the tabernacle (and later of the temple, in which case the dimensions were doubled) was a cube — ten cubits long, ten cubits wide, ten cubits high — one thousand cubic cubits. So too, the Holy City, New Jerusalem is described in Rev. 21:6 as "the city which lieth foursquare, the breadth and length and height thereof are equal" — twelve thousand furlongs, a mind boggling number, in every direction.

The one thousand year reign of Christ in Revelation twenty is not a number to be taken literally any more than the Psalmist's affirmation that "the cattle on a thousand hills are the Lord's" is intended to imply He owns only that many and no more. They are all His. The number is a symbol of completeness. The whole Christian era is embraced by the vision of John in Revelation twenty. Note that those who live and reign with Christ as "priests" do so "for a thousand years." But when the curse is no more (Rev. 22:4) and man is restored to the full fellowship of God, given again to eat of the tree of life, and God's name is on his forehead (that is, His authority is constantly kept in mind) there is then no more need for priestly ministrations. It is then said of the saints simply that "they shall *reign* with Him." But now it is said that they shall reign "forever and ever" — that is, unto the ages of the ages.

Other Facets of the Vision

The foregoing interpretation of the nature of the thousnd year reign is strengthened as other facets of the vision are considered. For example:

1. The thrones (plural). John says nothing in this chapter of seeing Christ in Jerusalem, seated upon the throne of a restored Davidic Jewish Empire. The reigning of Christ is mentioned only inferentially, in the sense that the throne occupants "live and reign with Christ."

2. The occupants of the thrones. These have judgment given to them. The meaning of this is not developed or explained in the text. Such texts as 1 Cor. 6:2, "Know ye not that the saints shall judge the world," and Dan. 7:22, "The Ancient of Days come, and judgment was given unto the saints of the Most High, and the time came that the saints possessed the kingdom," come to mind as one contemplates the verse in question.

The occupants themselves are further identified as a) those decapitated for their Christian witness and b) those who worshipped not the beast nor his image, and received not his mark upon their forehead or hand. The forehead is a symbol of the mind and the hand of service (See Ex. 13:16 and Deut. 4:8 for a possible basis of this symbol). Hence those who do not allow false systems to occupy their minds, and do not serve that which is evil are depicted.

Why did John single out from among the martyrs the decapitated? Why not those crucified, or garrotted, or burned at the stake, or torn asunder by wild beasts in the arena? Perhaps he does so because decapitation, the lopping off of the capitas (the head), the center of consciousness, self-awareness, rationality and will, is the most direct, dramatic assault upon human personality of any form of execution, so much so that to this day public execution of any kind is called capital punishment. Hence the imagery is a symbol of martyrdom per se. All Christian martyrs and martyrdom is embraced thereby.

3. Gog and Magog. Popular theory identifies Gog and Magog with Russia and Red China. In Ezek. 38:2 Gog is of the land of Magog, the chief prince of Rosh, Meshech and Tubal. Premillennialists see in Russia and Moscow derivatives of Rosh and Meshech. In their "Eastus vs. Westus" version of the battle of Armageddon Gog and Magog become the godless communist strongholds of Russia and Red China. Mention of "the uttermost parts of the north" (Ezek. 38:6) is supposed to strengthen this interpretation. East is expanded in this case to include that which is northward, but not of course "the uttermost parts of the north." The artic circle simply does not have the hordes of inhabitants necessary to accommodate the theory. In the ancient world Magog lay east of Scythia, to the north of the Caspian sea.

How did John interpret Gog and Magog? Quite differently. They are the nations in the four corners of the earth, v. 8. The mention of the earth's dimensions in that fashion is not intended to support an ancient concept of the earth's form, but rather as reference to the four points of the compass, east, west, north and south. John is speaking of the entire earth. No specific geographical designations or ethnic group are intended.

THE MILLENNIUM: REVELATION TWENTY

4. The war that was not—the Battle of Armageddon? The war that really turned out not to be one is thought by some to be the so-called battle of Armageddon. The term is a grossly overworked apocalyptic symbol in current eschatology. The name grows out of mention in Rev. 16:14-16 of "the kings of the whole world," v. 14, (presumably their armies are included, though not mentioned) being gathered together into a place which is called in Hebrew, Har-mageddon" (lit., Hill of Megiddo). Megiddo is a promontory overlooking the valley of Esdrelon, also known as the valley of Jezreel (Josh. 17:16, Judg. 6:33). A number of the bloodiest, most decisive battles of the Biblical world were fought in that locale. In World War I, General Allenby defeated the Turks there. Its dimensions scarcely lend themselves to an engagement of vast armies, as envisioned by sensationalists committed to literalism wherever possible. Neither do the changing patterns of warfare brought on by aerial and stratospheric technology correspond to the supposition that the battle of all battles will be fought on the ground in so restricted and vulnerable a site. The battle of Armageddon is best understood as an apocalyptic symbol of warfare per se, much as in modern times any one who suffers a crushing defeat is said to have met his Waterloo.

The alternative to the foregoing interpretation of Rev. 20:1-10 is to read into the text: 1) The regathering of Israel in Palestine, 2) Christ's kingdom headquartered in Jerusalem, with the Jews front and center; 3) the nations of the earth ruled by Christ and His saints, but hating Him and His rule insomuch that He must rule with a rod of iron even though Satan's influence is completely removed from the earth because he is absolutely bound and sealed off in the abyss for a thousand years; 4) all this preceded by only a partial resurrection day, that is, a resurrection only of the bodies of his saints; 5) the assumption that the Jews, with the Holy Spirit absent from the world, will turn out to be more effective evangelists than was the church with the help of the Holy Spirit and the power of the Gospel; 6) such incongruities as a) a restored temple, Levitical priesthood, and sacrificial system, b) angels now residing on earth, nonincarnated, and resurrected saints in glorified bodies, sustained by the viands of this physical world and dwelling alongside ordinary mortals, and c) whatever else is mandated for a literal interpretation of Old Testament prophecies. We shall have more to say of this latter observation in the next chapter.

Possibly a third option may be found in the work of Robert H. Mounce, *The Book of Revelation*, published by Eerdman's as a part of *The New International Commentary on the New Testament* series. Mounce has contributed a very scholarly commentary, correlating a considerable body of secondary (psuedepigraphical, rabbinic and other extra-biblical) literature. He attempts to be completely objective, and hence advances few conclusions, preferring the role of "the devil's advocate"; challenging the conclusions drawn by writers of the various schools of eschatalogical thought.

Chapter Five

THE KINGDOM OF THE MESSIAH

One's concept of the Messiah's kingdom will affect virtually every facet of end-time study. Two concepts predominate. One equates the church and the kingdom, for all practical purposes. Those so persuaded view Christ's kingdom as spiritual, "within," rather than "of this world." Insofar as His kingdom is concerned Christ's return is to claim His kingdom subjects, review their stewardship with a view to determining their rewards as they are then inducted into the eternal kingdom in which we shall reign forever and ever. I Cor. 15:25 informs us that for the present, that is, in this present age, "he must reign till he hath put his enemies under his feet" (even death, v. 26). "Then cometh the end, when he shall deliver up the kingdom of God, even the Father; when He shall have abolished all rule and all authority and power" (v. 24) except God (v. 27, 28).

The converse view is that the kingdom is not come, having been aborted by reason of the Jews' rejection of Christ, hence postponed until He returns with angelic reinforcement to establish again the throne of His father David, and rule the nations "with a rod of iron" (Rev. 19:15). The kingdom is thus viewed as an earthly political empire and is equated with the "thousand year" reign of Revelation, chapter twenty.

As with most Christian doctrines the New Testament teaching concerning Christ's kingdom is rooted in the Old Testament, hence the high pitch of Jewish expectancy. The fact is, the kingdom of the Messiah was the hallmark of Old Testament eschatology.

Two strains of eschatological thought are discernible in the Old Testament. One focused on the national hope of Israel as God's covenant people. This is so well known that it hardly calls for proof or elaboration. There was also a more transcendant form of messianic hope with universal, even cosmological expectations. The destiny of the Gentiles, and of the earth, and even of the heavens above, came within the scope of prophetic utterances.

In His covenant with Abraham, God promised that not only would Abraham and his seed be blessed, but they would be a blessing. In him, and in his seed, all the families of the earth would be blessed (Gen. 12:2, 3).

In the rainbow covenant with Noah, God promised never again to destroy the earth with water, affirming "while the earth remaineth, seed time and harvest, cold and heat, summer and winter, day and night shall not cease" (Gen. 8:22). The implications of that text are that the earth will not remain always. The next time God's wrath is poured out upon all the earth the result will not be just catastrophic; it will be utterly consuming. For the vehicle of judgment, we are to learn from later prophecies, is to be an all consuming fire.

The suggestion that the earth shall not be around forever runs counter to one of the cardinal doctrines of the Watchtower Society and the Armstrongites, and indeed of pre-millennialists in general. Isaiah 45:18 is quoted as proof the earth will be inhabited forever, although God did not exactly say that. He only said He made the earth "to be inhabited . . . He did not create it in vain." It does not bother them that they have aded the word "forever" to their interpretation of the passage, nor that the earth has for long been inhabited and therefore could hardly be said to have been created in vain. Nor does it bother them that Isa. 65:17 plainly quotes Jehovah as saying, "Behold, I create new heavens and a new earth: and the former things shall not be remembered, nor come into the mind." Peter quotes from this very text in the closing chapter of his second epistle, and interprets it as follows:

> But the day of the Lord will come as a thief; in which the *heavens shall pass away* with a great noise, and the *elements shall be dissolved* with fervent heat, and the *earth* and the works that are therein *shall be burned up.*
>
> Seeing these things are *all to be dissolved,* what manner of persons ought ye to be in all holy living and godliness, looking for and earnestly desiring the coming of the day of God, by reason of which *the heavens being on fire shall be dissolved and the elements shall melt with fervent heat?* But according to his promise we look for *new heavens and a new earth* wherein dwelleth righteousness (2 Pt. 3:10-13).

The context of the passage contrasts the partial destruction (the destruction of animal life, including man, save for those in the ark) wrought by the flood with the utter dissolution which shall be wrought by the consuming fire. But premillennialists are so insistent upon a literal interpretation of Old Testament prophecies they find it quite impossible to take the above prophecy literally, else they have no literal city of Jerusalem in which Christ can literally set up his millennial throne and rule over Israel and through them the world for a literal one thousand years. Thus, in theory, God will only "burn" the earth's crust "like a bride's biscuit," scrape the char, and replant the garden of Eden somewhere in the environs of Palestinian Jerusalem and rule there a thousand years. Then come the fireworks again, or some means of clearing the site for the new Jerusalem. For in conformity with the materialistic mentality which characterizes the theory, even heaven itself will be moved to earth — at least that part which shall accommodate the most of the redeemed. In Watchtower Society eschatology "the elect"— the one hundred and forty four thousand upper echelon of the Jehovah's Witnesses — these and these only go to heaven above to live with God. The rest of the redeemed dwell on earth below with Christ.

Such an interpretation is not altogether surprising. The Jews of Jesus' day were similarly caught up in a materialistic concept of the Messiah's kingdom. Though Hebrew prophecy was infused from earliest times with both facets of eschatological promise, universal as well as national, the Jews unfortunately were more concerned with their own national destiny than they were with the destiny of the nations. Hence the messianic predictions of the prophets came to be regarded as utterances made in the interest of the Jews only. The tragedy deepens when we note that the messianic hopes of Israel not only grew increasingly self-centered but increasingly materialistic also.

It is at this point that both Christ and the authors of the New Testament Scriptures came into conflict with the national self-interest of the Jews. And, we venture to add, they continue in conflict with the bulk of eschatological thinking of our own generation. How and why? Because of the appearance of One who laid strong claims to being the Messiah but who gave little if any support to their dreams of a revived political kingdom, a hermeneutical crisis arose. The crisis had to be resolved. Either Jesus of Nazareth's claim to be the Messiah had to be rejected, or the hope of the messianic kingdom had to be postponed. The unbelieving Jews took the first option. Premillennialists take the second. But Christ and the New Testament writers (including Christ's apostles) took the middle ground. They faced the crisis head on.

THE KINGDOM OF THE MESSIAH

What the Jews thought the prophets had predicted as an immediate accomplishment of the Messiah at His appearing was proclaimed by Christ to be spiritual in essence and developmental in accomplishment. That is to say, the coming of the kingdom was proclaimed to be something which takes place within men, not imposed upon them. The kingdom was to be ushered in and is extended through the preaching of the Gospel rather than imposed through carnal warfare. The Messiah's throne is to be at the right hand of the Father in heaven, not in a palace in Jerusalem. His kingdom is to be spiritual, not of this world. His subjects, like Abraham, are to confess themselves to be pilgrims and sojourners on earth, amabassadors in a foreign land. As Paul was later to so eloquently state it: "Our citizenship is in heaven, whence also we wait for a Saviour, the Lord Jesus Christ" (Phil. 3:20).

It was for this cause that Pilate found no fault in Him. When Jesus acknowledged that he considered Himself to be a king, but went on to explain His kingdom was not of this world, and therefore His subjects were not about to take up arms and fight (Jn. 18:36, 37); Pilate understood. Strange, strange is it not, that to this day multitudes who profess to take Him at His word do not understand what Pilate understood so readily. If Jesus had in mind the establishing of the kind of messianic kingdom the Jews had in mind, and premillennialists still do, Pilate would have had no choice but to order Christ crucified. Instead he sought to set Jesus free.

Mark this. It was not embarrassed theologians of some later time but Christ, and His inspired apostles as they followed His example, who reconciled messianic prophecy with Christian history by spiritualizing the messianic hope enunciated by the Old Testament prophets. Again we exhort: Mark this. It is as unacceptable to most prophetic interpreters of our day as it was to carnal Israel in Jesus' day, and for no little while to His twelve disciples also. Despite all that Christ and the New Testament authors have said to the contrary, promoters of end-time theology continue to insist upon a literal fulfillment of Hebrew prophecy. The fact is, there is little if anything that carnal Israel expected of the Messiah at His coming that is not expected by their modern counterparts at His second coming. If Jesus does not do for Israel, upon His return, precisely what the Jews expected of Him at His first coming the greater part of those professing to be looking for and earnestly desiring the coming of the Lord will be sorely displeased with Him. It was this that led the late inimical Sam Lappin to quip: "If Christ should come in the clouds at this moment, many who profess to be longing for His return would shoot Him for a blackbird."

There is undisguised irony evident in that gem of (shall we say) "occidental hyperbole"; obviously it is overstated to underscore a point. The point needs to be underscored. It needs more. It needs to be shouted from the tallest transmitters towering above our housetops. It is from thence we hear so much that is contrariwise today.

Jesus is even now on the throne of David, and has been since the day He ascended into heaven and sat down at the right hand of God. But His territory is neither gained nor governed by military or political power. "The kingdom of God is within you" (Lk. 17:21).

Hear it from the Apostle Peter. Speaking "as the Spirit gave him utterance" (Acts 2:4), Peter prefaced a quotation from one of the great kingdom prophecies of David (Psalms 110) by 1) an extended quotation from Ps. 16 in which

THE KINGDOM OF THE MESSIAH

David prophesied concerning the resurrection, and 2) an explanation of the same, saying:

> Brethren, I may say unto you freely of the patriarch David, that he both died and was buried, and his tomb is with us to this day. Being therefore a prophet, and knowing that *God had sworn with an oath to him, that of the fruit of his loins he would set one upon his throne;* he foreseeing this spake of the resurrection of the Christ, that neither was he (his soul) left unto Hades, nor did his flesh see corruption. This Jesus did God raise up, whereof we all are witnesses.

Now note the application:

> Being therefore by the right hand of God exalted and having received of the Father the promise of the Holy Spirit, he hath poured forth this which ye see and hear. *For David ascended not into the heavens: but he saith Himself,*
>
> > The Lord said unto my Lord,
> > Sit thou on my right hand
> > Till I make thy enemies
> > The footstool of thy feet.
>
> Let all the house of Israel therefore know assuredly that *God hath made him both Lord and Christ,* this Jesus whom ye have crucified. (Acts 2:29-37)

If Jesus was not already established on the throne of David, at God's right hand, then the Holy Spirit who ought to have known better, because He is the prime "mover" (see II Peter 1:21) of both testaments, not only misled Peter but failed to direct the historian Luke to correct the error. Better by far that we take issue with the interpreters of Scripture than with the Holy Spirit.

In his thought provoking paperback, *An Eschatology of Victory,* (Presbyterian and Reformed Publishing Co.) p. 205, Marcellus Kik writes:

WHAT THE BIBLE SAYS ABOUT THE END TIME

The trouble is that we have altogether a too materialistic concept of the millennial blessings. We fail to see that the greatest blessings are spiritual and they are in our midst. We are looking for a material kingdom, a material throne, and material prosperity. In this we fall into the same error with which our Lord had to contend with His disciples. We fail to see that the greatest millennial blessings are already in our midst.

He then cites several, not the least of which is the offering of salvation for all that call upon the name of our Saviour and the inclusion of the Gentiles in the covenant blessings of God. He suggests that as individuals Christians should ask themselves: "What more could the popular conception of the millennial kingdom give me than that which we already possess?" We have a Saviour who is our Prophet, Priest and King. God the Father is our covenant God. We have the forgiveness of our sins, not merely the forestalling of sin's penalty, but the remission of our sins. We have the Holy Spirit to indwell us and be our sanctifier and comforter. We belong to the church which is bride-elect of the Lamb. We are standing on Mt. Zion; we are citizens of that better country. We as well as the Old Testament saints belong to the commonwealth of Israel. We are no more strangers from the covenants of promise. We have eternal life and but await the Saviour to exchange the bodies of our humiliation for bodies conformed unto His glory. Could we gain the whole material world and lose these spiritual blessings we would profit nothing. We would have lost all that is worth the keeping, indeed all that shall abide. The absence of greater blessings is no fault of our Saviour king. It is due to a lack of faith and a warped sense of values.

Let us cease demanding of Christ that He prove His Divine Sonship by turning stones into bread and putting on spectaculars, as though he were a circus performer or staging an episode combining the best of Ben Hur and Star Wars.

The Church in Prophecy

The kingdom versus the church controversy owes much to the widespread use of the *Schofield Reference Bible,* a one man commentary so presented in format that the comments appear to be drawn naturally from the text of the Scriptures. To the contrary, Schofield, building on the foundation of Darby dispensationalism, has superimposed the ultra-dispensational dogma upon the Scriptures.

The Darby-Schofield hypothesis relegates the church to the role of a stop-gap measure, a kind of afterthought conceived by Christ to provide something to fill the gap between His return to the Father and his return to earth. The church is said to have no place in the minds of the Old Testament prophets. They speak of it therefore as "the mystery parenthesis." The prophet's saw only Christ's first coming and His yet to come earthly kingdom; thus His two comings are said to have been fused into one in the minds of the prophets. The church is regarded as "in the valley" beneath the sighting of the prophets who saw instead the higher ranges of God's purpose in Christ.

According to this bizarre thesis, what actually happened at Caesarea Philippi might be couched in contemporary jargon somewhat as follows: after eliciting from the twelve popular appraisals of His office and person, and Peter's classic confession of faith in His messiahship and Divine sonship, the conversation may have gone something like this:

Jesus: "Fellows, I have some good news and some bad news. First, the bad news. I am to be crucified, not crowned — at least not for awhile."

WHAT THE BIBLE SAYS ABOUT THE END TIME

Disciples: "That *is* bad news. We can't believe it. We won't stand for it."

Jesus: "It isn't all that bad. I'm going to surprise them. I will be raised from the grave."

Disciples: "That's good! That's great!"

Jesus: "It isn't all that good, at least not for you. I will be leaving you. In fact I'm going home to my Father."

Disciples: "That's bad; well, for us it is. We will miss you. You know we have just about forsaken all to follow you."

Jesus: "It isn't all that bad. You see, I plan to return."

Disciples: "That's good."

Jesus: "It isn't all that good. I may not come back for quite some time."

Disciples: "That's bad."

Jesus: "It isn't all that bad. I've got a job for you. To fill in the gap between my departure and my return I'm going to build a, uh, let me think a minute. I've got it. I will call it my church. And I will give you the job of setting it up. And Peter, I will put you in charge."

Peter: "That's great."

James and John: "Big deal. Mom always wanted us two to be your right and left hand men. We kinda had that in mind ourselves."

Jesus: "You are right about one thing, James and John. It isn't any big deal. And Peter, it isn't as great as you may think. The church won't do well. Not at all. But I've got to do something to fill in the gap until I can come back again. And so I've come up with this — my church. And my entering the gates of death will not prevail against my doing this. I will send the Holy Spirit to help you get it under way."

Admittedly, a bit of imagination has crept into the "text" of the conversation just reported, but no more imagination than called for by the Darby-Schofield "postponed kingdom" hypothesis.

For a scholarly but readable and readily comprehensible exposé of the hypothesis one will do well to consult Oswald T. Alllis' classic work, *Prophecy in the Church* (now available in paperback from Presbyterian and Reformed Publ.). Chapter six is particularly germane to the present inquiry.

The inquiry can be accomplished on a do-it-yourself basis if one has the use of a Bible which footnotes the Old Testament Scriptures cited or alluded to in the New. If one will open the Bible to the book of Acts wherein Luke traces the history of the church from its birth through the first generation, one can easily ascertain more than a score of Old Testament prophecies declared to be fulfilled by events of the church age then ensuing. This would hardly be possible if the church indeed is a "mystery parenthesis," an unscheduled and hence non-predicted development.

Among the salient references we may note the following. 1. Peter's positive identification of the descent of the Holy Spirit on Pentecost with the "it shall come to pass in the latter days," (saith Jehovah) prediction of Joel 2:28ff. Peter's *"this is that"* affirmation leaves no room for reassessment. 2. Peter's use of Ps. 110.1 has already been duly noted. It deserves to be called to mind at this point. 3. Psalm two, one of the most striking messianic kingdom Psalms is twice cited as being in the process of fulfillment, in Acts 4:25-28 and 13:33 (the second time by Paul). The scope of the Messiah's kingdom as stated in Ps. 2:8 finds its echo in Jesus' commission to the twelve in Acts 1:8.

An especially relevant text is found in Acts 3:24. In the course of Peter's sermon on Solomon's porch he calls attention to Moses' prediction in Deut. 18:15-19 that he would be superseded by "another prophet" to whom the people should hearken. The context makes clear that Peter would have his hearers understand that time had come. And in that very context he adds these significant words: "Yea and *all the prophets* from Samuel and them that followed after, *as many as have spoken,* they also have *told of these days."* Mark that. These days! The church age.

Time and space scarcely permit even the highlighting of the same phenomena as it abounds in the epistles. One text, however, deserves notice for it uses a part of the phrase invented by the ultra-dispensationalists — "mystery" — but not, take note, "the mystery parenthesis." Quite the contrary. Paul writes in Eph. 3:8-12 as follows:

> Unto me who am less than the least of all saints, was this grace given, to preach unto the Gentiles the unsearchable riches of Christ: and to make all men see what is the dispensation of *the mystery which for ages hath been hid in God** who created all things, to the intent that now unto the principalities and powers in the heavenly places *might be made known through the church* the manifold wisdom of God, *according to his eternal purpose which* he purposed in Christ Jesus.

To borrow a phrase from the apostle Paul, "What saith the oracles of God" (Rom. 11:4), i.e. what do the Scriptures have to say, stripped of the revisionist doctrines of men? We submit the following summary.

1. He was born the King of the Jews. Or at least the wise

---

* Note: The underscored phrase, "the mystery which for the ages hath been hid in God," is supposedly the key to the Darby-Schofield discovery. They did not read far enough. The apostle goes on to say that it has been God's "intent" all along to make known *through the church* His manifold wisdom according to His eternal purpose which He purposed in Christ Jesus.

men who came to see the Christ-child so thought (Mt. 2:2-9). Matthew, in reporting the fact, says nothing to infer they were mistaken in their esteem.

2. If He was not born to be King, or if so born God's purpose had gone awry, as late as the day of His crucifixion Jesus had not yet accepted the same to be so. Note, for example, His conversation with Pilate in John 18:33-38. And consider the implication of what is reported in Luke 23:37-43. Apparently Jesus considered Himself to be king right down to His dying breath. He was arraigned before Pilate for such a claim, and He did not try to lie out of it. However, when He made plain to Pilate the fact His kingdom was not the kind that Jews were wanting, (and most millennialists are still wanting and expecting), Pilate would have preferred to set Him free. He said he "found no fault" in Him. That is, no evidence of intended treason. Somehow the dying thief also seemed to sense what many yet refuse to understand. He received a precious promise from Christ because of it.

3. If Christ indeed belatedly conceived of the church as an ad interim measure, and so announced to His disciples at Caesarea Philippi, He behaved most strangely a few days later when He staged His triumphal entry into Jerusalem and accepted the plaudits of the populace who openly hailed Him as King. (See Mt. 21:1-11, Mk. 11:1-10, Lk. 19:29-40 and Jn. 12:12-19). To His inveterate enemies that was the last straw. Few things He might have done could have more angered and solidified them against Him.

4. If Christ conceived of the church as something different from the kingdom He surely must have confused Peter when He said, "Upon this rock I will build my church and the gates of hades shall not prevail against it. I will give unto

thee the keys of the kingdom . . ." If the church is not the kingdom, the keys Jesus gave to Peter and the rest of the apostles (See Mt. 18:18 and Jn. 20:23) must surely long since have rusted away from disuse. When are those keys going to be put to use? Or is there some truth after all to the fantasies and jokes which represent Peter as standing at the gates of heaven deciding who can enter and who can not?

Some try to ease the problem by making distinctions between the kingdom of heaven and the kingdom of God. The problem with that is we have three Gospels which are so closely parallel they can be called snyoptics. In reporting the same teachings of Christ the synoptists use the terms interchangeably. Matthew has a penchant for the phrase "kingdom of heaven," and Mark and Luke seem to prefer the phrase "kingdom of God." The reader-audience to whom they were directed accounts for this. To the materialistic Jews the phrase "kingdom of *heaven*" has obvious corrective value. To a polytheistic Roman and Greek society the phrase of *God* (singular) would likewise have a built-in corrective.

5. If the kingdom was to be postponed for centuries to come, now already postponed over 1900 years, Jesus must certainly have misled His disciples when He said there were some standing by who would not taste of death till they saw "the kingdom of God come with power" (Mt. 16:28, Mk. 9:1, Lk. 9:27). Where are those super Methusalahs, those hardy "bristle cone pine" human wonders who have not died and indeed will not die until they see Christ returned and enthroned in great power in His kingdom?

Again there are those whose theories embarrass them in the face of such predictions, and who desperately seek some way out of their dilemma. These try to make the word "generation" to have only a generic meaning, as referring to the Jewish race. Thus Jesus is saying only that there would still be survivors of the Jewish race when He returned to set up His kingdom. One wonders *what other races* may have been present when He made His announcement, that He should therefore have been obliged to say, there are *"some* of them that stand by . . ." How true is the adage which says: "Oh what a tangled web we weave when first we practice to deceive."

6. If the kingdom was postponed because of the rejection of the Jews how does one explain such a text as John 6:15? When He fed the multitudes in the wilderness the Jews apparently saw in Jesus the fulfillment of Deut. 18:15. The new Moses who could cause bread to materialize in the wilderness had come. God had raised up a new leader like unto Moses. Jesus therefore perceived that "they were about to come and take him by force, to make him king" (Jn. 6:15). How strangely He reacted, if He actually came to set up a material, political kingdom. It was when Jesus made known unto them that He had an entirely different kind of kingdom in mind that we read, "Upon this many of his disciples went back and walked no more with him" (Jn. 6:66).

7. Finally, as we have already had occasion to note, if the church is not Christ's kingdom then the Holy Spirit put the wrong words into Peter's mouth on the day of Pentecost. Peter plainly stated that Jesus was then occupying David's throne, howbeit at the right hand of God (Acts 2:29ff.).

Two Significant Vision Prophecies

Two significant kingdom prophecies illustrate the pains to which theorists will go to support their bizarre interpretations:

WHAT THE BIBLE SAYS ABOUT THE END TIME

Nebuchadnezzar's "image-vision" (Daniel, Ch. 2) and Daniel's own "seventy-week" vision (Dan. 9:24-27).

1. Nebuchadnezzar's Image-vision

The description of the awesome image which the king dreamed, but could not recall is described by Daniel in chapter two, verses 31-35, and interpreted in vs. 36-45. There can be no doubt about the identity of "the head of gold." Daniel took care of that. Babylon was the head of gold. There is no serious controversy over the identity of the other parts of the image, despite the fact Daniel did not specifically identify each of them. The "inferior" kingdom (the breast and arms of silver) is readily agreed upon as being the Medio-Persian empire that was soon to conquer and replace Babylon as a world power. The "belly of brass" is likewise generally recognized as the Grecian empire which became the next super power. Even the fourth, "the legs of iron with feet part iron and part clay," is readily agreed upon as being the Roman empire which superseded the Grecian.

What then is the problem? The problem is that Nebuchadnezzar saw not only the image but "a stone cut out of a mountain without hands" (cp. v. 34 and 45), which came rolling down the mountainside, apparently gaining mass and momentum as it came hurtling down. It smote the feet of the image (v. 34) pulverizing them and the rest of the image also, v. 35 (apparently symbolic of the manner in which each of the kingdoms had consumed the kingdom which had preceded), and the smiting stone itself became a mighty kingdom, becoming as it were, "a great mountain filling all the earth" v. 35.

Daniel's interpretation of that aspect of the king's vision

THE KINGDOM OF THE MESSIAH

was: *"In the days of those kings,"* (the kings represented by the legs of iron and feet part iron and part clay — the fourth great world power, the Roman empire):

> The God of heaven will set up a kingdom that shall never be destroyed, nor its sovereignty be given to another people, but it shall break in pieces and consume all these kingdoms, and it shall stand forever (2:44).

Why should that be a problem? It isn't unless one has a theory to defend which makes no allowance for a kingdom of God to be established in the days of the historical Roman empire. Ah, that is the problem. Dispensational millennialists refuse to accept the church as the "smiting stone" which became a kingdom growing to world wide proportions. The two are separated. The stone becomes Christ at His second coming, and then becomes His "millennial" kingdom. How is this arranged? The "prophetic clock," we are told, stops when the Jews are not in Jerusalem and remains stopped until they return. But that still poses a chronological problem. So the concept is modified to say that the clock stopped even before the fall of Jerusalem because of their rejection of Jesus' kingship. It stopped with the crucifixion, to remain stopped until the day that interpreters fix as the sure date of the Jews' return to Jerusalem. That sure date was once decided upon when the nation of Israel was granted re-occupation rights and self rule in Palestine by a special assembly of the United Nations in 1947. It has been adjusted from time to time to fit the chronology of end-time experts who believe they are able through minute study to zero in on the day (if not the hour) of Christ's second coming. In that they claim an expertise that Jesus said to be outside the domain of even the angels of heaven, and Himself as well (Mt. 24:36).

But the problem deepens. Daniel prophesied that the kingdom of the Messiah would be established in the days of the Roman empire. How do gap-hypothesis chroniclers resolve this problem? When Mussolini was "riding high" as El Duce of Italy, it seemed a way had been found for the theorists to crawl out of the hole they had dug for themselves. The Roman empire just had to be on the verge of being re-established, and Mussolini might very well be the beast rising out of the sea (Rev. 13:1-10). The end-time was assuredly at hand. But when Mussolini soon thereafter was "hanging high," and his empire dreams had burst, that changed things, but not for long. Never underestimate the imagination of end-time theorists, nor the shortness of the memories of the devotees of the cult.

The Armstrongites and others of similar persuasion would have us believe that the nations making up the ten nations of the Common Market of Europe represent a revival of the ten kingdoms which made up the Roman empire — spiritually, that is. (Now who is "spiritualizing" prophecy?) Thus God can soon start the prophetic clock ticking again, and the "smiting stone" can get rolling again, and the little girl and her pig can get over the sty and get home tonight! Pardon the satire. Things aren't going too well for the ten nation common market either.

Daniel's Seventy-week Vision

Is there further proof of this marvelous "mystery parenthesis" revelation. Indeed, there is. Daniel's vision of the seventy weeks (9:24-27) is handled in the same manner.

Again there is a wide consensus concerning the basic significance of the vision. The prophetical weeks are readily accepted as a time span covering 490 years, on the basis of Num. 14:34 and Ezek. 4:6.

According to the prophecy, the period would begin with the "going forth of the commandment to restore and to build Jerusalem" (Dan. 9:26). There were three such commandments. The one that seems best to fit the prediction is the one delivered to Nehemiah in 457 B.C.

Stage one of the vision was predicted to encompass seven weeks, forty-nine prophetic day-years. This corresponds to the number of years required to restore Jerusalem as a fortified city, complete with "streets and moat, even in troublesome times" (v. 25); 457 minus 49 brings us to 408 B.C.

Stage two was to be a nondescript period extending sixty-two weeks (434 prophetical day-years). Nothing is said of the events which should transpire during this period; it simply forms a time-bridge between the first seven weeks and the seventieth. Subtracting 434 from 408 B.C. brings us across the time divide to 26 A.D. This is precisely the year that Jesus was "anointed with the Holy Spirit and power," to borrow a phrase from Peter's discourse to Cornelius (Acts 10:38). With the baptism of Jesus, upon whom the Holy Spirit was seen descending and abiding (Jn. 1:33), "the anointed one" (Dan. 9:25) was formally presented as the Messiah (See Jn. 1:29, Mt. 3:16, 17.).

In the third and final phase of the vision, the seventieth week, we are told that "the anointed one" (Hebr., Messiah, Gr., Christ) would be "cut off" (v. 26, cp. Isa. 53:8). Moreover He would "make a firm covenant with many" that week, and *in the midst of the week* He would cause sacrifice and oblation to cease" (v. 27, cp. Hebrews 10:10-14).

While every facet of the prediction is not equally clear, enough is clear for understanding. Christ's ministry lasted "half a week" so to speak — three and one half years. He did indeed inaugurate a new covenant and made an effectual end of the sacrificial system. Granted that the Jews continued to offer sacrifices and offering until the time of the destruction of Jerusalem in 70 A.D., but insofar as God was concerned they were but empty ritual. Christ had already offered the once and for all sacrifice which alone could take away the sins of the world. The Hebrew writer touches upon this in a very subtle yet perceptive manner when he said: "in that he (Jeremiah, see 31:31ff.) saith, A new covenant, he hath made the first old. But that which is old and waxeth aged is nigh unto vanishing away" (Hebrews 8:13). Indeed it was. And indeed it did. With the fall of Jerusalem the whole sacrificial system ground to a halt.

Strangely enough, according to dispensational millennialism, the empty system will be reinstituted in the millennial kingdom. If Zechariah, ch. 14, the chapter so often used to describe the second coming of Christ and the inauguration of his postponed kingdom, is to be applied and taken literally, the direst of punishment (See 14:12, 13, 15, 17.) will befall any one in all the earth, regardless of nationality (See v. 16.) who does not go up to Jerusalem from year to year to keep the feast of tabernacles (v. 16-20). Moreover, if a literal construction, is to be placed on such prophecies, then Christ Himself will fall under the edict. Read Ezekiel 45:17 and 46:2-4.

If the kingdom of the Messiah is yet to be established, then not only is the church a stop gap measure, the whole Christian era is just a hiatus between Jewish epochs, and the same must be concluded concerning Christ's atoning death on Calvary. It is a lone sacrifice sandwiched in between two epochs of the Levitical sacrificial system.

THE KINGDOM OF THE MESSIAH

Returning to the seventieth week of Daniel's vision, we are informed by millennial theorists that the prophetic clock stopped. Where this time? At the end of the sixty-ninth week. When will it start again? When Christ comes "for" His saints and raptures them for a seven year rendezvous in the stratosphere. That's how it is decided the rapture episode shall last seven years. After that, Christ is free to descend *to* the earth to set up His long postponed kingdom. Marvelous! Scratch that. Preposterous!

The interpretations just reviewed are indeed so preposterous that upon first hearing such things many think we are just "putting them on," or that some unknown crackpot is the inventor of such far-fetched nonsense. But the fact is that many of the foremost prophecy buffs of our time teach such a system. Whoever it was that coined the phrase, "Truth is stranger than fiction," obviously never met a millennialist of the popular genus, or should we say, genius.

To appreciate what we have just taken note of, suppose you were a fledgling footballer of the Tank McNamara type, a draftee of the Los Angeles Rams. However, before you can appear in Los Angeles you receive a call that you have been traded to the Pittsburgh Steelers and are to appear in Pittsburgh the next day for assignment. You ask the General Manager of the Rams how far it is to Pittsburgh, your knowledge of geography having suffered as you went all out for football. He tells you it is 490 miles from your home in San Bernardino. That's better than you expected. You can make that by late evening, even staying within the speed limit.

As you are gassing your car, you ask the attendant the best way to Pittsburgh. He gives you a strange look, but advises that you take I-15 northward through the Cajon pass to Barstow. At the junction of I-40 turn right and put the hammer down. Barstow is just 49 miles up the road from where you are standing he tells you. Therefore, you head northward and 49 miles up the road you intersect I-40 and head east. You drive another 450 miles and begin to expect the lights of Pittsburgh to be illuminating the darkened sky. Instead you find yourself in the middle of the Arizona desert, somewhere between Winslow and Holbrook. You drive another 100 miles and the lights of Gallup, New Mexico, appear in the sky ahead. "This has to be Pittsburgh," you tell yourself. When you find that you have just entered New Mexico you call the head office of the Los Angeles Rams and demand an explanation. And you get one.

You guessed it. He had been reading his Schofield Reference Bible and got carried away. He forgot to tell you, it is actually about 2340 miles from San Bernardino to Pittsburgh, but when you reached Joseph City, 483 miles from your starting point on your odometer, you were supposed to disconnect the cable and drive to the City Limits sign of Pittsburgh. If you would then reconnect the cable, your odometer would then have registered exactly 490 miles. (Even if the road from Gallup was beset with detours it would still work out, wouldn't it?) Such are the wonders of the dispensational interpretation of Daniel, chapters 2 and 9.

Before moving on to other matters, we need to answer an objection to our own interpretation. If the 70th week of Daniel's vision is regarded as fulfilled by the three and one half year ministry of Jesus, doesn't that leave three and one half years of unfulfilled prophetic time? Not necessarily.

It was predicted of Christ that he would be raised the third day. How long did it take Him to come forth from the tomb? Did He make a day's work out of it? Or was he suddenly quickened from the dead, and came forth? If a contractor bids on a job calculated to take five weeks with the crew working shifts around the clock, must he keep them standing around at the construction site until the end of the thirty-fifth day, even though they may have completed the task specified in the contract by noon-time on the thirty-second day?

Every specification of the seventy-week prophetic vision of Daniel was fulfilled when Jesus completed His ministry and returned to the Father, having made a new covenant through His shed blood. If there is a seventieth prophetic week yet to be fulfilled, as demanded by the gap hypothesis, or even a half week, a seven or a three and a half year rapture is hardly a part of the prophecy. We venture to say of the seventieth-week what Jesus said of His atoning work on Calvary. "It is finished."

The King of the Jews

Contrary to so much that is being shouted from the transmitters towering over our housetops, Christ is king even now, yea even King of the Jews. But who is a Jew, spiritually speaking? Permit one of them, a renowned scholar among them, and an inspired Apostle besides, to answer that:

> He is not a Jew who is one outwardly, neither is that circumcision which is outward in the flesh; but he is a Jew who is one inwardly; and circumcision is of the heart, in the spirit not in the letter, whose praise is of God, not of man (Rom. 2:28, 29).

Hear him again in another place:

> Know therefore that they that are of faith, the same are sons of Abraham. And the Scripture, foreseeing that God would

WHAT THE BIBLE SAYS ABOUT THE END TIME

justify the Gentiles by faith, preached the gospel aforehand unto Abraham, saying, in thee shall all the nations be blessed. So then they that are of faith are blessed with the spiritual Abraham (Gal. 3:7-9).

And again:

For we are all sons of God through faith in Christ Jesus. For as many of you as were baptized into Christ have put on Christ. There can be neither Jew nor Greek, there can be neither bond man nor free, there can be no male or female: for ye are all one man in Christ Jesus. And if ye are Christ's then are ye Abraham's seed, heirs according to the promise (Gal. 3:26-28).

To the foregoing add also such texts as Romans 4:11, 12, 9:6-8, Ephesians 2:11-22, Gal. 6:16, Col. 3:11, Philippians 3:3, I Peter 2:9, 10. Recall too what Peter had to say at the birth of the church, citing Ps. 110:1 and declaring that the promise to David that God would set one upon his throne was already fulfilled in the resurrection and ascension of Christ (Acts 2:29-37).

It is written, "By the word of two or three witnesses a thing shall be established" (Deut. 17:6, Mt. 18:16, II Cor. 13:1). Of course the witnesses must be credentialized. The above cited witnesses have been. Their witness should settle the question concerning the church as it relates to Christ's kingdom.

Let us strike off the shackles of doom and gloom. Let us claim the victory we have in Christ. We are more than conquerors in Him that hath loved us. The kingdom of God is at hand, yea it is within you, even as He said.

> Rise up, O men of God.
> Be done with lesser things.
> Give heart and soul and mind and strength
> To serve the King of Kings.

Chapter Six

SIGNS OF THE TIMES

Don't you think we are living in the last days? That question is raised with each passing event which can be elevated by someone to destiny laden proportions as the fulfillment of end-time prophecy. Those who press the question, and they indeed press it, are generally sincere and concerned persons. They deserve therefore a candid answer. However, they are generally caught up in sensationalism and are as confused as they are concerned. That is all the more reason their question needs to be answered.

Neither "yes" (the expected answer) nor "no" is an adequate answer, although one could equivocate and answer either way with some degree of propriety. It bears mentioning that seldom is one simply asked what one thinks. The question is rarely phrased, "Do you think . . ." It comes across more pressingly: "Don't you think . . ."

How ought one to answer? I am personally inclined to respond, "Absolutely (pause) not!" Surprising? It generally is. Perhaps shocking would better describe the reaction. While the questioner is trying to recover from the shock I hasten to add, "No, I don't think we are living in the last days. I *know* we are." That usually shocks those who were not shocked before. But the answer is not given for its shock value, and it actually should not be so surprising.

One does not need to be a dogmatist to answer so assuredly. Neither does one need any special insight or a great store of Bible knowledge. All one needs is a Bible concordance.

The prophets of old had much to say about "the latter (last) days" and/or "the days (that shall) come." The latter of the two forms of expression is the least common, being peculiar to Jeremiah (See 23:5, 7, 30:3, 31:27, 31, 38. cf. Hebr. 8:8). Both forms of reference are applied by the

WHAT THE BIBLE SAYS ABOUT THE END TIME

New Testament writers to the Christian era. This is likewise true of Joel's expression, "It shall come to pass afterwards . . ." (2:28). Peter quotes Joel's prophecy in his sermon on Pentecost (Acts 2:17-21) and specifically declares it to be in the process of fulfillment.

The following Old Testament texts are commonly translated, "in the latter (last) days": Gen. 49:1, Num. 24:20, Deut. 4:30, 31:29, Isa. 2:2 (cf. Mic. 4:1), Jer. 12:4, 23:20, 30:24, 48:47, 49:39, Ezek. 38:16, Dan. 2:28, 8:19, 10:14, Hos. 3:5, Joel 2:28.

New Testament texts of special interest are: Acts 2:17 (cf. Joel 2:28), II Tim. 3:1,* Hebr. 1:2, 8:8 (cf. Jer. 31:31), Jas. 5:3, I Pet. 1:5, 20* II Pet. 3:3,* I Jn. 2:18, Jude 18.

Seven verses in John's gospel contain the expression, "the last day." (See Jn. 6:39, 40, 44, 54, 7:37,** 11:24, 12:48**.) Each of the texts manifestly relate to a pin point in time. Except for the two double-asterisked verses, the day of the general resurrection is designated. John 7:37 refers to the last day of the preparation for the passover, "the great day of the feast." John 12:48 refers to the day of the judgment.

To anyone who will take the time to look up the texts cited and read them 1) in their context and 2) as viewed by the New Testament writers, it should be obvious that the phrase "the latter days" is a general term for the whole post-Mosaic age. The simple truth is that we are living on the "western slope of time's divide." It has been so from the dawn of the Christian era.

If you have travelled any distance across the continent of North America, you came to a marker bearing the legend,

---

* The asterisk notes texts in which the term "the last days" is obviously used in the more restricted sense so common to present day jargon.

"Continental Divide." From that point up and down the continent every rain shower, every melting snowfield, is formed into rivulets, brooks and rivers flowing to the great oceans which flank the continent to the east and west. Theoretically, two rain drops falling an inch apart upon the summit of the great divide could end up as far removed from another as the east is from the west.

Chronology as well as continents has a dividing point. That point was reached over nineteen hundred years ago when Christ was born. Scripture and secular history unite in reckoning human history as summitted by the appearance of Christ. The Greeks tried to date time from the inception of their Olympiads, but failed. The Romans tried to date time from the founding of their Imperial city, and failed. Justinian tried to date time from the codification of Roman law, and failed. Las Plas tried to date time from the conjunction of certain stars, and failed. The French revolutionists tried to date time from the year one of their revolution, and failed. Many a world despot has dreamed of a new era being reckoned in terms of his brief impact upon the world. All these have failed. But what others have hoped for and sought after in vain, Christ did. On the brow of time He has stamped His name. All history is now reckoned in terms of his birth — Before Christ, B.C., Anno Domini, A.D., in the year of the Lord. Thus all time is now reckoned.

With this reckoning the Scriptures concur. The Biblical phrasing is somewhat different, but the frame of reference is much the same. The Biblical mode of expression is "the former times" and "the latter days," with Christ at the apex.

The book of Hebrews, a book which has been called the first comprehensive treatment of Christian doctrine, opens in this manner: "God having of old time spoken unto the fathers in the prophets . . . hath at the end of these days spoken unto us in His son" (Hebr. 1:1).

On the day of Pentecost following the consummation of Jesus' redemptive ministry, Peter explained the phenomena which brought a great concourse of people together by quoting these words from Joel: "It shall come to pass in the last days, saith God, I will pour forth of my Spirit upon all flesh." Then said he, *"this is that* which was spoken of by Joel" (Joel 2:28, Acts 2:17). Thus nearly two millennia ago Peter announced that those who were living then were living in the last days. In that Luke records that he spake "as the Spirit gave utterance" (Acts 2:4), we can dismiss any notion to the effect that Peter was simply carried away by the excitement of the occasion and was again displaying his penchant for speaking first and thinking afterwards. The fact is that a generation later, as an inspired penman borne along by the Holy Spirit, Peter wrote:

> Ye were redeemed, not with corruptible things, with silver and gold, from your vain manner of life handed down from your fathers, but with precious blood, as of a lamb without blemish and without spot, even the blood of Christ who was foreknown indeed before the foundation of the world, but was manifested *at the end of the times* for your sakes (I Pet. 1:18-20).

From these and other texts which could be listed we may conclude that we share this in common with the first generation of Christians — we are living in the last days.

What has this to do with the signs of the times? Much. Or are we to conclude that the exhortation to be looking for and earnestly desiring the coming of the Lord was actually only a teaser, an "unprofitable" Scripture until now? (See II Tim. 3:16.) Is ours the only generation for whom the warnings concerning the last days are valid? If the man of sin, the lawless one, and/or the antichrist is yet to be revealed, if the battle of Armageddon has not even begun, nor the coalition of nations effectuated who are to engage in it, if the great tribulation has as yet nothing in history which conforms to it, if the Roman empire has to be somehow restored, along with carnal Israel, and if many other happenings likewise must come to pass before Christ can come even secretly (for His church), much less come openly, actually and fully, then there is no way He could come as you read this, or at any time soon. And when He does, if only secretly for His church seven years ahead of the real thing, does this not provide sufficient warning for those left behind to repent? Or will the popular formula for instant salvation — only believe — be suspended for the duration of the rapture?

Approaching the matter from a different perspective, we are inclined to inquire: if the signs of Christ's coming are so singular and specific that Christ has to bide His time until every prophetical Scripture is literally fulfilled, and in the precise sequence established by the promoters, (hence ours is the only time in which this can happen) how does it happen that equally zealous prophecy buffs of other generations were able to relate so positively the same predictions to their day and circumstances? If they were all mistaken, and obviously they were according to the new crop of interpreters, might not the calculations and identifications of the present experts also prove to be wrong? To adapt an ancient question: can not Christ return without so much ado? Will not His coming be sensational enough? Will not the trumpet sound and the voice of the archangel, and the graves yeilding up their dead, and Christ appearing in the clouds in such a manner that every eye shall see him, and His saints caught up to meet Him — is this not enough? Must He wait until some one has the whole Divine order arranged, thus proving how precise and detailed end-time prophecies are, contrary to Christ's own prediction that no man will have figured it out right down to the day and the hour? Thanks be to God we need not be saddled with interpretive systems which make the return of Christ like the mechanical rabbit at a dog race, suddenly appearing just ahead, so tantalizingly near, but running ahead of the pack and then disappearing until the next time needed to get the pack off and running.

Let it be remembered that the predictions of Christ's *first* coming were so phrased that John the beloved apostle could say: "These things understood not his disciples at the first: but when Jesus was glorified, then remembered they that these things were written of him, and that they had done these things unto him" (Jn. 12:16). Perhaps we shall confess much the same thing when He comes in His glory, with His holy angels. Such, however, has not been the case with "sign" seeing soothsayers to date.

The History of "Sign" Seeing Soothsayers

Throughout the Christian era self-styled prophets, and often flowering sects, have arisen proclaiming the second coming of Christ to be at hand and themselves to be God's specially appointed witnesses to warn the world. Time, of course, has repeatedly proven all such "prophets" to be false. But that has never seemed to discredit them. Neither has it put an end to a parade of successors.

Prompt authoritative action on the part of the Apostle Paul may have prevented the rise of such a sect in the first generation of the Christian era. Of this Paul's Thessalonian letters bear witness. From Acts 17:11 it would appear that the Thessalonian Christians hardly may be regarded as diligent students of the Scriptures. Such lack has its price always. The Thessalonians were soon troubled by the fact that some of them had died without realizing the fulfillment of their hope that Christ would return in their lifetime. Obviously if some had already done so, others too might be thusly cheated, themselves for example.

Paul's first letter to the Thessalonians dealt directly with this problem. He would have them understand that when Christ returns those who had died in faith will be the first to meet Him. Only after the dead in Christ have been raised and caught up to meet Him in the air will the living saints be raptured (I Thess. 4:16, 17). First Thessalonians is unique in that every chapter closes with a reaffirmation of the fact that Christ shall come again. See 1:10, 2:19, 3:13, 4:13-18 and 5:23.

From Paul's second letter we learn the Thessalonians missed the point of the first one. Unfortunately they concluded that such repetition of the promise of Christ's return surely meant that the event was imminent. (See 2:1, 2.) Some obviously went so far as to quit working to devote themselves to waiting. (See. 3:10-13.)

Chapter two of Second Thessalonians contains some startling information. It is not startling because it is new information; to the contrary, Paul tells them he had at least hinted of the matter while he was yet with them in person. (See II Thess. 2:5.) But now he finds it necessary to tell them openly. Before Christ returns there must first be "a falling away" and "the revelation of the lawless one, the son of perdition, the man of sin" (vs. 3, 4). That which makes this revelation so startling is that for those to whom

Paul was writing and others who might chance to hear or read, the expectation that Christ could come at any time, or even relatively soon, was quelled. Apparently he had not stated the matter so bluntly when he was with them. To have done so would have been to set forth the doctrine of the second coming in a different light than the manner in which it is ordinarily articulated.

It is obvious that the intent of the Scripture is to so present the hope of the second coming of Christ that every Christian from the first generation until the last might live in the hope Christ's return might be in his lifetime, if not actually momentarily. Jesus' very succinct explanation of His parable of the watching servants tells us why this is so. (See Luke 12:35-48, particularly vs. 45, 46.) This is one of the few parables Jesus took occasion to explain.

Second Thessalonians, chapter two, does not seriously alter the manner in which the doctrine of the second coming of Christ is ordinarily presented. But it does pose an eschatological problem, as stated above. Perhaps there is a reason Paul seemingly allowed himself to be pressured into disclosing certain "signs" which will precede Christ's return.

Be it noted that even the two signs cited, 1) a falling away, and 2) the appearing of the lawless one, are set forth in sufficient ambiguity that almost from the beginning of the Christian era some possible identification could be considered. And throughout the history of the church a succession of apostasies and persons have appeared that could be so interpreted.

As for our day and generation, inasmuch as many such apostasies and persons have already come and gone and Christ has not yet returned, two conclusions are in order: 1. It ill behooves any one to say that Christ *cannot* come at any time, because "the Antichrist" has not yet been manifested. 2. On the other hand it ill behooves any one to say He *must* come right away because the apostasy is already upon us and some current character is obviously soon to be disclosed to be "the man of sin." These conjectures will be dealt with more fully under the caption, "Paul's Man of Sin."

Despite what we have noted, date setting has been the hallmark of a succession of self-styled prophets and sects and cults from the sub-apostolic era until now.

The Montanists arose in the middle of the second century, professing ecstatic visions announcing the imminent return of Christ. Their revelations created a great sensation, drawing many followers. Montanism flourished for more than a century. Time however cooled their fanaticism and eventually proved their prophets to be false.

The tenth century witnessed an outbreak of advent hysteria in the Latin church. Public and private buildings were permitted to decay, since "the dissolution of all things was at hand." Again time cooled the hysteria. Second and third generation converts became fewer and less committed.

The middle of the seventeenth century produced the Fifth Monarchy Men of England. The movement was so called because of its fanatical interpretation of the five monarchy vision of Nebuchadnezzar. They taught that the end of the four image monarchies was at hand and the God of heaven was about to establish the fifth monarchy which would destroy all rivals and continue forever. Thus persuaded they undertook to overthrow the English monarch to make room for the King of Kings. As ususal they insisted that all signs pointed to their time and season. After a second abortive attempt to overthrow the government (January

1661), Thomas Venner, leader of the sect, and a number of others were executed and the distinctive beliefs of the movement died out.

Shortly afterwards Edward Irving, a Scottish divine whose followers founded the Catholic Apostolic Church, became entranced by millenarianism. The Irvingites, as they were popularly known, boasted of "prophets," "revelations" and "confirming signs," not the least of which was "tongues." The latter has a familiar ring just now, does it not? The movement grew apace and spread to other countries. But again time took its toll. The "prophecies" failed and the "tongues" ceased. Disillusionment and spiritual lethargy followed in the wake.

In the new world the Millerites joined the procession of "sign" seeing soothsayers. William Miller, who drew about himself clergymen from virtually every denomination, set the time for the end of the world in the 1843-44 biennium. As the time drew nearer he narrowed the date of Christ's coming to October 22, 1844. The more zealous of his followers sold their farms or ceased planting or other employment, reminiscent of the problem Paul dealt with in Second Thessalonians, chapter three. October 22, 1844 was a long, long night for the Millerites.

Ellen Harmon (later Mrs. James White) who had risen to the status of prophetess sought to cover for him, explaining, "I have seen that the 1843 chart was directed by the hand of the Lord, and that it should not be altered; the figures were as He wanted them; but His hand was over and hid a mistake in some of the figures" (*Early Writings*, p. 64). And again: "I saw that they (the figures) were correct in their reckoning of the prophetic period; prophetic time closed in 1844" (*Spiritual Gifts, Vol. I.,* p. 107).

SIGNS OF THE TIMES

These are remarkable utterances. Though a prophecy professedly from the Lord failed, the blame is placed upon the Lord, and not his interpreters. God's hand was intentionally caused to hide some of the figures resulting in a therefore pardonable mistake of interpretation, but not a serious one. Miller's figuring was "still in the ball park" so to speak. It was the end of prophetic time, not Christ's return, that was fulfilled in 1844.

By this diversion the Millerites were able to hold a remnant of their devotees in suspense despite the miscue which disenchanted most of them. Later Mrs. White pronounced judgment upon the defectors and also their detractors throughout Christendom, saying: "As the churches refused to receive the first angel's message (Wm. Miller and his words) they rejected the light from heaven and fell from the favor of God" (*Early Writings,* p. 101).

This smacks of an adaptation of a doctrine introduced by a contemporary sect leader, J. N. Darby, founder of the Plymouth Brethren. Darby, you may recall, was the innovator of the notion that Christ's kingdom was thrust into a holding pattern, into postponement, because of the rejection of the Jews. Thus the prophetic clock stopped, awaiting His return at the end of the stop-gap era — the church age. According to Mrs. White the same thing happened again when the contemporaries of the Millerites rejected Millerism. God who had the foresight to see it coming purposely hid some figures thus obscuring the fact that Christ's millennial kingdom would be now further postponed, stopping the prophetic clock.

On the presumption that prophetess White's attempted cover-up had exonerated him, Miller set a new date for Christ's return, right down to the day and the hour. Or to be more specific, right down to the night and the midnight hour. Naturally it would have to be so. Literalism demands that Christ shall return at night, and midnight at that, despite the technical difficulties. In all such dogmatism there is a built-in egoism. The "sign seers" and their devotees to whom and through whom the warning is given invariably assume they are the center of God's concern and attention. Therefore the return of Christ will be so accommodated as to occur when the midnight hour comes to their particular locale. For them, and for them only, therefore does a literal fulfillment of the nocturnal appearance of Christ occur.

Miller's encore met with the blahs, even among the most devout of his depleted followers. Few neglected their fields or other pursuits that year and few spent the fateful night watching. It was at this juncture that the focus of Millerism shifted to sabbath keeping, hence the name by which the sect is known today, Seventh Day Adventists.

On the heels of the Millerites came the Russellites, followers of Charles Taze Russell, or "Pastor Russell" as he preferred to be addressed. The Russellites, alias the Millennial Dawnists, or International Bible Students, or the Watchtower Society, or Jehovah's Witnesses, were first organized in 1872. Undaunted by the failures of the sects which preceded them the Millennial Dawnists announced from the inception of their movement that the long awaited millennium was soon to dawn, hence the occasion of one of the names by which they have been known.

Eventually Pastor Russell took the plunge. He announced that all signs pointed to 1914 as the end of the age. The war clouds gathering over Europe gave credence to the forecast. But the world continued, the war dragged on. Russell died in 1916 tenaciously insisting his prediction would be vindicated, though his forecasts did not materialize as predicted. Meanwhile, with the war dragging on, the end of the age having not come, and no second coming of Christ, new leadership arose in the cult. "Judge" Joseph Franklin Rutherford took the reins from the ailing hands of Pastor Russell. As was true of the Millerites, a cover-up was conceived which never quite satisfied the less gullible. What really happened, the world was told, was not that the end of the world but the beginning of the final days, a sort of interim period, began in 1914.

Not only does the world continue, so do the Jehovah's Witnesses and their failing predictions. The late Robert M. Bell related how they swarmed across Tennessee, preying upon the mountain people and posting signs announcing "Jesus is coming soon." As time marched on the lettering faded beyond legibility and the posts rotted and toppled. All undaunted, with the advent of World War II, the JW's again swarmed over Tennessee sounding the alarm and posting their signs. But this time they used more durable lettering and materials, including steel posts set in concrete.

Beginning in 1966 readers of their bi-monthly publication, *Awake,* began to be conditioned for a new terminus announcement. In 1968 it was announced that "with all certainty" mathematical formula pointed toward the fall of 1975 as the long awaited end. As late as October 1968 the JW's were sticking with their prediction. An article in *Awake* included a buttressing quote from former U.S. Secretary of State Dean Acheson who said in 1960 that "fifteen years from today this world is going to be too dangerous to live in."

The best that can be said of the foregoing, and we use the word "best" with some misgiving, is that the scare tactics work. The ten year span, 1966-75, proved to be a banner decade for proselyting and evangelism. The number of

WHAT THE BIBLE SAYS ABOUT THE END TIME

baptisms began to increase almost immediately. By 1966 they had leveled out near the 60,000 mark, annually. In 1967 the number increased to 75,000. The momentum continued to build in the 1970's despite the fact that as the fateful year (1975) and its ominous autumn drew near, the head office coyly began to soft pedal its earlier prediction that the autumn of 1975 would be a watershed for life on earth as we have known it. In 1974 with the end of the world just around the corner there were nearly 300,000 baptisms, bringing the membership of the Watchtower Society to 1.9 million.

Following the 1914 miscue a number of disenchanted disciples deserted the sect. But there has been no great exodus discernible as yet since the 1975 repeat, although baptisms have again slackened. The coyness with which the 1975 date was promoted partly accounts for that. And so does a subtle wedding of the first miscue to a gross misinterpretation of the words of Jesus recorded in Mt. 24.34. The JW's insist that the year 1914 was indeed the beginning of the end. To that premise they join Jesus' prediction, "this generation shall not pass away till all these things shall be accomplished."

What is the connection? Actually there is none, unless one permits the JW's and their ilk to make up the rules for their numbers game as they go along. The rationale is as follows: 1) the *end* of the interim period (the beginning of the end) must come while the generation is still living that was alive in 1914, or at least a sizeable segment, the number to be decided by JW hierarchy. 2) Since the biblical term for a generation is defined by said hierarchy as three score years and ten (70 years), the very end of the end-time, including the rapture, great tribulation, and enthronement of

Christ in His millennial kingdom must all take place by 1984. Hence 1975 was the beginning of the last decade in which these things must occur. So they would have us know their prophets have been right all along. 1975 *was* a crucial year in the Divine time table.

Such is the stuff of which the "sign" seeing soothsayers weave the webs which ensnare the unwary. The pattern does not change; only the dates and procession of events and personalities.

Over and against the foregoing we set forth our own premise. There are no signs, none whatsoever in the popular sense in which the term is employed, by which we may discern the time of the end *prior* to the end. As it was in the days of Noah, so shall it be with the coming of the Son of Man. It is written of that generation "they knew not until the flood came and took them all away" (Mt. 24:39). So shall it be with that generation that shall be overtaken by our Lord's return.

The preaching of Noah provided no singular signs by which the dire event which he foretold could be discerned as impending. Neither were visions given through others to alleviate the void. The preaching of the Gospel is of the same order. The end of the age is clearly predicted, as certainly so as was the flood, but no singular signs are given — nothing that could pin point a given generation or event. We repeat, there are no signs predicted, nor should any be expected, Jesus' Olivet discourse so often cited to the contrary notwithstanding.

To express what has just been written is to provoke anger and resentment and invite scorn and contempt. Few doctrines are so dear to the hearts of prophecy devotees and so necessary to their theories as the teaching that one of the prime objectives of the Olivet discourse is to give the saints the signs whereby they may know of a surety when the day of His appearing draws nigh. But we boldly affirm there are no such signs given, neither in the Olivet discourse nor elsewhere. How, may we ask, could He have revealed such things to the twelve disciples when He plainly said that He Himself did not know?

To counter that He was only saying He didn't know the day and the hour, that is, the actual calendar date and the time of day, is to beg the question. It is highly doubtful that the disciples were asking that. They were wanting to know the signs of His coming, the order of events which could alert them that His coming was at hand. Jesus' answer was that only the Father knew that information. He was obviously right. Every interpreter who has ever used Matthew, chapter twenty-four to determine the signs of the beginning of the end has been proved wrong by the relentless march of time. With rough shod feet time has crushed every interpretative system that has used the chapter to discern the signs of Christ's coming. And thus far at least time has been the ally of those who believe the chapter was not recorded to serve that purpose.

JESUS' OLIVET DISCOURSE

No discussion of the signs of the times would be complete without due attention to Jesus' Olivet discourse, particularly as it is recorded in Matthew, chapter twenty-four, vs. 4-51. The discourse is repeated in a somewhat abbreviated form in Mark 13:3-37 and again in Luke 21:6-35. There are variations to be noted in each account. But Matthew's account is the one most generally cited as being more favorable to popular theory. Our discussion will therefore center on Matthew's account.

To understand Christ's Olivet discourse, which is no easy task, if indeed it will ever be fully understood this side of heaven, five things need to be noted.

1. The discourse is delivered in highly apocalyptic language — reminiscent of the rhetorical style used by the prophets of old to pronounce judgment upon various nations, including Israel. Such manner of speaking would be familiar to the Jews of Jesus' day, but hardly to our generation. We are steeped in literalism, in scientific analysis and precision; our language is crassly prosaic, and we have been told so often "God says what He means and means what He says," that we are ill-equipped mentally or emotionally to handle such a Scripture as the one before us.

Please do not jump to an unwarranted conclusion. I would be among the last to suggest we are not to take God's word seriously. But the truth is that though God says what he means, He doesn't always say it in the same way we would say it in this twentieth century. We therefore often misread Him. Truth is often more profound than ordinary language can express. The apostle John found it so when he attempted, even with the help of the Holy Spirit, to verbalize the visions given him on the isle of Patmos. Metaphors, and sometimes a whole flurry of figurative expressions, some of which would seem to contradict the others if taken literally, are employed to reach our hearts as well as our minds. We will have more to say about this as we move on.

2. We need to rid our minds of almost everything we are commonly told about this chapter. Most interpreters use it to teach the very thing Jesus devoted at least a part

of it to warn against. We have already touched upon this but it deserves repeating. If there is anything that ought to come through to us loud and clear it is the fact that the return of Christ will not come at an hour that can be pre-determined, neither from this chapter, nor from aught that is revealed to us elsewhere. It will come rather 1) like the flood, vs. 37-39, 2) like a thief, vs. 43, 44, and if verses 15-28 are referring to His coming (as is popularly taught) we can add a third warning: His coming will be like a bolt of lightning.

This is not to say His return will come about without any kind of prior announcement. That wouldn't be like the coming of the flood. That certainly was announced aforehand. In fact Noah was not only a preacher of righteousness (2 Pet. 2:5) who believed God's warning concerning things not yet seen (Hebr. 11:7), but he also manifested his faith in a striking manner. He built the mammoth ark through which he saved his household and condemned the world of unbelievers. But there were no signs cited, neither to *Noah* nor *through* Noah whereby the unbelieving and disobedient could make a mad dash for the ark at the last moment and be saved from the deluge. Jesus' simple summation of it is: "they knew not until the flood came and took them" (Mt. 24:39). And said He, "So shall be the coming of the Son of Man" (v. 37).

It is customary at this point for interpreters to interject mention of the violence and wickedness of the Noachial days, and to make that the point of comparison. Jesus did not do so. None of the things He mentioned (See vs. 38-40.) are suggestive of anything other than that life was going on quite as usual right down to the time that the flood came.

The context of the discourse needs to be kept in mind.

SIGNS OF THE TIMES

Beginning with chapter twenty-one events began to move toward a climax. The chapter opens with an account of the triumphal entry (vs. 1-11) followed by His second cleansing of the temple (vs. 12-16). Jesus then went forth from the temple to Bethany where he lodged for the night (v. 17). In the morning he returned to the city, visiting a curse upon a barren fig tree on the way (vs. 18-22). When he came again into the temple he was accosted by the chief priests and elders who demanded to know by what authority He had acted the day before, and who gave Him that authority. Those were fair questions, but those asking them were not fair. Jesus put them on the defensive, promising to answer their question if they would answer one, to which they agreed. He then thrust them upon the horns of a dilemma with his question concerning the baptism of John. That was a question they found too hot to handle. Therefore, after a huddle, they feigned ignorance. His adroit answer was, "And neither will I *tell* you by what authority I do these things" (v. 27). While they were still off balance he stung them with two parables, the parable of the two sons whom the father asked to work in his vineyard (vs. 28-32) and the parable of the wicked husbandmen (vs. 33-45). He took time to apply the lesson of both parables. Except for their fear of the multitudes they would have arrested Him then (v. 46).

Chapter twenty-two opens with the parable of the marriage feast (vs. 1-14). There seems to be an interlude at this point during which the Pharisees took counsel how they might ensnare Him in His talk (v. 15). The rest of the chapter details their efforts. A series of captious questions were thrust at Him. His answers left his questioners looking badly. In each case he turned the issue to put them on the defensive (vs. 16-33).

While they were still reeling He put to them the question, "What think ye of the Christ, whose son is he?" Ah, that was an easy one. They must have both smiled and sighed with relief as they answered, "The son of David." To their chagrin he asked them how then it was that David called him Lord, citing Ps. 110:1 as evidence. In embarrassed silence they hastily ended the exchange (vs. 41-45).

Chapter twenty-three is devoted to His denunciation of the scribes and Pharisees. Verses 1-12 were apparently addressed to the multitudes who had listened to the exchange recorded in chapter 22, but they were nonetheless spoken in the hearing of the Scribes and Pharisees. He then pronounced seven awesome woes upon the scribes and Pharisees, apparently addressing those words to them directly, in the hearing of the multitude (vs. 13-36). The chapter closes with His plaintive lamentation over Jerusalem (vs. 37-39).

Matthew, chapter twenty-four, takes up the story at this point. As Jesus again goes forth from the temple, the closing words of His lamentation must have been much on the minds of His disciples. What awesome import the words contained: "Behold, thy house is left unto you desolate." Could he be speaking of the temple? Once before (at the first cleansing of the temple) he had said something about the temple being destroyed. At the time His words were taken literally. Others who heard Him certainly did so, and John indicates the disciples did also and continued to do so until after His resurrection. Only then did they understand that he was speaking of "the temple of his body" (Jn. 2:19-22).

The disciples were apparently putting the two episodes together as they passed by the temple compound. His enemies had thought He was predicting the impossible when he taunted them, saying: "Destroy this temple and in three days I will raise it up again" (Jn. 2:19). It also seemed almost as incomprehensible to His disciples that the temple could be or even should be destroyed. They bade him pause and observe the immensity and sure foundation of the magnificent structure. Josephus records there were stones measuring fifty feet long, twenty-four broad and sixteen high. Jesus' answer was: "Verily I say unto you, there shall not be left here one stone standing upon another that shall not be thrown down" (24:2).

That really shook them. Apparently they made their way to the Mount of Olives in silence, or at the most questioning among themselves. When they reached the Mount of Olives they could no longer contain themselves. They came to Him with a flurry of questions: "When shall these things be? What shall be the sign of thy coming, and of the end of the world?" (vs. 3).

How many questions were the disciples asking? Three? Or were they asking but one question with three facets? To the twelve disciples such a destruction as He had predicted would befall Jerusalem and the temple might very well have come through to them as the announcement of the end of the world. Jerusalem was that important in the minds of the Jews, Christ's disciples not excepted.

Jesus answered by breaking their question into two parts, answering first their questions as they related to the fall of Jerusalem, and then directing their attention to His second coming and the end of the age. Note he did not separate the latter events as most theorists do. He dealt with His return and the end of the world as one event.

4. This brings us to the fourth guideline. We need to take note of the time-keys which divide and delineate the two sections of the discourse — vs. 29, 34 and 36. Verse thirty-four is pivotal, so let us begin there and move both ways.

Verse 34 reads: "Verily I say unto you, this generation shall not pass away until all these things shall be accomplished." That should settle the matter. Everything up to this point would seem to relate to events which would transpire within the lifetime of that generation, hence to the fall of Jerusalem and the closing out of the Jewish age.

This, by the way, is the second time Jesus is recorded as having spoken in this vein. In announcing the building of His church he said substantially the same thing. On the heel of Peter's confession of His Divine Sonship and Messiahship Jesus declared: "Upon this rock I will build my church" (v. 18), and added, "and I will give thee the keys to the kingdom of heaven" (v. 19).

In the text which immediately follows He again undertook to communicate to them the fact He was to be slain. Peter could not see how both of the things Christ was speaking of could be so. The one seemed to preclude the other, at least at any time in the forseeable future. In that regard Peter now has a lot of company. The Darby-Schofield gap hypothesis, so popular in current millennial theories, is evidence that many people still cannot see how Christ could possibly be crucified, depart from this earth, and yet be considered king. What can be the sense of praying, "Thy kingdom come, thy will be done, on earth as it is in heaven," when Christ's kingdom plans were aborted by the rejection of the Jews and He saw fit to take leave of the earth and has not yet returned? Jesus' answer was: "Verily I say unto you, there are some of them standing here [Note: some standing by then and there] who shall in no wise taste of death till they see the Son of man coming in His kingdom" (v. 28). Luke phrases it in this manner: "But I tell you of a truth, there are some of them that stand here, who shall in no wise taste of death, till they see the kingdom of God" (Lk. 9:27).

If the church is not the kingdom of Christ then where are those folk who were standing with Christ at the foot of Mt. Hermon that day? Are they now nearly two thousand years old with beards reaching all the way from Dan to Beersheba, having not died and will not die until Jesus returns to set up a mythological postponed kingdom?

Verse 34 of chapter 24 is of similar pronouncement. Note it once again. "Verily I say unto you, this generation shall not pass away till all these things be accomplished." That settles it. Within the life span of the generation then living the awesome destruction of Jerusalem, the downfall of the religious establishment and the cessation of its ancient rituals was accomplished. The events are described in vs. 16-28, and 29-31 in bold apocalyptical language. To attempt to interpret the verses literally is to add confusion to an already difficult chapter.

Verse 35 is a transitional verse. Recall that we have said verse 34 is pivotal. Verse 35 reads: "Heaven and earth shall pass away, but my words shall not pass away." When shall these things be? Let Jesus answer the question, v. 36.

Verse 36, another of the three time keys of the chapter, reads: But of that day and hour knoweth no one, not even the angels, neither the Son." I take that to mean not even Jesus Himself, the Son of God, much less Garner Ted Armstrong. And the Father is hardly to be construed as Herbert W. Armstrong, the Big Daddy of the Armstrong empire.

The phrase "that day" stands in sharp contrast to the expression, "those days" in v. 29, the third time-key verse of the chapter. Note what is said in v. 29. "Immediately after the tribulation of those days shall the sun be darkened, and the moon shall not give her light, and the stars shall fall from the heavens, and the powers of the heavens shall be shaken."

That really sounds like the end of the world, doesn't it? If that is what the verses are speaking of, then Jesus is quite unlike God the Father. He is an "author of confusion." He flip-flops back and forth, discussing the fall of Jerusalem and the end of the world in a diconnected jumble.

I must confess that verses twenty-nine through thirty-one long seemed to me to be speaking of the time of Christ's second coming rather than the fall of Jerusalem. But an entirely different light was shed on these verses by an afternoon spent with the Bible and a concordance, reading the language in which the Hebrew prophets described the demise of a number of nations of antiquity and of their rulers. I do not hesitate to say that the same exercise would convince all but the most inflexible readers that the possibility of another interpretation should be considered.

Note, for example, the language used in Isaiah 13:1-22 to describe the fall of Babylon. Particularly note vs. 9, 10. Taken in context the verses read as follows:

v. 1 The burden of Babylon, which Isaiah, the son of Amos did see . . . . v. 6 Wail ye, for the day of Jehovah is at hand . . .

v. 9 Behold the day of Jehovah cometh, cruel with wrath and fierce anger, to make the land a desolation, and to destroy the sinners thereof out of it. v. 10 For the *stars* of heaven and the *constellations* thereof shall not give their light; the *sun* shall be darkened in its going forth, and the *moon* shall not cause its light to shine. . . .v. 13 Therefore I will make the *heavens* to tremble, and the *earth* shall be shaken out of its place, in the wrath of Jehovah of hosts, and in that day of his fierce anger.

SIGNS OF THE TIMES

Note also the language Isaiah used to predict the downfall of nations, particularly Edom, in Isaiah 34. In vs. 1-4 he summons all nations and peoples to witness the awesome destruction, speaking as though it were already accomplished (in which case there would be no one left to witness), and concludes these opening verses by saying:

> v. 4 And all the host of heaven shall be dissolved, and the heavens shall be rolled together as a scroll: and all their host shall fade away, as the leaf falleth from the vine, and as a fading leaf from the fig tree.

The prophet then focuses his attention upon the destruction of Edom. Note particularly vs. 5, 9 and 10.

> v. 5 For my sword hath drunk its fill in heaven: behold it shall come down upon Edom, and upon the people of my curse, to judgment.
>
> v. 9 And the streams of Edom shall be turned into pitch, and the dust thereof into brimstone, and the land thereof shall become burning pitch. v. 10 It shall not be quenched night nor day; the smoke thereof shall go up for ever; from generation to generation it shall lie waste; none shall pass through it forever and ever.

Isaiah is not the only prophet to speak in such metaphoric phraseology. Note Ezekiel's prediction of the wrath of God to be visited upon Egypt, Ezekiel 32, particularly as it is phrased in vs. 7 and 8.

> v. 1 And it came to pass in the twelfth year, in the twelfth month, in the first day of the month, that the word of Jehovah came unto me, saying, v. 2 Son of man, take up a lamentation over Pharaoh, king of Egypt, and say unto him . . .
>
> v. 7 And when I shall extinguish thee, I will cover the heavens and make the stars thereof dark: I will cover the sun with a cloud, and the moon shall not give its light. v. 8 All the bright lights of heaven will I make dark over thee, and set darkness upon thy land, saith the Lord Jehovah.

WHAT THE BIBLE SAYS ABOUT THE END TIME

Jeremiah 15:9, Joel 2:10, 30, 31, 3:15 and Micah 3:6 employ the same imagery. Other apocalyptic symbols which likewise are not to be interpreted literally abound in the judgment language of Hebrew prophets.

The roots of the sun, moon and star imagery go back to the thirty-seventh chapter of Genesis. Joseph had two dreams which precipitated his brothers' most unbrotherly action against him. In the first dream (See Gen. 37:7, 8.) Joseph and his brothers were shocking grain. Lo, the shocks of each of his brothers did obeisance to his own. When Joseph related the dream to his brothers, despite the figurative language, they got the point. They found it shocking to say the least. "Shalt thou indeed reign over us? or shalt thou indeed have dominion over us?" they asked.

Joseph dreamed yet another dream (v. 9). In this dream, behold the sun and the moon and eleven stars made obeisance to him. Joseph told this dream to his father and to his brothers. His father rebuked him and showed resentment. "Shall I and thy mother and thy brethren indeed come to bow down ourselves to thee to the earth?" (v. 11). Note Joseph had not said a word about his parents and his eleven brothers. He mentioned only the sun, moon and eleven stars. But way back then, without the benefit of the prophetic writings and concordances to check out the possible meaning of such language, they were not the least bit hung up on literalism. Jacob saw the point. The sun and moon were himself and his beloved wife Rachel, the patriarchal and matriarchal heads of the budding tribes of Israel. And the eleven stars were the young princes thereof, the other sons of Jacob.

And so it may well be with the text in question, (Mt. 24:29). The sun and moon represent the house of Caiaphus

SIGNS OF THE TIMES

and of Herod, the religious and civil heads of the doomed nation. The stars falling from the heavens were the lesser rulers of the people, the scribes and Pharisees, the priests and elders. The shaking of the powers of the heaven is a prediction of the tottering and fall of the whole sacrificial and ritual system. Hebrews 8:13, written just ahead of the destruction of Jerusalem which brought a full end to the temple ritual and the sacrificial system, is a striking commentary on this phrase. In connection with the Hebrew writer's commentary on Jeremiah's prophecy of the new covenant and its more excellent sacrifice, he says: "In that he saith, A new covenant, he hath made the first old. But that which is becoming old and waxeth aged is nigh unto vanishing away." Indeed it was, and now has.

At a public forum in which chapter 24 of Matthew and chapter 20 of Revelation were under discussion my respondent stoutly contended that Mt. 24:29 could not possibly refer to the fall of Jerusalem. He read the verse slowly and with deliberate emphasis and added. "They (the sun, moon and stars) are still up there." That scored points with the premillennialists. But by the same rule we would have to rewrite Old Testament history. Isaiah's and Ezekiel's prophecies, noted above, could not then refer to the downfall of the nations to whom they were directed. The sun, moon and stars "are *still* up there." And the land of Edom is trodden by caravans of tourists year after year, who see no streams of pitch, no brimstone, no smoke going up for ever and ever. If the Bible is allowed to be its own interpreter, when read in the light of the prophecies couched in the same language style, and even using the same metaphors, Mt. 24:29 will be readily recognizable as fulfilled in the destruction of Jerusalem, 70 A.D.

WHAT THE BIBLE SAYS ABOUT THE END TIME

But what about verses 30 and 31? These verses also appear before v. 34 which we have declared to be pivotal. Verse 30 would be quite a problem were it not for the manner in which Jesus predicted the coming of the church age. His coming, in and through the church of which He is the head, is spoken of as "the Son of man coming in his kingdom" (Mt. 16:28).

When apocalyptic language is used, not so much to predict an event but to describe a state, or introduce an era, every facet of the prophecy is not to be regarded as demanding immediate fulfillment. Again permit Scripture to shed light upon Scripture. Note the prediction which Peter cited on Pentecost as being fulfilled that day, Joel 2:28-32 (Cf. Acts 2:16-21).

The multitudes were asking for an explanation of the phenomena they were hearing — "every man in his own language wherein he was born," though all the speakers were Galileans. By way of answer Peter quoted a prophecy predicting 1) the pouring out of the Holy Spirit upon "all flesh" — sons, daughters, young men, old men, servants and handmaidens; 2) wonders in the heavens, signs on the earth — blood, fire, vapor of smoke, sun turned into darkness, the moon into blood; and 3) the extension of salvation to "whosoever would call on the name of the Lord." Peter said of the tongues phenomenon, *"This is that . . . ."* that which we have just summarized.

It is worthy of note that no one answered him, "Oh yeah? Where is the vapor of smoke? We don't see any bloody moon. When is the eclipse of the sun to take place?" Neither did they ask for a demonstration of the other phenomena mentioned in the text — old men dreaming, young men seeing visions, daughters and handmaidens prophesying, gentiles receiving the outpouring of the Holy Spirit and salvation in the name of the Lord. They recognized the apocalyptic character of the text. Why is it so hard for our generation to do the same?

The predictions of Joel 2:28-32 actually span the whole of the Christian era. In a sense the era began when Christ in a forensic sense "made an end of the law" as he offered Himself as the perfect sacrifice on Calvary. This is likewise true of Mt. 24:30, 31. The focus is on the fall of Jerusalem, with which event the abrogated law came to a *full* end, as we have learned from Hebrews 8:13. Verses 30 and 31 are parenthetical. They take us down to the close of the church age, setting the stage for the consummation of the ages. The focus of the chapter is about to shift to that emphasis. The fig tree parable (vs. 32, 33) is a wrap-up of the first section. It serves as one more reference to the signs of the impending fall of Jerusalem.

Incidentally, much more is made of the fig tree parable than is warranted. In his helpful paperback, *Great Prophecies of the Bible* (Ralph Woodrow Evangelistic Association, Riverside, Calif.) Woodrow ably exposes the futurist interpretation which makes of the parable a prediction of the restoration of fleshly Israel to favored status as God's chosen people in Christ's "millennial" kingdom. The fig tree imagery, as contained in the Scriptures, is not complimentary of Israel. This will be discussed more fully in chapter ten.

5. Fifth and finally, the primary purpose of the Olivet discourse needs to be kept in mind if we are to understand its meaning. The discourse was not delivered to provide the apostles or ourselves a handy résumé of the signs preceding Christ's return. Of such, we repeat, there are none. The real purpose was to inform Christ's disciples of what they would need to know and share if they and the rest of

the Christian community residing in Jerusalem at its fall were to escape its awful tribulation and destruction. History bears out the fact the discourse served that very purpose, and did it well.

Josephus, Jewish historian, and one that could hardly be charged with writing from a pro-Christian bias, is our primary source of information. He related that Cestius, the Roman general, came from Syria and laid siege to the city. So successful was it, so horrible the hunger and anguish of the entrapped inhabitants, they were about to surrender the city when an inexplicable thing happened. Suddenly, for no known reason, Cestius lifted the siege and withdrew his armies.

The Jews, assuming Divine providence had intervened to spare the city, took no advantage of the respite to flee. It would have not been like them to do so. They were altogether too caught up in the nostalgia that still surrounds the very mention of the city.

With the Christians it was a different story. Their hearts were fixed on "the Jerusalem which is above" (Gal. 4:26). Thus the Christians, remembered Christ's warnings found in the Olivet discourse: "When ye see the abomination of desolation" (Mt. 24:15), "Jerusalem compassed with armies" (Lk. 21:20) — pagan hosts with images of their vain idols emblazoned on their shields and ensigns — standing at the very gates of the city, "*flee.*" Don't even take time to pack a few belongings. Get out while you may.

But how could they do that? What implausible counsel. How could one flee the city when they saw such a sign as has just been mentioned — the city encompassed by armies. Why did not Jesus give them a sign whereby they could know the siege was about to take place? During the height of the siege they must have pondered that.

SIGNS OF THE TIMES

Josephus tells us that some of the Jews thought to outwit the Romans. They dressed in their poorest clothes and went out through the gates disguised as beggars, having swallowed their gold and their jewels. But the crafty Romans slit their stomachs and stripped their bowels of their gold and jewels. These things were surely relayed to the besieged masses by the military guards who watched from the battlements of the city walls. Day by day the situation grew more hopeless. Then wonder of wonders, the enemy withdrew. It could be a trap. But the Christians did not so interpret it. They began to get the message of the Olivet discourse. They fled to the north, to the mountains of Perea and beyond the Jordan, even as Jesus had told them. Josephus reports that not one Christian lost his life in the fall of Jerusalem.

Soon after the Christians fled the city the siege was renewed, this time under the generalship of Titus. The most horrendous siege conditions in all the annals of history reduced the city to such desperation that the young and strong tore morsels of food out of the mouths of the weak and aged. One mother slew and roasted her own son and fed upon the corpse. The besieged inhabitants took to quarreling among themselves, castigating and placing blame for what was happening upon first one and then another segment of their society. Civil war and mad assault turned the city into a battlefield ere the Romans beat down the gates.

When at last the Romans stormed the gates they found they had little to do other than a little mopping up action here and there. As their eyes fell upon the riches of the temple they applied torches to the ornate structure, melting the gold by which it was so lavishly adorned. They then pried the great stones apart, toppling the walls to get at the gold which was melted into the crevices. The words of Christ, "not one stone shall be left standing upon another" (v. 2), were thus fulfilled.

Does one interject, "But what of the wars and rumors of wars? And the earthquakes in divers places, and famines? These, predicted in vs. 6 and 7, are assuredly signs of our times, and not omens of the fall of Jerusalem." Our generation can scarcely be credited with holding a premium on such things. And to say those signs did not mark the generation living in the shadow of the fall of Jerusalem is to contradict both Jesus and history.

As for the wars and rumors of War, *Clarke's Commentary, Vol. V.*, p. 227 cites *Josephus, Ant. v. xviii. c. é; War, b. ii. c. 10;* noting:

> v. 6 . . . as to *wars and rumors of war,* when Caligula ordered his statue to be set up in the temple of God, which the Jews having refused had every reason to expect a war with the Romans, and were in such consternation on the occasion that they even neglected to till their land.
>
> v. 7 *Nation shall rise up against nation.* This portended the dissensions, insurrections and mutual slaughter of the Jews and those of other nations who dwelt in the same cities together: as particularly at Caesarea, where the Jews and Syrians contended about the right of the city, which ended in the total expulsion of the Jews, above 200,000 of whom were slain.

He goes on to explain that the whole Jewish nation was thereupon so incensed they flew to arms, burned and plundered neighboring Syrian cities and villages, resulting in an immense slaughter of the people. The Syrians retaliated, taking no less a toll of the Jews. At Scythopolis alone they murdered 13,000. Other cities of Syria, in proportion, did likewise. At Alexandria (Egypt) the Jews and heathen fought, and 50,000 Jews were slain.

Clarke cites Bishop Newton and Dr. Lardner as corroborating his summary, and continues with verse 7, Mt. 24, saying:

"*Kingdom against kingdom.* This portended the open wars of different tetrarchies and provinces." He cites three different areas of conflict including civil war in Italy where Otho and Vitellius were contending for control of the empire.

As for *famines,* it needs only to be remembered that in Acts 11:28 Agabus is reported as having prophesied "a great famine over all the world, which came to pass in the days of Cludius." Tacitus and Eusebiius, among other secular historians of the antiquity, verify the report. Josephus (*Ant. b. xx. c. 2*) affirms its effects were so severe in Jerusalem that many died of starvation.

As for *earthquakes in divers places,* even without our modern seismographs and almost immediate world-wide news coverage, there were a sufficient number recorded in the immediate prelude to the fall of Jerusalem to fulfill the prediction. Meserve (*The Olivet Discourse,* San Jose Bible College, p. 25) notes: "Many authorities agree that perhaps never in an equal period of time in history did so many earthquakes occur, as in this period of forty years before the fall of Jerusalem." He cites the following authorities in a summarizing fashion:

> Alford enumerates these earthquakes as follows: 1. A great earthquake in A.D. 46, or 47; 2. An earthquake in Rome on the day Nero assumed the toga, A.D. 51; 3. One at Apamaea in Phrygia, and 4. one at Laodicea in Phrygia, A.D. 60; 5. One in Amporia, A.D. 62 or 63.
>
> Seneca mentions a surprising number of such calamities having occurred with great damage all over the empire.

His list includes proconsular Asia, Achaia, Syria, Macedonia, Cyprus and Paphus.

Tacitus also mentions several earthquakes in Crete; several in Italy, one at Rome and another at Campanen; in Phrygia at Apamea and Laodicea (as noted by Alford).

Adam Clarke adds to the list one mentioned by Josephus which occurred in Judea, accompanied by such violent storms that many believed it was some sort of sign. It would appear we do not have to await the impending return of Christ for the fulfillment of the dire warnings recorded in Matthew 24. This is not to say such events will be no part of the end-time. Were it so, the end-time would be much different from the times which have already come and gone, and the time in which we are now living. We mean only to say that if such are the signs of His coming He is long, long overdue.

What then are the signs of Christ's coming and of the end of the world? Hear it again from Jesus. He answered the question for the twelve in the same discourse we have been noting. "Of that day and hour knoweth no one, not even the angels, neither the Son, but the Father only" (Mt. 24:36). It shall be as in the days of Noah. Men will be eating, drinking, working, sleeping — in short, living as though there would always be a tomorrow; time to repent, time to get ready. "But in an hour when ye think not the Son of man cometh" (v. 44).

There will be no "early warning system," no time for last minute preparation, no secret rapture as a sure-fire warning one has but seven years at the most to prepare for His actual coming; no utopian millennium, no second chance for the Jewish nation, nor through them one last chance for the unbelieving Gentile nations. In a moment, in the twinkling of an eye, the dead in Christ shall be raised, and the saints raptured in their train. In the time it takes for a lightning bolt to flash in the eastern sky and be seen in the west, that suddenly will He appear.

Many other "signs" may be cited (if not sighted) which are not discussed in this book, but these are written that you may know that the signs of the times, our times, are no different than they have been at other times. There is no reason anyone should conclude Jesus *cannot* come soon, nor that He *must* come right away.

In the fulness of time God sent forth His Son. When that time is recycled Christ shall come again. Meanwhile it behooves us to look for and earnestly desire the day of Christ. It may be later than some think, or not as late as others think. Be that as it may, it is now some 1900 years later, and His coming over 1900 years nearer than when angels on Mount Olivet said to the eleven disciples, "This same Jesus shall come again."

Chapter Seven

THE APPEARING OF THE ANTICHRIST AND THE MAN OF SIN

Two terms, scarcely found in the Scriptures, receive much attention in current end-time interpretive systems — "The Antichrist" (Gr., *ho antichristos*) and "The Man of Sin" (Gr., *ho anthropos tes anomias;* literally, "the man, the lawless"). The first is a Johanine term found only in I John 2:18, 22, 4:3 and II John 7. The second, a Pauline term, is found only in II Thess. 2:3. A modified form, "the lawless one," (Gr., *ho anomos*) is found in 2:8. He is further defined as "the son of perdition" (Gr., *huios tes apoleias,* literally, "son of destruction"), 2:3, and thence described as "he that opposeth and exalteth himself against all that is called God or that is worshipped, so that he sitteth in the temple of God, setting himself forth as God" (v. 4).

The terms are quite commonly, though not always, equated. They are regarded as being two names for the same person. This is particularly so of those who see (the) antichrist as indeed a person, an individual who shall appear at the end-time. Such passages as Daniel 7:25, 8:25, 11:36 and Revelation 13:5 are cited as further references to *"the* antichrist" and "the man of sin."

The most common concept is that he will be some super malignancy who shall rise to power in the end-time and shall demand the worship of all mankind. His supreme offense will be the desecration of the temple (supposedly rebuilt at the time he appears) by setting up an idol-image of himself in the Holy of Holies.

The assumption of a rebuilt temple is one of several features of popular theory which helps to keep the actual expectation of Christ's return at some time removed — around the corner perhaps, but definitely not possible at any moment. The secret rapture hypothesis is one way the theorists have devised to dig themselves out of that predicament. The rebuilding of the temple and the appearing of the antichrist man of sin are projected as events which will take place in the seven year interim between Christ's supposed two "second comings." The Jews' outrage over the defilement of the temple, "the abomination of desolation," is conjectured to be the catalyst which shall trigger "the great tribulation." The "beastly" antichrist man of sin, in retaliation against those who have defied him, will loose his fury and great power in unprecedented persecution of the saints and whosoever does not worship him nor his image, and bears not his mark upon their foreheads and upon their hands.

Concerning John's Doctrine of (the) Antichrist

By way of response to the foregoing we choose to begin with a discussion of John's doctrine of (the) Antichrist. As one reads what John has to say about him (or *them;* see I John 2:18) it becomes immediately remarkable that John virutally strips the term of eschatological reference. (The) antichrist (pl.) have already appeared, and have manifested themselves in two distinct forms of doctrinal deviation.

To better understand what John has written on the subject one needs to be somewhat conversant with the gnostic heresy that was then flowering. As the Christian faith began to expand throughout the Graeco-Roman world it encountered various forms of a thought system generally lumped together under the name of gnosticism. The word is derived from the Greek word for knowledge, *gnosis.* It may be defined therefore as "the dogma of knowledge." The various forms of the dogma had for their common denominator the thesis that "salvation is to be attained through a rare kind of knowledge." It is not hard to guess to whom an inquirer was expected to turn to gain that special knowledge. Certain varieties of current end-time theory have an affinity to gnosticism. The Watchtower Society cult most certainly does.

Gnosticism was eclectic. It grew by absorption. The gnostics readily recognized that the Christian faith had much to offer. But they chose to adapt the Gospel to their own basic concepts, not vice versa. As early as mid-century of the apostolic era gnosticism began to challenge the church. Two of Paul's prison epistles, Ephesians and Colossians reflect an awareness of the threat. His pastoral letters do also. John, writing near the close of the apostolic age, dealt with the threat more directly.

Even a résumé of the heresy would fill many pages, and would not serve the purpose of this writing. We shall limit ourselves therefore to the two segments of the cult which prompted the apostle John to coin, or at least apply, the epithet "antichrist" to their teaching.

1. *Ebionism*

One branch of gnosticism, Ebionism, was the prototype of the form of Christology promulgated today by the Jehovah's Witnesses. The Ebionites did not hesitate to speak of Jesus as God; they simply did so with a small "g." They viewed him as a spirit being, but not one eternally with the Father. He was indeed "the first born of all creation," but not in the sense Paul employed the phrase. Paul used it metaphorically. He thus designated the place of honor which Christ regained via the resurrection. Though others before Him had been raised up, some by Him, He alone was raised to die no more and to become the resurrection and the life for all who come to God through Him. As the first born among the Hebrews held a special place of honor and privilege, so the resurrected Christ has regained the glory He had with the Father before the world was.

The gnostics who normally spiritualized virtually everything saw fit to interpret the phrase literally. They viewed him as a created being, the first and highest of creatures, but yet a creature. They had no qualms about the virgin birth but insisted nonetheless that only in the sense that the angels are called "sons of God" may He be so called. John's response is as follows:

> 18. Little children, it is the last hour (time): and as ye heard that antichrist cometh, even now have there arisen many antichrists; where we know it is the last hour. 19. They went out from us, but they were not of us; for if they had been of us they would have continued with us: but *they went out* that they might be made manifest that they all are not of us. 20. And ye have an anointing from the holy one, and ye know all things. 21. I have not written unto you because ye know not the truth, but because ye know it, and because no lie is of the truth. 22. Who is the liar but he that denieth Jesus is the Christ? This is the antichrist, *even* he that denieth the Father and the Son (I John 2:18-22).

2. Docetism

The other form of gnosticism with which John deals is known as Docetism. The Docetic gnostics took the opposite position. They recognized Christ as being eternally God, so much so that they could not believe He actually became incarnate. Their reasoning came from the backdrop of prevailing Grecian dualism which held that matter was essentially and inherently evil. The Docetists therefore concluded that Jesus could not have had a flesh and blood body and at the same time be the sinless One. Thus they hypothesized that His seeming incarnate life, including the phenomena of being touchable, and such ordinaries as eating, drinking, tiring, sleeping, hurting — these all were but an apparition, a kind of charade He carried on in order that mere mortals might thereby more readily identify with Him. They perhaps would not care to have it expressed that crassly, but such is the essence of what they taught. John responded to the teaching as follows:

> 1. Beloved, believe not every spirit, but prove the spirits, whether they be of God; because many false prophets are gone out into the world. 2. Hereby know ye the Spirit of God: Every spirit that confesseth that Jesus Christ is come in the flesh is of God: 3. And every spirit that confesseth not Jesus [the man, Jesus of Nazareth, the Word made flesh] is not of God: and this is the *spirit* of the antichrist, whereof ye heard that it cometh; and now it is in the world already (I John 4:1-3).
>
> 7. For many deceivers are gone forth into the world, *even* they that confess not that Jesus Christ is come in the flesh. This is the deceiver and the antichrist (II John 7).

The two forms of gnostic heresy designated as "antichrist" had one thing in common. Both were an assault upon the intrinsic nature of His person. Each made Him out to be something less, or other than, what and who He was. The Docetists would deny that they made of Him something less. They would make of Him something more than the New Testament writers represent Him to have been during His earthly sojourn. Be that as it may, they certainly made of Him something other than the Christ of the Gospels. Yet His humanity is as essential to His redemptive mission as His deity.

APPEARING OF ANTICHRIST AND MAN OF SIN

Of itself the term antichrist could be interpreted as a substitute for Christ, even an approved stand-in. The Greek prefix, anti, more commonly used to denote opposition, that which is "against," could be so rendered. But that is obviously not the meaning of the term as John employs it. And John is the sole employer of the term "antichrist."

John views the antichrist not so much as a person but as a doctrinal system (or systems) which assaults the true and full nature of the person of Jesus Christ. The systems were conceived and propogated by persons, but it was the mindset of such persons, and the expression thereof, which John calls the antichrist and the spirit of the antichrist. He does not use the term in the sense of a proper name. He speaks not of *the* Antichrist, but of antichrists.

Moreover, in John's use of the term, the antichrists of whom he spoke arose from within the Christian fellowship, and departed therefrom, not vice versa (I Jn. 2:19). This is a fact commonly overlooked by those bent on sensationalism. If we have oversimplified the subject, we have at least not perverted it or stretched it beyond the limits the textual data will support.

It would be presumptive, of course, to say no other doctrinal deviation could rightly be spoken of as "of the spirit of the antichrist," or that no individual could be rightly called antichrist, but not so presumptive as to insist that "the Antichrist" is indeed a person who is as yet to be revealed.

Paul's Doctrine of the Man of Sin

Paul's doctrine of the man of sin is somewhat enigmatic. It was interjected into the Thessalonian correspondence when they misread his consoling epistle (1 Thessalonians) and jumped to the conclusion that he was trying to tell them the second coming of Christ was assuredly at hand. In chapter two of II Thessalonians he informs them there must first be a falling away and the appearing of the man of sin, or lawless one.

This disclosure introduces no small problem. If the promises and warnings concerning Christ's second coming were couched in language intentionally vague, so as to keep every generation "on their toes," "looking for and earnestly desiring the day of Christ," Paul would seem to have changed that insofar as the Thessalonians were concerned, along with others who might read or hear what he revealed in his second Thessalonian letter. And the problem remains to this day if the man of sin has yet to appear.

There have been many periods of apostasy which could be regarded as fulfilling the first half of the prediction. In fact, except possibly for the first few months (or years at the most), there very likely has never been a time in the whole of the Christian era that did not witness a falling away of some degree. But not every few years, perhaps not even every century, has produced a malignancy of the magnitude of Paul's description of the man of sin. If he has not yet been manifested, then we are in the same predicament as the Thessalonians were placed in by Paul's second letter. Christ cannot come at any time now — unless we resort to the secret rapture escape hatch and say He will first come secretly for his saints. It is that which could happen at any time. But his actual coming will be delayed for some seven years to provide the man of sin a chance to appear.

The difficulty of that exercise in semantics is that Paul, who had already predicted the rapture (I Thess. 4:13-17), specifically says that "the coming of our Lord Jesus Christ, *and the gathering together unto him*" (the rapture) can not

APPEARING OF ANTICHRIST AND MAN OF SIN

be reckoned as at hand, except the falling away come first and the man of sin be revealed (II Thess. 2:1-3).

Four Questions to be Considered

To come to an understanding of Paul's teaching concerning the man of sin four questions need to be answered.

1. Is Paul's "man of sin" or "lawless one" just another name for John's antichrist? Are the two actually one and the same person?

2. Is the man of sin, whether equated with the antichrist or not, a person; that is, one specific individual? Or a system? Or perhaps a succession of persons within a system? Or a succession of systems all characterized by the same basic phenomenon — a time of full blown apostasy spearheaded and masterminded by some diabolic person or heretical movement?

3. Was this apostasy and man of sin relatively close at hand as Paul penned II Thessalonians, or something and someone that would not be manifested until near the end of the end-time? If the latter, was Paul aware of that? Or did he only know that an apostasy and super evil person would have to come before Christ could return? He speaks plainly enough concerning the reason the man of sin must first appear. High on Christ's priority list at His coming is the slaying of the man of sin with the breath of His mouth (v. 8).

4. What is, or was, or shall be, "that which restraineth"? (KJV, "letteth." This is one of several words in the KJV which have come to have an opposite meaning than the one carried in 1611.) The thought that Paul seems to be communicating is that something was holding the apostasy back and likewise holding in check the man of sin.

WHAT THE BIBLE SAYS ABOUT THE END TIME

Four General Interpretations

There are four general interpretations of the passage. These are not necessarily four attempted identifications of the man of sin, but general interpretative systems with regard to the passage of Scripture.

1. The Rationalistic. Liberal theologians see in this passage the old age syndrome. As men grow older they incline to lose the optimism of their former days and become somewhat dismayed, if not disillusioned; critical, if not cynical. The old days come to be regarded as "the good old days," and the new day, the day at hand or looming on the horizon is regarded with apprehension and distrust. Someone has written a bit of verse entitled *The Dogs*, which expresses the attitude here spoken of.

> My grandfather, noting the world's worn cogs
> Swears things are going to the dogs.
> His grandfather in his house of logs
> Was sure things were going to the dogs.
> His grandfather amid his daily jog
> Said things were surely going to the dogs.
> The cave man in his queer skin togs
> Just knew things were going to the dogs.
> So this is what I'd like to state;
> Those dogs have had an awful wait. Anon.

Liberal theologians have suggested Paul was having a bout with disillusionment. He had by now witnessed some defection among his own companions and observed what he could foresee as the beginning of schism and apostasy. He is allowing this to grow all out of proportion in his mind. The problem with that theory is two-fold. For one thing, the Thessalonian correspondence is generally recognized as

APPEARING OF ANTICHRIST AND MAN OF SIN

the earliest of Paul's writings. And even the last of his writings, yea, even when he is predicting apostasy, finds Paul still optimistic and at times even radiant in spirit. But rationalists have a ready answer for this. They simply date the Biblical writings to fit their theories.

2. The Preterit. The term is derived from the Latin *praeteritus*, "gone before." According to this view the things predicted are now history. There are two rival interpretations within the preterit school. The differences as they relate to the four main topics of the passage are as follows:

1) The Apostasy:
   a) The increasing apostasy and intransigence of the Jews
   b) The rising spectre of gnosticism
2) The Man of Sin:
   a) The Jewish hierarchy
   b) Simon Magus
3) The Restraining Power:
   a) The longsuffering of God
   b) The prayers of the saints
4) The Destruction of the Man of Sin:
   a) The fall of Jerusalem and end of the Jewish age
   b) The triumph of the Gospel.

3. The Progressionist. According to this system of thought, the prophecy continues in the state of *being fulfilled*, generally in and through the papacy. In this model, the meaning of the four aspects of the prophecy is as follows:

1) The Apostasy: The so called "Holy Roman Empire" that arose amid the ashes of Imperial Rome.

2) The Man of Sin: The Papacy. Not necessarily any one pope, although several have done more than others to expand the apostasy and to deserve the epithet.

3) The Restraining Power: Imperial Rome. As long as the Caesars were secure in Rome the papacy could not come to full flower.

4) The Destruction of the Man of Sin: Here the progressionists part company. Those premillennially oriented usually insist that the appearing of Christ personally in His second coming will occasion this. However, thorough-going premillennialists are rarely progressionists. Post and amillennialists generally regard the reformation, via the return to the Scriptures, as the power that is defeating the papal system.

4. The Futuristic. According to this school of thought the principal feature of the prediction, the revelation of the man of sin, is still in the future. The apostasy is generally acknowledged as being already at work in Paul's time, for that matter. (See v. 7.) And the restraining power, generally regarded as the Holy Spirit, is also thought to be at work; thus the position is not completely futuristic. Premillennialists make up the bulk of the futuristic school of thought. The four topics may be summarized as follows:

1) The Apostasy: A general falling away in the last days, a la the "days of Noah" syndrome as interpreted in premillennial theory — a time of violence, great wickedness and almost total unbelief.

2) The Man of Sin: The Antichrist, a super wicked and powerful atheistic ruler.

3) The Restraining Power: The Holy Spirit. According to this school of thought the Holy Spirit will be completely absent from the earth during the reign of the Antichrist.

4) The Destruction of the Man of Sin: Accomplished at Christ's second "second coming," His coming after the rapture "with his saints," and with His angels in flaming fire. The slaying of the Antichrist by Christ merely breathing

APPEARING OF ANTICHRIST AND MAN OF SIN

on Him is not always taken literally, but neither is it regarded as an apocalyptic expression. However the Man of Sin is destroyed, Christ will attend the matter personally.

The Crucial Question: Who or What is the Man of Sin?

The crucial question remains to be answered: Who or what is the man of sin? Answers have ranged from Nero to Nixon, and even Billy Graham. The Papacy, Luther, the Kaiser, Mussolini, Hitler, Kissinger and "Rev." Moon are among those who have been nominated to the dubious honor.

One of the most exhaustive and informational treatises on the subject can be found in *The Pulpit Commentary: Thessalonians - James* (Eerdmans). P.J. Gloag supplied the commentary of 1, 2 Thessalonians. An *Excursus on the Man of Sin,* pgs. 50-61, appended to his commentary on II Thessalonians, chapter 2, will be found especially illuminating.

Seven Deductions Which May Be Drawn

Despite the difficulties the passage presents there are seven deductions which can be drawn from the textual date:

1. There is, or once was, or there shall be a *man* of sin. It is sobering that this awesome being is a man, not the devil. Man, created in the image of God may be degraded into the image of Satan. But he is yet a man. It has been well said: "An evil man is more dangerous than a fallen angel, because he is nearer to his fellowmen."

2. The man of sin either arose (or shall arise) in a time of apostasy or accelerated it (or will do so when he comes), or perhaps both. It is not said that he precedes the apostasy and initiates it. Quite the contrary is indicated.

3. Both the apostasy and the appearing of the man of sin precede the second coming of Christ. It is not said that the second coming will follow soon afterwards, although this would seem to be the import of the prediction.

4. The mystery of lawlessness is at work prior to the appearing of the man of sin, but it is somehow restrained. Paul states he had spoken of this somewhat more openly when he was among the Thessalonians than the manner in which he now sees fit to write of it.

5. At His coming Christ will slay the man of sin by the breath of His mouth. This would seem to suggest that the appearing of the man of sin and the appearing of Christ in His second coming are somewhat close in point of time. However, the language at this point is obviously apocalyptic. Similar expressions are found elsewhere in apocalyptic literature. The expression is therefore capable of other interpretation.

6. It is said of the power and signs and lying wonders and deceit of unrighteousness manifested by the man of sin that it is God who is sending all this "because they believed not the truth." This is a rare instance in the New Testament of that form of speaking called "Hebrew verticalism." Jehovah's hardening of Pharaoh's heart and the sending of an evil spirit from Jehovah upon Saul are classic examples in the Old Testament. In Hebrew theology, the doctrine of the omnipotence, omniscience and omnipresence of God gave occasion for this mode of expression. If God is indeed all powerful, all knowing and everywhere present then nothing could happen without His knowledge and permission. If He knew it would happen (if not, He would not be omniscient) and did not prevent it though He *could* have done so (or else He would not be omnipotent), He must

APPEARING OF ANTICHRIST AND MAN OF SIN

therefore have willed it to happen, at least in a secondary sense. It somehow served His purpose. Thus Paul could speak of God giving a "working of error that they should believe a lie" because they had refused to believe the truth.

7. Paul's restraint in writing as openly as he had seen fit to speak of the matter when present in Thessalonica obviously gave the Thessalonians an edge over us in understanding this passage, unless there is something in history which can be definitely identified as the fulfillment of the prediction. This possibility should not be overlooked in the light of v. 7. He affirms the apostasy of which he spoke was already budding and would come to full flower when the restaints were lifted and the man of sin would be revealed. That would seem to place the fulfillment of the prophecy towards the beginning of the Christian era rather than the end.

In summary, two of the deductions would seem to be contradictory. The fifth, on the surface at least, seems to point to the second coming of Christ as the time of fulfillment and the seventh to a time much earlier in Christian history. Since the former seems to be fixing more certainly the time of fulfillment than does the latter we would be obligated to tip our decision in that direction were it not for the fact that that is the one facet of the prophecy which is couched unmistakably in apocalyptic metaphor. It is therefore the one which is the least demanding of literal interpretation.

The foregoing observations hardly solve the difficulties the passage presents but they should be helpful in evaluating the various theories one may encounter. Perhaps our first chore should be to deal with the supposition that the man of sin is to be equated with John's antichrist. When placed side by side for comparison they only appear to parallel on the surface.

WHAT THE BIBLE SAYS ABOUT THE END TIME

PAUL'S MAN OF SIN II Thessalonians 2:1-12	JOHN'S ANTICHRIST(S) I John 2:18-22, 4:1-6, II John 7
A. APPEARS IN A TIME OF APOSTASY, 2:3	A. DECLARED TO BE APOSTATES, 2:19
1. Exalts self, opposes all that is called God and is worshiped as God, v. 4.	(1. Only surface affinity, if any)
2. Sits in temple of God, setting forth self as God, v. 4.	(2. No parallel data stated)
3. His coming: according to the working of Satan with powers and lying wonders, v. 9.	(3. No parallel data stated)
4. And with all deceit of unrighteousness, v. 10.	(4. This could be inferred.)
(5. This could only be inferferred.)	5. Ebionites denied Christ's intrinsic deity, 2:22.
(6. This could only be inferred.)	6. Docetists denied Christ's incarnation, 4:1-3, II Jn. 7.
B. AN IMPENDING THREAT, 2:7	B. A THEN-PRESENT THREAT, 2:18
C. A POWERFUL BUT DOOMED FOE, 2:8	C. A NOT-AT-ALL INVINCIBLE FOE, 2:20, 21, 24-28, 4:4-6

By way of summary: (A.) Paul's man of sin is not said to be a defector from the Christian faith; John's antichrists (note the plural) are. Paul's man of sin is monstrously malignant; John only charges the antichrist with apostasy from the faith in the area of Christological concepts. (B.) The timing data can be reconciled. Paul's Thessalonian letters are generally accepted as among the earliest of the New Testament documents. John's epistles are among the last. At least forty years separate them. The threat shaping up near the mid-century mark could very well have materialized by the near end of the century. John, however, does not seem to deal with two problems, an apostasy and an egocentric maniac, but with a diversity of doctrinal differences. John's antichrist does not appear to pose the same peril as Paul's man of sin. In short the two passages have little in common.

It may be well to note that John grounds his confidence in the believers invincibility and triumph over the antichrists in the fact they had the unction of the Holy Spirit within, and the apostle's witness to the person of Christ as their basis of faith. We still do. Only as Paul's apocalyptic expression, "the breath of his coming," is interpreted as the Holy Spirit working through the Word of Christ can the manner in which the two foes are defeated be paralleled. In the larger sense of the term Paul's man of sin could be called *an* antichrist. And in the larger sense of the term John's antichrists could be called men of sin. But only in the context of futuristic end-time sensationalism can the two subjects be rolled into one.

The Man of Sin in History

Historically, Paul's prediction of the man of sin made a deep impression upon the early church fathers. References to it in their writings are numerous. They exhibit some degree of unanimity, particularly with regard to the identity of the restraining power. This was commonly agreed to be Imperial Rome. Paul's admonition to Christians to pray for their rulers that they (the Christians) might "lead a tranquil and quiet life in all godliness" (I Tim. 2:1), and to be in subjection to the higher powers "as ministers of God" to them for good (Romans 13:1-7), were commonly cited as evidence Paul so understood his prediction.

As for the man of sin, they viewed him as indeed an individual. Some saw him as the Antichrist, thus individualizing that subject also. The latter was due largely to the influence of Jewish eschatologists. Antiochus Epiphanes in the second century B.C. had profaned the temple by placing an idol therein. This rash act, the culmination of his diabolic persecution and harassment of the Jews, triggered the Maccabean revolt. The Maccabeans saw in Epiphanes the blasphemer predicted by Daniel (7:25). Jewish interpreters in the early post apostolic era saw in Epiphanes a type of Paul's man of sin and gave to him the name Armillus (in Hebrew) and Antichrist (in Greek). The Targum substitutes "Armillus" for "rasha" (wicked) in Isaiah 11:4 causing that messianic prophecy to read, "With the breath of his mouth he shall slay Armillus." This reading, combined with II Thess. 2:8 completes (in theory) the identification of Armillus Antichrist with Paul's man of sin.

One strain of Jewish eschatology developed the theory that in the last days an arch foe would arise, born of a marble statue in one of the churches in Rome. The Romans would acknowledge him as their king. He would wage war against Israel. Messiah ben (son of) Joseph would be slain, but Messiah ben David would appear and utterly slay Armillus and his followers.

Other identifications of the man of sin were soon to follow. In that Nero was the first Roman emperor to persecute the Christians, it was inevitable that he should have been regarded by many Christians as the man of sin. This presented several problems. The Roman empire had been rather effectively demonstrated as the restraining power which prevented the rise of the man of sin. The Roman empire had certainly not been taken away. And Nero's demise did

APPEARING OF ANTICHRIST AND MAN OF SIN

not fit the scenario. But soon a legend arose to the effect Nero was not actually dead, or that if he were he would be resurrected and return to earth as the Antichrist. Rev. 17:10, 11 was the basis of this conjecture. Nero was identified as the fifth of the seven kings who "are fallen" and the one who shall become the eighth king and spearhead the persecution which results in the Great Tribulation.

One historic interpretation persists. Long before the Protestant Reformation, the opponents of the Roman Catholic hierarchy, saw in the papacy the fulfillment of Paul's prediction. As early as the tenth century this identification was virtually universal among those opposed to the papal system. The Roman Catholic church arose amid the ashes of the fallen Roman empire. When the capital of the empire was removed to Byzantium, and the new capital, Constantinople, the city of Constantine, was established (306 A.D.) a power void was created in Rome. The budding hierarchy of Rome was quick to seize the opportunity this provided. By the time of the breaking up of the empire (475 A.D.) the papacy was fully established. The hordes of Barbarian invaders made any kind of established authority in the vast outreaches of the former empire welcomed above the anarchy that followed in the wake of the fall of Rome. The papacy was pleased to step in and assume the role of the Divine and sovereign head of the catholic (universal) kingdom of the God of heaven.

The blasphemy and arrogance and papal titles, and the wickedness and cruelty which later came to characterize the papacy, made the identification with the man of sin inevitable. The restraining power, Imperial Rome, had been removed. And the blasphemous man of sin had now appeared. It almost seems that the papacy took pains to fulfill every facet of Paul's prediction in II Thessalonians 2 and the signs of the apostasy he spoke of in his letters to Timothy, (I Timothy 4:1-13, II Timothy 3:1-5, 4:3, 4). The epithet, the man of sin, was well earned.

An imposing array of notables dared prison, torture and death to arraign the papacy as the man of sin and the beast of the apocalypse: Arnulph, at the Council of Rheims, 991 A.D.; Savonarola of Florence, Italy; the Albigenses, the Waldenses, Huss, Wycliffe, Luther, Calvin, Melanchthon, and Beza are but a few.

The papacy, of course, countered that the Protestants were the real culprits. The Greek church hung the label on the Mohammedans. Futurists have bequeathed dubious distinction to whatsoever super and not so super malignant person seems to be looming on the horizon. Just now there seems to be a lull in Man of Sinology. No prime candidate seems to be in the wings. One Middle East in Prophecy buff would likely pin the role on Jimmy Carter for his part in bringing about what might grow into an "Egyptian-Israeli coalition," were it not for the fact that Carter's political star is now waning. It takes something more sensational to sell ephemeral paper back quickies. In the interim one can always fall back on communism. The noted Tulsa evangelist plays it cool, keeping the focus on sensationalism and mystery. In his book, *How to be Personally Prepared for the Second Coming*, p. 36, he writes: "The Bible tells how, right in the middle of the rise to power, Antichrist will be assassinated. The devil will then make his big move. He will raise Antichrist from the dead in an attempt to reproduce the Holy Trinity."

We seem to be left with two options. We may join the end-time at hand futurists who stand ready to peer around the corner for us and give us a sneak preview of the real man of sin who will supplant the imposters who have tricked the peddlers in the past. Or we may adopt the historical approach which views the prophecy as in the process of fulfillment through the papacy.

In his book *Great Prophecies of the Bible*, to which we have previously called attention, Ralph Woodrow makes a strong case for the papal identification. In chapter 20 entitled "Paul's Prophecy — The Man of Sin," he devotes nine well documented pages to the thesis.

Woodrow begins by quoting Lenski on the meaning of the phrase, "except there come first a falling away," v. 3. In his commentary, *The Interpretation of St. Paul's Epistles, to the Colossians, to the Thessalonians, to Timothy and to Philemon*, p. 433, Lenski has said:

> This is an apostasy. It is, therefore, to be sought *in* the church visible, and not *outside* the church, nor the pagan world, in the general moral decline, in Mohammedanism, in the French Revolution, in soviet Russia, or in lesser phenomena.

Attention is called to the fact that the apostolic church was filled with truth and spiritual power as the book of Acts records. But towards the end of those days the apostles began to warn of coming apostasy (Acts 20:29, 30, I Tim. 4:1-3, II Peter 2:1-3). With the conversion(?) of Constantine, if not before, compromises were made with paganism. By the end of the fourth century what was then called the church was an apostate church, a fallen church, though politically speaking it had risen to great power. The apostasy which brought on the dark ages is generally recognized and well established in history as centered in Rome.

The Bishop of Rome rose to power claiming to be the Bishop of Bishops, the Father of all, hence the adoption of the title "papa" (Lat.), the Pope. In his *Dissertations on the Prophecies*, Thomas Newton reasons that if apostasy be rightly charged upon the church of Rome, "it follows that the man of sin is the pope, not meaning this or that pope in particular, but the pope in general, as the chief head and supporter of the apostasy. The apostasy produces him and he promotes the prophecy." (See Woodrow, p. 165.)

Woodrow amply supports his thesis that "the temple of God" mentioned in v. 4 of the prophecy refers to the church, not a restored Jewish edifice. Nine times in his teaching, Paul used the Greek word *naon* (temple). Woodrow is quite correct when he notes that "a careful study of every reference Paul makes to the temple of God reveals that he never applied this term to the Jewish temple" (p. 165). See Acts 17:24, I Cor. 3:16, 17, 6:19, II Cor. 6:16, Eph. 2:21, II Thess. 2:4. The word which commonly denotes the temple structure is *heiron*. Seventy-one times *heiron* is used in the New Testament to denote the temple at Jerusalem.

It is of interest that the word "sitteth," as contained in the expression, "sitteth in the temple" (v. 4), is a translation of the Greek word *kathisai*. Sitting implies a seat. This brings us to the term *kathedra*, familiar in the expression "ex cathreda." The expression is used to denote the Pope's utterances when he speaks *from* the Bishop's seat (cathedra). Pronouncements made from that "seat" are supposedly infallible, and orders issuing therefrom "bind on earth," the whole of the earth, what the Pope decrees.

The expression "sitteth as God" is not lacking in precedence. Ezekiel 28:2 records the king of Tyre, and Isa. 14:14 records the king of Babylon, as boasting in much the same manner as Paul's man of sin. Daniel 8:25 and 11:36, 37, Obadiah, v. 4, Acts 12:21-23 and Mt. 11:23 are also relevant. It would be no new thing for one to represent himself as God. Egomaniacs have done so for years. They still do.

APPEARING OF ANTICHRIST AND MAN OF SIN

Historically, popes have been guilty of this. The triple crown of the papacy is the visible symbol of the papal claim to rule not only the earth, but to have power over heaven and hell also. At the coronation of Innocent X, the following words were addressed to him by a cardinal who knelt before him:

> Most holy and blessed Father, head of the church, ruler of the world, to whom the keys of the kingdom of heaven are committed, whom the angels in heaven revere, and the gates of hell fear, and all the world adores, we specially venerate, worship, and adore thee.

To the foregoing quote cited by Woodrow (p. 168) he adds the following: "Moseri, a noted historian wrote: 'To make war against God, seeing the Pope is God and God is the Pope.' Decius is quoted as saying: 'The Pope can do all things God can do.' " Pope Leo XIII said of himself less than a century ago (1890):

> The supreme teacher in the Church is the Roman Pontiff. Union of minds therefore requires, together with a perfect accord in the one faith, complete submission of will to the church and to the Roman Pontiff, as to God Himself.

And in 1894 he declared: "We hold the place of Almighty God on earth."

As late as April 30, 1922, Pope Pius XI, in the Vatican throne room, declared to cardinals, bishops, priests and nuns who were on their knees before him, "You know that I am the Holy Father, the representative of God on earth, the Vicar of Christ, which means I am God on the earth."

There are many other such utterances, too numerous and lengthy to repeat. Does some one counter, the popes of today appear to be much more humble men? So they do.

WHAT THE BIBLE SAYS ABOUT THE END TIME

But they have a long way to go to conform to the image and mind of Christ. And there has to date been no public repudiation of the claims of their predecessors. Such change as we may see in both blasphemies and moral behavior are to be attributed to the lessening of politcal clout. Perhaps the breath of the mouth of Christ, His Spirit working through His word, is subduing even the papacy.

As for the wickedness which Paul attributes to the man of sin, the pages of history are black and bloody with the record of their exploits and deeds. Albert Barnes in *Barnes Notes* (Thessalonians - Philippians, p. 81-83) chronicles a list of crimes of which we shall make only scattered mention. Pope Vagilius waded to the pontifical throne through the blood of his predecessor. Pope John VIII (actually "Mother Joan") a female in disguise, was elected and confirmed to the papacy. Platinus says of her that "she became with child by some of those that were about her; that she miscarried and died on her way from the Laterian to the temple." Pope Marcellinus sacrificed to idols.

Some were so wicked that even their fellow apostates sought judgment against them. The Council of Constantinople decreed, "We have caused Honorius to be accursed; for that in all things he followed the mind of Sergius the heretic, and confirmed his wicked doctrines." The Council of Basil said of Pope Eugenius: We condemn Pope Eugenius, a despiser of the holy canons, a disturber of the peace and unity of the church, a notorious offender, a Simonist, a perjurer, incorrigible, a willful heretic." Pope John II was publicly charged with incest. Pope John XII usurped the papacy, spent his time in hunting, lasciviousness and monstrous forms of vice. He fled the trial to which he had been summoned, and was stabbed while in the act of adultery.

APPEARING OF ANTICHRIST AND MAN OF SIN

Pope Sixtus IV licensed brothels in Rome. Pope Alexander VI, according to a catholic historian, was "a horrible monster." His beastly morals, including monstrous incest with his daughter Lucretia, his insatiable avarice, detestable cruelty and furious lusts are described by a number of authentic papal historians. Need we say more. The papacy fulfills the prediction regarding the wickedness of the man of sin.

We would labor the point if we were to detail the fulfillment of every facet of the prediction. But one more deserves mention. The expression "he shall wear out the saints" (Daniel 7:25) suggests a process of long duration. It is at this point that Daniel introduces an apocalyptic time frame that is variously expressed in other apocalyptic utterances, viz., "A time, and times, and a half a time." This is elsewhere expressed as "a thousand two hundred and threescore (1260) days" (Rev. 12:6), and "forty two months" (three and a half years, Rev. 11:2). These expressions are commonly interpreted according to the "year for a day" principle (See Num. 14:34 and Ezek. 4:6.). Thus we have a predicted time span of one thousand two hundred and sixty years. This time span compares favorably with the period of history called the Dark Ages, the years of papal supremacy.

During the 1260 years of the Dark ages it has been estimated that over fifty million Christians were tortured and killed. Allow for shrinkage and the figure is still astronomical. It would take a Great Tribulation indeed for a latter-end Antichrist to do the same in three and a half calendar years, the time generally allotted him by premillennialists who take the figure literally in this instance to accommodate their rapture theory. In the light of the atrocities in Asia today it would ill behoove any one to say that such a massacre could not occur, with germ and nuclear arsenals and vast populations such as we have today. But we stoutly affirm we do not have to wait for some end-time Antichrist Man of Sin to appear and create such a holocaust in order for Christ to return and consummate the present order.

A Word of Caution

In closing this discussion a word of caution is in order. There is no ground for extending the foregoing application to the myriad of Roman Catholic followers throughout the world. The prophecy certainly does not. It is questionable whether the prophecy extends even to the entire hierarchy, or any of it short of the highest levels. It ill behooves anyone to indict the catholic people for the sins of the papacy, particularly the sins of the papacy past.

There is a sense in which the catholic masses are not the church. The church, technically, is the hierarchy, particularly the college of cardinals and the papacy. Catholics belong to the church as a team of oxen belongs to an Asian farmer, sheep to a shepherd, or cattle to a western rancher. It is conceded that the catholic populace make the papacy possible as cattle make possible the role of a rancher who burns his brand deeply upon them and does with them what he wills. Catholics have little if any control over the system to which they belong. They are the exploited, not the exploiters. They are to be loved and enlightened, as many have been — on both counts, to their liberation and salvation.

Moreover it is open to question whether every occupant of the papal seat is to be equated with the man of sin. The papacy was centuries in the making. Paul indicated the apostasy which would culminate in the man of sin was "already working" (v. 7) as he was writing. But the full blown apostasy that would grow from it was yet to come,

APPEARING OF ANTICHRIST AND MAN OF SIN

and the lawless one who would exploit it was yet to be revealed.

The papacy reached its zenith in the dark ages and was then smitten by the "*spirit* (Gr., *pneumati*, v. 8) *of Christ*" when He returned in the written Word via the reformation. The papacy began to wane through the agency of the Word, and is still waning. It has already diminished greatly. High ranking officials even at the cardinal level are questioning the infallibility of the pope, his role as Peter's successor, and other doctrines essential to the historic function of the papacy.

Unless one believes the spirit of Christ, working through His Gospel as proclaimed in His Name by spirit-filled men, is without the power to further reverse the Roman apostasy, we may conjecture that the coming of the Lord predicted in v. 8 may be interpreted metaphorically. The expression certainly may be in other passages in both Testaments.

It would be too much to expect that the Roman Catholic church will have ceased to exist when Christ returns. That will scarcely be true of other apostasies with which we now contend. Even if He should tarry for yet some time this likely will remain so. But when He comes in person He will "finish off" all perpetrators of apostasy, yea, even all those whose names are not found in the book of life (Rev. 20:10-15).

Chapter Eight

THE RUPTURE OF THE DOCTRINE OF THE RAPTURE

Strange as it may seem a doctrine barely mentioned in the Bible, and then not by the name by which it is popularly known, has upstaged the second coming of Christ in the hearts of multiplied thousands. Few doctrines "turn on" the average devotee of Biblical prophecy as does the modern doctrine of the rapture.

The doctrine is a "gut issue" in current end-time speculations. The very word evokes rapturous imaginations of sensational happenings calculated to frighten the wicked out of their wits, if not out of their wickedness, and promising the righteous transport somewhere out in the wild blue yonder for a three and one-half to seven year rendezvous with Christ on the proverbial "cloud nine."

It never seems to both the promoters of rapture rhetoric that not even the word "rapture," much less the greater part of what is being taught under that caption, is found in our Bible. Were one to look for the word in an exhaustive concordance of the Scriptures, whether Cruden's, Strong's, Young's or some other, not once will the word appear.

Thus we speak of the rupture of the doctrine of the rapture. When too much weight is put on too slight an abdominal muscle a rupture results. Altogether too much weight—the weight of far too many wild speculations—has been placed upon the slim Biblical data which men have ballooned and ballyhooed as the Biblical doctrine of the rapture.

Whence comes this captivating doctrine that has indeed upstaged the second coming of Christ in the hopes and expectations of tens of thousands, and thousands upon thousands of earnest believers? Has it no Biblical basis? It

THE RUPTURE OF THE DOCTRINE OF THE RAPTURE

has—some. The basic idea is there. But the rapture rhetoric so familiar to our times is largely the brain-child of doctrinarians who are still looking for the fulfillment of the seventieth week of Daniel's 70 week prophetical vision (Dan. 9:24-27). Proceeding on the "one day equals one prophetical year" premise (which of itself is not lacking textual support; see Num. 14:34 and Ezek. 4:6) but committed to the pseudo-exegetical juggling exercise known as the "gap hypothesis," Darby-Schofieldite millennialists have seven long overdue years of unfulfilled prophecy on their hands.

The cloud nine theory of the rapture provides an escape hatch for those who have locked themselves into the postponed kingdom dogma. How else do they conclude that the rapture will be an episode of either three and one-half or seven years duration, after which it is back to the old earth again for another thousand years at the least. Differences of opinion concerning the time slot into which the "great tribulation" fits accounts for the dividing up of the theorists into three camps, with two different projections for the duration of the rapture. There are "pre-tribulation," "mid- tribulation" and "post-tribulation" rapturists speculating within the framework of premillennialism. All of them agree the rapture ends with a return to earth. Even amillennialist Hoekama, *The Bible and the Future*, (Eerdman's, p. 168) seems to so believe. Commenting on the Greek word *apantesin,* translated "meet" in I Thess. 4:17, Hoekema says:

> On the basis of the analogy conveyed by this word, all Paul is saying here is that raised and transformed believers are caught up in the clouds to meet the Lord as he descends from heaven, implying that after this joyful meeting they will go back with him to the earth.

Were that what is implied, it would be better said that *He* will then go back with *them* to the earth. He Himself, however, has already said that when He comes it will be to receive us unto Himself that "where He is there we may be also" (Jn. 14:3). We know of course where He went (Lk. 24:51, Acts 1:9-11). And we know, of course, where He was when the martyr Stephen saw Him waiting to receive his spirit, (Acts 7:56). May "the analogy" one sees in a word set aside plain historical reporting? I think not. But I confess to find myself greatly outnumbered.

Obviously the average Christian is no more ready to leave the earth behind for good, for the new heaven and the new earth, than the Jews were ready to leave Jerusalem of Judea for the "Jerusalem that is above" (Gal. 4:26). How else may we explain the popular appeal of the Jehovah's Witnesses and the Armstrong empire teaching that all the redeemed of the Lord (save for 144,000 specially elect, according to the JW's) shall be literally "grounded" for all eternity on this dimunitive sphere, after it has been burned (and presumably scraped "like a bride's biscuit") — renovated, but never replaced.

What About the Rapture?

For the uninitiated, the epitome of modern rapture rhetoric is to be found in a bit of graffiti you may have seen at one time or another on a bumper sticker:

Warning: In case of the rapture this vehicle will be unmanned!

Indeed it will. Which one will not? But beyond that the case may not be at all what the driver of the vehicle nor the author of the bumper sticker graffiti had in mind. When all the Scriptures which bear on the subject are put together,

THE RUPTURE OF THE DOCTRINE OF THE RAPTURE

the facts are that not one of the five main features of popular rapture theory is true.

1. In the first place, it is the unsaved, not the redeemed, who are said to be the first that shall be taken out of this world. See the parable of the tares (Mt. 13:24-30 and 30-43), a parable which Jesus both spoke and explained. Note especially v. 30 and Jesus' own interpretation of the verse in vs. 40 and 41. (Incidentally, Schofield in His *Reference Bible* [commentary actually] saw fit to second guess Jesus. But we will deal with that later.)

2. In the second place, neither the rapture of the righteous nor any other event associated with the Biblical doctrine of the second coming of Christ will be such a secret thing a bumper sticker will be needed to advise that something unusual has happened. (See I Thess. 4:16, 17, II Thess. 1:7-10, I Cor. 15:50-58, II Peter 3:10.)

3. Thirdly, the rapture of the righteous is nowhere said to be a yo-yo affair, a three and one-half or seven year rendezvous somewhere in the stratosphere, after which the saints are again grounded for a thousand years, then airlifted again somewhere. But where? Where can they go while the heavens (not heaven, mind you, but the heavens, the skies) are passing away with a great noise, and the earth and the works that are therein are being burned up (but not actually, according to popular theory). Strangely, the literalists use a different criteria of interpretation when they come to this Scripture. Hence they prefer not to talk about the whereabouts of the reincarnated and raptured saints while the earth is being renovated for their re-entry and perpetual occupation.

4. Fourthly, nowhere is the second coming of Christ said to be a two-stage affair, with Christ on His first pass only

coming near enough to snatch up His saints, and then perhaps as much as seven years later coming all the way to the earth to set up a millennial kingdom "just like His father David's." The Scripture speaks only of one second coming, not a second and then a third. (See Hebr. 9:27, 28.)

5. Finally, nowhere is it taught in the Scriptures that the bodies of the righteous shall be raised a thousand years before the bodies of the wicked are resurrected. That is a gross misunderstanding of Rev. 20:4, 5 as has already been noted. The first resurrection of the Apocalypse is the resurrection to newness of life whereby we become "priests and a kingdom on earth" (Rev. 1:6, 5:10, 20:6). The bodily resurrection, the second resurrection comes at the end of the chapter (and of the present order). It will be the resurrection of both the just and the unjust at the same "hour," according to Jesus (Jn. 5:28, 29).

Aside from striking out on these five main points there isn't too much wrong with popular rapture reverie. But of course there isn't much left of it — except for what the Bible teaches.

What Does the Bible Say About the Rapture?

To understand what the Bible is speaking of we need to engage in a brief word study. We have complained that the popular word "rapture" is not in our Bibles. The derivation of it, however, is found in the Latin versions, and not without good reason.

The launching pad from which the doctrine of the rapture takes off is found in I Thess. 4:17 where it is written, "Then we that are alive that are left, shall together with them [the righteous dead who have just been resurrected] be *caught*

THE RUPTURE OF THE DOCTRINE OF THE RAPTURE

up in the clouds, to meet him in the air." The word rapture, as you can see, is not found in the passage, but the Greek verb *haparzo*, rendered "caught up," could acceptably be so translated. Our English word "rapture" is derived from the Latin *raptus*, the root meaning of which is to snatch or seize.

Thus the claws of birds of prey, for example the vulture, eagle, osprey, hawk, are called raptorial claws. They are designed to seize, to snatch up and carry away the hapless prey they swoop down upon. And for the same reason, the forcible assault of human vultures upon hapless and often helpless women and children is called "rape." This too is a rapture of a sort, but not the kind of rapture the text before us is speaking of.

The term also has positive and pleasant associations and applications. For example: Persons are said to stand at rapt attention when some momentous announcement is being made, or an especially moving challenge is being given. We speak of being enraptured and of experiencing rapturous delight when a breath-taking beauty of a wilderness scene, or the music of a great symphony, or an overwhelming religious experience snatches us from the humdrum and the common place and transports us, so to speak, into another world.

Unfortunately, the Biblical doctrine of the rapture has become so overlaid with wild and speculative theories one is tempted to suggest that we drop the word from our vocabulary. But that would just give the sensationalists an even more free hand to peddle their perverted theories.

There is a word found in our English Bibles which would serve as a suitable substitute. But it not only lacks the rapturous overtones which are evoked by the word "rapture," it also has come to be employed in a different context. We speak of the word "translation."

Hebrews 11:5 speaks of Enoch as having been translated. It is said of him that witness had been borne to him that before his translation he had been found well pleasing unto God, so much so that God "took" him. This is the sense in which the Greek word *harpazo* appears and the rapture should be understood. The text in Hebrews also speaks of the spiritual condition which is essential to such hope.

Two men of record, Enoch (Gen. 5:24) and Elijah (II Kings 2:11), one in each of the two previous dispensations, have been translated out of this world. That is to say, they were carried across the threshold which separates time and eternity, the temporal and eternal, without undergoing the experience of physical death.

The word is derived from the Latin prefix, *trans*, meaning "change" or "across" and a root word, *latio*, meaning "position" or "place." Hence the word means to change or bring across from one place to another. Enoch and Elijah were caught up, transported, translated entirely—body, soul and spirit. They were raptured, not for a few brief moments, as was Paul's spirit in his "Paradise vision" (II Cor. 12:3, 4), nor for a mere seven years at the most, as in popular rapture theory. They were taken up from this earth altogether and forevermore. Elijah appeared perchance in a vision, along with Moses, to Christ and three disciples on the Mount of Transfiguration, but the record in Kings reports that he was taken up "into heaven." He was not then obliged to return later to dwell on earth. This is the core of the Biblical doctrine of the rapture.

Unfortunately the words "translate" and "translation" are now somewhat narrowed in their application. They are most readily associated with the process of carrying the thoughts expressed in one language into words of equivalent meaning in another language. This is a legitimate use of the term, but it is not exhaustive. The term applies as readily to the transporting of mortal beings from this world into the world beyond.

Going back to I Thessalonians 4:13-17, the Greek word *harpazo* describes an experience such as we have just noted. And it shall be the experience of every redeemed human being, whether deceased or alive at the time of Christ's return. Thus the Bible does speak of what may be rightly called the rapture.

The Greek word *harpazo* is found thirteen times in the New Testament while it is instructive to note each instance of its use, only two of the texts speak of an event which is germaine to our discussion. We have italicized the translation of the Greek verb *harpazo*.

1. Mt. 11:12 reports Jesus as saying: "From the days of John the Baptist until now, the kingdom of heaven suffers violence, and men of violence *take* it by force."

2. Mt. 13:19. In the parable of the sower Jesus said, "When one hearing the word of the kingdom understandeth it not, then cometh the evil one and *snatches away* that which was sown in the heart" (cf. v. 4).

3. John 6:15. Here it is said that after Jesus had fed the multitudes in the wilderness, "they were about to *take* him *by force* and make him to be king." As we have noted, this text scarcely supports the theory on which the postponed kingdom, gap hypothesis is constructed.

4. John 10:12. In the parable of the good shepherd it is said, "The wolf cometh and *snatches* them" (the sheep deserted by the hireling).

5. John 10:28 contains the phrase, "No one shall *snatch* them out of my hand."

6. John 10:29 adds, "And no one shall *snatch* them out of the Father's hand." These are among the proof(?) texts for the doctrine of eternal security. The text says nothing to the effect the sheep are powerless to desert His fold, or go astray and be snatched by beasts of prey after they do.

7. Acts 8:39 states that "the Spirit *caught* away Philip" after he baptized the Ethiopian eunuch. Were He guided by the spirit which is so visibly at work in evangelism today He would have departed sooner.

8. Acts 23:10. Here we are told the chief captain, fearing lest Paul should be torn to pieces, "commanded the soldiers to go down and *take* him *by force*" from among the hostile Jews, and bring him into the castle.

9. Jude 23 speaks of saving some, but barely, as it were "*snatching* them out of the fire."

10. Rev. 12:5 speaks of the man-child of the woman pursued by the dragon as "*caught up* unto God."

11. II Cor. 12:2 finds Paul speaking of a man, probably himself, "*caught up* even unto the third heaven. The first heaven in Hebrew cosmology was the atmosphere which surrounds the earth, the air in which the birds of the heavens fly about. The second was the stellar skies in which the sun, moon and stars move about. The third was the spirit world (Paradise, see v. 4.).

12. II Cor. 12:4. Paul, speaking in the same context, alters the expression slightly, speaking of the man as "*caught up* into Paradise."

13. I Thess. 4:17. We are now back to the basic text. Here Paul speaks of the saints which are alive in Christ's coming being *caught up* with the righteous dead whom He has just resurrected "to meet (Him) in the air."

THE RUPTURE OF THE DOCTRINE OF THE RAPTURE

These thirteen texts are illustrative of the sense of the word *harpazo*. Actually, only the last text cited deals directly with the snatching of saints out of this present world and transporting them into the world and life beyond. From this one text, however, five important facts concerning the rapture are clear.

(1) The event shall take place at Christ's coming, period. Not just the first phase, His reentry into the atmosphere to return actually forty-two months to seven years later, but the entire event shall take place at His coming.

(2) His coming apparently will be a rather noisome event, for He is said to come "with a shout, with the voice of the archangel and the trump of God." This hardly speaks of a secret affair.

(3) The dead in Christ will be raised but moments ahead of the snatching up of the living saints. See also I Cor. 15:51, 52.

(4) Both are to be taken up into the clouds, as Christ was when he ascended unto His father. So shall it be with the saints.

(5) Those caught up to meet Him in the air shall be with Him forevermore where they shall be with Him was explained to the twelve in the upper room (John 14:1-6).

This hardly conforms to popular conceptions of the rapture. From whence come such notions we have previously taken note of: 1) the rapture will be secret — and at night, always, and apparently everywhere at once; 2) that it is to be a forty-two month to seven year rendezvous in the air; 3) that the unsaved will be left behind wondering where a lot of people have gone they once knew and saw; 4) that at the close of the airlift Christ will come yet again, this time all the way down to the ground to set up his long postponed millennial kingdom; and 5) that the righteous dead shall be resurrected a thousand years ahead of the wicked?

WHAT THE BIBLE SAYS ABOUT THE END TIME

Are there other Scriptures which perchance do not use the word *harpazo* but speak of the event from which we may learn all these things? At this point there comes to mind a question that was put to the renowned Bible scholar, G. Campbell Morgan, by Paul G. Jackson, reported in *Christianity Today,* Aug. 31, 1959, p. 16, 17.

> *Jackson:* After your long and full study and extensive exposition of the Bible, do you find any Scriptural warrant for the distinction which Bible teachers draw between the 2nd coming of the Lord *for* his own (the rapture) and the coming of the Lord *with* his own (the revelation) with a time period of 3-1/2 to 7 years between?
>
> *Morgan:* Emphatically not! I know this view very well. In the earlier years of my ministry I taught it and incorporated it in one of my books (*God's Method With Man*). But further study so convinced me of the error of this teaching that I actually went to the expense of buying the plates from the publisher and destroying them. The idea of a separate and secret coming of Christ is a vagary of prophetic interpretation without any Biblical basis whatsoever.

That confession is a classic but altogether too rare example of intellectual honesty. It was also a costly one. Not only did Morgan suffer the loss of further revenue from the sale of his book, and perhaps the loss of some friends and followers, he paid money out of his pocket to gain control of the plates and destroyed them to prevent further circulation.

It is a sad commentary on the greater part of prophecy peddlers that they show no similar misgivings for their errors. Even when time has proven their dates and identifications wrong, there is rarely a confession, not often even an attempted cover-up. That would call attention to their error. New identifications, new dating charts are quickly whipped

THE RUPTURE OF THE DOCTRINE OF THE RAPTURE

up to keep attention focused on the exciting events which are just around the next corner. Thanks to the gullibility and short memories of those who thrive on excitement and suspense, their suppliers on the money side of the game proceed with game plan number twenty-nine, then thirty, then thirty-one, etc.

Father Time has often caught up with the likes of Father Armstrong, but either their followers are quick to forget what they were told would surely come to pass or Barnum was right about a new crop of suckers being born daily. Perhaps both are true. But God the Father must one day be reckoned with. That will be "the day of the Lord" of which His prophets have so repeatedly warned.

But let us hear the other side. At least it will demonstrate we aren't just fighting the proverbial straw man. H. L. Wilmington sets the tone for the other side of the argument in his book, *The King is Coming*. On page 12 under the caption, "False Views of The Rapture," Wilmington puts at the head of the list "the view that the rapture and the second coming of Christ are the same thing." Of that view he has written:

> *False.* At the rapture Jesus comes in the air *for* His church, while at the second coming He comes *with* His saints to the earth.

By way of proof(?) Wilmington cited Jude, vs. 14, 15 and Rev. 19:11-16. Unless those are typographical errors, Wilmington is assuming his readers to be fully as gullible as I have suggested they are.

Dr. Robert Strong, writing in *The Presbyterian Guardian* (February 24, 1942) affirmed:

> By the rapture is meant the sudden and possibly secret coming of Christ in the air to snatch away from the earth the resurrected bodies of those who have died in faith, and with them the living saints.

WHAT THE BIBLE SAYS ABOUT THE END TIME

Speaking in much the same vein, the "Reverend" Jesse P. Silver, author of *The Lord's Return*, stated on p. 260:

> Quickly and invisibly, unperceived by the world, the Lord will come as a thief in the night, and catch away His living saints.

So writes also Herschel W. Ford in his tongue-twister titled book, *Seven Simple Sermons on the Second Coming*. On p. 51 he says:

> The rapture will be a secret appearing, and only the believers will know of it.

Oral Roberts, erstwhile Divine healer and charismatic evangelist, now hospital and university enterpriser, wrote in his book, *How to be Personally Prepared for the Second Coming*, p. 34:

> His appearance in the clouds will be veiled to the human eye. He will slip in, slip out: move in to get his jewels, and slip out as under cover of night.

It seems more likely that it is Oral Roberts who has slipped.

The classic expression of this line of reasoning is found in the oft quoted words of Richard W. DeHaan of the *Radio Bible Class*. Among others, Lorraine Boettner, in his book *The Millennium*, p. 172, 173, quotes from a DeHaan broadcast of November 1954, these oft parroted words:

> One of these days, as sure as this is the Word of God, those who have pled with you, who have warned you, who have prayed for you, will be missing. The preacher will be gone, mother will be gone, wife will be gone, and the baby's crib will be empty.
>
> Oh, what an awakening that is going to be. Imagine, getting up some morning and your wife is not there, and you call for her, but there is no answer. You go downstairs but

THE RUPTURE OF THE DOCTRINE OF THE RAPTURE

> she is not there. You call upstairs to your daughter asking her where mother is, but no answer from her. Your daughter is gone too.
>
> You ring the police, but the line is busy. Hundreds and thousands are calling up, jamming the telephone lines. You rush out of doors and bump into a pal of last night's wild party. He is as white as a sheet. He is out of breath and stammers a few words, and bawls out, "My wife is gone. My *brother* is gone and I don't know where they are."

Note: The italicizing of the word "brother" is an editorial addition. It was beginning to appear as though DeHaan was trying to tell us that except for preachers only women and children would be raptured. The quotation continues:

> Down the street runs a woman shrieking at the top of her voice, "Some one has kidnapped my baby." And in a moment the streets are full of people, weeping, crying, and howling over the disappearance of loved ones.
>
> What has happened? The Lord has come, like a thief in the night. He has quietly stolen away those who trusted Him, like Enoch, and no one is left behind to warn you any more, to pray or show you the way.

That ought to just about wrap it up, should it not? Is it not written, "At the word of two or three witnesses a thing shall be established" (Mt. 16:18, II Cor. 13:1, Deut. 17:6). The problem is, none of the voices we have just heard echoed are the voices of witnesses. They are the voices of fanciful theorists. And what they have fancied is diametrically opposed to what is written by those who were witnesses of Christ and who wrote by Divine inspiration.

Two Questions are In Order

Two important questions are in order. When these are settled the other issues readily fall in place.

WHAT THE BIBLE SAYS ABOUT THE END TIME

1. Is the rapture to be a "hush, hush" happening, a nocturnal meeting of a secret society? Note that in all the fanciful descriptions it always takes place at night. Despite the fact night only covers half the earth at any one time, all are supposedly raptured at midnight. We are not told whether this will be on standard or daylight saving time. Are we to assume the rapture is to be strung out over a twenty-four hour period, and occur in 24 stages, with the proverbial cloud nine poised in space, standing stationary above the earth for one whole revolution of the earth below? Only so could the emptying of the graves and the rapture of the living saints happen everywhere at the stroke of midnight. Of course no one actually says that. But what is said implies it.

All that aside, where does the idea of a secret and quiet rapture originate? Certainly not from Paul who has written most of what we can learn about it. He wrote:

> The Lord himself shall descend from heaven, with a shout, with the voice of the archangel and the trumph of God: and the dead in Christ shall arise first, then we that are alive, that are left, shall together with them be caught up in the clouds, to meet the Lord in the air (I Thess. 4:16, 17).

Unless we are to assume that contrary to Paul's expectation both the Lord and the archangel will be having a bout with laryngitis and the heavenly trumpeter will have a sore lip and can't blow his horn, the rapture should be quite a noisy affair from the heavenly side. And on earth below, the excitement of the resurrected saints and the raptured living saints caught up to join them alone ought to occasion a crescendo of excitement such as no stadium or colosseum ever knew. Is that one reason Christ descends with angels in his entourage — to muzzle his resurrected and raptured

THE RUPTURE OF THE DOCTRINE OF THE RAPTURE

saints so that they can't make a sound?

Peter says much the same thing as Paul, though not focusing attention on the rapture of the saints but on the coming of Christ. Peter has written:

> The day of the Lord will come as a thief; in which the heavens shall pass away with a great noise, and the elements shall dissolve and burn with fervent heat, and the earth and the works therein shall be burned up (II Pet. 3:10).

Since the holocaust of Hiroshima, it is not uncommon for sensationalists to predict the igniting of the earth's atmosphere by the unbridled use of nuclear bombs. They can hardly have their cake and eat it too. Nuclear explosions are hardly muffled affairs. The contradiction between Biblical prophecy and human theory at this point is one of the reasons theorists have seen fit to separate the rapture and the second coming.

But did not Peter just say Christ would come as a thief in the night? And did not our Lord say the same? (Mt. 24:43) and Paul also? (I Thess. 5:2). Indeed they did. But the comparison obviously has nothing to do with stealth and silence, only with suddenness and unexpectedness. Christ did not say He would be a thief. He would only behave like one, and that in but one respect. His coming would be when least expected.

Instead of teaching His coming would be unnoticed and only certain ones would be "in the know," He specifically warned that we should be wary of those who teach any such thing. Hear Him, as he speaks in the Olivet discourse (Mt. 24:23-27):

> If any shall say unto you, Lo, here is the Christ, or here; believe it not. For there shall arise false prophets . . . so as to lead astray, if possible, the very elect. Behold, I have told you beforehand. If therefore they shall say unto you,

Behold, he is in the wilderness; go not forth: or Behold, he is in the inner chambers: believeth it not. For as the lightning cometh forth from the east and is seen in the west; so shall be the coming of the Son of man.

As noted, the words just cited belong to that portion of the discourse which relates to His coming in judgment upon Jerusalem. But His words in the later portion of the chapter make it equally plain when He has come again in person there will be no more secrecy about it, not even of the date. Paul's use of the thief analogy is very interesting. Having just told the Thessalonians that the Lord would descend in a tumultous fashion, he writes (I Thess. 5:1-4):

But concerning times and seasons, brethren, ye have no need that aught be written unto you. For ye yourselves know perfectly that the day of the Lord cometh as a thief in the night. When they are saying, peace and safety, then cometh sudden destruction, as travail upon a woman with child, and shall in no wise escape. But ye brethren are not in darkness that that day take you as a thief,

In this passage Paul combines a second analogy. Labor pains, though not by any stretch of the imagination unnoticed, and certainly not something wholly unexpected, come suddenly upon a woman with child. As with the thief analogy, the comparison can be pressed too far, having Paul predicting that one can almost pinpoint the day when the Christ will again be "born" so to speak into this world. Paul's point is that since a pregnant woman cannot know the time that labor pains shall overtake her, she tries not to be found in circumstances which would endanger her life and the life of her unborn child. Neither should we be found in circumstances that would embarrass us should Christ come suddenly

THE RUPTURE OF THE DOCTRINE OF THE RAPTURE

"as a thief in the night." It is in this respect the metaphors meet.

2. Our second question has to do with the order of events at Christ's coming. Will He come twice, once to gather to Himself His saints in the event called the rapture, leaving the unsaved to go through the Great Tribulation and whatever else the theorists may put into their charts? And will He then come *with* his saints in an event called the revelation, delaying the resurrection of the wicked until he has enjoyed a thousand years of iron rule over their living counterparts upon the earth in the course of His millennial kingdom?

This is precisely the point Schofield attempts to establish in a footnote on p. 1016 of his commentary *Reference Bible:* "At the end of the age, the tares are set apart for burning, but *first,* the wheat is gathered into the barn." In saying that, Schofield is commenting on the parable of the tares. It so happens that Jesus, the author thereof, also has commented on the parable, having seen fit to interpret it for His disciples.

The parable is found in Mt. 13:24-30 and explained in vs. 37-43. In vs. 28-30 we are told that when the servants discovered that tares had been sown among the wheat they inquired of the householder whose field it was and whether they should pull up the tares. He ordered that it not be done, for in attempting to do it they would pull up the wheat also. Therefore said He:

> Let them grow together until the harvest; and in the time of the harvest I will say unto the reapers, gather up *first* the tares, and bind them in bundles and burn them: but gather the wheat into my barn (v. 30).

The word "first" has been underscored in Schofield's commentary and in Jesus' own words to underscore the contradiction between the two. In Christ's explanation of the parable He expands what He has already said about the tares, as follows:

> The harvest is the end of the world; and the reapers are angels. As therefore the tares are gathered up and burned with fire; so shall it be in the end of the world. The Son of man shall send forth his angels, and they shall gather *out* of his kingdom all things that cause stumbling, and them that do iniquity. And shall cast them into the furnace of fire. There shall be the weeping and gnashing of teeth (vs. 39-42).

In the parable of the dragnet, found in the same chapter of Matthew, Mt. 13:47-50, Jesus seems at first glance to place the two main events in the opposite order. But read it carefully.

> Again, the kingdom of heaven is like unto a net that was cast into the sea, and gathered of every kind: which, when it was filled, they drew up on the beach; and they sat down, and gathered the good into vessels, but the bad they threw away. So shall it be with the end of the world. The angels shall come forth, and *sever* the wicked from among the righteous, and shall cast them into the furnace of fire.

And so it is also with the familiar flood analogy. At the time of the flood, who was taken? And who was left when it was all over? The same also happened with the destruction of Sodom. Luke reports Jesus as saying, "But the same day that Lot went out of Sodom, it rained fire and brimstone from heaven, and destroyed them all. Only Lot and his daughters were left at the end of the day. Even so, Jesus said, shall it be when the Son of man is revealed" (Lk. 17:28-30).

THE RUPTURE OF THE DOCTRINE OF THE RAPTURE

There is surely some good reason behind the repetition of the phrase, "in the end of the world." Note that the total harvest is reaped in the end of the world, not the wheat long before the tares. The net filled with both good and bad was drawn up on the shore for sorting. The bad were cast aside, the good were placed in vessels. The tares were first bundled and burned, and the wheat then gathered into the barn. Fortunately, the angels are the reapers, so we can be assured the harvest event shall follow the script of the Scriptures and not of the revisionists.

Actually, which is taken first is an academic question. It will all happen too closely together to make any real difference. This is true also of the resurrection of the righteous dead and the rapture of the righteous saints. In either case, while the one precedes the other, yet it all takes place the same day (Lk. 17:28-30), even the same hour (Jn. 5:28, 29), yea, even "in a moment, in the twinkling of an eye" (I Cor. 15:51, 52).

A question not so readily answered remains. When will the rapture be? A simplistic answer can be given. Since the harvesting of the saints is the predominate feature of the rapture, the time therefore is "in the end of the world." The parable of the tares makes that clear. But the question is now only pushed back one step. When will that be?

In the Olivet discourse Christ is quoted as saying, "This gospel of the kingdom shall be preached in the whole world for a testimony unto all the nations; and then shall the end come" (Mt. 24:14). Whether this relates to the end of the Jewish age or the end of the world is not a matter which seriously affects the answer to the question at hand. If it refers to the fall of Jerusalem, then obviously it happens before the end of the world.

WHAT THE BIBLE SAYS ABOUT THE END TIME

In Col. 1:23, before the fall of Jerusalem was quite near, Paul wrote: that "the hope of the gospel" which they heard had already been "preached in all creation under heaven." Obviously he was speaking synecdochally. There is no reason to believe that every living person on earth had by that time heard the Gospel. By the same token we may conclude that Mt. 24:14 does not demand that every living person had to hear the Gospel before Jerusalem could be destroyed, or must do so before Christ can return to earth. If the latter is what Mt. 24:14 is saying the rapture is now further removed from imminent possibility than it has been at other times. Evangelization of the earth's populace simply is not keeping up with the birthrate.

Further discussion of the indefiniteness of the time of Christ's return and the reason God has so planned it will be reserved for the next chapter. There the other side of the rapture-return of Christ "coin" will be examined.

In conclusion, how are we to define the rapture? Precisely what is it? What purpose is served by it? It is precisely what Jesus said it would be, and Paul indicates it indeed shall be. It is the harvest time of the redeemed in Christ, viewed from the perspective of the Divine purpose. It will be the gathering of the resurrected and transformed saints, those who died in Christ (and perchance the Old Covenant saints who died in faith and faithfulness, looking for the Messiah), and of the living saints who are alive at His coming.

As our Lord was "taken up" and received out of sight and "into heaven," to sit down at the right hand of God, so we shall be received up into the clouds and transported by Him into the realms of glory, to sit down with him in the eternal kingdom prepared from the foundation of the world. Thus did our Saviour say:

THE RUPTURE OF THE DOCTRINE OF THE RAPTURE

In my Father's house are many mansions. If it were not so I would have told you. For I go to prepare a place for you. And if I go and prepare a place for you, I will come again and receive you unto myself: that where I am, there ye may be also (Jn. 14:2, 3).

Where He is, there shall we be! Just exactly where is He? Still in the clouds somewhere? That's not where Stephen saw Him. That's not where John saw Him. That's not where Peter said He was as he proclaimed the Gospel on Pentecost. That's not where the writer of the epistle to the Hebrews said that He is. Hear him: "When he made purification of our sins (He) sat down at the right hand of the Majesty on high" (1:3). There we shall be also, come the rapture. Even so, come Lord Jesus.

Chapter Nine

WHEN HE COMETH

In the parable of the servants watching, (and of some who did not, but ought) Jesus exhorts us:

> Let your loins be girded about, and your lamps burning; and be ye yourselves like unto men looking for their lord, when he shall return from the marriage feast; that, *when he cometh,* and knocketh, they may straightway open unto him. Blessed are those servants, whom the Lord, *when he cometh* shall find watching . . . (Lk. 12:35-37a).

We are to be watching, did He say? Only watching? No. When Jesus finished the parable Peter said: Speakest thou this parable unto us, or even unto all?" And the Lord answered:

> Who then is the faithful and wise steward, whom His Lord shall set over his household, to give them their portion of food in due season? Blessed is that servant whom His Lord *when he cometh* shall find so doing. Of a truth I say unto you, that he will set him over all that he hath. But if that servant shall say in his heart, My Lord delayeth his coming, and shall begin to beat the menservants and the maidservants, and to eat and drink and be drunken; the Lord of that servant shall come in a day when he expecteth not, and in an hour when he knoweth not, and shall cut him asunder, appoint his portion with the unfaithful (vs. 42-46).

When He cometh! Yes, when He comes. Not if and when, if ever — but when. "I will come again," Jesus said (Jn. 14:3). The doctrine of the second coming is not borne of wishful thinking. It roots in Divine promise.

Barely over a generation ago our nation was facing one of its darkest hours. The Japanese militia, exploiting to the full the advantage gained by their successful sneak attack

WHEN HE COMETH

upon Pearl Harbor (December 7, 1941), were hopscotching across the vast array of islands which make up the Archipelago of the South Pacific.

On orders from President Roosevelt, General McArthur bade goodbye to his brave and beleagured troops on Bataan and was spirited away in a PT boat, under the cover of darkness, just ahead of the fall of Corregidor and the Philippines. The parting words of McArthur were grim, resolute and dramatic: "I shall return."

And return he did. From the relative safety of Australia, Douglas McArthur, assigned the general command of the allied forces in the pacific theatre, mapped out a strategy which in sixty days stalled the Japanese advance and by the fall of 1942 made the resurgence and ultimate triumph of the allied forces a dynamic reality.

Some 1900 years ago, in another dark and foreboding hour another great leader bade goodbye to his followers. But He left not to leave them to die that He might carry on but Himself to die that they might live for evermore. Before leaving them He too promised to return. "I come again" (*palin erchomai,* Jn. 14:3). And return He will.

Does some one say, "McArthur promised to return to Bataan and did. Christ has not yet returned"? That is very true, but it is not the whole truth. McArthur belonged to the realm of time and decay. Whatever he would do had to be done soon or not at all. Already he has been so long dead as to be all but forgotten. Were it not for those dramatic words which have made him legendary, his name would be much less familiar today. Jesus belongs to the sphere of the eternal. It is His office and appointment to sit at the right hand of God until his enemies, even death, are made the footstool under his feet. His coming again, as was true of His first coming, will be in the fullness of time, as viewed from the Divine perspective.

Does one complain, "But 1900 years, going on two thousand, is a long time to wait"? Long in whose sight? It is not too long in the sight of the eternal God to whom a thousand years is as a day (II Peter 3:8), as a watch in the night, as yesterday when it is past (Ps. 90:4). Let it be remembered that even were Bishop Usher's dating to be taken at face value, it has not yet been even half as long a time since Christ promised to return as the time which elapsed between the first Messianic promise (Gen. 3:15) and the birth of Christ in Bethlehem. That needs to be kept in mind if we are to see Biblical prophecies in proper perspective.

Perspective Defined

Perhaps we should take the time to define the term perspective. It appears so often in end-time discussions. Perspective is to time and space what context is to literature and speech. Webster defines it as "the ability to see things in their true relationship," and "as a point of view which provides for an understanding and a basis of judging things or events, particularly as they relate to one another."

Suppose you were asked in what direction the Mississippi River flows. You would of course answer, "southward," for you are able through maps, if not through actual sightings, to view its course in perspective. But suppose you were an early explorer, coming upon the river for the first time at random point along its way, having no idea where it begins or where it ends. You might regard its possible source and destination differently. At times it flows eastward, sometimes even northward. In fact northward is the

WHEN HE COMETH

direction it first takes, and that for a good many miles after leaving Lake Itasca in northern Minnesota. It then turns eastward and loses itself for a time in Lake Bemidji. Only after that does it begin its southerly sojourn. Over and over again, in its upper reaches the Mississippi virtually loses its identity as a river and would seem to be a lake or chain of lakes. Towards the end its meandering is often similar to the configuration of old fashioned ribbon candy. Only as we view the river in perspective can we understand why the Indians called it "Missi Sippi," (the Great River).

There comes to mind a day when traversing a ribbon of concrete spanning a Dakota prairie, I suddenly realized that for some time, no matter where I looked, there was not an object of any kind to be seen silhouetted above the flat horizon. A 360 degree sweep of the eyes saw not a tree, nor bush, nor post or pole, no machine or beast. Were one born in that area hundreds of years ago, and had never traveled more than a walking day's journey from that spot, one would have little difficulty accepting the flat earth theory of the earth's form. The fact is it would be difficult to conceive of any other. There was nothing to provide perspective.

So it is with time. If the globe on which we live rotated on its axis at twice its present speed, but took twice as long to orbit the sun, have you any idea what that would do to your sense of time? Your concept of a day and of a year? Or suppose you, like many of earth's creatures were born, matured, mated and died in one season fixed somewhere between early spring and late fall. What would that do to your sense of time? Such thoughts must be kept in mind if we are inclined to quarrel with God, and begrudge His seeming delay in keeping His promises. Time is not a commodity of which God is in short supply.

WHAT THE BIBLE SAYS ABOUT THE END TIME

May I confess, even with such thoughts as we have just considered helping me, I am still just about as impatient as the next person. We are much like commuters at a way station, most of whom have set their watches by different clocks. Some have re-adjusted theirs both forwards and backwards time and again to conform to first one cocksure chronologist and then another. Thus every bus that appears on the horizon, and everything that looks as though it might be one, is hailed by someone as just what we have been waiting for.

Does one complain that in view of the title of this work we seem to be so slow in getting around to what the Bible actually says about the topics suggested by the chapter headings? That is true. But there is a reason.

Not only has "the enemy sown tares among the wheat," well meaning theorists (speaking kindly) have planted bramble bushes along every path that leads to the topic at hand. Thousands have been caught and are "hung up" on one briar bush or another, or hopelessly trapped in the thicket — the thicket of millennialism, or tribulation, or Zionism, or Anglo-American Israelism, or secret rapturism, or postponed kingdomism, or Antichristism, or the battle of Armageddonism to name a few.

When were you last asked the simple question, "Do you believe Jesus is coming again?" That is too simple. The question today is, "Do you believe His coming will be pre-millennial?" Or "Do you believe in a pre- or post-tribulational rapture?" Or "Do you believe the effort of the Jews to recolonize their homeland is the fig tree putting forth its blossoms?" Or "Do you think so and so may be the Anti-christ?" etc. And every crisis that arises or threatens in the Middle East is the harbinger of the battle of Armageddon.

WHEN HE COMETH

The second coming of Christ is constantly being upstaged by such speculations.

There is an old saying that "one cannot see the forest for the trees." That could well be revised to read: "One cannot see Him Who is unto dying sinners as the Tree of Life for the thorn thickets of preferred human interest — the yo-yo rapture briar patch, the gap-hypothesis (postponedus kingdomus) thorn bush, the battle of Armageddon (eastus vs. westus) bramble thicket, etc. One is reminded of an old nursery rhyme which makes about as much sense, or nonsense:

> There was a man so wondrous wise
> He jumped into a bramble bush
> And scratched out both his eyes.
> And when he saw his eyes were out,
> With all his might and main,
> He jumped into another bush
> And scratched them in again.

No way! It wouldn't work. The first jump might have accomplished the stated result, but not the second. Besides, He really wasn't very wise. Far from it, he ought to have circumvented the thicket. But perhaps it was a hedgerow, stretching far to either side. Then he should have gotten a machete and cleared a path through the briars. That is what we are attempting to do in this work. We are not through the thicket yet, but we can see daylight ahead — even the day of the Lord, His coming.

The Certainty of Christ's Coming

One of the most certain facts of history is that Christ once came to earth to purchase unto God with His own blood a people for God's possession. One of the most certain facts of prophecy is that He will come again to gather unto Himself those that have washed their robes and made them white in the blood of the Lamb. These He shall present unto the Father as His bride, His chosen. There are three witnesses to the fact of Christ's coming:

1. The witness of the New Testament writers. As surely as the authors of the New Covenant Scriptures are trustworthy, that sure we may be that Christ will come again. With the possible exception of the little one chapter epistle of Jude, every New Testament writer bears witness of our Christian hope.

The synoptic evangelists, Matthew, Mark and Luke record parable after parable in which the return of Christ is the over-riding theme. A few are: 1) The dragnet, Mt. 13:47-50; 2) The household watching, Mk. 13:33-37; 3) The nobleman and the pounds, Lk. 19:11-27; 4) The servants watching, Lk. 12:35-48; 5) The tares, Mt. 13:24-30, 36-43; and 6) The ten virgins, Mt. 25:1-13. Besides these and others, all three synoptists gave large place to Jesus' Olivet Discourse in which He answered His disciples' questions concerning both the end of the Jewish age and also the present age at His coming. See Mt. 24:3—25:46, Mark 13:3-37 and Lk. 21:8-36.

To the apostle John we are indebted for his designation of the second coming as a purifying hope (I Jn. 3:3). We are the more indebted to him for the recording of Jesus' farewell address in the upper room. Included therein is one of the most treasured of all His sayings:

> In my Father's house there are many mansions. If it were not so, I would have told you. I go to prepare a place for you. And if I go to prepare a place for you, I come again, and will receive you unto myself that where I am there ye may be also (Jn. 14:2, 3).

WHEN HE COMETH

The authors of the epistles have, with but one exception, clearly enunciated the hope and promise of Christ's coming. Peter, Paul, and James and John all bear testimony. And if the author of the epistle to the Hebrews is none of these, nor one of the others named, we have yet another witness. He has written:

> Inasmuch as it hath been appointed unto men once to die, and after this cometh the judgment; so Christ also, having been once offered to bear the sins of many, shall appear a second time, apart from sin, to them that wait for him unto salvation (Hebr. 9:27, 28).

Peter's witness to the second coming of Christ is primarily set against the backdrop of the mockers and doubters. Peter, who aforetime was scarcely a man known for patience, reminds his readers that God is not bound by our time tables. "A day with the Lord is as a thousand years and a thousand years as a day . . . But the day of the Lord will come as a thief" (that is, at a time when men least expect it). "What manner of men then ought we to be?" he asks. The answer is: We should be persons who, "in all holy living and godliness (are) looking for and earnestly desiring the coming of the day of God" (II Peter 3:8, 10-12).

Paul has much to say about the second coming of Christ. It is to him that we are indebted for the designation of Christ's return as "our blessed hope" (Titus 2:13).

Paul's first epistle to the Thessalonians is unique in that it is not only the first epistle to be written (except perhaps for the epistle of James) but all five chapters close with an affirmation of our Lord's return: In chapter one he praises them for having "turned from idols to serve a living and true God, and to wait for the return of His Son from heaven" (vs. 9, 10). In chapter two he rejoices over them, saying: "What is our hope, or joy, or crown of glorying? Are not even ye, before our Lord at his coming" (v. 19). Chapter three concludes with a prayer on their behalf, the last line of which entreats that they might "establish (their) hearts unblamable in holiness before our God and Father at the coming of our Lord Jesus with all his saints" (v. 13). Chapter four contains the classic rapture text to which we have already given much attention (vs. 13-18). Chapter five draws toward a close with this beautiful benediction: "The God of peace sanctify you wholly: and may your spirit and soul and body be preserved entire, without blame, at the coming of our Lord Jesus Christ" (v. 23).

James, the brother of our Lord, also speaks concerning this hope. In chapter five, vs. 7, 8 he writes:

> Be patient therefore brethren, until the coming of our Lord. Behold, the husbandman waiteth for the precious fruit of the earth, being patient over it, until it receives the early and latter rain. Be ye also patient; establish your hearts: for the coming of the Lord is at hand.

Thus it is again witnessed that Christians of that first generation, even the inspired penmen of New Covenant Scriptures, lived in the hope that Christ's coming was near. Does this raise the spectre of doubt? That is really nothing new. Peter indicated it was so from the beginning. Mockers derided the promise of Christ's first coming when God's time table did not fit their own.

The epistle of Jude, partly because it is so much like chapter two of II Peter, and partly because he comes so close to doing so, is often included among the writers witnessing to the second coming. See vs. 18-21.

WHEN HE COMETH

There can be no doubt about it. The authors of the New Covenant Scriptures join in concert and with confidence to proclaim that Christ will come again.

2. Our Lord Himself bore witness to this blessed hope. His words are the basis of it. As surely as He is the way and the truth and life, just as surely shall He return.

In His farewell address to the disciples the night in which He was betrayed He made the fact of His imminent departure from this world our assurance He shall return. His words will be readily called to mind (Jn. 14:1-3).

As has been mentioned already, Christ made the fact of His return the topic, the theme, of many of his parables. Anyone familiar with the synoptic gospels can easily expand the list. His Olivet discourse, as has also been noted, deals in part with this great theme (Mt. 24:35-51).

3. We have also the witness of angels. Their testimony is that as surely as Jesus was seen ascending into the heavens, that surely will He be coming back again, and in the manner in which He was seen ascending.

Angels played a significant role in the life of Jesus. They not only announced His birth beforehand, but they attended His birth. On that hallowed night angels appeared unto shepherds keeping watch over their flocks. Luke writes concerning them:

> An angel of the Lord stood by them and the glory of the Lord shone round about them, and they were sore afraid. And the angel said unto them, Be not afraid, for behold, I bring you glad tidings of great joy which shall be to all the people; for there is born to you this day in the city of David a Saviour who is Christ the Lord. . . . And suddenly there was with the angel a multitude of the heavenly host, praising God, and saying, Glory to God in the highest, and on earth peace among men in whom he is well pleased (Lk. 2:9-11, 13, 14).

Even as angels witnessed His coming to earth, they witnessed as well His ascension. Luke reports that after the resurrection, after Jesus had appeared unto many throughout the space of forty days, Jesus led His disciples out until they were at a point of Olivet overlooking Bethany. There He commissioned them to preach the Gospel to every nation. After that, He blessed them. And while His hands were yet lifted in blessing, "he was parted from them, and was carried up into heaven" (Lk. 24:50, 51).

In the book of Acts, Luke resumes the narrative at that point and adds these significant words:

> And when he had said these things, as they were looking, he was taken up, and a cloud received him out of their sight. And while they were looking steadfastly into heaven, as he went, behold two men stood by them in white apparel; who also said, Ye men of Galilee, why stand ye looking into heaven? This Jesus, who was received up from you into heaven, shall so come in like manner as ye beheld him going into heaven (Acts 1:9-11).

And that is only half the story. Even as a choir of angels came to earth to sing of his birth, angels gathered on the ramparts of heaven to witness His return to glory. The closing verses of Psalm 24 are generally recognized as a prediction of Jesus' homecoming. The great choirs whose anthems filled the temple sang these words antiphonally as the ark of the covenant was carried into the temple on the day that magnificent house was dedicated to Jehovah. The language of the Psalm depicts the triumphal return of a mighty conqueror. Thus they may be regarded as a prophecy of the return of Christ, the mighty conqueror, who had triumphed over sin and death and the devil, as He was welcomed home to sit down at the right hand of the Majesty on high.

WHEN HE COMETH

Taking our cue from the temple ceremony in which Jehovah's regal residence in the midst of his people was feted in the dedication of the temple, and celebrated thereafter thrice annually in the great home-coming festivals, I view the angels of glory gathered on the ramparts of the city of God as Jesus returns to the Father. And the angels on the one side of the gates of splendor raise their voice in song, saying:

> Lift up your head, O ye gates,
> And be ye lifted up, ye everlasting doors:
> And the King of Glory will come in.

And the angels on the other side of the heavenly portals respond, antiphonally:

> Who is the King of Glory? (And answer:)
> The Lord strong and mighty,
> The Lord mighty in battle.

Again those on the left hand sing out to the keepers of the gates below, as though they and the gates were one:

> Lift up your heads, O ye gates,
> And be ye lifted up ye everlasting doors,
> And the King of Glory will come in.

And again the angels on the right hand respond, antiphonally, saying:

> Who is the King of Glory?

And as Christ the mighty conqueror of sin and death and the grave and devil, enters the gates, now thrown open wide, to sit down at the right hand of His Father in His throne, the whole angelic chorus on either side of the gates, and the heavenly beings throughout the celestial city, lift up their voices in one great crescendo of song:

WHAT THE BIBLE SAYS ABOUT THE END TIME

> The Lord strong and mighty,
> The Lord mighty in battle,
> HE IS THE KING OF GLORY.

We confess to having turned on our own sanctified imaginator as we attempted to enter fully into the spirit of the Coronation Psalm. We present it not as a doctrine that must be believed but as an effort to dramatize the honor that is accorded our Lord in the realm of glory. The songs which are found in the Apocalypse well support this appraisal. See, for example, Revelation 5:9, 10, and 12 and 13b in the context of the whole of the chapter.

In view of the honor and glory and praise that is accorded Christ in Heaven, we can better appreciate why, against the backdrop of His return to earth in judgment, Peter should ask, "What manner of persons ought we to be in all holy living and godliness, looking for and earnestly desiring the coming of the day of God!" (II Pet. 3:11b, 12a).

There can be no doubt about it. Jesus is coming again. No facet of the future, no fact of Scripture, is more certain.

The Time of His Coming

Only the time of Christ's return, not the fact of it, is uncertain. But there is good reason for that. There are at least two which deserve mention:

1. The uncertainty of the time of His return tests our faithfulness. This is perhaps best stated in the parable of the faithful and unfaithful servants which we placed at the head of this chapter. Peter, be it recalled, asked for an explanation. Jesus' answer is:

> Who then is the wise and faithful steward whom his Lord shall set over his household, to give them [his fellows] their

portion of food in due season? Blessed is that servant whom his Lord when he cometh shall find so doing . . . But if that servant shall say in his heart, My Lord delayeth his coming: and shall begin to beat the menservants and the maidservants, and to eat and drink and be drunken, the Lord of that servant shall come in a day when he expecteth not and in an hour when he knoweth not, and shall cut him asunder, and appoint his portion with the unfaithful (Lk. 12:42, 43, 45, 46).

Paul, in his Philippian letter, pays those beloved saints a high compliment which the foregoing parable calls to mind. Such adages as: "Out of sight, out of mind," and "When the cat is away, the mice do play," are non-descriptive of the Philippians. He commends them for their faithfulness apart from his presence among them and encourages them to keep it up, saying:

So then, my beloved, even as ye have always obeyed, not as in my presence only, but now much more in my absence, work out your own salvation in fear and trembling, for it is God who worketh in you both to will and to work, for His good pleasure. Do all things without murmurings and questionings; that ye may be blameless and harmless children of God in the midst of a crooked and perverse generation, among whom ye are seen as lights in the world, holding forth the word of life; that I might rejoice whereof to glory *in the days of Christ,* that I did not run in vain, neither labor in vain (Phil. 2:12-16).

A mother once related this story. Her husband, a business accountant, lived a very routine life. Day after day, year in and year out, except for Sundays and major holidays, he boarded the same trolley at the same corner (just a few doors from their house) and rode to work. At the close of the working day he got off at the same corner, at the same time, give or take a few minutes. Their son, when barely more than a toddler, began to sense the time his father would be coming home and would come in the house to wash up a bit, and change clothes if needed to make himself presentable. He would then run to the corner to meet and greet his beloved daddy as soon as he stepped to the curb.

One day there came a break in the father's schedule. His employer saw fit to send him to a branch office for a few days to look into some matters for him. He was informed he should pack in the expectation of being away for several days, how many he could not predict. But he was to stay until he had the matter under control.

That night the father explained to his wife and son he would be leaving early the next morning and did not know when he would return. It could be in two or three days, or it could be a week, or even more. But he would return as soon as he could get away to do so, whether morning, noon or night. As it turned out, he was gone a full week, arriving home on the evening of the seventh day.

In telling the story the mother related that their son missed his daddy so much, and was so anxious to meet him and greet him at the earliest possible moment, and was so anxious to look presentable when his daddy returned from his important business assignment that he kept himself in a state of readiness day and night. "And that," the mother said, "changed almost every waking moment. It kept him clean for a week."

For children of God one need not labor the point. In his first epistle, John speaks of the expectancy of our Lord's return as a purifying hope, saying:

WHEN HE COMETH

We know that if [when] he shall be manifested, we shall be like him; for we shall see him as he is. And every one that hath this hope set on him, purifieth himself, even as he is pure (I Jn. 3:2, 3).

2. There is also another reason the time of Christ's return is left uncertain, preceded by no signs so singular one can chart the course of events and anticipate the time of His return. Because the facts are otherwise, every generation of Christians has known the joy and hope of the thrilling expectation that the return of Christ could be in their lifetime. We have noted that hope was held by even the first generation of believers. It certainly should be our hope today.

There is a joy in expectation of good things to come. In our home, when we are expecting company, especially our children, other loved ones, or friends from afar, we go to special pains to have our house in order. I even tidy up the garage. My wife lays in extra stores of food stuffs, including special goodies she knows that various ones enjoy. We keep the porch light burning in the evening, and the drapes open wide. Every car that is heard coming down the street heightens our anticipation. Anyone of them could be the one. One will be.

In a way, there seems to be a greater thrill at the arrival of those we are waiting for when we only know we may expect them, but know not the day nor the hour. The extended preparation, the mounting anticipation are joys exceeded only by the realization, the fulfillment of our fond hopes.

And so it is with the hope of our Lord's return. It makes not for idleness, but for faithfulness and preparation. John was so right. "Every one that hath this hope fixed on Him, purifieth himself, even as he is pure."

WHAT THE BIBLE SAYS ABOUT THE END TIME

The Manner of His Coming

We now consider what the Bible says about the manner of His second coming. This is an important question, for such expressions as "the coming of the Lord," "The day of the Lord," "the coming of the day of Christ," or "of God," or "the day of visitation" have various shades of meaning. This is the case even when the same phrase is used in verses quite closely adjoined (See Mt. 16:27 and 28.).

Sometimes in the prophetic writings the day of the Lord is seen as a day when God will bring swift destruction upon a nation, or nations. Obadiah, for example, in vs. 15, 16 describes the doom of Edom as the coming of the day of Jehovah. Isaiah spoke in the same manner of the destruction of Babylon (13:9-11). In an extended prediction Zephaniah (See 1:14—3:8.) likewise describes the coming of God's wrath in universal judgment. At other times the expression may include a promise of redemption or of a visitation of grace as in the remainder of the book of Zephaniah (3:9-20) and Joel 2:28-33. Sometimes the two are intermingled as in the fourth chapter of Malachi.

Jesus spoke of His coming sometimes as the coming of judgment (Mt. 24:37, 39), sometimes in glory and recompense (Mt. 16:27); and sometimes in and through the progress of His kingdom (Mt. 16:28). We do well, therefore, to ask what kind of coming is to be expected from such predictions as Jn. 14:3, "I come again," and Acts 1:11, "this *same* Jesus . . ." (KJV); lit. "This Jesus, the one having been taken up from you into heaven, thus will come in the way you beheld him going into the heaven."), and from the words in Hebrews 9:28 where the phrase "a second time" is applied to the promise of His return. We conclude:

1. His "second" coming will be *personal*. He will not be coming in and through a representative as Elijah's predicted return (Mal. 3:1, 4:5) was fulfilled in John the Baptist (Mt. 11:7-14). The language of Acts 1:11, noted above, makes this point clear. The words spoken by Peter in Solomon's porch do the same. See Acts 3:19-21:

> Repent therefore and turn again that your sins may be blotted out, so that there may come seasons of refreshing from the presence of the Lord: and that he may *send the Christ* who hath been appointed for you, *even Jesus*, whom the heaven must receive until the times of the restoration of all things whereof God spake by the mouth of his prophets that have been from of old.

Paul, who came to the apostleship as a child untimely born shared this same knowledge. In the classic rapture passage he declares that "the Lord *himself* shall descend from heaven" (I Thess. 4:16). Phil. 3:20, "Our citizenship is in heaven from whence also we wait for a Saviour, the Lord Jesus Christ," underscores this hope, as does also Col. 3:4, "When Christ, who is our life, shall be manifested [Gr., *phanerothe*, "make visible, show forth, cause to be seen"], then shall ye also be manifest in glory." The coming of Christ will be personal, actual.

2. His second coming shall be *visible*. The text just cited from Colossians (3:4) affirms this. John, in the Apocalypse, is more specific. "Behold, he cometh with the clouds, and every eye shall see him" (Rev. 1:7). When the sphericity of the earth first came to be known this verse presented somewhat of an interpretation problem, but no more. When untold millions encircling the globe watched simultaneously as Neil Armstrong set foot on the moon one quarter of a million miles away, the problem was solved. If human ingenuity can accomplish such a feat, think not that the Godhead will

find it difficult. Christ's second coming will be visible — universally, instantaneously.

3. His coming will be *heavenly,* that is, in the air. He is not coming to stand again upon the earth, or to dwell or reign here. He is coming to gather His people, to resurrect the dead out of it, and they and the living saints from it (I Thess. 4:16, 17, 18). Our citizenship is in heaven. We are but strangers and sojourners on earth. That is not going to change at His coming. Our citizenship is not going to be transferred. The saints, as citizens of heaven, are going to be translated like Enoch and Elijah, popular theory notwithstanding. Romans 3:4 is still in the Bible, and still valid.

The Purpose of His Coming

The second coming of Christ will signalize the consummation of the ages. It is written, "Him, the heavens must receive [Gr., *dechashai,* receive in the sense of accepting to hold, to keep] until the times of the restoration of all things" (Acts 3:21). Such an expression as "the times of the restoration of all things" can hardly refer to some interim period. It describes a final state, the end toward which all God's redemptive work is moving. In short, Jesus is not coming to set up a stop-gap postponed millennial kingdom. He is coming to receive His kingdom, that is, to receive His kingdom subjects. Remember, His kingdom is *within* us (Lk. 17:21).

The parable of the nobleman recorded in Luke 19:12-27 makes this point quite clear. The opening lines set the stage for the drama illustrated.

> A certain nobleman went into a far country to receive for himself a kingdom, and to return. And he called ten servants of his, and gave them ten pounds, and said, "Trade ye herewith till I come." (But his citizens hated him, and sent an

ambassage after him, saying we will not that this man reign over us.) And it came to pass, when he was come back again, *having received the kingdom* [obviously the one he went to receive] that he commanded those servants unto whom he had given the money to be called to him, that he might know what they had gained by trading (vs. 12-16).

There is no way that the parable which unfolds from this setting can be fitted into the premillennial theory of the second coming. Jesus is that nobleman. He indeed went away to a far country — into heaven above — where "he sat down on the right hand of the Majesty on High" (Hebr. 1:3) and was thereby "seated on his [David's] throne" (Acts 2:30) in "the Jerusalem which is above" (Gal. 4:26).

In due season He shall return — not to dwell again in a land where "his citizens hated him and sent an ambassage after him, saying, we will not have this man reign over us" (Lk. 19:14). (See Mk. 15:12-14, Jn. 19:14, 15.) Such was the reception He had from His own countrymen (Jn. 1:11) and still receives from most of the world He came to save (Jn. 1:10, 11, I Tim. 4:10).

Moreover, His return to earth is not to set up a kingdom. He has already received one, as is explicitly stated in the text (v. 15). The purpose of His return, as is also explicitly stated, is to call to Himself for an accounting those He had entrusted with His affairs (Lk. 19:15-27).

Christ's return to earth in the fulness of time will be to accomplish three things:

1. He is coming to receive to Himself, by resurrection and rapture, those good and faithful servants whom he shall reward by according them entrance into that "eternal kingdom which the Father has prepared from the foundation of the world" (II Pet. 1:11, II Tim. 4:18, Mt. 25:34). Other

rewards will be forthcoming, as deserved (Rev. 20:13, 22:12). Eternal life is the gift of grace (Eph. 2:5-10).

2. He is coming to judge the world, by a universal resurrection and judgment (Jn. 5:28, 29, Mt. 25:31-46, Rev. 20:11-15).

3. He is coming to bring to an end this present cosmic order, as a prelude to "the new heavens and the new earth, wherein dwelleth righteousness" (II Pet. 3:7-13, Rom. 8:18-23, Rev. 20:11—22:5). This is not to be construed as a mere facelift. See Isa. 65:17; II Pet. 3:10-13.

The Hebrew word translated "heavens" signifies "the expanse," the infinitude of creation which stretches out, out, out in all directions. Our word "heavens," from a root which means something heaved or piled up (as a gopher mound, for example), was applied by our ancestors to the arch of the skies, as viewed from below. It is not a satisfactory translation of the Hebrew *shamayim*.

The word "earth" is not to be construed as applying only to this globe. It would apply to our place of habitation wherever that might have been or shall be. If God had seen fit to place us on any one of the myriads of heavenly bodies the Bible would still read the same from Gen. 1:1 onward. If it should then be that we might catch a glimpse of this miniscule speck in the star-lit skies, we would not call this "the earth." That is what we would call our global habitation. We would more likely call this globe "mini."

And so it is that we are told at Christ's coming this earth shall be "burned up," and the heavens shall "dissolve with fervent heat." But according to His promise, "we look for new heavens and new earth wherein dwelleth righteousness" (II Pet. 3:10-13).

Conclusion

And so we close. When He cometh, when He cometh, to make up His jewels — all His jewels, precious jewels, His loved and His own — what manner of persons ought we to be? What manner of persons will we be? Rev. 22:11 has something to say about that which has awesome implications. Verses 12, 14, 17 are filled with great promise for the faithful.

Were you to sense somehow His coming would be in the next moment, would you be found looking for and earnestly desiring to see Him? Or would the very thought send a shaft of fear through your soul. Will you be among those who shall cry unto the rocks and the mountains to fall upon you as though they could hide you from the sight of God and of Christ (Rev. 6:16). Or will you cry out with apostle John, in the words with which the Scriptures draw to a close: "Amen, [even so], come, Lord Jesus!" (Rev. 22:21).

Chapter Ten

SIGNIFICANT AND NOT SO SIGNIFICANT END-TIME TOPICS

As originally conceived this chapter was to serve as a basket to pick up the fragments from previous chapters. We now see that to do that job thoroughly we might end up with "twelve baskets full." That would give disproportionate attention to the many "catch words" and popular phrases which have been stretched into major doctrines of end-time discussion. We feel obliged therefore to be selective. It is likely that one or more topics of interest may be left out. We have not intentionally slighted any topic we consider to be of vital importance or essential to the understanding of what the Bible teaches about the end-time.

A recent Eerdman's publication, *The Bible and the Future*, by Anthony B. Hoekema (c. 1979) has just come into my hands. An examination of its contents finds it to be embracive, voluminous, well documented and indexed, written in good taste and excellent literary style. While overlapping much that we have written and prepared for inclusion in Part Two, it touches upon several facets of eschatology we have not the time nor inclination to review. Much of what appears there underscores and augments the conclusions expressed in this work. But on several points a different conclusion is advanced. Those portions have been examined quite carefully. No reason has been found to alter what we have prepared for publication.

The divergencies of opinion expressed by author Hoekema I believe to be answerable, and in many cases have been, or shall be, in the remaining chapters. His scholarly work deserves reading and reflection. We recommend that it be read in the same manner as this one, namely: "searching the Scriptures daily to see whether these things be so" (Acts 17:11).

SIGNIFICANT AND NOT SO SIGNIFICANT END-TIME TOPICS

The Regathering of Israel

One of the basic presuppositions which strongly influences the charting of the end-time concerns the popular view of the future of Israel. This is perhaps best stated by the redoubtable dispensational scholar and administrator of Dallas Theological Seminary, John F. Walvoord. In his book, *Israel in Prophecy,* at least as late as his 1974 reprint, Walvoord continues to champion a position which he labored in his earlier work, *The Millennial Kingdom* (1959). Walvoord's thesis is that after the Gentile church has been raptured from the earth the partial hardening of Israel will be taken away. As a nation Israel will then be converted. This is presented as something that will take place almost immediately upon the "second" second coming of Christ — the so-called "revelation" or "appearing," as distinguished from the "rapture," the so-called secret coming of Christ. In the revelation "every eye shall see Him, and those (Israel) that pierced Him, and all the tribes of the earth (the lost tribes of Israel scattered among the nations) shall mourn over Him." Christ will then rule over converted Israel from a throne in Jerusalem for a thousand years. To complete the hypothesis of a literal fulfillment of the Abrahamic "land grant" prophecies, Israel will be regathered in their ancient homeland during the millennium.

Walvoord believes the land grant promises to Abraham were unconditional. The repeated loss of the homeland of the Jews is no problem to him. While allowing that individual Israelites may suffer the loss of Abrahamic blessings and promises, he affirms the covenant to Abraham is inviolable, irrevocable. (See *Israel in Prophecy,* pgs. 34-43.) He and others so persuaded base this upon Gen. 17:7, 8 where God tells Abraham the covenant is an "everlasting covenant," and the land promised him shall be an "everlasting possession."

We have already taken note of the fact the battle so briefly mentioned in Rev. 20:9 is symbolic, not literal. Thus John sees fit to pick up the names Gog and Magog and use them symbolically. The "beloved city" is certainly not "Jerusalem that now is" (Gal. 4:25) but "the Jerusalem above that is free" (Gal. 4:26). Granted, most interpreters disagree, and insist it has to be carnal Jerusalem, the so-called "holy city." But the writer of the epistle to the Hebrews has a better idea.

> Ye are not come unto a mount that might be touched, and that burneth with fire, and unto blackness, and darkness, and tempest, and the sound of a trumpet, and the voice of words; which voice they that heard entreated that no word more should be spoken unto them; for they could not endure that which was enjoined . . . but ye are come unto Mount zion, and unto *the city of the Living God, the heavenly Jerusalem,* and to innumerable hosts of angels, to the general assembly and church of the first born [ones] who are enrolled in heaven, and to God the Judge of all, and to the spirits of just men made perfect, and to Jesus the mediator of a better covenant, and to the blood of sprinkling that speaketh better than that of Abel (Hebr. 12:18-20, 22-24).

Biblical scholars would do well to spend an afternoon with an analytical concordance researching the biblical usage of the Hebrew word *olam,* and its Greek counterpart, *aion.* Most of them would be aghast to learn that while *olam* is translated by such words as "ever lasting," "ever more," "for ever," "eternal," "perpetual," "always," etc., it really does not refer to endless duration. It simply means

SIGNIFICANT AND NOT SO SIGNIFICANT END-TIME TOPICS

"age-lasting." And its Greek counterpart, *aion*, normally means an "age." A number of the ages referred to by the words obviously were not very long lasting. (See Deut. 23:2, Jonah 2:6, Josh. 8:28, Isa. 34:9, 10, II Ki. 5:27.) The sabbath law, the greater part of the Mosaic system, including its rituals, sacrifices and feast, were all appointed "for ever," to be observed "in all your generations," even "perpetually." Unless we are under Divine mandate to restore sabbath keeping and the rituals of the temple, we would do well to correct our theology to conform to what the Bible really has to say about the duration of various enactments, institutions, etc. (See Ex. 31:16, 17, 12:14, 17, Lev. 16:34, 23:11, 41, 24:8, 9, Ex. 40:15, II Chron. 2:4, etc.)

There is no reason to believe that *olam* means something different in Gen. 17:7, 8 than what it does in the scores of other places it is used in the Old Testament. Would the "land grant" literalists want to argue that even throughout the endless ages of the world beyond the present cosmic order that Israel is supposed to dwell in the land area promised to Abraham? There are some who probably would. A few among them, e.g., the Armstrongites keep the Sabbath. But beyond that they are quite selective in the "olam ordinances" they choose to keep. Tithing pays off for the establishment, as the life-style of Father Armstrong bears witness, but the sacrificial system would be a bit too messy.

We affirm the promises to Abraham were plainly conditional. This is so from the outset. (See Gen. 12:1-3 and 17:1, 2.) It seems strange indeed that a land Israel lost through disobedience is presumably to be regained while still unbelieving and disobedient. If any one thinks that the Israelis are keeping the covenant God made with Moses, a trip to the "Holy Land" would soon dispel that notion. Not even the core of the covenant, the decalogue, is kept as commanded. Even Walvoord, as gung-ho an Israeli watcher as one can find, who looks hopefully to the Zionist movement for signs to support his restoration theory, admits: "It soon becomes evident (to visitors) that the religious life of Israel is to some extent one of outward form. The religious exercises are devoted primarily to revival of their traditions . . . and the application to some extent of moral standards. For Israel their religion is one of works rather than of faith, and their redemption is to be achieved by their own efforts" (*Israel in Prophecy*, p. 24). Isn't that what led to their downfall in the first place?

History of the Hebrew Nation

A brief recounting of the history of the Hebrew nation is in order. It begins some four thousand years ago when God called Abram to leave Ur of the Chaldeas for a land He would show him. After some delay Abram, whose name was changed to Abraham, arrived in the land God had promised him. But he showed no disposition to possess it. He seemed much more occupied by God's promise to give him an heir. He continued tenting and lived as a pilgrim in the land. For a time he departed Canaan and sojourned in Egypt, but he later returned to Canaan. At the age of 86, Ismael was born to him of Sarah's Egyptian handmaid, Hagar, at Sarah's instigation. This was not what God had in mind. When Abraham was 100, Sarah, who was now 90, bare Isaac.

Isaac and Jacob continued in the nomadic tradition of Abraham (Hebr. 11:9). When a famine came over the land

SIGNIFICANT AND NOT SO SIGNIFICANT END-TIME TOPICS

Jacob and his entire family (75 in all) forsook Canaan for Egypt where they were providentially provided for through his lost son, Joseph. Apparently Israel, as Jacob was now called, and his children were not too keen on reclaiming their inheritance in Canaan. They remained in Egypt some 430 years (Ex. 12:40, 41). Only under the heavy hand of oppression did they want out, and they were scarcely out of the land before they began to second guess their decision.

After forty years wandering in the wilderness they finally entered Canaan. But not yet did they fully possess the land. They neglected to drive the inhabitants out, as directed by Jehovah, and paid for that by almost ceaseless harassment, oppression and armed conflict. For three hundred years they were ruled by magistrates (judges) during which time their lot worsened.

Approximately one thousand years removed from the promise to Abraham, under King David Israel finally completed the conquest of Canaan. Following the death of Solomon, Israel's third king, the monarchy divided. Ten tribes seceded from the union to form the northern Kingdom. They took with them the name Israel. The southern kingdom, consisting of the tribe of Judah and the minuscule tribe of Benjamin, became known as Judah. The divisions were also sometimes known by their capital cities, Samaria and Jerusalem.

In the year 721 B.C. the Assyrians captured and laid waste the Northern Kingdom. The inhabitants were slain or carried into exile. Most of the latter were dispersed among other captive nations. Intermarriage so thinned the blood line as to justify the designation, "the ten lost tribes of Israel." Apart from Anglo-Israel fantasy, they no longer exist as a distinguishable ethnic populace.

WHAT THE BIBLE SAYS ABOUT THE END TIME

With the destruction of the Northern Kingdom, the name Israel was again readily applicable to the kingdom of Judah. Someone has well said, "The only thing we learn from history is that we don't learn anything from history." Such is the story of the Jews. In 586 B.C. the sins which caused Jehovah to permit the destruction of the Northern Kingdom had become so rampant in Judah that God permitted Babylon to carry Judah into captivity.

For seventy years the land of Canaan was virtually stripped of the seed of Abraham. But God had a messianic purpose in Israel. Thus the Jews were spared the fate of the Northern Kingdom. Under the leadership of Zerubbabel, Ezra and Nehemiah, the remnant was restored to their homeland. The reconstruction of Jerusalem was largely financed by a sort of proto-type Marshall plan gratuity.

The history of Israel continued to be precarious. Under Alexander the Great the Macedonians swept over the land. Then came the rule of the Selucid kings, and later the Syrians. In 167 B.C. the Maccabean revolt against their oppressors, sparked by the blasphemous action of Antiochus Epiphananes, brought harsh reprisals. In 63 B.C. Pompey established Roman rule. From then to the fall of the Roman empire Israel, remained a vassal state of Rome.

It was during the Roman rule that the messianic hope of Israel became focused on a political emancipator. The messianic claims of Jesus Christ of Nazareth were weighed against this hope and were found wanting. Therefore, the Jews rejected Him as their Messiah. A forty year grace period, or so it would appear, was extended. Then came the judgment of Jerusalem that Jesus had predicted. In 70 A.D. Jerusalem was utterly destroyed. One and a quarter million Jews were slain. When rebellion continued to manifest itself in the hinterland despite reprisal measures, the utter desolation of Judea was ordered in 135 A.D. Approximately one thousand cities and towns were left in ashes. Except for a few scattered families who managed to escape captivity or slaughter, the survivors were dispersed.

From 135 A.D. to modern times the Jews have made their homes among the nations. In the eighth century the Arabs took possession of the land. The Frankish crusaders regained a foothold but were defeated by Saladin in 1187 and driven out. In 1517 the Turks took control and Palestine became part of the Ottoman empire and remained so until the defeat of the Turks by the British in 1917. The League of Nations gave Britain a mandate over the land.

The Zionist movement which currently dominates the Jewish establishment in Jerusalem began in the late 1800's. In 1871 a feeble feeler effort was made to establish a Jewish colony in Palestine. There was not one Jewish settlement in the whole of the land. A more concerted recolonization movement was initiated in 1881. In 1897 Theodor Herzl unmasked the Zionist movement, openly acknowledging its aim: "To reclaim Palestine as the home of the Jews, and to make it secure by public law." By the outbreak of World War I the colonists had grown from the 25,000 who had entered the land in 1881 to 60,000.

The Balfour Declaration of the British parliament, November 1917, fanned the hopes of the Zionists. The declaration affirmed: "His Majesty's government views with favor the establishment in Palestine of a national home for the Jewish people." But rather than risk the wrath of the Arabs the declaration was not implemented.

In the midst of the Second World War Britain issued a declaration setting forth the conditions for a Jewish state in Palestine. By then nearly one half million Jews were in the land. Severe restrictions were now placed on further Jewish colonization, and Arab consent was made a part of the formula. This was a bitter pill for Zionism. But the Nazi slaughter of some six million Jews tipped the sympathy of the western world toward the Jews. The wily Arabs sensed this coming and formed a league of Arab states (1945) to oppose Jewish expansion. The British then saw fit to unload the problem in the lap of the United Nations. The UN recommended the partitioning of the land, and it was done.

As the British relinquished their control, on May 14, 1948, Israel proclaimed itself an independent state within the boundaries prescribed by the UN. War flamed immediately. Egypt, Iraq, Jordan, Lebanon, Saudi Arabia and Syria joined in an attack upon Israel. Israel acquitted herself well militarily, despite the odds. Casualities, however, were heavy on both sides. On January 7, 1949, the UN arranged an armistice, the terms of which permitted Israel to keep the land gained in the conflict. This was a bitter decision for the United Arab Republic. Thus the land continues to seethe with unrest and with sporadic outbreaks of hostility. Guerrila warfare maintains almost constant harassment for Israel. The decisive and impressive victory of Israel in the Six Day War, June 5-10, 1967, has made the UAR wary of open warfare. But there is little peace in the land where citizens greet one another and bid farewell with the word *shalom*, that is, "peace."

The foregoing résumé of Jewish history is essential to put into perspective the issue of the restoration of Israel to its homeland. The truth is that in the nearly four thousand years from the call of Abraham until now the seed of

SIGNIFICANT AND NOT SO SIGNIFICANT END-TIME TOPICS

Abraham has not even occupied the promised land, much less controlled it for as much as half the time. Not even Abraham, to whom the promise was given, nor Isaac, nor Jacob, "heirs with him of the same promise" (Hebr. 11:9) took the land grant promise as seriously as modern interpreters.

The Belated Salvation of All Israel

As we have already noted, one of the basic presuppositions which strongly influences the charting of end-time prophecy has to do with the role of Israel in the consummation of the ages. Along with the view that Israel will be regathered in its ancient homeland is the theory that in the end-time all Israel will be saved. This is conceived as something that will happen in the immediate aftermath of Christ's "second" second coming. Romans, chapter 11, is the basis of this doctrine, augmented by numerous Old Testament predictions. Some would phrase it otherwise. Old Testament prophecies are said to be the basis of the doctrine and Romans, chapter 11, assures us of its fulfillment. In either case, according to this point of view, the Jews will be given a second chance to accept Christ while He is dwelling in their midst. Thus in effect they will be walking by sight and by signs, and not by faith. To those committed to literalism, a seemingly formidable argument can be marshalled in support of the presupposition. Verses 11, 12, 15, 22-26 of Romans 11 are the verses most often cited.

The doctrine of the ultimate salvation of fleshly Israel has some tangent interpretations. The Anglo-American cults have a special appeal to white supremacists. These think themselves to have the best of two worlds. We white folk, particularly of Anglo-Saxon ancestry, are "the ten lost tribes of Israel," and hence heirs of the promises to the seed of Abraham. This supposedly explains why first Great Britain and then the United States grew to greatness and prosperity. Mormonism, Armstrongism and a variety of lesser known cults are deeply rooted in this doctrine.

An understanding of the clause, "and so all Israel shall be saved," (Rom. 11:26a) is crucial. The clause obviously serves as the conclusion of an argument which has preceded. "and so" we do well to review what has been written leading up to v. 26. The context of the verse embraces three chapters of the book of Romans, chapters 9-11.

The theme of Romans, chapters 9-11, is God's seeming rejection of Israel in punishment of Israel's seeming rejection of Christ. We have interjected the word seeming into the two clauses because the point of Paul's extended argument is that the rejection was not total, absolute, nor final on either side.

Résumé of Romans 9

In chapter 9 Paul begins his discussion by baring his soul. He has great sorrow and unceasing pain in his heart over the state of his people (v. 1). So much does he love them that he finds himself wishing he could be accursed in their stead (v. 2). In vs. 3-5 he details the inheritance that was once theirs by birthright as Abraham's seed.

Beginning with v. 6 he introduces the point on which he is to elaborate. Things are not as bad as they may at first seem. All is not lost. The word of God has not come to nought. "All Israel" is not lost. Bear this in mind. Nearly three chapters later (see 11:26a) Paul will use the words "all Israel" again, as he concludes the argument he is now starting.

SIGNIFICANT AND NOT SO SIGNIFICANT END-TIME TOPICS

Immediately Paul defines what he means by "all Israel." If we miss his definition here where he introduces the term, we will surely misread him in 11:26 where he concludes his argument using again the same expression. Note carefully as he defines the term, (9:6b): "They are not *all Israel,* that are *of Israel.*" Does that sound like double talk? To the Jews it ought not. Their acqaintance with the case of Ishmael and Isaac, and their antipathy to their Arab kinsmen should have helped them understand what Paul is saying. Thus he develops his argument by citing the case of Abraham and his seed, saying: (v. 7) "neither because they are Abraham's seed, are they all children of Abraham." Why not? This is surely double-talk, or is it? Hear him out as he finishes the verse: "but in Isaac shall thy seed be called" (cf. Gen. 21:12). Ah, then Paul is not introducing into the Scriptures and hence into the mind of faith a new concept. God told Abraham the same thing hundreds of years ago. In v. 8 Paul continues to explain: "That is, it is not the children of the flesh that are children of God: but the children of promise are reckoned for a seed." Having said that, he proceeds to identify the promise, v. 9: "For this is the word of promise, according to this season will I come, and Sarah shall have a son" (cf. Gen. 18:10).

Now that an illustration drawn from the exalted father of the Hebrew nation has been set before them, Paul moved a generation forward and applied the principle to the sons of Isaac (vs. 10-12). Just as God did not consider Himself bound to go with the first born of Abraham, neither was He obliged to work through the first born of Isaac. Paul explains that God made this decision before the twins were born, and therefore before either of them had done "anything good or bad" (11a). This is where God's foreknowledge enters in; it is the basis of God's foreordaining predestination.

In vs. 14-19 Paul proceeds to explain himself, lest it be made to appear that God's choice of Jacob over Esau even before they were born was an arbitrary decision. The argument is not readily clear to minds unacquainted with what is called Hebrew verticalism. Since we have previously defined this term in an earlier chapter, and illustrated it by the case of Pharaoh, we will not repeat the same here.

Verses 19-24 continue the argument in the same vein. Paul is further cautioning man, the creature, against second-guessing, challenging or criticizing the all-wise God, the Creator.

In vs. 25-32 Paul cites the prophets Hosea and Joel to show that what has taken place was known beforehand, and that God had actually exercised restraint and mercy— else Israel would have been left without seed: and "become as Sodom and Gomorrah," (v. 29). Further, he states that Israel was to blame for what had happened. They had sought the outward righteousness of the law rather than the righteousness of faith (cf. Phil. 3:2-11, particularly, vs. 8, 9).

Résumé of Romans 10

In chapter 10 Paul much more clearly demonstrates that God had not acted arbitrarily. Generally speaking, Israel is lost because Israel rejected 1) Christ when He was with them, and 2) the Gospel of Christ that was afterwards proclaimed, with Israel as the first to be privileged to hear it.

Chapter 10 opens as did the ninth one, with Paul expressing his heart's desire and supplication to God for Israel, that they should be saved (v. 1). The thesis of the closing paragraph of chapter 9 is now expanded. The Jews were complimented for their zeal, but not for the focus of it. They

SIGNIFICANT AND NOT SO SIGNIFICANT END-TIME TOPICS

continued to seek the righteousness of the law, though "Christ made an end of the law unto righteousness, unto every one that believeth" (v. 4). At this point he has picked up again the theme of the book of Romans — justification through "the obedience of faith" (See 1:5 and 15:26. Cf. Ch. 6, particularly vs. 12, 13, 17, 18). Not faith alone, but the obedience of faith, is the manward condition of justification (Cf. 10:9, 10, 13).

Verses 11-21 underscore the argument. Salvation is not offered arbitrarily, nor restrictively. Far from it. By way of proof he notes:

> Whosoever believeth on him shall not be put to shame. For there is no distinction between Jew and Greek: for the same Lord is Lord of all that call upon him: for whosoever shall call upon the name of the Lord shall be saved (vs. 11-13, cf. Isa. 28:16).

That should settle it. There is then no distinction in God's mind between Jew and Gentile. The one is not totally rejected in order to make room for the other. God's rejection of the Jews is based on their rejection of His grace. God has not behaved as an unfaithful husband. Israel has behaved as an unfaithful bride. Vs. 16, 20, 21 reminds them that Isaiah foretold Israel's unbelief in 53:1 and 65:1, 2.

Vs. 12 of chapter 10, cited as it is in the context of vs. 8-17, deserves special attention. If the obtaining of salvation is offered without distinction to Jew and Gentile, then a future period of time in which only Jews will be gathered in, or in which Jews will be saved in a way that is different from the way in which Gentiles have been, is ruled out. This is the heart of chapter 10. If one misses that, he is in trouble.

In the closing verses of the chapter Paul makes it clear that God's punishment was not a hasty decision. It should not have been unexpected (see v. 19). In the Song of Moses, Israel's great lawgiver predicted as much in his farewell address (Deut. 32:21). Moreover, the stated prediction anticipated the Gentiles would be used of God in the process. Thus Moses cried: "Oh that they were wise, that they understood me, that they would consider their latter end" (v. 29). Note the context of the prophecy indicates the phrase, "their latter end," relates not to an end-time prediction, but simply a future condition, and certainly one that has been and continues to be fulfilled.

The Crucial Chapter — Romans Eleven

Now concerning the crucial chapter, chapter 11. William Hendriksen has rightly noted that in this chapter Paul demonstrates that the rejection of Israel was neither absolute nor unqualified. That is, it is neither total nor irrevocable (*Israel in Prophecy*, Baker Book House, p. 36 and context). The rejection Paul deals with is a two-way street. Overlook that and much of the meaning of this chapter is lost.

As to the first premise, Paul opens chapter 11 by citing his own example as exhibit A., (v. 1; cf. Phil. 3:4-11). Paul then cites a bit of history. There was a time when Elijah considered himself a loner (vs. 2, 3), but God straightened him out on that (v. 4, cf. I Ki. 19:14, 18). In v. 5 Paul states the same situation still presents itself, but hastens to explain that this is due to the grace of God and not the worth or work of man (v. 6). God does not quickly give up on his people.

This introduces the second premise. Just as *all* Israel at

SIGNIFICANT AND NOT SO SIGNIFICANT END-TIME TOPICS

no time rejected Jehovah, even so at no time has Jehovah rejected all Israel. Of that fact the book of Acts is our witness. On the day of Pentecost, from among the multitudes whom Peter charged with having slain the Messiah by the hands of lawless men, three thousand answered the call to repent and be baptized in the name of Jesus Christ for the remission of their sins (Acts 2:23, 36-38, 41). In chapter 4 we are told the number of man came to be about 5,000 (v. 4) and in chapter 6, the number of disciples in Jerusalem is said to have been multiplying, and a great number of the priests were obedient to the faith (vs. 1, 7).

In every church of record that was established by Paul, the apostle to the Gentiles, except perhaps Philippi, the first converts were Jews—even in Gentile cities.

Currently the "Jews for Jesus" movement is enjoying signal success, so much so that Jewish leaders are expressing grave concern. *Time* magazine for June 12, 1972 (p. 67), carried an article quoting Shlomo Cumin, Campus Rabbi at UCLA as estimating six to seven thousand young Jews are converted to Christianity every year. Abe Schneider, a California Jewish Christian evangelist, is reported as having noted more converts of Jews to Christianity in the preceding nine months than in the previous twenty-three years. Obviously God has not totally rejected Israel, nor has Israel totally rejected Christ as the Messiah. Paul speaks only of a "hardening in part" (11:25, cf. v. 7). The same phrase could certainly be applied to the Gentile world, and currently the ratio of conversions in the two groups would likely be surprisingly comparable. This is particularly so with respect to the more sophisticated Gentile nations. If this be a sign of the times, so be it. Time has a way of establishing truth and toppling error in its own season.

Returning to chapter 11 and beginning with v. 7 Paul introduces an application of Moses' prediction cited in v. 19 of chapter 10. Simply stated, the word and the will of God have always had a two-fold effect. Some are hardened; some are saved. Paul illustrates this by citing the example of Israel (v. 10). Again he uses the language of Hebrew verticalism. The Jew, familiar with the Old Testament, could or should understand this. From the positive side the following bit of verse illustrates the principle of theistic verticalism:

> Back of the bread is the cook and the flour,
> Behind the flour, the wheat and the mill:
> Behind the mill, the sun and the shower,
> The soil and the Father's will. (anon.)

The labeling of earthquakes, floods, tornados, tidal waves, lightning bolts, and other natural phenomena as "acts of God" illustrates the principle from the negative side. Both fit the thought form of Hebrew theology. Jehovah being Lord God omnipotent, all-wise and everywhere present, all things which happen, whether good or ill, are not only known to Him, but foreknown, and somehow serve God's over-all purpose.

The remainder of chapter 11 is devoted to an explanation of what the apostle calls the "mystery" (v. 25) of God's will. As used in the Scriptures a mystery is something previously hidden but now revealed. For example, in Ephesians 3:1-13 Paul employs the term as he speaks of the inclusion of the Gentiles in the church as set forth in the preceding verses of that epistle (2:11-22). He does so again as he speaks of God's purpose as it was being fulfilled through his own special calling and ministry. (See Eph. 3:4 and 9.) He is doing the same here in Romans 11:11-15.

SIGNIFICANT AND NOT SO SIGNIFICANT END-TIME TOPICS

In vs. 16-24 he furthers the explanation by means of an elaborate parabolic analogy. He uses two olive trees, one which has been carefully cultivated, and the other which had been left to grow wild. The unbelieving Jews, as unfruitful branches of a cultivated tree, have been broken off that fruitful branches may be grafted in.

To any one familiar with grafting it will be readily understood that the wild olive tree is not "wild" in the sense it was of an entirely different stock, inherently inferior; else grafting its branches into the cultivated tree would have profited nothing. To overlook this is to make Paul appear ignorant of basic horticultural knowledge. Yet this is commonly done to make it appear there is something inherently special in being a Jew. Only covenantly has this ever been so. Such is the thrust of Romans chapter 2 and the conclusion he draws from it (3:1, 2). Again we say, only covenantly has the Jew ever been advantaged, and now that advantage has been taken away. The new covenant makes no distinction between Jew and Gentile (Rom. 10:12, Gal. 3:26-29).

To continue with the analogy, Paul 1) does not say that *every* branch was broken off the olive tree which represents Israel. He was not, even though he had been, "a blasphemer, and a persecutor, and injurious" (I Tim. 1:13). 2) Neither does Paul say that at some future time the ingrafted Gentile branches will be reckoned as having borne all the fruit God wants from them, and they shall thereupon be broken off and replaced by the Jews. It is true that Paul envisions a time when more of his countrymen will believe, and therefore be grafted back into the tree. 3) But Paul does not say that "all (fleshly) Israel shall some day replace even the Gentiles that are of spiritual Israel, the latter being taken away that the former may be grafted in, "and so all Israel shall be saved." 4) Nothing is said to the effect that both Jew and Gentile do not nor cannot grow and bear fruit on the same stock. They did in the first century. Why must it be presumed it will not be so in the end-time?

It is true that the Gospel came through the Jews (Jn. 4:22, Rom. 3:1, 9:4) and was proclaimed first to the Jews (Rom. 1:16, Lk. 24:47, Acts 1:8, 2:5, 14, 22, 39, 20:21, 26:17, 20). However, at the Jerusalem conference Peter declared:

> Brethren, ye know that a good while ago God made choice among you, that by my mouth the Gentiles should hear the word of the Gospel and believe. And God who knoweth the heart bare them witness, giving them the Holy Spirit, even as he did unto us, and he made no distinction between us and them, cleansing their hearts by faith (Acts 15:7b-9).

Likewise, when Paul was called to be a special minister to the Gentiles, and when after much heartache and suffering at the hands of his countrymen Paul declared, "Henceforth I will go unto the Gentiles" (Acts 18:6), he introduced no different requirements; neither did he set aside ought that had been required of the Jews. Incidentally, many dispensationalists say that he did the latter. Baptism for remission of sins was then suspended. They are mute when asked if it shall be reenacted when their hypothesized exclusive time of the Jews is ushered in. But Paul knew nothing of this. There are not two different olive trees bearing fruit for God, at two different periods in Christian history. Jewish Christians and Gentile Christians are nourished by the same stock. This is the particular emphasis of Rom. 11:18: "Glory not over the branches: but if thou gloriest, it is not thou that beareth the root, but the root thee."

SIGNIFICANT AND NOT SO SIGNIFICANT END-TIME TOPICS

The "Fullness" Doctrine

But what about the expressions, Israel's "fulness" (11:12) and "the fullness of the gentiles" (11:25) and "the fullness of time" (Gal. 4:4); what do these terms mean? Are we to understand that when the time of the fullness of the Gentiles is come in, then the Gentiles are to be phased out, the hardening of Israel shall end, and the time of the fullness of Israel shall begin? That is not what Paul has said. That has to be read into these terms.

This brings us back to the basic question with regard to 11:26, "and so all Israel shall be saved." There are three interpretations which receive some acceptance:

1. The clause refers to all fleshly Israel, literally, yet not altogether literally. That is, no one really believes that all fleshly Israel of all generations will be saved. It is therefore argued that the clause predicts a significant if not total ingathering of those Israelites living at the second coming of Christ and the onset of the millennium. This is open to challenge. If the term is to be taken literally, as referring to end-time fleshly Israel, we hardly see that one generation can be regarded as the salvation of all Israel. Is the expression literal, or is it not? If "fullness" means "a full number," as many pro-Israel interpreters believe, is that number one that is really not so full after all? a number so small that one last generation can fill Israel's quota?

2. Others believe the clause refers to the total number of fleshly Israel that *will be saved* in the full course of God's redemptive system, and not to the totality of fleshly Israel either of all time or at the end-time. Calvinist interpreters, reasoning from the bias of the doctrine of election, necessarily take this view. Not being Calvinistic I find this view as unacceptable as the dogma that would seem to require it.

3. Others believe the clause refers to spiritual Israel, "the Israel of God" (Gal. 6:16) as interpreted by Paul in such texts as Rom. 2:28, 29, Phil. 3:2-4, Gal. 3:6-9, and the chapters of Romans under review, particularly 9:6-8. In this view the clause is applied to the whole history of the Gospel proclamation, rather than an end-time windfall harvest. I can live with this view.

Taken in context the eleventh chapter of Romans seems to suggest a time when fleshly Israel will be less hardened, and hence more responsive to Christ. This could be. If so, the question rises, how much more responsive? Totally? If that be required, or if the term "all Israel" be only interpreted as referring to Israel *generally* in the end-time, then it would seem that nothing short of the appearing of the Son of Man in power and glory, with His holy angels, could accomplish this. Should we buy this? Must the whole package be accepted, including a literal millennial reign of Christ in Jerusalem with the Jews front and center? The text certainly says nothing from which that could be inferred.

As popularly interpreted, the terms, "the fullness of time," "fullness of Israel," and "fullness of the Gentiles," smacks too much of crass literalism and even of quotas. It is hard to conceive of God systematically ripping pages off of a colossal cosmic calendar until He comes to a certain date He has previously decided upon. When such a date showed up some 1900 years ago, God said to the Logos, "The fulness of time is at hand. We've got to get things started down on earth for your incarnation." By the same token it is difficult to conceive of God keeping a watchful eye on the counters registering the flow through two giant turnstiles. And when what Hoekema calls "a full number," the Calvinistic definition of the Greek *pleroma* (fulness), appears on the counter

SIGNIFICANT AND NOT SO SIGNIFICANT END-TIME TOPICS

of the Gentile gate, God orders the gate closed. Also, when the predestined number is registered at the Israeli turnstile, He closes that gate. "And so all Israel shall be saved!"

Admittedly Calvinists have not expressed the idea so crassly, but that is the essence of predestination. It is the occasion for the substitution of the term "full number" for the Greek word *pleroma*, fullness.

Incidentally the JW's have a somewhat similar hang-up in their semi-literal interpretation of the number 144,000, made up of 12,000 from each of the twelve tribes (See Rev. 7:4-8). An examination of the passage reveals that the twelve tribes are not exactly as we have known them. Joseph replaces Ephraim, even though he is represented by Manasseh. And the Levites, the priestly tribe which did not figure in the numbering of the tribes originally (See Num. 2:33), apparently replace Dan.

We raise still another objection to the literal interpretation of Rom. 11:26a. The text does not say, "And *then* all Israel shall be saved." Were Paul wanting to communicate that, either *tote* or *epeita* would have done so. *Houtos* describes the *manner* in which something is done, not the time. This is a key to the interpretation of the clause. The interpretation which rises from it is compatible with the principle Paul introduced beginning with 9:6b and summarized in 10:12 — "There is no distinction between Jew and Gentile!

Peter said the same at the Jerusalem conference. (Again see Acts 15:7-11.) Jew and Gentile are not dealt with differently. Descendants of Abraham, whether through Isaac or Ishmael; the seed of Isaac, whether through Jacob or Esau (if there be identifiable survivor's of Edom's destruction); the children of Jacob, whether of Judah, Joseph,

Benjamin, Levi, or whomever, will be saved as the Gentiles are saved, and in the same age of grace, or not al all.

The following diagrams, the first that of Hoekema (*The Bible and the Future*, p. 145), may serve to illustrate the manner in which Romans 11:26 is diversely interpreted:

Calvinistic Amillennialism

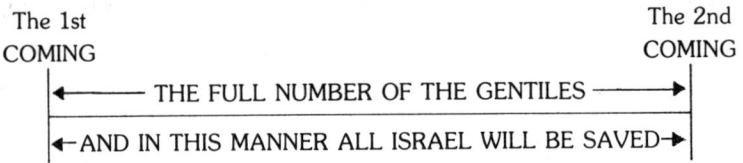

Dispensational Premillennialism

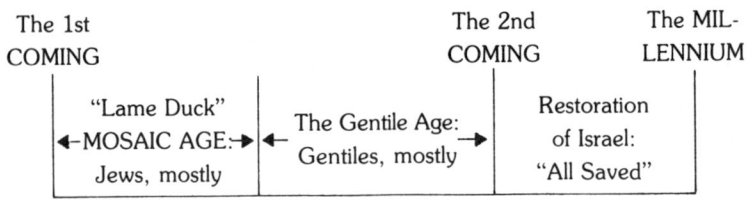

Author's View

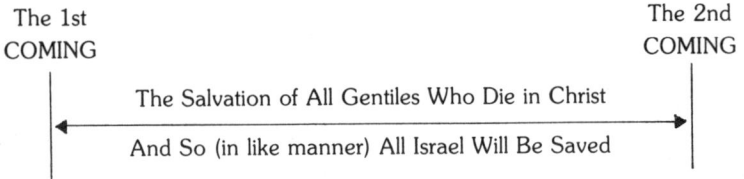

The Great Tribulation

The great tribulation is a subject which seems to appeal to the morbidity of man. A gory traffic accident will tie up

SIGNIFICANT AND NOT SO SIGNIFICANT END-TIME TOPICS

traffic for miles. The carnage of an earthquake or holocaust will draw multitudes to the site, and sight. Gruesome headlines sell newspapers. If the Indianapolis 500 does not produce one pile-up and near casualty many racing enthusiasts leave the track disappointed. Thus it should not come as a surprise that the more gory, gruesome and ghastly the great tribulation can be depicted the better copy it will make for publishers, promoters and pulpiteers with an eye on the proceeds.

The topic of the great tribulation has this to its advantage: the phrase can be found in the Scriptures (once, Rev. 7:14). Twice is found mention of "great tribulation" (Mt. 24:21 and Rev. 7:14). Taken in context the two references do not appear to refer to the same time. The addition of the definite article in Mt. 24:21 is an interpreter's gloss. Jesus told his disciples, "In this world ye have tribulation" (Jn. 16:33). The book of Acts records the fact they did. Acts 14:22 indicates that is regarded as the norm. The epistles confirm this. (See Rom. 5:3, 8:35, 12:12, II Cor. 1:4, 7:4, I Thess. 3, 4, II Thess. 1:6, Eph. 3:13; cf. Jas. 1:2, I Pet. 4:12, 13.)

The word "tribulation" (Gr. *thlipsis*) appears twenty times in the New Testament. A comparable term, *tsarah*, the Hebrew word for distress, is commonly translated tribulation in Deut. 4:30, Judg. 10:14, and I Sam. 18:19 and 26:24. Such passages as Dan. 12:1, Joel 2:1-3 and Jer. 30:5-7, though not using the term tribulation, describe a time of distress which tribulationists equate with "the great tribulation" of which they have so much to say.

Those who see fleshly Israel at the center of Biblical prophecy right down to and through the end time combine Deut. 4:30 and Mt. 24:21 to put the Jews front and center in an end-time tribulation event which they determine to be "the great tribulation." From Jer. 30:5-7 they gain the phrase, "the time of Jacob's trouble" which they identify as another form of expression relating to the same thing. Thus the role of Israel in end-time prophecy is further established according to this construction.

The phrase, "the abomination of desolation" is wrenched from its context, wherever found or thought to be alluded to, and likewise equated with the great tribulation dogma. If this identification be allowed the subject is simplified. But it turns out to be something else than the promoters would make of it. That is not unusual. The context in which the phrase appears is Christ's Olivet discourse in which he responded to His disciples' questions concerning the fall of Jerusalem, His return and the end of the world. Mt. 24:15 and Mark 13:14 contain the expression, "the abomination of desolation." With which of the foregoing events do they associate the term? That is a moot question. But Luke pretty well settles it, and on the best authority.

Luke also records the Olivet discourse and gives particular attention to the desolation predicted (Lk. 21:20). The expression under review is an apocalyptic term drawn from Dan. 9:26, 11:31 and 12:11, wherein Daniel speaks of an "abomination that maketh desolate." Luke, in interpreting the sense in which Jesus used it, apparently recalled the warning of Christ he recorded in his preceding chapter:

> For the days shall come upon thee, when thine enemies shall cast up a bank about thee, and compass thee round, and keep thee in on every side, and shall dash thee to the ground, and thy children with thee, and they shall not leave in thee one stone upon another; because thou knowest not the time of thy visitation (Lk. 19:43, 44).

The foregoing is a vivid and unmistakable prediction of the siege and destruction of Jerusalem. In reporting Christ's words in the Olivet discourse, Luke explains the phrase, "abomination of desolation" in this manner: "When ye see Jerusalem compassed by armies, then know that the desolation is at hand" (21:20). He then cites Jesus' prediction of the awesome desolation that would come upon Jerusalem (vs. 21-28). But all this is too simple to satisfy end-time sensationalists. Who would send a dollar, or two dollars, or who will make it five to get a transcript of a radio or TV broadcast to learn that?

Briefly, the Biblical doctrine of tribulation has a three-fold application: 1) The sufferings of Israel in times past and the tribulation they shall continue to suffer in consequence of their disobedience; 2) The suffering of Christians for Christ's name sake. For example, John in the introduction to the book of Revelation, speaks of himself, as follows: "I John, your brother and partaker with you in the tribulation and kingdom and patience which are in Jesus" (Rev. 1:9). And the innumerable multitude of saints whom he saw standing before the throne and before the Lamb are identified as "they that come out of the great tribulation" (Rev. 7:14). The fact they are further identified as those having washed their robes in the blood of the Lamb, together with the vastness of their company, would indicate that the great tribulation of which John speaks is not the near genocide tribulation predicted for the Jews in Matthew 24. 3) The delivering of Divine punishment upon the wicked in recompense for their affliction of the saints and disobedience to God is described by the same Greek term (II Thess. 1:6-9).

Tribulation trumpeters will agree that the term has a wider application than their fondness for the term, "the great tribulation," would suggest, but they quote Mt. 24:21 to indicate there will be one time of tribulation greater than all the rest. That could be. But that which it could be might well be what has already happened in fulfillment of what Christ said.

Several authors who take exception to the theory that the great tribulation is an end-time event suggest the Greek word *megale* can have two meanings, extensive (in point of time) and intensive (in terms of degree). In the scores of places the word appears in the Greek text of the New Testament our reading did not turn up a single clear cut example. However, Jesus not only graphically described the destruction of Jerusalem, but He went on to say that Jerusalem shall be trodden down by the Gentiles until the time of the Gentiles has come to a full end (Lk. 21:23, 24).

It is not necessary to stretch out the tribulation of the Jews over the course of the church age to find in the fall of Jerusalem and its aftermath the fulfillment of Jesus' prediction. In his *Wars of the Jews*, Josephus has chronicled a story of horror, suffering, bestiality and slaughter that is awesome to contemplate. For example consider the following excerpts:

In Jerusalem, the Zealots, the leaders of the revolt against Rome, "fell upon the people (who disagreed with them) as upon a flock of profane animals and slit their throats." Over 12,000 eminent citizens died in this manner. The terror is said to have been so great no one had the courage either to weep openly or bury the dead. Those who did suffered the same fate (*Wars*, IV., 5:3).

The slaughter is said to have continued until the entire outer temple was "overflowed with blood." 8,500 bodies accumulated in one day. Ministering priests were stripped naked and thrown to the dogs. Even those who had come with sacrifices were slain, and their blood sprinkled the altar.

SIGNIFICANT AND NOT SO SIGNIFICANT END-TIME TOPICS

Bodies of both the priests and the profane were intermingled with the carcases of beasts in lakes of blood in the courts of the temple (Wars, V., 1:3). "No method of torture or of barbarity was omitted" (Wars, V., 1:5).

Josephus then describes the famine which befell the city as the siege continued. Those that went forth from the city at night, whether seeking to escape or in search of food, were caught and crucified within sight of the walls, until the number was so great there was "not enough room for the crosses, nor crosses for the victims." Several were often nailed to the same torture stake (Wars, V. 11:1, 2).

Within the city the famine devoured whole households and families. The lanes of the city were full of the bodies of the dead. "The multitudes of carcases that lay in heaps one upon another was a horrible sight, and produced a pestilential stench" (Wars, VI. 1:1).

When the city fell the warfare spread to the countryside. It is estimated as many as one and a half million Jews were slain. But aside from the slaughter, the hunger and suffering of the children and aged, the bestiality of Jew against Jew as rival factions attempted to fix blame for their plight, venting their frustrations and despair and disillusionment even upon their own household, plus the awesome agony of spirit knowing they had been forsaken of God and delivered to their enemies — all add up to give credence to the appraisal of Christ: "For there shall be great tribulation such as has not been from the beginning of the world until now, no, nor ever shall be" (Mt. 24:21).

One does not have to risk the wrath and reproach of literalists by suggesting Jesus' words are an example of Hebrew hyperbole. There are many examples of such in the Bible, especially in apocalyptic passages. Jesus was not above using the emphatic device to underscore His teachings, even in non-apocalyptic settings. See Mt. 5:29, 30, Lk. 14:26. Be that as it may, the fall of Jerusalem is demonstrably the fulfillment of the predicted time of great tribulation.

It is worthy of note that the synoptic evangelists, writing but a decade or two before the fall of Jerusalem, gave prominent place to Jesus' prediction of imminent destruction and tribulation. But John, writing a decade or two afterwards saw fit to record Christ's warning concerning tribulation only in broad genereal terms: "In this world ye have tribulation. But be of good cheer. I have overcome the world" (Jn. 16:33).

The doctrine of the tribulation has been greatly complicated by the Darby-Schofield gap-hypothesis. This has given rise to three schools of thought: 1) Some teaching a pre-tribulation rapture, 2) others a mid-tribulation rapture, 3) still others a post-tribulation rapture. How did the rapture get into the mix? The words of Mt. 24:22 are cited: "Except those days be shortened no flesh would have been saved, but for the elect's sake they shall be shortened." The words "no flesh" are supposed to prove this prediction has to be universal, that it cannot refer to one segment of the world's populace. Somehow literalists with a doctrinal axe to grind have never discovered the Biblical usage of synecdochal reference. So we are told this must take place at the second coming. Before accepting that, one will do well to read the next two verses. Verses 23, 24 distinctly warn against setting this prediction in the context of His return. "Don't believe it," He warns.

One of the bizarre facets of the Darby-Schofield school of thought is the thesis that the Holy Spirit will be absent from the earth during the tribulation. Yet, these would have

SIGNIFICANT AND NOT SO SIGNIFICANT END-TIME TOPICS

us believe that a Jewish remnant which survives the tribulation will turn to God, be sealed, and go forth to preach the gospel of the kingdom. And this remnant, minus the Holy Spirit, minus the word of the cross, minus the power of God unto salvation which is in the gospel of the death, burial and resurrection of Christ, will prove more effective in three and one half years than Holy Spirit led Christians will have been throughout the whole of the church age.

We have neither the time nor disposition to labor this point further. For a thorough and illuminating discussion of the great tribulation we cite chapter IV of Boettner's classic review of the major millennial theories in his book, *The Millennium*. While not fully agreed at every point we very much agree with his conclusion: "Nowhere in the Bible is the word tribulation used in connection with a seven year period at the end of the age, either while the church is still on earth, or after the church has been removed from the earth" (p. 176, 177).

In his book *Great Prophecies of the Bible*, Woodrow devotes two chapters to the subject. Chapter 9 presents in considerable detail the historical evidence which identifies Christ's prediction with the fall of Jerusalem. Chapter 10 is devoted principally to a careful word analysis.

For those who prefer it spelled out in simple terms we recommend a booklet by George C. Miladin, *Is This Really the End?* Miladin provides an "analysis of *The Late Great Planet Earth*" (Hal Lindsay) including a chapter critiquing Lindsay's Great Tribulation theory. He writes perceptively and plainly.

Refutation of the position that the warning of Jesus had direct reference to the fall of Jerusalem proves difficult to premillennialists. Their final refuge is found in the view that

WHAT THE BIBLE SAYS ABOUT THE END TIME

Biblical prophecy often has a two-fold fulfillment, immediate and future. Thus the fall of Jerusalem is said to be but a prototype of an even greater tribulation at the end of the church age. The apostle Paul took a much less gloomy view when he wrote:

> Who shall separate us from the love of Christ? shall tribulation, or anguish, or persecution, or famine, or nakedness, or peril or sword? . . . Nay, in all these things we are more than conquerors through him that hath loved us (Rom. 8:35, 37).

Fig Tree Figments

The Olivet discourse contains a parablette — a brief analogy drawn from the budding of a fig tree, and all the trees. By reason of the context in which the passage is found it has intrigued the End-time Sign Company. Their goal is to post the sign of the fig tree all along the King's Highway.

From the literature produced by the fig tree fanciers one would expect to come up with some fruitful information about the second coming of Christ. But upon comparing what we read from their publicity department with what is contained in the Scriptures we find that most of what they have to say is a figment of the imagination. Fig-tree theology, generally, is about as barren as the Bethany fig tree (Mt. 21:18).

As it was with Jonah and the gourd vine that shaded him for a day, it is not given us to curse the fig tree parable which we did not write, which appears in a sentence or two of the synoptic gospels and is never again mentioned in the Scriptures. If we have anything to say by way of criticism, it should be against the words of men and not the Word of Christ.

Matthew and Mark record the parable in almost identical

SIGNIFICANT AND NOT SO SIGNIFICANT END-TIME TOPICS

words. We cite Matthew's version, and bracket the differences in Mark's gospel.

> Now from a fig tree learn her parables: when her branch is now become tender, and putteth forth its leaves, ye know that the summer is nigh. Even so ye also, when ye see all these things [Mark: "when ye see these things coming to pass"] know ye that he is nigh, even at the door (Mt. 24:32, 33, Mk. 13:28, 29).

Luke's version pretty well strips the fig tree of any special "specie" significance when compared to any other tree. He records the words of Jesus somewhat more fully. (The italics indicate significant differences in the wording of Luke when compared to Matthew and Mark.)

> And he spake to them a parable: *Behold* the fig tree, *and all the trees,* when they now shoot forth, ye see it and *know of yourselves* that the summer is now nigh. Even so ye also when ye see these things coming to pass [cf. Mk. 13:29] know ye that *the kingdom of God is nigh.*

Two important clues to the interpretation of the parable are seen in the differences between the Lukan version and the phrasing of Matthew and Mark. Luke is generally recognized as writing later than the other two. Having carefully researched his data (Lk. 1:3) as well as being recognized as an inspired penman, it would appear that Luke has been constrained to add an explanatory note here and there by way of clarification. He does so twice in this brief parable.

The most widely touted interpretation of this passage is that the fig tree symbolizes the nation of Israel. In his *Reference Bible* Schofield says that the fig tree parable is "a prophecy that Israel shall bud again" (p. 1028). Tens of thousands who use the Schofield "Bible" regard his comments to be almost as sacred as the King James text which he employs as the basis of it. Such persons are predisposed to regard the Zionist movement as the budding of the fig tree. Therefore the founding of the state of Israel in 1948 is regarded as a sure sign that "He [the coming of Christ in person] is nigh, even at the door" (Mt. 24:33, Mk. 13:29).

But there are some problems with that interpretation, some serious problems in fact. For example:

1. The Old Testament is devoid of fig-tree analogy of Israel; therefore, we have no reference point there. If Jesus had wanted to compare Israel to a tree, the olive tree would have served His purpose better. *Cruden's Concordance* notes that the olive tree "is often used as a figure for Israel" (p. 461). The word "often" overstates the case, but the premise is demonstrable, however not from the Old Testament. It is interesting that Cruden makes no similar claim for the fig tree, though the fig tree is mentioned much more often in the Scriptures.

2. In the New Testament there are only three cases in which the fig tree could conceivably be regarded as a symbol of Israel. Not one of them is helpful to the Schofield interpretation.

(a) The fig tree Christ cursed on the road leading from Bethany to Jerusalem received the direst of curses: "Let it bear fruit no more for ever" (Mt. 21:19). There is that word "for ever" again. If the literalists insist in taking the English translation of *aion* literally, as they commonly do elsewhere, then Israel is doomed to be barren throughout all the endless ages. This text does not help the Schofield hypothesis.

(b) In Luke 13:6-9 another fig tree parable of Jesus is recorded. A certain man had a fig tree planted in his vineyard. It proved to be unfruitful. After three years of disappointment he ordered his vine dresser to cut it down. "Why should it encumber the ground?," he asked. The vine dresser suggested the tree be given another year. He would dig about it and dung it. If then it bore no fruit, he assured the man he would surely cut it down. There the parable ends, as written. Or does it? Does not the history of Israel finish writing the account of it? Many see in the words, "Behold, these three years I came seeking fruit on this fig tree, and find none" (v. 7), as allusion to the three years of Christ's ministry. If this fig tree is a symbol of Israel, and a good case can be made for that, then the tree was assuredly given the axe the following year. Israel certainly did not become fruitful in Christ's final year of ministry. Far from it. It is of interest that Jesus does not suggest that the fig tree in the parable ever became fruitful. From the history which follows the fourth year of grace for the tree in the parable was extended to include forty years for Israel. But Israel was then cut down. The nation was not permitted any longer to encumber the ground it then occupied.

(c) This leaves only the Olivet fig tree text. There is nothing in the passage to identify it with the nation of Israel. If so, then "all the (other) trees" (Lk. 21:29) would have to refer to all of the Gentile nations. Their budding is as much the sign that is to be looked for as the budding of the fig tree. An old adage comes to mind: "That which proves too much proves too little."

3. A third major difficulty of the Darby-Schofield hypothesis presents itself. Luke specifically identifies the budding of the fig tree with the coming of the kingdom of God, not Christ the Son of God (Lk. 21:31). Here the dispensationalists would agree in a sense, but not in fact. Their postponed

kingdom hypothesis which we refuted in chapter five demands that the second coming of Christ precede the coming of the kingdom of Christ. So the text can be harmonized to fit Darby-Schofieldism after all. But not quite. For according to that thesis the kingdom of Christ is not the same as the kingdom of God. We stoutly differ with them. The Gospel writers, as we have seen, use the terms interchangeably to cite the identical sayings of Jesus. The difference which Schofield draws between the two terms does not help in his effort to identify the Olivet fig tree with Israel, or else Luke's version has to be rejected as in error.

4. A fourth difficulty remains. The very next verse quoted by each of the three synoptic writers quotes Jesus as concluding the parable with these words: "Verily I say unto you, *this generation* shall not pass [away, Lk. 21:32] till all [these things, Mt. 24:34, Mk. 13:30] be accomplished." That stamps the dateline. The same thing was said by Jesus of the founding of His church (Mt. 16:28, Mk. 9:1, Lk. 9:27).

It is at this point that we are treated with an example of how far men will go to defend a theory once they have committed themselves to it. Those of the gap hypothesis genre can find but one refuge from their dilemma. They would have us believe that in the six texts cited, touching two of Christ's important pronouncements, "generation" does not mean "generation"; it means race. (cf. Schofield, p. 1034). Thus Jesus is saying that the Jewish race will not pass away until they see Him returning in glory to set up his long postponed millennial kingdom.

That's interesting. If the Jewish race is to survive "until" that happens, what happens to them thereafter? Do they cease to exist, at least as a race? The "gap" gang might still escape their dilemma by suggesting that is when the distinction

SIGNIFICANT AND NOT SO SIGNIFICANT END-TIME TOPICS

between Jew and Gentile shall cease. But their problem is that their theory affirms the distinction will then be even greater, with the Jews being the chief evangelists and filling the principal offices in the millennial kingdom.

The Scriptures will not sustain such weaseling with words. Matthew, the most Jewish oriented of the four Gospel writers, uses the word *genea* (generation) thirteen times: Mt. 1:17 (4 times), 11:16, 12:39, 41, 42, 45, 16:4, 17:17, 23:36, and 24:34. In none of these texts can the word "race" be substituted for "generation" without doing violence to the text. The same is true of the 28 other times the word appears in the New Testament.

Once again we see the necessity of rightly dividing the word of truth (II Tim. 2:15). This is not easily done in the Olivet discourse. However, this is due to the want of understanding of the nature of apocalyptic language. Even those who have managed to read themselves out of the morass of premillennialism are frequently found suggesting Jesus is jumping back and forth from first one subject (the fall of Jerusalem) to another (His second coming). We suggest you read again chapter six, noting what was said of time keys included in the text of Matthew 24.

In this present chapter we have attempted to clear away the accretion of misinterpretations which have attached themselves to the parable of the trees. The question may now be fairly asked, "What do I see in the text?"

A parable, of course, is an illustration. Jesus was using an illustration his disciples, as outdoors men, could readily understand. A budding tree, whatever its specie, is a sign that "spring has sprung" and "summer is nigh." Thus He was telling His disciples that when they should see the things He had enumerated, they should know the fall of Jerusalem was at hand. What things?

WHAT THE BIBLE SAYS ABOUT THE END TIME

Beginning with chapter 23 he detailed one by one the sins of the nation as these focused in their blind guides. If the blind lead the blind, will they not both fall into the pit? Schofield spoke aright when he said, "It is the way of history. Judgment falls upon one generation for the sins of centuries. The prediction was fulfilled in the destruction of Jerusalem, A.D. 70" (Marginal note, p. 1032). How true! How fitting to the case at hand! Israel had sown to the flesh, and of the flesh was reaping destruction. The disciples certainly understood Jesus to this point. They were not ignorant of the law of cause and effect, sowing and reaping.

In chapter 24 the thesis continues in response to the disciples' questions. The signs of the fall of Jerusalem were summed up in apocalyptic symbols. When they should see the abomination of desolation which Daniel predicted, explained by Luke as "Jerusalem compassed with armies" (Lk. 21:20), and when they should see the power structure of the Jewish establishment failing, the house of Herod and the house of Caiaphas, the civil and religious heads of the nation eclipsed, no longer able to give any semblance of guiding light; and the lesser lights, the scribes and Pharisees, the priests and elders derelict also, to say nothing of the emptiness of the whole ceremonial system of the now abrogated and annulled Mosaic law, they should know of themselves (Lk. 21:20) the city could not survive. They should flee at the first opportunity. The opportunity came. The Christians fled. The unbelievers deemed the crisis had passed. They perished when the siege was renewed.

Thus the parable was obviously understood by the Christians for whose sake the entire discourse was delivered. And the predictions made were fulfilled, except for two. These remain for the time of the end: 1) Christ will return and 2) there will be no equally obvious signs to warn anyone the time of His return is at hand. Be ye therefore ready, ready always, for in an hour ye think not, the son of man cometh.

Agog over Gog and Magog

Prophecy buffs are all agog over "Gog and Magog." That figures. The terms sound sinister and mysterious. And besides, Ezkeiel devoted two chapters (38 and 39) to their role in an apocalyptic battle against "my [God's] people, Israel," coming "as a cloud to cover the land" (38:16).

Assuming, as most of them do, that fleshly Israel (the Israeli) rather than the spiritual Israel (the church) will occupy God's attention in the last day, Ezekiel's prophecy is thereby brought forward and made an end-time prediction. To be consistent in this, (1) Israel will have to be dwelling securely in the land, 38:14; (2) a fantastic temple will have been rebuilt, chs. 40-42; (3) the sacrificial system of the law of Moses will have been restored, 39:17-20, 40:38-43, 43:18-27; and (4) the Levitical priesthood will be restored (40:46, 43:19) and their ancient ritualistic duties renewed (43:20-28), including both teaching and judging God's people (44:23, 24).

And as though all that were not enough, (5) "the Prince of the people" (the Messiah, no less) will be a party to all this (45:17), even to the extent that (6) he will have to prepare for himself a *sin offering* (45:22, 23) and burnt and peace offerings (45:24, 25, 46:12). Moreover, (7) he, the Prince, will be obliged to stand aside while the priests prepare his burnt and peace offerings (46:2-5), and all this shall be done on "the Sabbath day" (46:4, 12).

Apparently Hal Lindsay found all this no problem. At least he affirms the temple will be in existence and the sacrificial system restored (*The Late Great Planet Earth*, p. 152). His rationale is that since the Romans destroyed the temple it will have to be restored under some form of restoration of "the Roman culture." That is an interesting phrase. One would expect literalist Lindsay to say "the restored Roman empire." In substituting the word "culture" he seems to be following the lead of Armstrong whose *Plain Truth* magazine affirms the ten nations of the Common Market of Europe are "the revival of the Roman empire, spiritually." Now look who is "spiritualizing" Hebrew prophecy.

Are we to understand that Armstrong and his World Wide Church of God are right after all? Except for the sacrificial ritual which is a bit too messy to suit the life style of the high-living cult leader, and the prominent role of the priests which Armstrong would find a bit threatening to his own near-Messiah profile, Armstrongism pretty well goes along with Lindsay.

But what saith the Scriptures? If Ezekiel 38-45 is indeed an end-time prediction, Paul ought not to have written the epistle to the Galatians. Or was the mistake of the Galatians only that they were born 1900 years too soon? To the Galatians, who had "become entangled again in a yoke of bondage" (5:1), though apparently they were only pushing ritual circumcision (5:2) Paul had some serious things to say: (1) They had removed to another Gospel (1:6, 7). In so doing (2) they were bewitched (3:1), and no longer obeying the truth (5:7). Moreover, (3) they were severed from Christ and (4) fallen from grace (5:4).

The book of Hebrews has much to say about this. The Christian faith and its institutions are not an interlude sandwiched between two epochs in which the law of Moses and its institutions are supreme. Christ is a superior priest to the Aaronic order (5:1-10, 6:13-20, 7:11-28, 8:1-5). He is the mediator of a better covenant (8:6-13), the minister of a better sanctuary (9:1-10), offering a better sacrifice (9:11-28, 10:1-25). Moreover, that sacrifice which He offered actually accomplishes what the sacrifices under the law only typified (9:6-10). It was offered "once for all" and "obtained eternal redemption" (9:12). Thus He does not have to offer over and over the same sacrifices which could never take away sins (10:1-11). "But He, when He had offered one sacrifice for sins for ever, sat down at the right hand of God, henceforth expecting till his enemies are made the footstool of his feet. For by one offering he hath perfected for ever them that are sanctified" (10:12-14).

There is more to be said, but that should be enough to establish the point. To make the prophecy of Ezekiel apply to the end time is to make a shambles of the New Testament revelation. And if one does not apply the passage literally to the end-time, then Gog and Magog are reduced simply to apocalyptic symbols of warfare, which is precisely the manner in which the only New Testament reference to them uses them. (See Rev. 20:8.)

The name Gog first shows up in the Scriptures in an extended genealogical table which prefaces the book of I Chronicles, (chs. 1-9). In I Chron. 5:5 Gog is listed as a descendant of Reuben. He is next mentioned in Ezekiel (See 38:2, 3, 16 and 39:1.). Magog first appears in the Scriptures in Gen. 10:2 where he is identified as a son of Japheth and hence a grandson of Noah. Magog also appears in the genealogical table prefacing I Chronicles (1:5). He too is then mentioned in Ezekiel (See 38:2, 39:6.). By this time Magog has come to be the name of a land and is no longer the name of a person.

Neither Gog nor Magog are mentioned again in the Scriptures until we come to Rev. 20:8. In this reference neither is a person, nor is either of them a nation as such. Together they constitute an apocalyptical term which John takes occasion to define for us, lest someone make the very error that Lindsay and his like repeatedly make. John defines Gog and Magog as "the nations which are in the four corners of the earth."

In Ezekiel, Gog is "of the land of Magog," and "the prince of Rosh, Meshech and Tubal" (38:2). He is predicted as coming out of "the uttermost parts of the north" (38:15), along with his hosts, "all of them riding upon horses." Salem Kirbhan in *666* takes this literally and accepts the interpretation that Russia is the territory spoken of. He states that Russia is raising horses by the thousands and ten thousands, because "horses can go where tanks cannot." He fails to mention that airplanes and guided missiles can go where horses cannot, or at least they can do so much more speedily, and carry infinitely more power of destruction. But he too subscribes to the theory that the Bible must always be taken literally wherever it can be so interpreted. From this point of view, to apply logic is to put reason ahead of revelation. Thus Kirbhan suggests that the phenomena described in Rev. 9:12, the darkening of the third part of the sun, moon and stars, could be caused by hundreds of thousands of cavalrymen sweeping down off the steppes of Russia in such numbers that their horses' hooves so tear up the earth that the dust cloud raised obscures one third of the sky.

Lindsay and Wilmington likewise employ select literalism to fill in where the Scriptures are silent. Wilmington, for example, (*The King is Coming,* p. 130) presents the line of reasoning that has caused Gog and Magog to be identified

SIGNIFICANT AND NOT SO SIGNIFICANT END-TIME TOPICS

as a Russian invasion of Israel. (1) Since Gog is said to come from the uttermost parts of the north, that would have to be Russia. Greenland which extends even farther to the north than Russia was of course unknown to Ezekiel, and presumably to the Holy Spirit who otherwise could have scaled Ezekiel's description down a bit. (2) Magog, the grandson of Noah, migrated to a land north of Palestine. Russia happens to be one of the lands, a part of which lies north of Palestine. Where else Magog may have wandered is immaterial, as indeed is the fact that migration seemed to be a way of life for the people of the ancient world. (3) Linguistically, Rosh, according to Wilmington, "may be" the root of the modern name Russia. Meshech sounds like Moscow, and Tubal could be the Russian province of Tobelesk.

Wilmington's linguistic argument is really a study in fanticized phonics. Why might not Rosh be identified with Rossa (Sweden), for that is way, way up north. Or "maybe" Ruse (Ruschek), a place in Bulgaria. He did not come up with a possible phonetic identification of Magog, although that one would be easy. There is a place in Quebec, Canada, which bears that name. Perhaps Canada will be involved in the assault against Israel. Remember that John identified Gog and Magog as the nations in the four corners of the earth. Thus Meschech could be Mexico, or "maybe" Merzig, or Mueslwitz, Germany. The possibilities are many and fascinating.

It is strange that the New Testament predictions of the end-time are not nearly so enlightening as the prophecy of Ezekiel. How is it that Ezekiel saw fit to skip over the whole of the Christian era and turn his attention to the consummation of the ages, a task which would seem to better suit the purpose of John and the Revelation he was instructed to write.

Chapter Eleven

CONCERNING DEATH AND DYING

We have defined eschatology as the study of the endtime as it relates to 1) the life we now live in the flesh and 2) the present cosmic order. Eschatology has two focal points. One is personal; the other is cosmic. The onset of physical death poses a crisis to our personal existence. The second coming of Christ will mightily affect the whole cosmic order.

Thus far this study has dealt with the events which will be precipitated by the second coming of Christ. The heavens and the earth will undergo catastrophic change. This is no less true of the human race, including the countless generations which have occupied the earth ahead of those living at the time of Christ's coming. But long before the return of Christ triggers cataclysmic changes in the universe and the present social order as we now know it, we may be caught up in an event of great eschatological significance. We may die before Christ returns. Innumerable hosts have done so, including millions who have looked for and earnestly desired the coming of the day of the Lord. We may be called upon to join them.

The cosmic order is so well established and scientists say it has so long endured, it is easy to say with the mockers of Peter's day, "Where is the promise of his coming? Since the fathers fell asleep all things continue as they were from the beginning of creation" (II Pet. 3:4). To the cynic, the passing of some 1900 additional years does not make the day of the Lord seem nearer. It actually seems to confirm the cynicism of the mockers who have gone before them. It is relatively easy to give no thought to the end of the present cosmic order.

CONCERNING DEATH AND DYING

But how about our personal end-time? Many choose not even to think about their own demise. But this is not so easily accomplished. Death occurs so often. It happens to so many persons we know. We can not drive the subject from our minds and have it remain so. Murder is so rampant and accidents are so often fatal that one does not have to wait till the aging process manifests itself to be very much aware of the fact we are going to die. A fanatical belief in the soon coming of Christ might convince one he might escape death. But unless He indeed does come very very soon, most of us shall find our first encounter with eschatological reality will be experienced in physical death.

The Certainty of Death

The book of Ecclesiastes, sometimes called "the most pessimistic book of the Bible," contains one of the most sobering sayings ever written: "The living know they shall die" (Eccles. 9:5). There are many things we do not know, and things we may never know. But this we know — we are going to die — unless our Lord comes quickly (i.e. soon, not just suddenly).

Aside from Enoch and Elijah, one person only in each of the two previous dispensations, every descendant of Adam has died or will do so in due time — except for those who shall be alive at Christ's coming.

As a child I had a school teacher who infuriated me by her response to our childish complaint, "Do we have to do this or that?" She invariably answered, "No, you don't have to do anything but die." That came across as a very morbid view of life. I cast about in my mind to think of some exception to what she said, and could find none. Perhaps that is what infuriated me so. She was right. The only thing one has to do is die.

In order not to die, at least not right away, there are some things we can do to keep body and soul together. But one does not have to do any of them. One can put a plastic bag over one's head and bring to a halt even the involuntary process of breathing. One can do many things to hasten death. But no matter how good the care we give to our bodies, and regardless of how careful we are to stay out of harm's way, at best we can only delay death. Let's face it. We are going to die. Sooner or later the rider of the pale horse will draw along side of the car or plane in which we are riding, or drop in on us where we are staying, and shall draw his sword and run us through. It's not too happy a thought, but we had better take thought and prepare for death. For we are going to die.

A salesman is said to have dreamed he had an encounter with death. In his dream death overtook him at eventide, just as he was completing one of his regular rounds. The dream was so real he awakened in a cold sweat and could not go back to sleep. As he contemplated his dream it occurred to him it might be a Divine warning for him to change his ways. That prospect was almost as upsetting as the prospect of dying.

Towards morning the thought occurred to him he might be able to outwit death. Instead of changing his ways he might change his work routine. In his dream he had seen the very time and place where death seemed to be awaiting him. So instead of running his eastern loop, which was coming up next on his schedule, he decided to turn it over to his assistant. He would then expand his westward circuit.

CONCERNING DEATH AND DYING

In that way he would not even go near Boston, the place he saw himself dying in his dream.

At daybreak he called his assistant and informed him of his decision, but not the reason for it. His assistant was delighted to be assigned to so lucrative a sector of their sales district. That taken care of, the crafty salesman headed west. The day went well. Orders were taken at every stop. By mid-afternoon he had already sold his usual volume of merchandise. He decided not to press his luck. Why not turn in early and miss the evening traffic rush. He would thereby alter another of the circumstances of his disturbing dream.

As he wheeled into the hotel parking garage and was about to turn his car over to the attendant he felt a sudden rush of cold air behind him. It was startling. In his dream the same sensation was felt just before a careening car rammed into his own and took his life. "It can't be," he heard himself saying, "It can't be. Some one has just opened an outside door and let in a blast of wintery air." But it wasn't winter. It was a mild autumn day. Suddenly, a car out of control came hurtling down a parking ramp and headed straight for him. In the brief moment twixt the crushing impact and his last breath be found himself looking into the surprised face of death.

"What are you doing here?" Death asked. "I had scheduled an appointment with you in Boston later this afternoon, and was wondering how I was going to keep it."

The story was but a dream — a dream in two parts, to be exact. But the point of the story is no dream. "It is appointed unto every man once to die" (Hebr. 9:27). No manner of conniving on our part is going to cheat death out of his due. Only in Christ, and that at His coming, can we gain victory over death. Meanwhile, death reigns. From Adam until now it has been so. And so shall it be until the last trumpet shall sound, and the dead are raised incorruptible (Rom. 5:14, I Cor. 15:50-57).

Indeed the living know they shall die — not the day nor the hour, nor the place where it will occur, but the fact. I find it sobering to consider I have already lived two, perhaps three times as long as I have any reasonable expectation to believe I shall yet live. I have long since reached life's summit and find the forces of degeneration and decay quickening their pace as they take me down the ever steepening slope toward a yawning grave.

The New Testament counterpart to Ecclesiastes 9:5 is Hebrews 9:27. "It is appointed unto every man once to die, and after this cometh judgment." This text adds still another ominous note to what has been said. We not only shall die: we shall then be judged according to the deeds done in the body. II Cor. 5:10 states the fact quite plainly: "We must all be manifest before the judgment seat of Christ to receive the deeds done in the body, according to what we have done, whether good or bad." Mark carefully what is said there. Certain doctrinarians would have us believe otherwise. That should not surprise us. Once a falsehood is told or believed others must follow and be accepted as a cover-up for the first. This is no less true in theology than in other realms of thought and communication. The "once saved, always saved" dogma requires the pretzeling of a good many Scriptures of the order of II Cor. 5:10, Hebr. 9:27, and Rev. 20:12, 13.

The subject at hand is much too serious a subject to ignore or embellish with fantasy. Death is not only a personal experience awaiting us along life's pathway: it is a prelude to judgment.

Precisely What Is Death?

What constitutes death? What lies beyond it, if anything? Webster defines death as: "1) an act or event in which one dies, 2) the state of being dead." That doesn't help much, does it? Nothing particularly perceptive is told us there. So death is an act or event in which one dies — the state of being dead. You knew that already.

Of the two definitions we are more concerned in this study with the latter: the state of being dead. Precisely what is that state? What lies beyond it, if anything?

The act or event itself is not too fearsome to contemplate. The fact that untold millions before us have managed to accomplish the act quite successfully, or have otherwise been involved in the event, suggests that each and every one of us can and probably will do likewise. The fact that some have managed to die with dignity and serenity suggests that perhaps we can do that also.

No particular insight into the meaning of death can grow out of a word study of the subject. The Hebrew *maveth*, the Greek *thanatos* and the etymology of our English word *death* offer no particular insight.

The only way one can understand the subject beyond its physical manifestation is to note what the Scriptures have to say. Only the Scriptures can shed any light on the state of the soul, the id, the ego — that part of our being that is the subject of our self-awareness.

Several widely read books on death and dying have appeared on the market, notably the work of Elizabeth Kubler

Ross, *Death and Dying* and Raymond Moody, *Life After Life*. The popularity of such books is readily understandable. Not only do they fortify the instinctive longing of the human soul for life beyond this life, and thus seem to be in harmony with a major tenet of the Christian faith, they also leave the general impression that dying is a beautiful experience regardless of one's life style or relationship to Christ. That certainly is not in harmony with either traditional Christian belief or Biblical pronouncements.

The first intimation is readily welcomed by many who are nominally Christians but who need the constant assurance of "scientific" confirmation and/or subjective experience. Even to such the second intimation ought to run up the warning flag. The popular "tunnel to the light" reports run contrary to the Davidic "valley of the shadow of death" imagery (Ps. 23:4). Moreover, the intimation that one's life-style and relationship to Christ are irrelevant is in direct contradiction to the whole thrust of the Scriptures with regard to the state of the dead.

In an article entitled "The Enemy" (*Psychology Today*, August 1970, p. 37) Edwin S. Schneidman has some pertinent remarks concerning the so-called "after life" experiences reported by persons who supposedly have "lived again" (in this life and sphere) to tell of their interim "death experience."

> Where either consciousness or loss of consciousness (including death) is involved, we must distinguish between *your* private experiences and *my* private experiences. You (privately) can experience my (public) death; we can both (privately) experience some one else's (public) death: but neither of us can experience his own (inexperienceable) death. You can never actually *see* yourself unconscious,

hear yourself snore, or experience your own being dead, for if you were in a position to have these experiences you would not, in fact, be unconscious, asleep or dead.

If you can never experience your own death;, it follows logically you can never experience your own *dying*. "Now, wait a minute," you might say. "Granted that I cannot experience my being dead but obviously I am still alive while I am dying and, unless I am unconscious, I can experience that." No, the fact is that you can never be *certain* you are dying. "Dying" takes its only legitimate meaning from the fact that it immediately precedes death.

One may think he is dying, and survive. In that case he wasn't actually dying. He was only in a state, or amid circumstances which, if not reversed, would lead to death. One can very keenly experience the belief he or she is dying. The experience can be interpreted as an actuality. But unless one actually dies the experience was but the working of the fears which can grip the human mind. Such fears can be remembered when the crisis is past only because the brain in which such thoughts were at work was actually alive, and the thoughts thereof were recorded therein.

Are we suggesting there is no consciousness after death and apart from the cerebrum? No, that too would run contrary to both traditional Christian belief and Biblical teaching.

The human mind is capable of amazing adjustments to circumstances. Daily we tune out various stimuli, even those which bombard our minds at the level of distraction. We can attune our senses, or direct our minds apart from any sensory stimulation of the moment to areas of interest of our own choosing. Our ability to go to sleep amid noise and confusion is an exercise of the mind.

WHAT THE BIBLE SAYS ABOUT THE END TIME

A man and his wife were thrust into a situation in which they were obliged to live near a plant where a large raucous engine staccatoed away day and night. The first night they thought they would never get to sleep. But they did. Weariness took care of that. The next night sleep came somewhat more readily, and they slept less fitfully. The time came when they could carry on conversation without any overt effort to override the noise of the engine, and could nap in the day time and sleep at night without sense of distraction. One night after the couple was sound asleep the engine suddenly stopped. The husband bolted upright in bed and is reported to have cried out in startled tones something to the effect, "What's all that silence?"

The mind learns to handle pain in the same way. And the body evidences a built-in mechanism to assist the mind in doing so. A toothache is an intermittent discomfort because the nerve tends to retreat from the pain-inducing area of decay. As the advancing decay again makes contact the nerve retreats further. Short of an abscess, the process may be repeated again and again. The same result of course can be achieved by the use of drugs. But the mind, without such aid, can achieve wonders in the area of the threshold of pain, discomfort and sundry distractions.

Lewis Thomas M.D., President of New York's Memorial Sloan-Kettering Cancer Center, noted scientist as well as physician, reports a number of such wonders in his bestseller, *The Medusa and the Snail* (Viking Press, 1974-79). In a *Reader's Digest* condensation (October 1979, pp. 97-100), under the title "Warts, Brains and Other Astonishments," Dr. Thomas mentions some of the wonders he has observed and his thoughts as he pondered over them. For example, despite the fact that warts have about them the look of toughness and permanence, they can be made to go away by willing that they go away. In effect they can be ordered off the skin by the mind, under hypnotic influence. And the achievement can be accomplished even without first rubbing the wart with an old dishrag and burying it (the dishrag, not the wart). Persons with multiple warts can mentally order specific warts to go away without affecting others on which the mind has not concentrated. And that is in spite of the fact warts are caused by a virus, not merely an aberration of the skin cells.

But it is in the area of pain control that the power of the mind holds particular interest in the context of this chapter. Physicians have noted that a sense of euphoria sometimes comes over persons whose bodies are wracked by such torments as ravaging diseases, crippling injuries and extensive burns. This has been observed taking place apart from anesthetics, tranquilizers and other drugs.

It has been suggested that peptide hormones, called endorphins, are released by brain cells and these substances attach themselves to the surfaces of the cells responsible for pain reception. The hormones are said to have the pharmacalogic proprieties of opium. Pain ceases. Dr. Thomas cited the example of "the worst accident" he ever witnessed, a World War II event. Two MP's were trapped in a crushed jeep. Only their heads and shoulders were visible amid the twisted steel which crushed bones, penetrated flesh and tore muscles and organs. Despite the fact both were mortally wounded they remained conscious and conversed with those who sought frantically to pry them from the wreckage. When asked how they felt they replied they felt fine. Their concern was for the men in the troop carrier into which they collided. When told that the troops were all right the two men died quietly.

Others, observing similar phenomena, have suggested that the mind tends to retreat from unpleasant reality as the nerve of a decaying tooth retreats from advancing decay. When the mind achieves that goal, as it often does when one who is seemingly faced with certain death resigns to that eventuality, a sense of euphoria, of general well-being may sweep over the soul. The subject generally drops off into a deep sleep, in marked contrast to the state (both physical and mental) from which relief has been gained. In such a case the patient sometimes undergoes what is interpreted afterwards as a death experience in which sensations of peace, pleasure, beauty and light are recalled when the subject later awakens to reality.

Such observations strike me as a better explanation of the experiences cited in popular "death experience" fast sellers. At the least such explanation is not clouded with the anti-Scriptural construction of currently popular circulation. And it is not servile to the false hope so eagerly sought and accepted by those whose life styles provide no Biblical warrant for the prospect of an afterlife of sweetness and light.

It is of no small interest that when certain psychic phenomena is in vogue, suddenly it becomes epidemic. Many begin to share precisely the same experience. When attention is later focused on some other psychic expression, that becomes the experience most often imagined, manifested or reported. This observation covers a wide range of human experience. 1) Teen age girls shrieking and swooning en masse at an Elvis Presley concert, 2) The changing pattern of behavior at the reception(?) of the Holy Spirit from one generation or decade to another—rolling on the floor, fainting into the arms of a waiting attendant who then laid the zapped novitiate upon a sheet already thoughtfully spread in place, the tongues phenomenon, etc., and 3) the irrational behavior of masses incited to riot and violence. These and other examples of programmed "response" or imaginings may be cited. The sudden increase of a stereotyped "death" experience is another.

So much for the more unusual aspects of death and/or what is being called a "death experience." Let us now return to the more normative aspects of the subject. Some consideration needs to be given to the phenomena which occasioned the language that is the chief Biblical support for the doctrine of soul sleeping. A case can be made for the doctrine provided one limits the textual data to those Scriptures which deal only with the phenomenal (public) viewable aspects of death.

We shall review the doctrine of soul sleeping in the light of the Scriptures in chapter twelve. For the present the phenomenal and physical aspects of the subject need to be considered. Logically, any experience outside the body (including apartness from the brain, the center of consciousness), would have to be somehow communicated to the memory bank of the person reoccupying the "resurrected" physical organism. We have no Biblical data to support the notion this has ever occurred, save for the instance of Christ. The Scriptures report a number of resurrections. It is significant that none of the resurrectees is reported as discussing anything that was "experienced" in the interim twixt death and the resurrection. Insofar as the Biblical record is concerned even Jesus related to no one anything He may have experienced between the time He "bowed his head and gave up the ghost" and "arose on the third day." Incidentally, He also is not recorded as having communicated anything He experienced before He became incarnate. There is possibly a relationship between the two.

The apostle Paul's "Paradise vision" (II Cor. 12:1-4) is sometimes cited as paralleling the "life after life" experiences reported by such writers as Ross and Moody. If so, Paul apparently could not speak as authoritatively, decisively or confidentally as modern claimants. Yet he had to his advantage the power of Divine inspiration. If it is given unto us to be instructed by those who have died and returned to live again in the flesh, somehow God failed to see the wisdom of such. None of the resurrectees of Biblical record are reported as having related his "after death" experience. Thus we have no authenticated and interpreted "after death" experiences. Even if we allow Paul's "Third heaven/Paradise" vision to be such, it is still to be noted his only "revelation" to us concerning the happening is that he "heard unspeakable words which it is not *lawful* for man to utter" (v. 4). Are we to suppose that "law" has since been repealed? Or is it only that one is not allowed to speak of the *words* one hears? Have the *sights*, particularly "the light at the end of the tunnel," now become "non-classified information" to be spoken of freely?

Therefore we return to the basic question. When body functions cease and the brain is no longer viable, hence no longer available as the vehicle of consciousness, self-awareness, thoughts, emotions, volitions, etc., what then? Only from the Scriptures can we learn the answer to that question. Therein we quickly come to see that death is far more complex than the mere physical phenomenon we call by that name. Death appears to have a number of different aspects.

CONCERNING DEATH AND DYING

1. There is first of all the common physical phenomenon, the total cessation of the life processes including brain activity. Phenomenally speaking, from the materialistic viewpoint, that is all there is to it. But Biblically speaking, the death of which we are now speaking involves much more. It is the separation from the body of a surviving non-material entity called (somewhat interchangeably) the *soul* or *spirit*. When the body dies, when brain waves cease, when the processes which animate the body are no longer operable, the soul or spirit departs. And where does it go? What is the state or condition of the person, the conscious entity which once dwelled within the body and used it (the brain included) to achieve its ends? To that inquiry we shall address ourselves shortly.

2. The Scriptures also speak of a "second death" — the irrevocable banishment of body, soul and spirit into hell. Revelation 20:6, 14, 15, among other texts, speak of this awesome judgment as the ultimate punishment not only of the despicable trinity of the nether world — the devil, the beast and the false prophet — but of all those whose names are not found written in the book of life. Of that we shall have much more to say in a later chapter.

3. Death is also spoken of in a figurative or metaphysical sense. Extended separation of any kind is called death. Thus in the parable commonly called the parable of the prodigal son, the father said of him upon his return: "This my son was dead, and is alive again" (Lk. 15:32). Soldiers unaccounted for among the dead and captured, husbands and others who disappear and are not heard of again, after so long a time may be declared "legally dead." A sustained adultrous relationship is recognized by the Scriptures as effectuating the same sad state of affairs which results when the body of a mate is lying in the grave.

4. Again, in a figurative sense, those separated through sin from the fellowship and favor of God are said to be dead in trespasses and error. Such is the point of the illustration just cited. In a sense it is an even more serious aspect of spiritual death, and the occasion for the second death.

5. Finally, those who repent of sin and are baptized into Christ for the remission of sins are said to "die unto sin," and to be raised to walk in newness of life (Romans 6:4ff.).

The Origin of Death

Insofar as man is concerned the origin of death is chronicled in Genesis, chapters 3 and 4. Unanswered by the Garden of Eden account are such questions as whether death of any kind existed before the transgression of Adam and Eve, and whether those two were in any sense subject to death before they were banished from the garden and cut off from the tree of life.

Concerning the first question, artists have long painted pictures of the Garden of Eden and lions, tigers and the like grazing alongside such docile creatures as lambs and fawns. This idea grows out of the wedding of such texts as Romans 5:12 with kingdom prophecies such as Isaiah 11:6-9, and 65:25.

Romans 5:12 reads: "Therefore as through one man sin entered into the world and death through sin, so death passed unto all men, for all sinned." Of itself this text speaks only of the origin and occasion of human death. But Isaiah 11:6 reads:

> And the wolf shall dwell with the lamb, and the leopard shall lie down with the kid; and the calf and the young lion and the fatling together: and a little child shall lead them. And

the cow and the bear shall feed; their young ones shall lie down together: and the lion shall eat straw like the ox, and the suckling child shall play on the hole of the asp, and the weaned child shall put his hand on the adder's den. They shall not be hurt nor destroyed in all my holy mountain: for the earth shall be filled with the knowledge of Jehovah as the waters cover the sea.

Isaiah 65.25 speaks in much the same vein. Again mention is made of the lion eating straw like the ox, and erstwhile carnivores and docile creatures feeding together, with hurt and destruction non-existent in all Jehovah's holy mountain.

The line of reasoning is that if this is the way it is going to be in Christ's millennial kingdom (the kingdom and the millennium hypothesized in popular theory) that is the way it must assuredly have been in the Garden of Eden. The insistence upon literal interpretation of apocalyptic language invariably predisposes interpreters to so reason.

If such a line of reasoning be allowed, then it follows that all animals were originally created herbiferous, and shall become such once again. It is further assumed that all species of animals that we know of, including all the fearsome creatures which are extinct, roamed about in the Garden of Eden, and none preyed upon another.

Such assumptions have some basic problems which need to be considered. Not the least of these is the fact that Paul informed Timothy that a mark of apostasy would be the forbidding of the eating of meats which "God created to be received with thanksgiving . . . for every creature of God is good, and nothing is to be rejected" (I Tim. 4:3, 4). Was mankind created to be a strict vegetarian and one of the benefits of Adam's sin is that we can now enjoy steak, roast beef, southern fried chicken, etc.?

If animals did not feed on other species, much less upon their own kind, as creatures of the rivers and seas are obliged to do, then we would be forced to hypothecize that some degree of evolution has taken place generally in the anatomical structure and gastronomic apparatus of birds, beasts, creeping things and such as move through the paths of the seas. If not, we must ask what purpose was served by the talons and hooked beaks of the birds of prey, and the fangs and claws of the carnivores by means of which they can rip open the tough hides and tear asunder their hapless victim? And what purpose was served by the venom and constricting coils and hinged jaws by which snakes can kill and swallow whole creatures two or three time their own girth? Were all those blood thirsty carnivores created later? Or did they evolve from docile vegetarians?

Aside from such questions, where does the Bible say that carnivores roamed freely in the Garden of Eden, but in a quiescent non-aggressive state? And where does the Bible say the whole earth was like the Garden of Eden? The Genesis record says: "Jehovah God planted a garden eastward, in Eden, and there he put man whom he had formed" (Gen. 2:8). Later we read "He drove out the man: and he placed at the east of the garden of Eden, the Cherubim, and the flame of sword which turned every way, to keep the way to the tree of life" (3:24). This suggests the garden may have been walled or otherwise secluded and rendered relatively private and protected. Be that as it may, to assume there was no death of any kind prior to the sin of Adam and Eve is to make the Bible say something it does not.

A still more important question centers in the significance of 1) the warning concerning the tree of knowledge of good and evil and 2) the role of the tree of life in both the garden of Eden and the restored Paradise. See Gen. 2:9, 16, 17; 3:3, 22-24 and Rev. 2:7; 22:2, 14, 19.

CONCERNING DEATH AND DYING

Concerning the tree of the knowledge of good and evil God is said to have warned, "in the day thou eatest thereof thou shalt surely die." Eve informed the serpent God had said they should not even *touch* it, lest they die" (Gen. 3:3). Her words were probably an overstatement. In the throes of temptation, struggling to maintain her defense, it is understandable that she should speak thusly. Many a teenager has told his or her temptor(s), "I wouldn't dare do it. My dad would *kill* me."

What kind of death was God speaking of? We have noted five different usages of the term in the Scriptures. What kind of death passed upon Adam and Eve "in the day" they ate of the forbidden tree? If the Hebrew word *yom*, translated *day*, is to be taken literally as referring to a 24 hour solar day (as many insist the word is to be understood, especially when a specific day is spoken of), then physical death would seem to be eliminated. Adam lived some 800 years even after the birth of Seth.

According to the dogma of original sin formulated by Augustine and still taught by Roman Catholic and Calvinistic theologians, the death spoken of was primarily spiritual death. That such was indeed the immediate effect would be hard to gainsay. And the fact that physical death followed inevitably and consequently, however long delayed in consummation, is likewise quite obviously true.

But unfortunately the dogma of original sin goes beyond the Divine record. According to the dogma, Adam and Eve not only died spiritually that day, but in consequence all their posterity by "ordinary generation" are born dead in sin. The phrase enclosed in quotation marks is taken from a creedal statement of the dogma, and was obviously inserted in said creed to "take Christ off the hook," so to speak.

Christ alone being thereby exempted, the theory is that the entire human race is automatically and inescapably saddled not only with physical consequences of Adam and Eve's transgression, but with the actual guilt thereof as well. All are said therefore to be born sinners, depraved and hellbound from the moment of conception. If I understand Calvinism aright, that guilt was affixed upon us, one and all, in the foreknowledge and determinate counsel of God from the day Adam and Eve sinned, and even before that by reason of God's foreknowledge and predestination. The dogma finds its classic expression in the official confession of the Presbyterian Church in the U.S.A. (Revised edition, 1939, p. 25, 26)

> By this sin (eating of the forbidden fruit) they (Adam and Eve) fell from their original righteousness and communion with God, and so became dead in sin and wholly defiled in all the faculties and parts of body and soul. They being the root of all mankind, the guilt of this sin was imputed and the same death in sin and corrupted nature conveyed to all their posterity descending from them by ordinary generation. From this original corruption whereby we are indisposed, disabled, and made opposite to all good, and wholly inclined to evil, do proceed all actual transgressions.

One could hardly say any thing worse of the devil himself than what is there said of a newborn child. No wonder the practice of infant baptism(?) was introduced almost immediately into the doctrine and practice of the heirs of Augustinianism. As we have already noted, in theology as well as elsewhere, once a falsehood is told and/or accepted, other falsification must quickly follow in attempted cover-up of or accommodation to the first one. In this case infant baptism (so called) proves to be just the tip of the iceberg.

CONCERNING DEATH AND DYING

There are at least three problems which immediately grow out of the assumption that Adam and Eve, in dying spiritually, automatically passed spiritual death upon all their posterity save the virgin born Messiah.

1. This would assume Adam and Eve were never restored to God's fellowship, having apparently committed in one act of transgression unpardonable sin. Whether or not they were pardoned we are not told. But in clothing them with skins of animals it could be conjectured that animal sacrifice such as we find incumbent upon Cain and Abel (Gen. 4:1-7) began with Adam and Eve. At least Eve considered herself to be to some degree within the favor of God. When her first son was born she said: "I have gotten a man with the help of Jehovah" (Gen. 4:1).

2. If all Adam's posterity are born spiritually depraved, how are we to account for the righteousness of Abel? and of Enoch? and of Elijah? to name a few. Moreover, if infant baptism (so called) is for the remission of Adamic guilt then how does Adam's guilt get back into the genes and chromosomes of those baptized to be automatically transmitted to the next generation? Is the guilt of the sin remitted, or is it not? If it is not remitted through infant baptism (so called), what about through believer's baptism? (See Mark 16:16, Acts 2:38, Ro. 6:3-5, Col. 2:12, Gal. 3:27, I Pet. 3:21, etc.) Or, of those of the faith-only persuasion let us ask: If we become new creatures in Christ (all things being made new, the old things passed away, II Cor. 5:17), being "born anew," (this time "from above," by the Spirit no less and thus "saved by grace through faith"), how does it happen that all this Divine operation working in the heart of "the elect," plus the atoning blood of the cross, is cancelled out by one act of transgression on the part of Adam? Is Adam

so much greater than Christ that the new nature received from Him who is alive and well, seated with all authority at the right hand of God, is still powerless to prevent the corrupt nature and guilt of Adam and Eve from creeping right back into our innermost nature, to perpetuate the guilt of Adam's transgression even unto the children of the most devout Christians? Was the Psalmist mistaken? Does Jehovah actually always chide? Does He really keep his anger forever? (Ps. 103:9). Was Jeremiah, along with others who expressed similar assurances of Divine pardon, mistaken in announcing that when God forgives He also forgets our sins? (Jer. 31:34).

The answer to such questions is to be found in a reexamination of the Scriptures, and not in the dogma that foisted infant baptism(?) upon the church. Infants are not born saddled with Adamic guilt. We live in a world in which we are cut off from the tree of life, and hence are subject to physical death. And we live in a world in which we are subject to temptation, as was Adam, or else we would not be free moral agents. And as Adam did, his descendants also do. We sin. Thus it is written, "As in Adam [not because of] we all die, so in Christ we are all made alive" (I Cor. 15:22).

3. This brings us to the third objection to the dogma under consideration. If indeed all die in Adam spiritually, that is if all are born into a state of spiritual death just because of one solitary act of (Adam's) transgression, then the Universalists are right in teaching that all mankind will be saved because of one solitary act of Christ. The second half of the verse cited in the paragraph above is surely as true and embracive as the first.

CONCERNING DEATH AND DYING

Let us face it. If all men are constituted sinners, condemned to eternal death just because Adam sinned, then the "second Adam" is no match for the first. He gave it a good try, and died in doing so. But the effect of Adam's transgression is ever so much more extensive than the effect of Christ's redemptive act on Calvary. Certainly every human being born into this life does not become a Christian, much less did His death on Calvary automatically make alive in him (spiritually, or otherwise) all who lived on earth and died before He came. To assume either is true would be to make a shambles of the Biblical revelation. If all the myriads of persons who have or shall occupy this earth are condemned to hell just because of one solitary act of Adam, then how is it that the one solitary act of Christ (See Hebr. 9:24-28.) does not cancel that condemnation and accomplish the salvation of all men apart from their personal involvement?

If the death which passed on to mankind is reckoned as physical death, Paul's argument in his resurrection treatise (I Corinthians 15) makes sense. It can scarcely be contradicted that the resurrection he speaks of there is the resurrection of the body. It follows, therefore, that the death which the second coming of Christ shall cancel is physical death. In fact Paul speaks of Christ's own resurrection from the grave as "the firstfruits" thereof.

Physical death is certainly not incongruous with man's nature. This was true of man even before the fall. Man is a creature, not the creator. He is inherently temporal, not eternal. Partaking of the tree of life apparently could and would change that. According to God's own words, even sinful men could "live for ever" if allowed to "put their hand to the tree of life" (Gen. 3:22-24). God very judiciously put an end to that possibility. He drove Adam and Eve from the garden, guarded the approach to the tree of life, and then removed the tree from this earth. Why He left the tree for a time we can only conjecture. It could be that leaving it for a time, guarded by the cherubim and flaming sword, served as a vivid object lesson. Undoubtedly the sweat and toil to which man was now subjected was accompanied by fatigue. If at all perceptive, they should have gotten the message. How soon they sensed the aging process was setting in and would end in death we have no way of knowing. Obviously there was soon sufficient observational data all around them and working within them that the tree which was now denied them no longer served a useful purpose. How wistfully and longingly Adam and Eve must have looked in the direction of the tree in the midst of the garden, "so near (so tantalizingly near) and yet so far." Be that as it may, the awesome judgment of which God forewarned and which their severance from that tree enforced, passed on to Adam and Eve in a sense the day they sinned. Dying, they would now surely die.

Death is so indigenous to man as a creature of clay that we actually start dying the moment we start living. Even in the womb this is so. Two forces are ever present in us — life and death, development and degeneration, growth and decay. For a time the forces of life, growth, development and strength override the forces of death, arrestment, degeneracy and decay. Then comes a time when the two seem to reach a balance. But then, at first slowly, then with quickening pace the forces which consummate in death take over.

The most oft repeated phrase in Genesis is "and he died." At first death came slowly after several hundred years. But eventually death took its toll. Obviously the wages of sin required several generations for their cumulative effect to be felt with awesome accelerating force. The warning given to Adam and Eve is most provocative. Literally it reads: "Dying, thou shalt surely die."

Upon the separation of Adam and Eve from the tree of life, at first by their banishment from the garden, and later by the removal of the garden itself along with the tree, death passed inevitably upon all mankind. It is worthy of note that God did not club Adam and Eve to death. He did not zap them with a bolt of lightning, nor poison them, nor cause a wild beast to devour them. The earth did not open and swallow them, nor did a volcano rain fire and brimstone upon them. He did not send a plague or pestilence upon them. He simply separated them from the tree of life.

From that day on Adam and Eve were like fish snatched out of the water, or rosebuds in a vase. A fish out of water appears to be very much alive. Such action, such flopping about! But soon the gills extend and close laboriously. Then the gilling slows down. The jaws move more slowly, and it dies. Its doom was sealed when it was cut off from the environment for which it was made.

So it is also with a rosebud in a vase. The bud proceeds to blossom as though it were still a part of the bush on which it grew. It appears very much alive. But it is dead. Soon the petals will fade and fall. The leaves will turn yellow and drop off the stem. The rosebud was doomed to an early and certain demise when it was severed from the bush. The bristle cone pines of the California coastline are known to have a life span of two or three millenniums. Yet when a branch is cut off it withers and dies.

One is reminded of the prodigal son. He wasted his father's substance "in riotous living" (Luke 15:13). Living? So he thought of it at first. But not for long. His father never considered it living. "This my son was dead and is alive again" (v. 24). So said the father when at last the "poor sucker got off the hook" (so to speak) and made his torturous way back home. There he was "alive again."

There is still another factor which bears on the question as to whether physical death or spiritual death, or both, is the death spoken of in the Genesis account of the fall of man. In Paul's two expositions on the subject (I Cor. 15:20-26 and Romans 5:12-21) physical death is the death Paul specifically speaks of as resulting from Adam's transgression. That physical death was included is seen in the fact that the penalty pronounced upon Adam closed with the dismal sentence: "In the sweat of thy face thou shalt eat bread till you return unto the ground. For out of it you were taken: for dust thou art, and unto dust thou shalt return" (Gen. 3:19). It is this death, phsyical death, that passed on to Adam's posterity as a universal judgment. Spiritual death is personal — personally attained (if it be that one could call such an "attainment"). Spiritual death is the result of personal transgression for the simple reason that guilt is personal. Ezek. 18:1-4, 20 makes this fact clear.

Chapter Twelve

THE INTERIM STATE OF THE DEAD

Bang! You are dead, with a bullet in your brain. What then? Is there any part of you that survives? Is there some entity which continues to exist conscious of its identity and able in some way to relate to the life you now live in the flesh? This is a crucial question. The answers may be summed up under three heads: 1. Nihilism. 2. Innate immortality views. 3. Conditional immortality views.

1. *Nihilism*

Atheists, and even some Deists, believe that no part of man except for his progeny and influence survives physical death. Once dead, "like Rover, we are dead all over." Human consciousness — indeed, all thought — is conceived by materialists to be but the effluvium of the brain. Thus when brain waves cease and the brain cells begin to decompose, the brain can never again function. There can be no consciousness, no thought whatsoever arise therefrom. Death ends all.

Materialists are quick to point out that the brain is the first part of the human organism to start the process of decay, and the part in which decay advances the most rapidly and irreparably. Even on this side of death, we are told, brain cells once damaged are irreparable. New cells are not formed to replace brain cells which are damaged or destroyed. Phenomenally speaking, the argument is impressive. That is exactly what appears to happen.

Neuro-surgeons have probed the brain and identified the seat of consciousness, the areas which are related to the five senses, the control centers for the various functions of the body, etc. Through electrical stimulus via needles probing the brain, a subject, fully conscious through the process, can be made to recall events of the past — some of which have been long buried deep in the sub-conscious mind. Sights, sounds, smells and other sensations, including the emotional factors which were a part of the original experience, can be caused to come again to the mind. Moreover the manipulating experimenter can stimulate and activate various functions of the body. The subject's hands can be moved at the manipulator's instigation. The eyes may be closed and opened. Other parts of the body likewise will respond in simplistic movements to the imposed stimuli. But there is one thing the neuro-surgeon can not do. By his probes he can not cause the subject to *will* to do the things his imposition upon the brain causes to happen. The subject of the experiment describes the experience as being like an operator seated at the control panel of a complicated machine he or she is accustomed to operate, with a second party reaching over one's shoulder and taking one's hand in his. As the subject's hand is then manipulated to press the various buttons, closing and opening switches, etc., the subject is aware of what is happening, but remains completely aware of the fact that what is being done is not arising from one's own will.

Thoughtful neuro-surgeons sense that the human soul, the source of one's own volition, and self consciousness, does not respond to the probes and artificial stimuli. Moreover, the soul appears not to be identical to the brain but uses the brain as the manipulator in the experiment does, only much more expertly, extensively and directly. The elusive will — elusive, that is, to the manipulator — but at the full command of the subject, is a metaphysical entity

THE INTERIM STATE OF THE DEAD

which defies the ability of the experimentors to locate, explain or control. That metaphysical entity which is so inseparably linked to one's own self-awareness and personal identity is what Christians believe to be the soul, and which Christians believe survives the death of the body.

It is worthy of note that the "stream of consciousness" theory by which atheistic materialists have sought to explain human consciousness along phenomenal lines is open to question at almost every point. The brain does not merely register and respond to sensations which are emptied into it through the five senses. The brain is capable of originating thoughts which have nothing to do with the current stimuli. We can control our thoughts even in the face of strong stimuli from without. We are not the victim of the strongest sensation or stimulus of the moment. We can willfully shut out of our consciousness pain, loud noises, bright lights and other potential distractions and give attention to thoughts not even suggested by our present circumstances. We can stop a train of thought at will and start a new train of thought totally irrelevant to what we have been thinking of and without any relevance to present circumstances.

In short, human thought cannot be adequately accounted for by any materialistic formula. Only in its simpler form can it be so explained. It is granted that we normally think about the things of which we are made aware through our five senses. God has created us so, for obvious reasons. But man, the thinker, does not derive his thoughts solely from the stimuli which press upon him as the five senses are activated in the course of our constant encounter with the physical universe.

As Christians intellectual honesty compels us to candidly acknowledge that: 1) our hope of conscious life after death is rooted and grounded in the Biblical revelation. 2) Aside from the thoroughly documented account of the resurrection of Christ we have no objective experiential data to which we may appeal. There are no contemporary resurrectees with whom we can converse. The claimants of the Moody-Ross genre include no one who was "dead" long enough for the brain to decompose. 3) As Christians we can offer no scientifically attestable explanation of how a human being can continue to think and be conscious of self-identity apart from the body and even apart from the brain. Our whole thinking process has been so closely linked with the life we now live in the flesh and the functioning of the brain that thinking is suspended when anesthetics and/or injuries affecting certain brain tissues put the seat of consciousness to rest.

But there are two sides to every coin. We may also call attention to the fact there are certain aspects of human thought for which science can provide no objective explanation. Mere materialistic explanations, observations and formulations fail to account for all aspects of human thought. Christians are not alone in clinging "by faith" to certain subjective conclusions concerning human consciousness. The differences are: 1) we admit it, and 2) the basis of our faith rests in Divine revelation, not merely on a mind-set bent on rationalizing even the things which transcend reason.

Christians do not claim Christ's resurrection was a normative human experience. It was not so either then or now. Unusual phenomena marked facets of His life in the flesh from conception to the closing event of his earthly sojourn. It is because of such phenomena that we believe Him to be the Son of God. The apostle John candidly confessed that selection of "the things" he included in his Gospel was evangelistically oriented. Said he, "Many other things did Jesus in the presence of his disciples which are not written in this book, but these are written that ye may believe that Jesus is the Christ, the Son of God; and that believing ye may have life in his name" (Jn. 20:30, 31).

There is another side to that also. When the docetic segment of the gnostic cult began to teach that Christ did not really become flesh, but only appeared to do so, John in subsequent epistles declared such a notion to be "of the spirit of the antichrist." (See I John 4:1-3. Cf. II John 7.) Christ's true manhood is as much a basic doctrine of the Christian faith as is His deity. It was the *man* Christ Jesus who was raised from the dead to be "the firstfruits of them that sleep." The metamorphosis of which Paul speaks in his resurrection treatise (See I Cor. 15:35-58.) was delayed in Christ's case to call attention to that fact. Thus when His first appearance to His disciples "affrighted" them, in that they "supposed him to be a spirit" He said to them, "See my hands and my feet, that it is I myself: handle me, and see; for a spirit hath not flesh and bones as ye behold me having" (Lk. 24:39).

If God could raise up, very much alive, the tortured and crucified body of Christ, and present Him to the disciples as the very person they had known Him to be before His death, we can believe His promise: "Because I live, ye shall live also" (Jn. 14:19). The degree of decomposition is not a factor. When deprived of oxygen for only a few minutes irreparable damage is done to the brain, the seat of consciousness — irreparable, that is, short of the power of the resurrection. Thus Paul declared in the passage cited above: "Behold, I show you a mystery. We shall not also sleep [die] but we shall all be changed, in a moment, in the twinkling of an eye, at the last trump: for the trumpet shall sound, and the dead shall be raised incorruptible, and we shall be changed" (I Cor. 15:51, 52).

The Christian doctrine of the resurrection is the antithesis of the nihilistic doctrine of materialistic atheism. It is also the only credible alternative thereto. The resurrection of Christ is the one well documented event of human history which provides a rational basis for man's longing for immortality.

2. Innate Immortality Views

According to the doctrine of innate immortality, as taught by orthodox Christian traditionalists, the soul of man is innately (inherently) immortal; hence it is interminable and indestructible. The same is generally held of man's resurrected body — of the bodies of the unjust as well as of the redeemed.

The doctrine of innate immortality (of the soul, at least) is shared to some degree with spiritualists and various pagan religions, including some animists. By and large the doctrine is equated with religion per se. There are exceptions. As noted, some Deists, some even in the context of the Christian faith (speaking loosely), deny life beyond the life we now live in the flesh.

Innate immortality views fall into two main classes, with several sub-classes. We shall make brief mention of pagan oriented views and then proceed to evaluate the variant views within the larger context of the Christian faith.

A. Pagan Oriented Views

1. *Transmigration of souls.* The teaching of the transmigration of souls is traceable to the ancient Egyptians, and

beyond them to other less notable cultures. Currently the teaching is more readily associated with Hinduism and Buddhism. But again less notable cultures teach various forms of the theory. It is quite common to the animistic religions of primitive tribes in various parts of the undeveloped countries of the world.

Basically, the belief is that the soul never dies. It simply migrates and changes residence. In its new mode of existence it is limited to the nature of the beast, bird, reptile, insect — or whatever it is assigned to indwell, even trees and flowers. The latter is believed to be a romantic outgrowth of the observation of trees and flowers growing out of gravesites.

Most varieties of the teaching find their moral compulsion in the belief that a good life — that is, a life well pleasing to the gods — is rewarded by rebirth into a higher form of life. And an evil (displeasing) life is punished by rebirth into a lower form of existence. The value system, however, is often incongruous. Primitives and others who worship snakes, cows and other creatures naturally consider the object of their worship to be a higher and more desirable life form than their own.

Aside from the Christian doctrine of the resurrection of the just and the unjust — the just to live anew in glorified bodies in the paradise of God, and the wicked to be cast into the lake of fire with the devil, the beast and the false prophet the teaching has nothing in common with the Christian faith.

2. Reincarnation. Reincarnation is the doctrine that departed souls may (and some do) reenter this world in the form of another person. Some of these are believed to be aware of having had a prior existence as another person.

The widely publicized Bridey Murphy story of a few years ago is evidence that the teaching is not limited to savages dwelling in abysmal ignorance and squalor.

The concept is thought to originate in an attempt to understand the phenomena of dreams in which a person appears to undergo real life experiences outside the body. Souls came to be regarded as small enough to leave the body through the mouth or nostrils. The former was the more general hypothesis in that it obviously provided more latitude in assuming the form of the soul. In some cultures the soul is viewed as a snake. In others the soul was viewed as a mouse-like creature, a shrew or a bat or a weasel. The Greeks commonly thought of the soul as flying and depicted it as a butterfly. This view was widely dispersed throughout all Europe and has persisted until fairly recent times. In the wake of the Christian faith, the soul came to be regarded as a dove. Poles bearing replicas of doves were erected on Lombard graves. The ancient Egyptians believed the soul to have the form of a hawk.

Cultures which conceived of the soul entering and leaving the body through the nostrils viewed its form as insect-like, possibly because insects (particularly flies) appear in profusion when a corpse remains in a viewable situation.

Basic to the concept of reincarnation is the postulate that if the soul can leave an individual during sleep and return again it surely should be able to enter and be reborn into the body of a new born baby.

The doctrine of reincarnation and the transmigration of souls are often intermingled. The distinction is not always clear. The two are dealt with as variant forms of metempsychosis and frequently discussed together under that title in general encyclopedias.

THE INTERIM STATE OF THE DEAD

Aside from the Christian doctrine of the resurrection of the just and the unjust in the last day, reincarnation as it is popularly conceived has little in common with the Christian faith. In the Christian doctrine of future life, we continue into the next life very much aware of being the same person we are in this present life. And we are dealt with as such in the Great White Throne Judgment (Revelation 20:11-15).

B. Traditional Orthodox Views

The three major branches of Christendom (Roman Catholic, Greek [Eastern] Orthodox and Protestants) teach as a common core of faith the doctrine of innate immortality. It is also a teaching of many of the cults. That the trichotomy of man includes an "immortal soul" is reckoned to be so axiomatic that the concept is rarely questioned despite the fact the term appears nowhere in the Bible. But the near unanimity of teaching ceases when the exact state of the soul between death and the resurrection is considered. Five distinct views have again wide acceptance.

1. *Soul sleeping.* According to this teaching the soul exists in a deep coma between death and the resurrection. The Seventh Day Adventists are the chief proponents of this concept, but the view is also shared by others. Rare is the denomination which does not have at least a few among them who hold to the doctrine of soul sleeping.

Proponents of the theory are able to marshal some imposing arguments. The Scriptures abound with references in which death is spoken of as sleep. A number of Scriptures can be cited which seem to indicate the "sleep" is so deep that the dead are completely oblivious not only to the world from which they have departed, but of their current state as well. Phenomenally speaking, the theory certainly "appears" to be plausible. As a bit of verse puts it:

> We thought her dying as she slept
> and sleeping when she died.

The theory deserves consideration. The textual data is too extensive to be ignored. But that is also true of other textual data from which a quite different conclusion can be drawn. We are scarcely at liberty to be selective. The Scriptures must be harmonized. The following texts bearing on the state of the soul after death point up the complexity of the problem.

Death as an Unconscious State	Vs.	*Death as a Conscious State*
1. Without awareness of earth events, Job 14:21		1. With awareness of earth events, Lk. 16:19-31, especially vs. 22-28
2. Without knowledge, emotions, work or wisdom, Eccles. 9:4-6, 10		2. A place of mourning and pain, Job 14:22, Lk. 16:24, 28
3. Without remembrance, Ps. 6:5, 88:12, 146:4		3. A place of remembrance, Lk. 16:25, 27, Rev. 6:9-11
4. A place of silence, Ps. 88:10, 115:17		4. A place of speech, Lk. 16:19-31, Rev. 6:9-11
5. A place of prolonged sleep, Job 14:12 (See notes below.)		5. A place of watchful waiting, Isa. 14:9-11, Rev. 6:9-11

Death as sleep is a metaphor found throughout the Scriptures. It is first introduced in Deut. 31:16, unless Job is regarded as the oldest book of the Old Testament, as Jewish tradition has it. In that case the metaphor was first used in

THE INTERIM STATE OF THE DEAD

Job 14:21. The books of the kings speak repeatedly of death as sleep. David's death is spoken of in this way: "And David slept with his fathers, and was buried," (I Kings 2:10). Cf. I Kings 11:43, 14:20, 31, 15:8, 24, 16:6, 28, 22:40, 50, II Kings 8:24, 10:35, 13:9, 13, 14:16, 22, 29, 15:7, 22, 38, 16:20, 20:21, 21:18, 24:6. See also Daniel 12:2.

The New Testament also employs the metaphor. See Jn. 11:11-14, Acts 7:60, 13:36, I Cor. 15:6, 18, 51, I Thess. 4:13, 14, II Pet. 3:4. The metaphor belongs to that category of speech which is called "phenomenal," that is, "pertaining to appearance." It is descriptive, not definitive. We speak in phenomenal terms when we speak of the sun rising and setting, when in fact the earth is turning on its axis. In the process the portion of the earth from which we are viewing the skies above is turned first toward the sun and then away from it. Although we live in an age of science, we continue to use the phenomenal expression. So do scientists.

The key to the seeming contradiciton in the Scriptures we set in contrast above is to be found in the fact the references which speak of death as sleep employ phenomenal language. Passages such as Ecclesiastes 9:4-10, Job 14:21, and others of like nature describe what one sees. Those who go into their "last sleep" register no emotion, express no response as the mourners gather about their casket.

It is worthy of note that the various passages cited in support of the deep coma view of the state of the dead are all taken from poetic stanzas. Poetry is generally addressed to the emotions more than to the mind. Feeling is more in the forefront than fact. This is not to say that facts are misrepresented. They simply are not as subjected to cold objective analysis.

Against the theory that the dead are in a comatose state from which nothing can awake them short of the resurrection trumpet on the last day, the following Scriptures need to be added to those already cited in refutation of the soul sleeping dogma: 1) The account of the reappearance of Samuel at the behest of the witch of Endor, I Sam. 28:11-19, 2) The hope expressed by David concerning his deceased son, II Samuel 12:23, (cf. Ps. 23), 3) The reappearance of Moses and Elijah in a conversational context, Matthew 17:1-3, Lk. 9:30, 31, 4) Christ's preaching to the "spirits in prison," I Pet. 3:19, 5) A score of references to demon possession in the Gospels, and four such in Acts.

It does not serve our present purpose to discuss demon possession. But should it be found that the demons spoken of were disembodied spirits of wicked men returned to earth, that would be but another indication that the dead are not "conked out" for the duration. Whatever the demons were, it is worthy of note that only evil spirits from the other realms of existence were desirous of taking up residence on earth in what ever way they could. Samuel was quite piqued that he should be called upon to reappear. "Why have you disquieted me, to bring me up?" he asked (I Sam. 28:15). His words suggest he was in a restive state, but not necessarily unconscious in that state. Jesus' depiction of Lazarus in Abraham's bosom is of similar implication.

2. *Compartmentalized Sheol-Hades Concept.* This concept of the interim state of the dead has been the view most widely accepted throughout the ranks of the Restoration Movement. The view follows closely the implications of the parable of the rich man and Lazarus (Luke 16:19-31). Since life apparently is going on as usual among the living, the implication seems to be that the setting of the parable is this

THE INTERIM STATE OF THE DEAD

side of the end-time. Lazarus has been carried away by the angels into Abraham's bosom (v. 22). The rich man has gone down into hades where "he lifts up his eyes, being in torment, and sees Abraham afar off, and Lazarus in his bosom" (v. 24). Between the two states (abodes of the dead) "there is a great gulf fixed," and it is declared to be uncrossable (v. 26).

The two states are interpreted as intermediate states, not the final state for either the just or the unjust. But they serve as a foretaste of the final states to which each leads. The concept is commonly diagrammed somewhat as follows:

THE INTERMEDIATE STATES OF THE DEAD

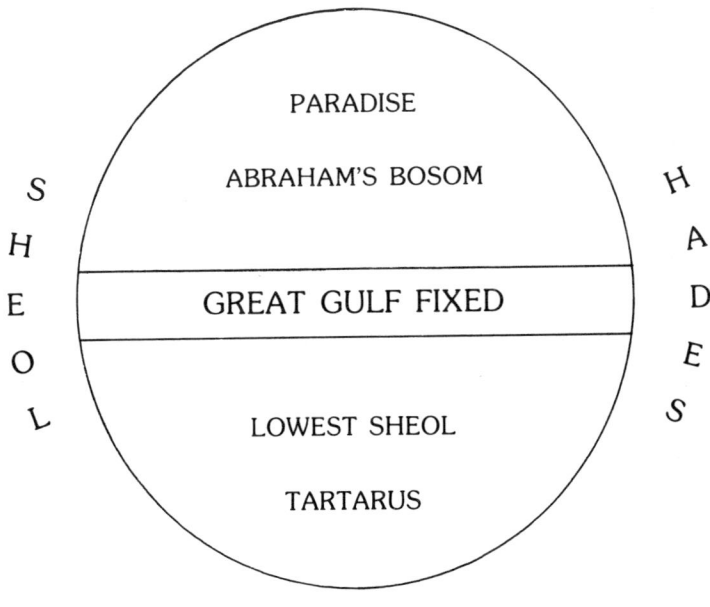

WHAT THE BIBLE SAYS ABOUT THE END TIME

Not the least of the difficulties which accompany a study of the subject is the fact that the King James translators saw fit to translate four different words by one and the same word — hell. The four are: sheol, hades, gehenna and tartarus.

Sheol appears sixty-five times in the Hebrew text of the Old Testament. The KJV translates it "grave" thirty-one times, "hell" the same number of times, and "pit" three times (Num. 16:30, 33, Job 17:16). Revisers commonly translate the word (שְׁאוֹל to sheol) in poetic passages, retaining "grave" and "pit" elsewhere. The ASV transliterates it consistently throughout. The Greek Septuagint (LXX) generally rendered it ᾅδής (hades - "unseen"). The New Testament writers followed the lead of the Septuagint when quoting O.T. passages which contain the word "sheol." For example, see Acts 2:27, 31, I Cor. 15:55.

Hades (Gr. ᾅδής) is used eleven times in the New Testament. Only once does the KJV render it "grave" (I Cor. 15:55). In that context translators could hardly do otherwise. But in the other ten passages the KJV uses the word "hell." (See Mt. 11:23, 16:18, Lk. 10:15, 16:23, Acts 2:27, 31, Rev. 1:18, 6:8, 20:13, 14).

Gehenna (Gr. γεέννα, literally, "valley of hinnom") appears twelve times in the New Testament (Mt. 5:22, 29, 30, 10:28, 18:9, 23:15, 23:23, Mk. 9:43, 45, 47, Lk. 12:5, Jas. 3:6). The KJV uniformly translates this word "hell" also, as do most other versions. Some prefer to transliterate it, "gehenna."

Tartarus, a Greek word by which they referred to the "abode of the wicked dead" is used only in II Peter 2:4. The context scarcely justifes the KJV transating the word "hell." In doing so the translator acted in obvious violation of the

THE INTERIM STATE OF THE DEAD

context, as the rendering of the word "hades" as "hell" would have been in I Cor. 15:55. In doing so, however, they have a lot of company. The ASV, RSV, NIV and many others do the same. If such is the proper translation then the angels that sinned have spent all the intervening years in the lake of fire, from whence they will be called forth for judgment in the end time, and promptly returned. The passage however continues to explain that in being cast down into Tartarus they were "committed to pits (Gr. *siroi*) of darkness, to be *reserved unto judgment*." The manner in which modern translators follow the lead of the long standing "authorized" version indicates how difficult it is to even notice an error of translation, much less correct it, when the error is well suited to a prevailing theory which probably occasioned the manner of translation in the first place.

At the time the KJV was first introduced the liberties taken by the translators in using the word "hell" so freely was not necessarily as confusing as it proves to be today. Back then the word had a much wider meaning. Actually it was the Old English equivalent of our modern word "hole." Like its modern counterpart it carried a number of different meanings. Most of them related in some way to a cavern, pit or other dark and foreboding place. Just as one who deals in furs is called a furrier and one dealing in coal was called a collier, a man who patched "hells" in a roof after a "hell" storm was called a "hellier."

Therefore some three hundred years or so ago the word "hell" was commonly used to refer to any dark or foreboding place. A grave could be referred to by that term without readers or hearers automatically envisioning "the lake of fire which is the second death" (Rev. 20:15). The hole dug in the ground to receive the body of a deceased loved one is certainly a foreboding place. A prison, dungeon, lunatic asylum, or a valley such as the valley of Hinnom outside of Jerusalem with equal propriety could be spoken of as "hell" three or four hundred years ago. That is no longer so.

In the intervening years the word has come to have a much more restricted connotation. Aside from being a handy curse word, seemingly suited for all occasions (along with "heck," its sissified substitute), in our time "hell" has a fairly settled meaning. When used seriously rather than profanely, its use conjures up visions of the awesome lake of fire judgment reserved for sinners (and the devil that deceived them) in the last day.

In the interest of clarity and more exacting usage, only the Greek word *gehenna* should be translated hell. *Sheol* and its Greek counterpart, *hades*, refer to the temporary abode of the dead, both of the righteous and the unrighteous, partitioned by the great gulf fixed between them. "Lowest Sheol" (Deut. 32:22) might well be spoken of as "Tartarus," being the abode of the wicked dead reserved unto judgment (II Peter 2:4). The upper division may be provisionally called "Paradise" (II Cor. 12:4, Lk. 23:43), or "Abraham's Bosom" (Lk. 16:22, 23). The latter is a Hebrew metaphor holding a special meaning for Jews, the former is a Persian word for a place of delight.

The abode of the righteous dead, as we have just said, is to be only provisionally spoken of as Paradise. The term is used in Revelation 2:7 with reference to the final abode of the saints, the site of the tree of life. Its use by Jesus in Lk. 23:43 and by Paul in II Cor. 12:4 is obviously relative. Compared to lowest Sheol (Tartarus) the upper chamber is indeed Edenic, a garden of delight. That Jesus was not promising the dying thief the two of them that very day would be going to heaven is made manifest by Jesus' words to Mary (Magdalene) following his resurrection: "I have not yet ascended unto the Father: but go unto my brethren, and say to them, I ascend unto my Father and your Father, and my God and your God" (Jn. 20:17).

Some would avoid the obvious import of Luke 23:43 by repositioning the comma, in an attempt to have Christ say to the penitent thief, "I say unto you *today*, you shall (some day) be with me in Paradise." Such a juxtapositioning of the time reference is patently absurd. Once it is clarified that "hades" and "hell" are not two words for the same place or state, hence Jesus did not go to hell in the interim twixt his death and the resurrection (creedal statements to that effect notwithstanding), and once the notion is overturned that the Sheol-Hades interlude is a comatose state, there is no further need for such a juggling exercise.

But what about Peter's reference (I Peter 3:19, 20) to Christ preaching to the imprisoned spirits of the disobient antedeluvians? Many able scholars believe this was accomplished figuratively, through Noah. But even when the passage is taken as a literal account of what Jesus did while His body was entombed, the text poses no great problem. If Abraham could converse with the rich man across the intervening gulf of Hades, Christ would surely be able to accomplish a somewhat similar feat.

There are some who insist the parable has nothing authoritative to say to us concerning the state of the dead. They would have us believe it is to be interpreted allegorically. Jesus is said to be simply accommodating Himself to contemporary Jewish notions concerning the state of the dead in order to predict in veiled terms the downfall of the Jewish nation from their privileged position and the receiving of the Gentiles into His grace. The interpretation is artificial and forced. If the parable is not to be taken as an accurate portrayal of what it seems to be speaking of, we have no way of knowing that. Nowhere did He say anything to the contrary. In this study we confess that the intermediate state of the dead concept has much to commend it to our consideration.

3. *The Semi-Intermediate State revision.* Most premillennial interpreters, and not a few others, subscribe to a revision of the compartmentalized Sheol-Hades concept. In the semi-intermediate state revision it is taught that at Jesus' ascension the upper sector of Hades, Paradise (Abraham's Bosom), was taken up into heaven. Several scriptures are cited in support of the viewpoint.

In Ephesians 4:8 Paul (quoting Ps. 68:18) wrote: "When he ascended on high, he led captivity captive and gave gifts unto men." This is interpreted as saying that when Jesus passed into the heaven he swept by the abode of the righteous dead, and took them, along with Paradise itself, with Him into heaven. The wicked dead, according to the theory, were left captives in lowest Sheol, and continue so to this day. Col. 2:15, the parallel passage in the companion epistle, is seldom cited. It does not lend itself as readily to the relocated saints hypothesis. The context of Ps. 68:18 likewise provides no basis for the interpretation currently forced upon it.

II Corinthians 5:6-9 is a key text in the semi-intermediate state revision. There Paul speaks of being absent from the Lord while present in the body. He affirms, "we are willing rather to be absent from the body, and to be at home with the Lord." I can relate to that. The prospect is exciting. But Paul does not exactly say the two things spoken of — being 1) absent from the body, and 2) at home with the Lord — occur simultaneously. It might be inferred without doing violence to the text, but such an inference by no means exhausts the possible interpretations.

In a sense the time factor is immaterial. At death we enter into a timeless, eventless state. Thus to be absent from the body is to be at home with the Lord. This side of the rapture that is the sequence of events, insofar as the saints are concerned. And it may very well be that the second event will seem to follow immediately. To those of the soul sleeping persuasion that is certainly their expectation. They believe we shall go to sleep in death and awake in resurrection, and will not have the slightest idea of whether our sleep has lasted a moment or a millennium. But one does not have to subscribe to the soul sleeping viewpoint to hold to a very similar hope. Unless one projects the categories of time and space into the future state one does not need to accept either soul sleeping or a relocated upper Sheol to accept II Cor. 5:8 at face value.

John 3:18 is a third text used to support the semi-intermediate state revision. There it is written: "He that believeth in him [Christ] is not judged." Does that mean they will never undergo a judgment experience of any kind? The verse which immediately follows in the Corinthian passage cited above most certainly seems to affirm otherwise. II Corinthians 5:10 reads: "For we must all be made manifest before the judgment-seat of Christ: that each one may receive the things done in the body, according to what he hath done, whether it be good or bad." Rev. 20:11-15 says pretty much the same thing.

Is God "the god of confusion" after all? (I Cor. 14:33). The key to what may seem at first to be a contradiction is to be found in the context of John 3:18. The words "judge," "judged," and "judgment" are used in the sense of condemnation proceedings, and the state of being condemned. Those in Christ shall not be subjected to condemnation proceedings, nor shall they be condemned. But to say their work in no sense shall be judged would be to say that their works will neither be recognized nor rewarded.

John 3:18 is a favorite proof text of those who teach the doctrine of "the security of believers" as an absolute irrevocable state, "no matter what," once one believes in Christ. If believers are in no sense to be judged, ever, there of course would be no point in their waiting out the consummation of the ages in some intermediate state. Thus reasoning, it is assumed that believers at the time of death proceed immediately to heaven as disembodied ethereal entities who must wait there the consummation of the ages in a sort of "neither fish nor fowl" state of being. That is to say, they will have neither bodies terrestial nor celestial. Yet it is assumed they will nonetheless co-exist among those whose form is commensurate with their estate. Such a conjecture is open to challenge.

I Thessalonians 4:14 is another text used to support the conjecture. Their reasoning is along these lines: When Christ returns to rapture the living saints and resurrect the bodies of the dead in Christ, how could "God bring with Him (Christ) those that are fallen asleep in Jesus," unless their souls have already been received into heaven? Suppose we answer that question by asking another. "Bring *who where*? and *when*? Who? The saints (that is, the souls of the saints) who have fallen asleep in Jesus? That is what the text might be made to seem to say. But if so, how about all those sainted "souls" of the ages prior to His ascension, which according to the theory in question Jesus is supposed to have taken with Him into heaven? When are they going to be brought down out of heaven to get their resurrected bodies? If the popular theory we are questioning is left unchallenged we have a problem. In fact we have three problems to be settled.

We have asked the question, "Who?" and received not a satisfactory answer. Let us consider the second question, "Where?" Where will God bring the saints who return with Jesus — back to earth to be grounded here for a thousand years? That is not what is said. The context makes that clear. The verse immediately preceding sets forth the question which is answered in II Thess. 4:14 and following. The question: "What about those Christians who had hoped to see the return of Christ but died with their hope unrealized?" Paul's answer is, in effect: "Don't fret about that." Let it be remembered that the death of Jesus was likewise a blow to the faith of many who had hoped in Him during the days of his flesh. Recall the words of the Emmaus road disciples, "but we hoped it was he who should redeem Israel" (Lk. 24:21).

Paul wrote to the Thessalonians, "If we believe that Jesus died and rose again, even so them that are fallen asleep in Jesus will God bring with him" (II Thess. 4:14). Who will bring who where? The text does not say Christ will bring the souls of the Christian saints down out of heaven to earth below. The text says *God* will bring with him (Jesus) those who have fallen asleep (died) in Jesus. Where? Where God will *bring* Jesus when He accomplishes the mission for which He is sent — not where will God *send* Him!

WHAT THE BIBLE SAYS ABOUT THE END TIME

According to Acts 3:20, 21 the heavens must receive Christ "until the times of the restoration of all things." When that time comes, the text proceeds to inform us, God will again "send [not bring] the Christ." I Thess. 4:13-18 tells us why. God will send Him to receive, by rapture and resurrection, those Christ has redeemed. And God will *bring* them, together with Christ, to be with Him in glory. See John 14:3.

According to Paul's resurrection treatise (I Corinthians 15) there are bodies terrestial and bodies celestial. Neither inhabits the realm of the other. Christ emptied himself of the form (Gr. *morphe*) of God and took upon himself the form (*morphe*) of man (Phil. 2:6, 7). He thus was "made flesh" preparatory to sojourning among men on earth. Are we to suppose that among the celestially bodied hosts of heaven there are now multitudes of disembodied saints? Are the innumerable hosts of saints who died in the pre-Christian era, and all the saints in Christ who have died since, now in heaven in a disembodied state? Such conjecture is contrary to the whole order of creation, both visible and invisible, as it is delineated for us in the Scripture.

Rather than assume that Christ emptied Paradise (or swept Paradise and those therein up with him, when He ascended into heaven), it is much more reasonable and Biblical to believe that he will sweep by Sheol-Hades on His return from heaven. At the voice of the archangel, and the trump of God, the souls of the dead in Christ shall enter the transformed bodies which shall rise from the graves and from the sea (Rev. 20:13). As full-orbed beings (body, soul and spirit) the saints shall be readied for entrance into that celestial city whose builder and maker is God.

THE INTERIM STATE OF THE DEAD

Neither I Thessalonians 4:13-18, nor I Corinthians 15 deals with the nature of the resurrected bodies of the wicked dead. It would be presumptuous and folly for us to do so. Such folly and presumption has been dared by others who have written and spoken on the subject. We care not to join them.

4. *The Limbo-Purgatory hypothesis.* According to Roman Catholic theology the souls of the dead are assigned forthwith to Limbo, Purgatory or Hell (*The Catholic Encyclopedia,* Vol. XII, p. 575).

Purgatory (from the Lat. *purgare* - to purge, purify, make clean) is defined by *The Catholic Encyclopedia* as "a place or condition of temporal punishment of those who though departing from this life in God's grace are not entirely free from venial fault, or have not fully paid the satisfaction due to their transgressions" (Vol. XII., p. 575). Such punishment is said to be due even after sin itself has been pardoned by God. Presumably purgatory eventually purges whatever defilement has been inbred by original sin, or such personal defilement as has lingered on, though forgiven.

The 1961 *Encyclopaedia Britannica* notes that: "Such souls continue to be members of the church; that they are helped by the suffrages of the living — that is, by prayers, alms, and other good works, and more especially by the sacrifice of the mass" (Vol. 18, p. 775B). It is also noted that although they are detained in purgatory until "the last farthing is paid" (Mt. 5:26), their salvation is assured.

The doctrine is supported chiefly by reference to II Maccabeess XII, 42 seq. where mention is found of prayers for the dead. Fourteen apocryphal books of the inter-testamental period are accepted as canonical by Catholics, and are included in the Catholic Bible. Incidentally, this was also true of the translators of the King James Version of the Bible. They were, therefore, originally included therein by the authority of the King. In fact by royal edict a punishment of one year in prison and a thousand dollar fine was levied upon those who sought to publish the "authorized" version otherwise. Considering the fact that England was then but one step removed from Catholocism, the decree is understandable. Fortunately it was repealed and the spurious books deleted.

The Eastern Orthodox Church also affirms a somewhat similar dogma. The Longer Catechism of the Orthodox Church state: "Such souls as have departed with faith but without having had time to bring forth fruits meet for repentance may be aided toward attainment of a blessed resurrection by prayers offered in their behalf" (*Encyclopaedia Britannica,* Vol. XVIII, p. 575B).

Mormon theology, in substituting " 'baptism' for the dead" in the place of prayers for the dead is similarly deluding the bereaved with a false hope and teaching a doctrine that is seriously at variance with the Scriptures. It is plainly written in the Scriptures that apart from one's personal acceptance of the righteousness of Christ in lieu of one's own, there is no salvation. It is written: "As I live, saith the Lord, to me every knee shall bow, and every tongue shall confess to God. So then each one of us shall give account of himself to God" (Rom. 14:11, 12).

Such perversion of Biblical doctrine as is exhibited by the three schools of thought we have cited might be expected to precipitate a strong reaction. Indeed they have. And in conformity to the pendelum principle, it is manifested in an over-reaction. This is well illustrated by the contributor of the *Brittanica* article from which we have quoted. His comment is: "Rejection of an intermediate state after death follows the Protestant idea of salvation by faith as logically as the doctrine of purgatory results from the Catholic idea of justification by works." (*Ibid*)

If by the phrase, "the Protestant doctrine of justification by faith" is meant the currently popular extremist dogma of "justification by faith *alone*," the writer may be right in what he has said, but not so in what he has implied. No Biblical teaching is to be rejected and replaced with some other to provide an extremist alternate to an extremist fallacy. Such an alternate also will be fallacious. Rejection of the *Biblical* doctrine of an intermediate state after death by no means follows logically the *Biblical* doctrine of justification by faith.

Here is a case in which two negatives do not make a positive. They only make two postulates, both of which are in error. Such a poor exercise in logic both positions are. We refuse to be intimidated by pressure from either extreme.

We have almost left limbo "out on a limb" as we turned aside to consider the relevance of certain other facets of Romanist dogma. In Romanist theology there are two limbos to be noted. *Limbo Patrum* (of the fathers) is said to be "the place where those were detained who died before the atonement of Christ" (*The New Schaff-Herzog Encyclopedia*, Vol. 6, p. 490). It is believed to have ceased to exist when Christ "went and preached to the spirits in prison" (I Peter 3:19). Recall that current Protestant theory holds that the same thing happened to Abraham's Bosom when Christ ascended into heaven.

If indeed the subjects of Christ's enigmatic preaching mission are said to have received *any* benefit therefrom much less salvation (of which things the text actually says nothing), the verse is far too limited in terms of those who were addressed to accommodate the "fathers" of the whole of the pre-Christian era. How often so much is made of so little.

Limbo Infantrum (or pueorum) is said to be "the place where the souls of infants dying without Christ are detained." (*Ibid*) It is taught there is no actual suffering there. Though they are excluded from the "Beatific Vision" of Heaven, they exist also outside the borders of Hell. The Scriptures have very little to say about the state of deceased infants. The cherished and comforting tradition that the innocent go to heaven, or shall in the last day, is based on inferences drawn from a very few and quite meager texts, such as: 1) the ambiguous hope David expressed concerning his deceased son born of Bathsheba (II Sam. 12:23), 2) Jesus' likewise ambiguous remark concerning "little children," to the effect that "to such belongeth the kingdom of heaven" (Mt. 19:14) and 3) his enigmatic statement that "in heaven their angels do always behold the face of my Father" (Mt. 18:10). The most direct statement which can be cited is found in the words with which He closes the Parable of the Ninety and Nine recorded in Matthew's Gospel. In the verses which immediately follow the above cited quotation He says, "Even so it is not the will of your Father who is in heaven that one of these little ones should perish" (v. 14). Of that we may be sure. But a similar expression is found with reference to all mankind (II Peter 3:9). If Mt. 18:14 is to be offered as a proof text that all "little ones" shall go to heaven then II Peter 3:9 may be offered as proof that eventually all mankind will go to heaven. Indeed the text is so used by the Universalists. It is as positive in its affirmation concerning the will of God as is the other.

In concluding our discussion of Roman Catholic theology concerning the state of the dead, we observe that in several

THE INTERIM STATE OF THE DEAD

respects it appears as an inverted model of the popular evangelical model. The semi-intermediate state revision of evangelicalism holds that the irrevocably redeemed (those who have "trusted" in Christ) go directly to heaven. In Catholicism the irrevocably dammed (those who "die in stubborn rebellion against God") go directly to hell. In the evangelical model the wicked are retained in a holding place (Hades), from whence they are to be brought forth in the last day and judged, then cast into hell to be tormented forever. In the Catholic model it is those marked for heaven who are detained in a holding place (purgatory). These, given the help of the suffrages of the living — alms, masses and the like — may gain release from their temporal state to enjoy the Beatific Vision of heaven forever.

Roman Catholicism seems to have no clear doctrine of a final judgment embracing all mankind. In a sense this is true also of evangelicalism. The one almost seems to be a studied attempt to balance out the other. In the papal system the irrevocably dammed are heisted off to hell at the time of death to suffer there forever without benefit of trial or formal judgment. In the popular evangelical system the irrevocably redeemed (eternally secure believers who put their "trust" in Christ) are hoisted up to heaven at the time of their death to enjoy bliss forever — and this too without benefit of formal judgment. About the only difference in the format, aside from who the persons are and the nature of their final estate is that in the evangelical model the ascent into heaven by the redeemed is viewed by many as only a temporary expedient. More and more it is being taught that at the rapture they will be called upon to leave heaven and come back to earth for a three and a half to seven year space-shuttle type experience in the clouds. After that they shall be obliged to put in a thousand years on earth. Moreover the kingdom which they are to share is faulted in that it is actually a rod of iron affair with Christ's kingdom subjects rebellious at heart and biding their time for an opportunity to revolt. The kingdom is said to be further marred by an earth-encircling war precipitated by the loosing of Satan. And that is not all. More commonly it is also being taught that the redeemed shall never return to heaven. Heaven (of a sort) will be shriveled and miniaturized to earth proportions and brought down and implanted upon earth. "So shall we ever be with the Lord," according to popular theory. With such a view we dissent vigorously.

5. *The Universalist View.* Universalists appear to have no definitive doctrine of the interim state of the dead. Their focus is on the final state. As their self-designation, Universalists, implies they teach that all mankind will be saved in the end. Those who die in ignorance, unbelief and disobedience will be given a second chance after death. The time and circumstances are not made clear, but be such as it may, it is conjectured that the ignorant will become knowledgeable, the unbelieving will become convinced, and the disobedient, upon being made aware of the reality of the world beyond this one, its glories and joys, will act quickly to fulfill any requirements necessary to have a share in the eternal kingdom of God. Apparently the graciousness of God in giving all another chance will be appreciated so much and the riches and delights of heaven will be so attractive that one and all will take full advantage of the second chance given them.

Those who believe what has just been said are by far more numerous than the membership of the Universalist churches (Societies). As one might expect the doctrine of universal salvation without regard for what any one may have done (or may be) in this life offers little incentive for evangelism. If God will save everyone anyhow, somehow, why concern ourselves with the lost? Likewise the position taken offers little incentive for indoctrination and edification. Christian growth and church growth suffer sorely when it is taught that those who give themselves to the pursuits of this life will be saved without exception in the end. A screen title of a few years ago says it well— *"All This* (this world and its pleasures) *and Heaven Too."* Thus despite the popular appeal of the doctrine, the Universalists Societies are experiencing negative "growth." Reduced to less than 50,000 members 20 years ago, they escaped the threat of extinction by a merger with the Unitarians. Together they numbered only about 185,000 members in 1968.

The rationale for universalism is as follows: 1) The character of God demands that all shall be saved. Since Jehovah is a God of love (I Jn. 4:8, 16), merciful and gracious, slow to anger and abundant in loving kindness (Ex. 34:6, Ps. 108:8), One who does not always chide, neither keeps His anger forever (Ps. 103:9), and the judge of all the earth, He can be counted on to do right (that which is just), according to Abraham (Gen. 18:25). It follows that God could not and will not punish anyone for ever. A sentence to an eternity of punishment for a few years of wrong doing is incompatible with God's self-revelation of Himself in the Scriptures and in Christ Jesus.

2) Secondly, the Universalists note the words of II Peter 3:9, the parallel to one of the chief proof texts whereby Evangelicals teach the universal salvation of deceased infants (Matt. 18:14). Peter affirms "God is not willing that *any* should perish, but that all should come to repentance."

Universalists insist the term *any* is all inclusive, children and adults as well as infants, the wicked as well as the innocent.

3) Thirdly, by way of answering those who object that II Peter 3:9 only expresses God's desire, not His will in a determinate sense, Universalists cite Paul's argument in Romans 5:12-21 and I Corinthians 15:20-28 in which Christ is contrasted with Adam and presented as the second universal federal head of the human race. Universalists use these texts in much the same way that doctrinarians, both Catholic and Protestant theologians, use these Scriptures to teach the dogma of original sin and its corollary (the corollary of the dogma, that is), Total Hereditary Depravity. The logic and textual data used by the Universalists is at least as good as that used by the traditional dogmatists of the Augustinian genre. But the logic of neither is good enough to set aside the scores of Scriptures which serve to correct both extremist and perverse doctrines. These are discussed at length in the appendix, *The Big Lie: A Compilation and Analysis of the Deviations of Doctrine and Perversions of Practice Arising out of the Dogma of Original Sin.* (See pp. 330-350.)

The foregoing analysis and critique completes the survey of the variant views relative to the interim state of the dead. The survey was prefaced by an appraisal of nihilism. It seems equally appropriate to supplement both with a brief statement of the doctrine of conditional immortality, a point of view sometimes confused with sheer annihilationism and often disparaged as but a disguised form of various "no hell" theories, as for example, the "poof" theory of the Jehovah's Witnesses.

THE INTERIM STATE OF THE DEAD

3. *Conditional Immortality Views*

As an alternate to the foregoing schools of thought, strict annihilationism (nihilism) and innate immortality, there are those who offer an option called conditional immortality. The view is not regarded as a compromise, nor as a mediating position. Nonetheless it has some affinity with each of the two more prevalent views. To those cast on the horns of a dilemma, particularly with regard to the fate of the wicked, the doctrine of conditional immortality may provide a viable option and clarify a number of perplexing questions.

Basically, the doctrine affirms: (1) Life is a gift of God, sustained in the flesh through the processes of nature He has ordained and ever subject to His will. "In Him we live and move and have our being" (Acts 17:28). (2) Man is of himself mortal. Only the Creator "*hath* immortality" (I Timothy 6:16). (3) Mankind a) originally was "enclothed," so to speak, with immortality in that he had access to the Tree of Life (Gen. 2:9, 16); b) lost that privileged estate through Adam (Gen. 3:22-24) and became not only subject to death, but passed under sentence of death (Gen. 2:17, 3:19, 22); c) may regain the right (that is the promise to that right) of eating again of the tree of life through "the first resurrection" (Rev. 20:5b, 6, 22:14), the resurrection from the death of sin (Eph. 2:1-8, Rom. 6:2-11, Col. 2:12, 13); d) may realize the promise of God and actually regain the lost estate by the *resurrection* and/or transformation of the body (the second resurrection), and the *rapture* (I Cor. 15:20-55, I Thess. 4:13-18).

(4) The redeemed, though not innately immortal, may again "put on" immortality (lit., enclothe, Gr. *endusetai*, cf. Gal. 3:27. See I Cor. 15:53, 54.) (5) Unlike our Creator,

the everlasting "I am" who "only hath immortality," man the creature is subject to death, and always has been so, else there would have been no reason for the tree of life in Eden before man sinned. But unlike the other creatures that share this earth with us man has a spirit which came from God (Gen. 2:7, Eccles. 12:7). Man's spirit survives the death of the body (Acts 7:59, Lk. 16:22, 23). (6) The spirit of man, tabernacled in the body, through the second resurrection, the resurrection of the just and the unjust in the last day (Jn. 5:28, 29) shall appear before God in a great forensic judgment (Rev. 20:11-15).

(7) Subsequent to the judgment the unjust shall be cast into hell where they shall be punished according to their works, no more, no less (Rev. 20:12, 22:11, 12, II Cor. 5:10). The ultimate punishment is that to which they have ever been subject, (being creatures not the Creator) — annihilation (Rom. 6:23, II Thess. 1:9, 10, Mt. 10:28).

(8) The redeemed in Christ likewise appear before God in the final judgment, but unto commendation, not condemnation. By the grace of God and through His righteousness, not their own, they are privileged to enter into the new paradise, to eat of the tree of life, and in effect enclothe themselves with immortality (I Cor. 15:53, 54).

There are variants of interpretation among those who hold to the doctrine of conditional immortality, as with every other doctrine. We take occasion to note briefly two. (1) the materialistic kingdom — instant annihilation theory, and (2) the grace redemption — equitable punishment model. In both models it is only the unjust who shall be subject to extinction. The two views differ in their view of the fate of the wicked in that the latter holds the wicked are not forthwith and immediately annihilated. They "suffer punishment" in the lake of fire "according to their works." God does not withdraw His "life support systems" (Acts 17:28) until His holy and righteous justice is fully satisfied. Extinction (the loss of being) is the ultimate, rather than the immediate, punishment of those cast into hell.

Such a concept obviously runs contrary to more traditional views of man as innately immortal and hence absolutely indestructible. It nevertheless must be noted in a discussion seeking to be comprehensive in setting forth the variant views of the state of man subsequent to physical death.

1. *The Materialistic Kingdom — Instant Annihilation Theory.* The principal advocates of this theory are the Jehovah's Witnesses. The view follows the Scriptures to the extent that they recognize two major classes of people, the saved and the lost. However, they divide the saved into two castes: 1) "The little flock," (the 144,000 "elect" of their sect, the "Spirit begotten") and 2) "the Great Multitude." The first will be privileged to go to heaven where they shall live and reign with Jehovah. The second group represent the over-run of JW's. The magic number which the Russellites, or "Millennial Dawnists" were shooting for when the sect first began was 144,000. That number having long since been passed while Jehovah keeps embarrassing them by postponing the end of the world, they are obliged to make room in their theory for all the extras which now swell the ranks of their sect. These will spend eternity down here with Christ. Inasmuch as the JW's bait their hook with the perennially popular material-kingdom-right-down-here construction of end-time prophecy they find a lot of folk predisposed to buy their thesis when they show up at the front door. Christ, as a fellow creature (according to JW theology) will be Lord of this fire-purged, scraped and refurbished earth.

The wicked, at Christ's coming are immediately annihilated upon the sentence they receive at the last judgment. For them it is "poof" and it is all over in an instant as they are cast into hell and consumed like a blade of grass. Malachi 4:1 is treated as though it were of itself the whole of Jehovah's revelation concerning the wicked.

Armstrongism. The core of belief which marks the "World Wide Church of God," being kindredly Jewish, materialistic, and geocentric, and even more Jewish oriented, is closely parallel to the Jehovah's Witness scheme except for the caste system. Both constructions have some affinity with Rabbincal eschatology of the inter-testamental period.

2. *The Grace Redemption — Equitable Punishment* model is not, to our knowledge, the official position of any denomination, college or publishing company. It certainly is not the view of College Press, nor of its clientele generally.

The view follows basically the eight (8) point outline by which the general doctrine of conditional immortality was presented earlier. The variant now under discussion, the grace redemption — equitable punishment model, is so named because of its twofold emphasis: 1) The eternal bliss of the redeemed in Christ is theirs by grace and not according to their deserving. Those saved are such as have accepted the offer of Divine grace on God's terms. There may be degrees of reward in heaven, according to man's works. (See Mt. 5:12, 10:41, 42, Lk. 6:23, I Cor. 3:8-15 and such parables as the parable of the talents, Mt. 25:14-30, and of the pounds, Lk. 19:11-27, among others.) But "eternal life" is "the free gift (Gr. charisma) of God in Christ Jesus" (Rom. 6:23).

2) The second part of the title for the viewpoint under consideration is chosen to emphasize the punishment of the wicked will be an equitable punishment, individually assessed,

not a class judgment meted out to all as though the lost were all alike from the twelve year old lad who died while yet wrestling with the decision to accept Christ to Adolph Hitler—and even Satan, the beast and the false prophet. Proponents of the view are fully persuaded that salvation is only in Christ, and is extended by the grace of God in this life only. Hence those who die out of Christ go to hell. But some are, as it were, "beaten with few stripes, others with many" (Lk. 12:47, 48). Subsequently, having refused, ignored or been ignorant of the grace whereby they might have been saved through Christ, God ultimately withdraws from them whatever life support system(s) He may have used to sustain them in hell until His justice could be satisfied.

In brief, the view is that in the consummation of the ages the redeemed in Christ "through the exceeding riches of God's grace, in kindness towards us in Christ Jesus" (Eph. 2:7) shall "enter by the gates into the city" (the heavenly Jerusalem), where they shall enjoy the right to partake of the tree of life (Rev. 22:14). They will thus "put on" what Christ "hath" as One within the Godhead—immortality (I Cor. 15:53, 54, I Tim. 6:16). The unsaved shall "suffer punishment, even eternal destruction from the face of the Lord and the glory of His might (II Thess. 1:9). The punishment they shall "suffer" (feel, be aware of, be sentenced to endure) shall be according to their works, that is, according to the guilt for which they are personally accountable (Ezek. 18:20).

According to this view, the punishment of the wicked is non purgatorial, hence non redemptive. That is to say, it is not to burn out the dross, or otherwise condition them for entrance into heaven. It is punitive. And like capital punishment at the end of solitary confinement on death row it is finalized in death, hence final—everlasting. Proponents of the view do not pontificate, much less guess or assume to assess, the duration of the conscious aspect of their exposure to God's awesome judgment. They simply believe that the *wages* (Gr. *opsonion*, what one has *earned*) of sin, as opposed to the *free gift* (Gr. *charisma, unmerited favor*) of God (Rom. 6:23) will be delayed in the decree of God's judgment only by the degree of conscious punishment individually merited — as determined by a wise and just and merciful God — no more, no less (II Cor. 5:10, Rev. 20:12, 13, 22:11, 12).

Conclusion

In conclusion we can hardly say with the inspired penman of the book of Ecclesiastes, as he brought that literary monologue to an end: "This is the end of the matter; all has been heard." But we can share with him in his closing admonition, and the basis for it: "Fear God and keep his commandments; for this is the whole duty of man. For God will bring every work into judgment, with every hidden thing, whether it be good, or whether it be evil" (Eccl. 12:13, 14).

Many of the matters we have treated are worthy of further study. Indeed all has *not* been said, nor could it be said in a volume of this size. I trust my frankness will not be interpreted as closemindedness. No attempt has been made to hide behind the views of other writers, so as to disclaim personal responsibility in the event of disputation. For the most part I attempted to state my personal assessment of the various topics investigated. If readers are surprised at some of the things which have been written as a result of months of painstaking research, permit me to candidly acknowledge, I too am surprised. It has been a learning experience.

THE INTERIM STATE OF THE DEAD

Solomon once said, "much study is a weariness to the flesh" (Eccles. 12:12). To that observation I can add a hearty amen. On the other hand, it is stimulating to the soul. But it can also be quite upsetting to no end of preconceived and settled conclusions. We are all victims of what the late Dr. John Ralls so often called: "I-thought-you-checked-it" syndrome.

Permit me to close on a clear, positive note. There are certain facts which deserve to be re-emphasized. As Christians ours is a privileged state: Consider what awaits us should death overtake us ere Christ returns to claim His own:

1. At death the redeemed pass into a restive, quiescent state of comparative peace and tranquility — so much so they are represented in figure as "fallen asleep in Jesus" (I Thess. 4:14). The metaphor is not to be pressed too far. It is a relative expression. While they are said to "rest from their labors" (Rev. 14:13) it would be to overstate the case to say they are in a state of suspended animation, or hibernation. They certainly are not in a comatose state. Neither of the redeemed or the unredeemed can such be said. A number of Scriptures indicate a measure of consciousness, awareness, exists in the Sheol-Hades state: See I Sam. 28:11-19, Isa. 14:9, 10, Ezek. 32:31, Lk. 16:19-31, Rev. 6:9-11.

2. Man's final destiny is fixed at the point of physical death (Heb. 9:27, II Cor. 5:10, Rev. 20:12, 13, 22:11, 12). For the Christian this is a comforting thought. "To be absent from the body is to be at home with the Lord" (II Cor. 5:8, 9). While the fullness of that blessed estate awaits the resurrection and redemption of the body, our glorious destiny is fixed at the moment of death — if not before! "The Lord knoweth them that are his" (II Tim. 2:19). The separation of the redeemed and the unredeemed into the two compartments of Sheol-Hades is immediate. The day of judgment

is forensic, declarative, not an information gathering occasion. God's righteous judgments shall be vindicated before the assembled universe. It is written that "the books shall be opened" (Rev. 20:12) and every man shall be judged according to the things written in the books, according to their works" (Rev. 20:12, 13). The reading of the record is not to inform the Judge. It is to vindicate the judgment He has already exercised in gathering His own into Abraham's bosom, (the Jewish metaphor for the state of the redeemed) or Paradise and the consigning of the wicked to lower Sheol (Tartarus).

3. Finally, the hope of the redeemed at long last shall be "eternally secure." This is underscored by an impressive array of Divine promises and pronouncements. Those troubled by fears lest the redeemed in a restored paradise shall repeat the debacle of Adam and Eve should consider these blessed assurances:

1) This corruptible and mortal being shall put on incorruption, immortality (I Cor. 15:53, 54).

2) To assure this promise the redeemed in the renewed paradise of God will have full access to the tree of life (Rev. 2:7, 22:2, 14).

3) The redeemed, unlike Adam and Eve, and ourselves in our present state, will no longer have physical bodies as a prime avenue of temptation (I Cor. 15:44, see context vs. 35-38).

4) Moreover, Satan, the deceiver and tempter, along with the beast and false prophet, and as many as have served him, will be consigned to the lake of fire "for ever and ever" (Rev. 20:10).

5) By way of contrast, the redeemed will dwell in the City of God, new Jerusalem, prepared for those who love and obey Him (Jn. 14:2, Hebr. 11:11-16, Rev. 22:14).

THE INTERIM STATE OF THE DEAD

6) As though that were not enough, in the new Paradise of God He will no more be but an eventide visitor, as in Eden. He shall *dwell* with His people — not just "in spirit," nor just symbolically, as in the wilderness tabernacle, nor only through some representative person. "God *Himself* shall be with us" (Rev. 7:13-17, 21:3).

7) "There shall be no more curse" (Rev. 22:3).

8) "And death shall be no more" (Rev. 21:4). Both death and hades shall be cast into the lake of fire (Rev. 20:14).

9) Moreover, God's name (authority) shall be on our foreheads (that is our mind). This is the ultimate fulfillment of the prophecy of Jer. 31:33. And we shall "serve him" (Rev. 22:4 & 3). This is the counterpart of the basis on which the judgment of God is said to be visited upon the unredeemed. In speaking of them as having the mark of the beast upon their forehead and their hands, the one being a symbol of the mind and will, the other of service, it is said of them that their minds were given over to Satan and they served him instead of the living God, our Maker.

10) The climax of these assurances is that which concludes the third and final tabloid view given John of the final state of the redeemed. We shall "live and reign (with God and the Lamb) for ever and ever" (Gr. from the ages unto the ages) Rev. 22:5. Thus it is written:

> When this corruptible shall have put on incorruption, and this mortal shall have put on immortality, then shall come to pass the saying that is written, Death is swallowed up in victory, O Death, where is *thy victory?* O Grave, where is thy *sting?* The sting of death is sin, and the power of sin is the law. But thanks be to God who giveth us the victory through our Lord Jesus Christ. Wherefore, my beloved brethren, be ye steadfast, unmovable, always abounding in the work of the Lord, forasmuch as as ye know your labor is not in vain in the Lord (I Cor. 15:54-58).

Appendix

Excursus on Original Sin

THE BIG LIE

LIBERALISM

CATHOLICISM **FUNDAMENTALISM**

- Ritualism
- Assumption of Mary
- MARIOLATRY
- Immaculate Conception
- Works of Supererogation
- **SALVATION BY WORKS (ALONE)**
- Sacradotalism
- Baptismal Regeneration
- "Water Salvation"
- Confirmation
- **INFANT BAPTISM**

- Ethicism
- Social Progress
- THE SOCIAL GOSPEL

- Eternal Security
- "Raise your Hand"
- Just "believe ye have received"
- *Faith* based on "Experience"
- **SALVATION BY FAITH (ALONE)**
- Praying Through
- The Mourner's Bench
- Altar Calls
- Calvinism
- "Free Grace"
- Election
- **PREDESTINATION**

TOTAL HEREDITARY DEPRAVITY

DOGMA OF ORIGINAL SIN

A Compilation and Analysis of the Deviations of Doctrine and Perversions of Practice Arising Out of the Dogma of Original Sin.

APPENDIX - THE BIG LIE

The most noxious seed ever sown in the soil of the Christian faith is the dogma of original sin. Every branch of the Christian doctrine of salvation has subsequently been corrupted. Some one has said, "one of the nicest things about telling the truth is that one doesn't have to remember what has been said." On the other hand, telling a lie is like stepping off onto a ski slide. There is no stopping until one hits the bottom. The bigger the lie the more precipitous the slide. For every lie that is told, another, and another, etc., etc., etc., must be told. Such is the history of the "big lie" in denominational dogma.

The dogma of original sin produced the doctrine of total heredity depravity — the teaching that man is by nature, in consequence of Adam's transgression, dead in sin from the moment of conception. This doctrine is generally attributed to "Saint" Augustine who lived in the latter half of the 4th century. Historians, however, point out that Augustine should only be credited with the particular form of the doctrine attributed to him. He was a compiler, not an originator.

A Jewish sect as early as the Exilic period is known to have taught a doctrine of similar import. This is attested by the vigorous refutation of such contemporary prophets as Jeremiah and Ezekiel (See Jer. 31:29, 30 and Ezekiel 18, particularly vs. 1-4 and 19, 20). Notwithstanding the thoroughness and finality of the prophet's refutation the teaching persisted, supported by false application of such passages as Exodus 20:5 and Psalms 51:5.

The Jewish form of the doctrine sought only to provide excuse for man's personal wickedness. It was argued he came by it naturally. Father was a sinner, his father was a sinner, his father, also, etc., etc. The phrase that was coined to express this was a cute one — "The fathers have eaten sour grapes and the children's teeth are set on edge" (Ezek. 18:2; cf. Jer. 31:29, 30). The modern behavioristic school of psychology would find in the ancient Jewish sect minds kindred to their own.

The Augustinian doctrine is a perversion of deeper dye. Not the consequences only, not even just a susceptibility or tendency to sin, but the very guilt of Adam's sin — this too is transmitted unto all generations through the process of procreation! This is the big lie in denominational dogma — the most noxious seed ever sown in the soil of the Christian faith. Behold how every branch of the Christian doctrine of salvation has been corrupted by it.

Part I

APOSTASIES CULMINATING IN THE DOCTRINE OF SALVATION BY WORKS (ALONE)

INFANT BAPTISM

Out of the doctrine of total hereditary depravity grew the practice of infant "baptism." (Quotation marks may be omitted, insofar as the mode is concerned at the outset, for the Roman Church as well as the Greek branch in Augustine's time immersed, and continued to do so for several centuries afterwards.) If the doctrine of total hereditary depravity be allowed then infant "baptism" becomes mandatory even if it isn't commanded, alluded to or allowance made for it, in the New Testament. As soon as it began to be believed that "there are babes in hell not a span long" (because of the transmission of Adam's guilt) mothers began to clamor for their babies to be admitted to the rite of baptism.

APPENDIX - THE BIG LIE

The reason is not hard to understand. If babies are born sinners, then (since baptism is for the remission of sin)* obviously babies should be baptized at the earliest time possible.

SACERDOTALISM, BAPTISMAL REGENERATION, ETC.

Out of the practice of infant baptism arose a cluster of closely related perversions of Christian doctrine. Obviously the "baptism" of infants posed a problem. In that infants can not fulfill the requirement of faith (Mark 16:16) it was necessary to reason around this requirement. This was accomplished (1) by attributing "priestly" powers to the officiating ministers (sacerdotalism, the basic ingredient of the Romanist hierarchial system), or (2) by assuming that the faith of believing parents sanctifies their children, through baptism. The logical outgrowth of such reasoning is the doctrine of baptismal regeneration (water salvation, as it is sometimes scornfully called).

Our brethren, in this the heydey of the faith only cult, are often charged with teaching and practicing baptismal regeneration. To make such a charge is to neither understand the terminology employed nor the teaching and practice of our people. Baptismal regeneration is a necessary corollary of infant baptism. In our insistence upon believer's baptism we reject the very conditions that necessitate such a doctrine. No, not the baptism of penitent believers "for the remission of (personal) sins" (Acts 2:38) but the "baptism" of unwitting (and often unwilling) infants for the remission of Adam's sins — this is "baptismal regeneration."

---

* NOTE: The notion that "baptism for remission of sins" violates the principle of justification by faith is of much later origin, being a reaction to the doctrine of sacerdotalism which arose out of the practice of infant baptism.

John 3:3-5 clearly informs us we must be spirit begotten (regenerated by the Holy Spirit) as well as be born of the water to enter into the kingdom of heaven. Thus we insist that baptism be reserved for those who have first been evangelized by the Christian gospel, who profess their faith in Christ thereby, and who come repentantly surrendering body and soul to the Lord Jesus Christ.

CONFIRMATION

Another outgrowth of The Big Lie is confirmation, as practiced throughout the Paedo-baptist denominations. In a society where it was customary for the parents to make life's greatest decision for their children, even to their occupations and partners in marriage, it was not at all difficult to develop this corollary to infant baptism also. The child, "baptized" without his (or her) knowledge or consent, upon reaching the age of accountability was required to confirm (personally accept) the decision the parents had made for him.

SALVATION BY WORKS

The "leaven of the pharisees" (Matt. 16:6), the doctrine that salvation is secured by ritual was infused into the "lump" of Christian doctrine by the foregoing development. Two divergent movements have grown out of such a notion — Roman Catholicism and Protestant Liberalism.

ROMAN CATHOLICISM

Roman Catholicism represents one end to which the doctrine of total hereditary depravity has led. Besides the foregoing a number of kindred errors peculiar to the papist system have arisen. The doctrine of the immaculate conception (introduced to spare the Christ child the guilt of Adam's transgression) and more recently the doctrine of the assumption of Mary are contingencies. Purgatory, works of supererogation and a number of other encrustations are other contingencies. The bridge between these and the Augustinian dogma is the sacerdotal system.

Protestant Liberalism

Protestant liberalism has avowed to cut itself adrift from all tradition, to seek truth wherever it may be found. But the road to salvation blazed by the papists is the road these would travel also. Only the vehicles in which they would have us travel differ. These too expect to find salvation (whatever that may mean to a liberal protestant) *by works*.

Ethicism and sociology replace the vehicles in which the Romanists expect to ride up to the pearly gates. Liberal protestants may not be too sure the road they are traveling leads to eternal life in that "better country," but to whatever ultimate goal they do expect to arrive, if any, they are sure the way to get there is by "works of righteousness which we do ourselves" to borrow a phrase from Paul, in which he denied the very thing the liberals avow! (Titus 3:5).

AUTHOR'S NOTE: The tracing of the doctrine of salvation by works is not a difficult task. The lines of dependency, especially in the papal system, are clear; and are generally conceded. That protestant liberals share the concept of salvation by works is a fact of common knowledge, although it may not be as generally recognized that they are indebted to the Romanists for the development of the idea. In Part Two we wish to show that 20th century Fundamentalism also, in its teaching of "salvation by faith alone" is likewise an outgrowth of the same basic error.

The doctrine of salvation by faith (alone) stands today as the antithesis of the

— continued next page

WHAT THE BIBLE SAYS ABOUT THE END TIME

Part Two

APOSTASIES CULMINATING IN THE DOCTRINE OF
SALVATION BY FAITH (ALONE)

(Synopsis of Part One)

In Part One we trace the dependency of the papal doctrine of salvation (by works) upon the dogma of original sin. We showed too that modern protestant liberalism is nourished from the same stock. In the instance of the latter the dependency is akin to such a growth as mistletoe, a vegetable parasite which derives its life from the tree upon which it feeds.

The doctrine of salvation by works as developed by the papists is an offshoot of sacerdotalism, which is an offshoot of infant baptism, an offshoot of the doctrine of the total hereditary depravity of man, growing out of The Big Lie — the dogma of original sin.

Modern protestant liberalism is in no sense native to such a system, but like any other parasite it has enough affinity to that upon which it feeds to sustain itself thereby. The affinity in this case is the doctrine we have taken pains to expose. Whether the doctrine be in its papal form (salvation by ritual) or its protestant form (salvation by social progress) it is utterly false to the Christian doctrine of salvation.

---

doctrine of salvation by works (alone, or otherwise), but the roots thereof are the same. Fundamentalists simply represent another offshoot of the same parent stock. Not since Adam and Eve ate of the forbidden tree and introduced sin and death into this world has one act of man had such dire consequences as the introduction into the church of the dogma of original sin. In Part Two we propose to refute this dogma and discuss also the other branch thereof — 20th century Fundamentalism.

336

APPENDIX - THE BIG LIE

In Part Two we wish to examine the tenets of fundamentalism, and to show its dependency likewise upon The Big Lie. It has been truly said, "The old serpent, the Devil, has a forked tongue!"

THE DOGMA DEFINED

The dogma of original sin finds its classic expression in the official confession of the Presbyterian Church in the U.S.A.:

"By this sin (eating of the forbidden fruit) they (Adam and Eve) fell from their original righteousness and communion with God, and so became dead in sin, and wholly defiled in all the faculties and parts of body and soul. They being the root of all mankind, the guilt of this sin was imputed and the same death in sin and corrupted nature conveyed to all their posterity descending from them by ordinary generation. From this original corruption whereby we are indisposed, disabled, and made opposite to all good, and wholly inclined to evil, do proceed all actual transgressions." (Revised edition, 1939, p. 25, 26).

PREDESTINATION

Such a dogma calls for action — strong, immediate action — on the part of God, or man, else all would be lost. No worse thing could be said of the devil himself than the dogma has said of all Adam's race. One branch of theology has man taking the initiative to spare the race the guilt and condemnation of Adam's transgression. By the introduction of the practice of infant baptism the depraved child is supposed to be provided a way of escape. Another branch of theology has God taking the initiative. With this branch we now wish to deal.

Some such doctrine as predestination seems a logical necessity if the major premise of the dogmatists be allowed to stand. If a child is born "dead" in sin, "utterly indisposed, disabled and made opposite to all good," nothing the child could possibly do, or ever hope to do, could count for righteousness. The fact is, these theories would remind us, a dead man can't do anything! He must first be made alive, and that is a Divine prerogative and function. Thus these theorists would have us believe salvation is wholly of God, and not by anything which we may do ourselves. Our fate is wholly in the hands of God who has predestined (predestined, foreordained) all things.

How then shall anyone be saved? This is a matter of God's arbitrary election. God, being both just and merciful, elects some to be lost, others to be saved. All deserve to go to hell in consequence of the guilt of Adam. Those whom God elects to go to hell receive their just dessert. Those whom God elects to go to heaven are just as deserving of hell but God, to show Himself merciful, elects that they be saved. This is the Calvinistic doctrine of salvation. Calvinists would dignify this farce by calling it the doctrine of the Divine Sovereignty of God. He arbitrarily elects some to participate in the "free grace" of Christ's "finished work on Calvary." He elects, equally as arbitrarily, to allow others to be lost, that His justice may also be vindicated.

The Mourners' Bench*

Out of such a theory came the mourners' bench, altar calls, and "praying through" ceremonies so common to the fundamentalist movement. Herein is one of the paradoxes of

---

* See addenda at the close of this Excursus.

fundamentalism. While professing to believe in salvation by faith alone rather than in "works of righteousness which we do ourselves," they have devised a system all their own, having no relevance to the New Testament record of conversion.

Instead of an open confession of Jesus as the Christ the Son of the Living God, fundamentalists instruct sinners to "raise your hand" (while every head is bowed and every eye is closed). That the New Testament provides no authority for such a procedure seems to bother them not at all.

When as many as can be persuaded at a given service to raise their hands have indicated they would have the evangelist pray for them the altar call is given. They are now exhorted to show they "mean business" by coming to the mourners' bench to be prayed through. This is generally required as a deliberate alternative to Christian baptism. The latter would be "a work." But praying through is not a work! How deceived and deceiving can these deceivers be? That which is of faith ("faith cometh by hearing and hearing by the word of Christ," Rom. 10:17) is called a work, and that which is altogether a work of righteousness which men do of themselves, being not by commandment of Christ but by order of fundamentalist evangelists, is pawned off as salvation by faith alone!

Salvation by Faith Alone

There is no such thing as salvation by faith alone, not even in the practice of those who shout such a doctrine from the tallest transmitters towering above our housetops. Fundamentalists have substituted works of their own devising for "the obedience of faith" (Romans 1:5, 6:16-18, 16:26). "Raise your hands," "come to the altar," "pray through," "say, pray for me . . . (name of the evangelist.)" These "works" are required of every seeker for salvation, after which they are told, "just believe you have received." Salvation by faith alone is only a catchy phrase to "catch" the ignorant and unsuspecting. The doctrine itself was conceived as a necessary corollary to the doctrine of election whereby it is assumed God "gives faith" to those upon whom His "free grace" has been "elected" to fall. His Divine Sovereignty foreordains who is to be elected, who is to be omitted. We may agonize and plead and pray at the mourners' bench for God to give us faith, but we dare not "confess with our mouth Christ Jesus as Lord" and "be baptized for the remission of sins." That would be to minimize the grace of God. Salvation could not be the "free gift of God" if we would so work for it. Apparently praying through, sweating it out on a mourners' bench, is not work. But simply yielding oneself, body and soul, to the will of God so completely that one can be represented as having died, and been buried, and raised to walk in newness of life — that's work! Can you believe it?

Eternal Security

The cap sheath of this strange mode of reasoning is the doctrine of Eternal Security — "once saved, always saved." It is not generally recognized how necessary this doctrine is to the anti-be baptized cult. In order to hold that salvation is by faith alone these theorists have to teach that not only baptism, but "continuing steadfastly in the Apostles' doctrines, fellowship, the breaking of bread and prayers," and other aspects of the Christian life likewise are just "electives." They may determine the extent of reward in heaven, the size and splendor of our mansion, but not our entrance into heaven itself.

APPENDIX - THE BIG LIE

FAITH BASED ON EXPERIENCE

That such doctrines are completely at variance with scores of scriptures does not seem to disturb the fundamentalists one whit. Theirs is a "faith" based on "experience." That experience may be, and often is, a form of self-hypnosis, experienced under the emotional strain and suggestion of the "prayer workers" whose wailing and entreating and exhorting destroys all power to reason. This experience, nonetheless, is made a basis for belief that one has been gloriously and everlastingly elected to salvation, brought under the blood of Christ, and glory bound.

CONCLUSION: Astronomers used to believe that the earth was flat, that it stood still, and that the sun, moon and stars revolved about it. Error of such magnitude led to so many difficulties that when King Alphonso of Spain was being instructed by his court astronomers, he shook his head and said, "Even I could have told the Creator of a better plan."

The difficulties were not with the Creator's plan. They were due to man's false reasoning. When Copernicus, some years afterward, demonstrated the true nature of the solar system the difficulties of which King Alphonso complained were solved.

In like manner the myriad of errors growing out of the Big Lie will never be solved by arguing with our religious neighbors about infant baptism, baptism for remission of sins, predestination, election, etc. The Big Lie itself must be exposed, and God's truth be made clear. The axe needs to be laid to the root of this noxious weed that has become as a great tree.

SUPPLEMENT: The foregoing remarks are not intended to be scholarly or exhaustive, but rather to summarize and expose in terms the ordinary person can understand the terrible fruitage of The Big Lie. As a supplement to the foregoing, a critical analysis of the nature and effect of Adam's transgression is hereby appended.

THE DOGMA OF ORIGINAL SIN

We have reviewed the devious doctrines growing out of The Big Lie — the dogma of original sin. In this supplement we wish to examine the dogma directly. This is no great task, provided that we limit ourselves to the teaching of the scriptures on the subject. The sin of Adam, and the direct and immediate consequences are discussed in Romans 5:12-21 and I Cor. 15:21, 22. An incidental allusion to Adam's transgression is found in I Tim. 2:14.

ADAM'S SIN

From Genesis 3 we learn Adam and Eve ate of the forbidden fruit as an act of willful disobedience. The immediate consequence was that "their eyes were opened." Inasmuch as the tree they had eaten of was the tree of knowledge of good and evil, the inference is that they passed from the state of innocency into the state of moral accountability. In this regard they exhibited a sense of shame at their physical nakedness and set about to cover themselves as best they could. They apparently had no evil imaginations prior to their temptation and fall. The second consequence was that they were "afraid" when they heard the voice of God and immediately undertook to hide themselves as best they could.

WAS ADAM ORIGINALLY IMMORTAL?

At this point we need to note man was not created immortal. Were this so, what purpose would have been served by the tree of life? The fact that subsequent to their transgression they were barred from the tree of life is evidence the perpetuity of their lives was conditioned upon access to that tree. By the sweat of his brow Adam might, and did, eke out a living for himself and his bride for a time, but it was a losing battle. He died, as his posterity have done. Thus God had warned: "Of the tree of knowledge of good and evil, thou shalt not eat of it, for in the day thou eatest thereof *dying, thou shalt surely die"* Gen. 2:7. (Italics indicate the more exact meaning of the Hebrew text.)

Adam and Eve came under the sentence of death when they sinned. Like a fish thrown into a stagnant pool, gilling laboriously to escape impending death, so Adam and Eve now turned out of the garden into the cursed earth beyond the gates of Eden, by toil, sweat and pain "lived" for some time and even begat children, but death was inevitable. Inasmuch as the garden with the tree of life was subsequently removed from earth all Adam's posterity passed under the sentence of death.

DID ADAM DIE SPIRITUALLY?

Did Adam and Eve die spiritually the day they sinned? This may be allowed, for sin separates from God (Isa. 59:2) and the basic idea in the Biblical usage of the word "death" is that of separation. The separation of the soul from the body is called death. (This is physical, ordinary death.) The ultimate and final separation of the soul from God, after the judgment, is called "the second death" (Rev. 20:14). The New Testament refers to those in this present life who are separated from God by reason of sin as "dead through trespasses" (Eph. 2:2, 5). Reasoning from the dogma of original sin, fundamentalists are inclined to interpret the term in its literal sense, that is in the sense of one being without life, feeling, sensibility, consciousness, inclinations, capacity to act, etc. In such case the sinner is thereby rendered wholly dependent upon the "quickening" grace of God to even so much as have the capacity to believe on the Lord Jesus Christ, to know and love God, trust in Christ for salvation, etc. But this is a decided and obvious misuse of the figure of speech. We repeat, the basic idea in the Biblical usage of the term is that of separation. In the sense in which the scriptures use the term we may allow that Adam and Eve entered the state of spiritual death upon becoming transgressors.

ARE WE ALL BORN "DEAD" SPIRITUALLY?

Are all men "born dead" spiritually in consequence of Adam's transgression? This is the paramount issue involved in this discussion. Exponents of the dogma of original sin teach that all are "stillborn" spiritually. This is a strange wresting of the scriptures. Adam and Eve suffered physical death in consequence of their sin but their descendants certainly are not all born dead (physically), *else the race itself would have died at the stem.* On what basis must we assume all are born dead *spiritually?* Neither by analogy nor by any Word of the Lord may we draw such a conclusion. Paul's statement in I Cor. 15:21, 22 can not rightly be so construed. If spiritual death is the death he is speaking of, then all men will be saved. The text reads: "As in Adam all die, so also in Christ shall all be made alive." The Universalists are no more in error in using the first half of the verse to teach universal redemption through Christ than are the dogmatists in using the first half of the verse to teach universal Adamic guiltiness. They are no more wrong, *but they are also no more right.*

I Corinthians 15:21, 22

The context of I Corinthians 15:21, 22 makes it unmistakably plain that the death spoken of is physical death, for the resurrection spoken of is certainly the resurrection of the body. Here we do have a parallel. All die (physically) in Adam. And all are made alive (physically) in Christ. Hear ye Him: "The hour cometh, in which all that are in the tombs shall hear His voice, and shall come forth; they that have done good unto the resurrection of life; and they that have done evil unto the resurrection of judgment" (John 5:28, 29).

Romans 5:12-21

Romans 5:12-21 is not so easily explained, at least not in so few words. But when explained in the light of the doctrine of inherited guilt a far greater difficulty is raised than any that are explained thereby. It is impossible to escape the doctrine of universal redemption if universal guilt is reckoned as passing upon men in consequence of Adam's transgression. Not all parts of Paul's analogy are readily comprehensible but this much is plainly propounded: Everything that has been "passed upon" man by reason of Adam's transgression is canceled by the gracious act of Christ. To the extent Adam's sin is said to affect us, to the same extent Christ's righteousness is said to nullify that effect. The same number of persons affected by the one are said to be affected by the other. If the solitary act of Adam *condemned all men* to spiritual death (apart from any personal accountability) then one solitary act of Christ *redeemed all men,* apart from any personal, individual accountability. Since all men are not "saved" just because Christ is Savior, all men are not sinners just because Adam was a sinner. The one state of being or relationship is no more automatic nor universal than is the other. What Paul is actually saying is not that we inherit Adam's guilt, but simply that Adam introduced sin, condemnation and death into the world. Thus Christ came to bring righteousness, justification and eternal life. To say more than this is to say too much. *If the guilt of Adam's sin is the ground of our condemnation then Adam is greater than Christ, for more by far are thereby "made sinners" (if this interpretation be allowed) than are "made righteous" through Christ.*

Guilt vs. Consequences

The dogmatists fail to distinguish between the consequences of an act and the guilt of that act. The children of adulterers, drunkards, murderers, thieves and such like suffer many of the consequences *but none of the guilt.* Exodus 20:5 is often cited to support the doctrine that guilt is inherited. The passage reads, "I Jehovah, thy God, am a jealous God, visiting the iniquities of the fathers upon the children, upon the third and upon the fourth generation of them that hate me." But the next verse reads, "and showing loving kindness unto thousands [of generations, *see marginal note*] of them that love me and keep my commandments."

Ps. 51:5 is the classic scripture used to support the doctrine of inherited guilt. "Behold I was brought forth in iniquity, and in sin did my mother conceive me." If every distress wrought cry in the Psalms were to be taken as a basis of

APPENDIX - THE BIG LIE

Christian doctrine the confusion would be even greater than it now is. Was David stating a truth that is to be interpreted as being universally applicable? The words were spoken after his own great sin of adultery. He undoubtedly was reminded of a point of law recorded in Deut. 23:2, "A bastard shall not enter into the assembly of Jehovah; even to the tenth generation shall none of his enter into the assembly of Jehovah." From Ruth 4:12-22 and Matt. 1:2-6 we find that David was of the tenth generation to arise from the base fornication of Judah (See Genesis 38:24-30.). Contemplating his own great sin of like nature David may well have surmised himself to be born and conceived in sin.* But the distressed cry wrung from the heart of the guilty king is hardly a basis for Christian doctrine, especially since the only scriptures he could possibly appeal to in support of such excuse for his folly is a part of the law that was nailed to the cross and made of no effect by Christ's redemptive death.

THE PROPHETS' ANSWER

Scriptures such as Ex. 20:5 and Deut. 23:2 apparently were as misconstrued by the Jews as they are by dogmatists of our generation. The Jews found in such scriptures excuse for themselves. "We can't help it. We are born that way." Yea, "The fathers have eaten sour grapes and the children's teeth are set on edge" (Jer. 31:29, Ezek. 18:2). Therefore God, through His prophets, cried out: "As I live, saith the Lord Jehovah, ye shall not have occasion any more to use

---

* The word David used for "conceive" is not *harah*, the common word for human conception, but *yacham* — animal "heat." This is the sole such use of *yacham* in all the Bible.
 In this context that needs to be noted.

this proverb in Israel" (Ezek. 18:3, cf. Jer. 31:29). Having thus spoken God announced through Jeremiah the coming of a new covenant (vs. 31-34) which the Hebrew writer declares to be fulfilled in Christ (Heb. 8:8-13), and through Ezekiel God declares:

> The soul that sinneth, it shall die; the son shall not bear the iniquity of the father, neither shall the father bear the iniquity of the son; the righteousness of the righteous shall be upon him, the wickedness of the wicked shall be upon him (Ezek. 18:20).

This should end the matter. Unfortunately it has not done so. Thus one more observation is in order. The practice of infant baptism arose to meet the emergency created by the dogma of original sin. Noting the fact that the scriptures teach baptism for the remission of sins, the baptism of infants was introduced to remit the inherited sin of newborn babes lest they should die in infancy and thus dying (physically) before they were old enough to be evangelized they should go to hell by reason of being spiritually dead also. But note that every consequence of Adam's sin, real and imaginary, Biblical and traditional, continues in force *after baptism*. Male children, "baptized" as well as unbaptized, must battle weeds in every garden, lawn or field they may have to till. They must sweat, toil and die. Female children likewise suffer the same lot imposed upon Eve, "baptized" or not! What kind of remission of sin is this that remits the sin but wreaks out vengeance upon the remisees nonetheless?

Does one say, it is not the physical consequences of Adam's sin but the inherited guilt that baptism remits? The issue is unchanged. If baptism is for the remission of inherited guilt how is it then that the offspring of those who

APPENDIX - THE BIG LIE

have been baptized still inherit Adam's guilt? Is Adam's guilt remitted or isn't it?

This is too much. It is assumed that infants inherit the sin of Adam and therefore must be baptized. Yet they remain cursed with that guilt despite baptism to pass it on to the next generation. Does God thus mock us?

The dogma of original sin is the biggest lie Satan has told since the day he told the first lie to the hapless pair he caused to be driven out of Eden. "He is a liar, and the father thereof" (Jn. 8:44). Only the world's biggest liar could have conceived The Big Lie which has proven to be the most noxious weed ever sown in the soil of the Christian faith—the Dogma of Original Sin.

THE MOURNER'S BENCH

Whence is it? Is it of God, or of man?

Charles G. Finney, celebrated evangelist of the early 19th century and President of Oberlin College, delivered a series of lectures on evangelism in 1838 which, by popular demand, was made available to the general public in book form. Fleming H. Revell & Co. secured publishing rights. A copy of the second edition, entitled *Revivals of Religion* dated October 22, 1868, is before me.

Evangelist Finney, probably more than any other man, popularized the mourner's bench (or anxious seat, as he preferred to call it) as he led the vanguard of revivalists in the Great Religious Awakening that swept Europe and America a century ago. On pages 254-56 of the 1868 edition, Mr. Finney wrote in defense of the anxious seat. The following quotation is taken verbatim from p. 254. Speaking of an "awakened sinner," Mr. Finney wrote:

If you say to him, "There is the anxious seat, come out and avow your determination to be on the Lord's side," if he is not willing to do so small a thing as that, then he is not willing to do *anything*, and there he is, brought out before his own conscience. It uncovers the delusion of the human heart, and prevents a great many spurious conversions, by showing those who might otherwise imagine themselves willing to do anything for Christ, that in fact they are willing to do *nothing*.

The church has always felt it necessary to have something of the kind to answer this very purpose. In the days of the apostles *baptism* answered this purpose. The Gospel was preached and those who were willing to be on the side of Christ were called on to be *baptized*. It (baptism) held the precise place that the anxious seat does now, as a public manifestation of their determination to be Christian.

Mr. Finney goes on to state that there were those who opposed the "anxious seats," but countered by saying, "in modern times those who have been violently opposed to the anxious seat have been obliged to adopt some substitute, or they could not get along in promoting a revival." Note, there is no appeal for evangelists to return to the apostolic practice of baptism, only a defense of the premise that some kind of substitute is necessary "in modern times" to the promotion of a revival.

Appendix

THE NATURE OF MAN
Who Am I?

By Don DeWelt

Introduction

1. Before we consider the end events of this world we *must see* ourselves in proper perspective in "our world." If we do not, we shall not be able to understand nor appreciate what God is doing, has done, or will do.

2. From several perspectives, there is *no greater question* than, "Who am I?" Notice: (1) As to origin: whom am I, an animal or something more and different? (2) As to purpose: am I indeed responsible to God and to my brother? (3) As to destiny: am I like all other creation locked-in to live out a short span of time and then cease to exist, or is my existence here but the vestibule of the whole house of life in the world to come?

3. Our interest in this lesson has to do with nature, essence or essential being. Who am I intrinsically?

4. Our study shall begin and center on Genesis 1:26 and 2:7, but it will consider many other related texts.

5. We need to attempt a definition of terms. What does the Bible mean when it says, "Let us make man in our *image* and after our likeness"? We use the plural here, i.e., let "us" make man in "our" image, because our Lord and the Holy Spirit were involved in this creative act. Speaking of the one who existed with God and was God, John says, "without Him was not any thing made that hath been made" (John 1:3), and Job 32:8 states "the breath of the Almighty giveth him understanding." When God shared His nature with man He was sharing spirit because the nature or essence of

God is spirit. Our Lord said, "God is spirit" (John 4:24). God is "the Father of the spirits of all men" (Numbers 16:22). To look for the likeness of God in man is to look for spirit. I Thessalonians 5:23 discusses the whole nature of man. "And the God of peace himself sanctify you *wholly*; and may your *spirit* and *soul* and *body* be preserved entire, without blame at the coming of our Lord Jesus Christ." Cf. Heb. 12:9.

Let us discuss the whole man. For sake of emphasis we will reverse the order found in I Thessalonians 5:23.

I. The Body. You are Body.
   A. Made of the dust of the earth.
      1. This can be scientifically established by simply chemically analyzing the component elements of the human body and the component of a clod of dirt. The same chemical elements appear in both. There are more chemical elements in the earth than in the body of man, but all the elements in man's body are of the earth, earthy. (We have facetiously observed that mixed with a little water your name is mud.)
   B. There are many references to the body of man in the Bible. It is called:
      1. "a tabernacle" (II Corinthians 5:1ff). The tent house of the nation of Israel is in this use. The temporary nature of this house is emphasized. It will soon dissolve or deteriorate and be laid aside.
      2. "a mortal body" (Romans 8:12, 13). This indicates that the sentence of death has already been passed on this body. "Mortal" means subject to death; when one is "mortally" injured or wounded we know he will die as a result (Cf. 5:12).

3. "your body." Since you are not wholly body but an occupant of the body, you are personally responsible for its use (Cf. I Corinthians 6:17-19).
4. "corruptible body, dishonorable, weak, and natural" (I Corinthians 15:42-44). In the context each of these words describe the temporary nature of your body. Your body is corruptible inasmuch as it will one day be food for the worms. It is dishonorable for one day it will let you down, and compared with the honorable glorified body we shall one day receive, it is indeed dishonorable. How weak and fragile is the body of man as compared to the bodies of a number of animals or even that of the bodies in the physical world about us. Our bodies are natural in contrast to the supernatural body we shall one day receive.
5. "The body of our humiliation" (Phil. 3:21). This is how we were made a little lower than the angels (Hebrews 2:7ff) and in this sense were humiliated by the body in which we live. This was for the purpose of giving us advantages never given to angels. It was not for angels that God sent His son, but for all men. In the death of our Lord He delivered *all* men from the grave. "As in Adam *all* die so in Christ shall *all* be made alive" (I Corinthians 15:22; Romans 5:12ff). The death that passed on to all men was physical death. Jesus has provided deliverance for all men (i.e. the bodies of all men) from the grave (John 5:23ff). Our bodies will one day be fashioned like His resurrected body. This earthly house will one day return to the dust from whence it came (Genesis 3:19). Whereas I am body, there is much more to me.

II. *The Soul.* You are Soul. (Please notice we can say of you that you *have* a body and in a sense you *are* a body, but we can never scripturally say you *have* a soul; we must always say *you are soul.*)

"And God breathed into his nostrils the breath of life and man *became a living soul"* (Genesis 2:7).

Please notice what happened on the garden floor of Eden: after God finished the fashioning of the body of Adam, Adam lay inert and dead, for as the body apart from the spirit (of man) is dead so was Adam dead because he was only body (Cf. James 2:26). What did God breathe into Adam? The answer can be expressed in several ways: God breathed into the dead body of Adam His own image or likeness. Adam was not like God physically because "God is Spirit." God breathed into the dead body of Adam a part of Himself or spirit, for "God is the Father of the spirits of all flesh." All men are "His offspring" (Acts 17:28); i.e., all men share the nature of God. Plainly put, God breathed spirit or a part of Himself into the dead body of the first man.

Now get this: Why are not all men exactly identical? If God is *one,* a perfect harmonious being, wouldn't all men share that oneness or harmony and be perfectly identical? The answer is in the fact that when the spirit or nature of God or "the breath of life" entered the body *something happened!* Man *became a living soul.*

The soul of man was a result of the uniting of the spirit of man with the body of man. The soul is the by-product of the entrance of the spirit into the body. We could say that the image of God (spirit) was effected by its entrance or uniting with the body, and man *became* a living soul. He *was* body and he *was* spirit, but he *became* soul. The soul is man's distinctiveness.

APPENDIX - THE NATURE OF MAN

It shall be easier to understand this definition if we proceed to the second generation of man. After the creation of a body for man, God provided a means in man and woman for the continuation of the human race. Please notice very carefully the process: the bodies of Cain, Abel and Seth began in the womb of Eve. The seed of the woman was fertilized by the sperm of man.

The first seed of Eve to be fertilized by the sperm of Adam was the body of Cain. How is it that Cain was not identical in his outlook and response to life as his mother Eve and his father Adam? Because something *more* happened when he was conceived in the womb of Eve than the mere forming of a living earthly body. The medical biological definition of the act would be conception, but what really happened was that God once again shared a portion of himself and sent a human spirit into the womb of Eve. When this spirit of Cain united with the genetic combination provided by Adam and Eve, *the soul or life of Cain became.* Cain did not look at life in the same way as Adam or Eve because he had a different set of genes and in this sense a different kind of body than either of his parents. What was true of Cain was also true of Abel and Seth and all men and women since. There have never been two genetic combinations just alike since the garden of Eden.

Man is essentially a spirit being, but each man has a distinctiveness; this he has from or in his soul. No one looks at life just the way you do or I do because there has never been a body like the one formed in the womb of woman just like the one formed for us. When God shared His likeness or spirit with our bodies, there was the creation of   a soul ! i.e., one of a kind, wondrously and marvelously made (Ps. 139:13ff). We do all have the same capacities, and we do share inclinations or proclivities from our parents, but in a very real sense each of us and all of us are uniquely distinctive. Our soul is that distinctiveness. After offering this somewhat technical definition of soul, we can appreciate more than ever the wide use made of this term in the Bible:

A. The term "soul" is used to identify the whole man, i.e., "seventy-five souls" (Exodus 1:5). Because each man is distinctive and is identified not only by his body but by the way he expresses himself, the term "soul" could well be applied to the total person.

B. The term "soul" of man is sometimes used interchangeably with "spirit" of man. Since the soul is but the personal modification of the Spirit we can see why the terms are used interchangeably. Several times "the soul" is referred to as separate from the body. In these references *the spirit* is under consideration, but since man is a spirit-soul being, i.e., man's soul is but the personal expression of his spirit, we can thus see why this is done.

C. The term "soul" is used in a derogatory sense. We mean that the "soulish" man is in contrast to the "spiritual" man.

The explanation of this is easy with the above definition before us.

The soulish man is the one totally interested in his own outlook; he wants to express his own independence and distinctiveness. He either does not know he is essentially spirit or does not care. The emphasis is on the fact that man has a separate identity in his soul. The spiritual man is one who recognizes himself as the creation of God, created in God's likeness and able to express himself in the wondrously unique way that God and his parents and the world around him have given him.

Neither the body nor the soul of themselves are sinful; i.e., they were not created or born in sin. Each man lives as a wonderfully created spirit-soul being in a clay tabernacle. He *does* sin, but not because he is soul or body. "The soul that sinneth it shall die" (Ezekiel 18:4). Each man in his own unique way of himself and by himself sins; his soul is himself, his single individual self. Essentially he is a spirit soul, the image or Spirit from God, beautifully modified by the body in which he lives. When *he* sins *he* will die, not physically but *eternally* for he is an eternal being. This leads us to the third part of our definition.

III. *The Spirit.* You are spirit. We have made full circle on this definition of man's nature. Man is body, man is soul, but apart from spirit man is *nothing! Please note:* Man's capacity to see, hear, feel, and know are all capacities of his spirit. God is Spirit; God sees, hears, feels, and knows. God is a self-conscious being; so is man for he shares the likeness of his Creator.

Let's examine the triune nature of man in the example given us by our Lord in Luke 16:19-31: "There was a certain rich man."

A. *As to his body*: "he was clothed with purple and fine linen and fared sumptuously every day."
B. *As to his soul*: He evidently didn't express his distinctiveness in a way that pleased God; he was

"soulish" in the sense that he lived to "do his own thing" and cared not for man or God.

C. *As to his spirit*: Since all *the spirit's capacities are expressed by or through the soul with the body* his spirit-soul ended up in torment.

What happened to him when he died? He simply moved out of the clay house he lived in for the few short years of his life. He was a spirit being whom God had sent into the womb of his mother. When he united with the genetic combination provided by his mother and father, he *became* a separate distinctive being, a living soul. He looked at life somewhat like his parents, not only because he lived with them and his five brothers, but because he lived in the body they gave him, and his spirit was modified and identified by this union. Yet he was a responsible one-of-a-kind individual, a spirit-soul person alive in an earthy house called a body. One day he moved out; he was separated from the body and lived apart from the body instead of in it. That separation is called *death* (Cf. James 2:26; II Corinthians 5:1ff.). Since man feels with his spirit through his soul by his body the rich man was well able to feel the flame apart from his body.

The ability to see, hear, speak, think, and feel were all of his spirit. The particular way or expression of such capacity was that of his soul. While in the body such capacities were exercised by the body, but since origin of such functions are of the spirit through the soul, he was well able to exercise them apart from the body.

Since man shares the nature of God man's capacities are limitless! What did Jesus mean when He said, "Ye are Gods" (Cf. Jn. 10:34)? Was He not saying that we

APPENDIX - THE NATURE OF MAN

all share the nature of His Father and can exercise some of His capacities? We only use an infinitesimal part of our total spirit-given abilities. Man has learned to think of his nature as being made up of two parts: (1) the self-conscious life, those sensations and responses we receive and give in our daily life, and (2) his subconscious life, all those sensations, thoughts, and reactions which have dropped down into our memory.

Nothing is forgotten it would seem. Like the brothers of Joseph we would like to forget some events, but let a crisis arise like it did with them and our subconsciousness will bring into our consciousness a long forgotten event. Such capacities are those of the human spirit. The subconscious is as much a part of our spirit as our self-consciousness is. As a matter of fact the subconscious is a much larger part of our spirit than our self-consciousness.

Perhaps we could best understand our nature by a comparison with the illustration following: the triune nature of man is clearly seen in this glass. The glass represents the world in which we live. Each of us has his own world in which he or she lives. Our body is represented by the water. It is itself made up of chemicals. When the spirit enters the body, represented by the dye, it is changed or modified by its contact with the water or the body and becomes the soul represented by the ink. We could say that we are body or water; we could say we are spirit or dye; or we could say we are soul or ink!

WHAT THE BIBLE SAYS ABOUT THE END TIME

Ten Sober Conclusions Based on This Lesson

1. All men are created in the image of God. Their response to their environment produces the change we see in their lives.

2. As eternal, conscious beings, there is no purpose in life that does not begin and end in God and His Son Jesus Christ.

3. Our responsibility here has eternal consequences.

APPENDIX - THE NATURE OF MAN

4. We shall never lose our conscious eternal existence. We only transfer from this life to the next.
5. We are only one heart beat away from eternal torment or eternal comfort.
6. We shall await in the unseen world as conscious eternal spirit-soul beings our resurrection when we shall be given our eternal bodies.
7. To influence one person to accept salvation in Christ is worth more than all the effort we could give.
8. We could expect a completion in the world and life to come of all we have begun in this life and world.
9. We shall know each other as individuals since we never lose our identity. We only transfer our address.
10. We have been blinded by Satan to the real world.

Answers to Questions from Students at Ozark Bible College about Birth and Conception

1. Where in the Bible does it say God's spirit unites with the sperm and egg at conception?

The fact that man is alive and his life comes from God (Gen. 2:7; Psa. 139:13-17; Job 27:3; 38:4; Eccl. 12:7), added to our knowledge of how this life begins in conception, should help us to answer this question. Man is a spirit being (I Thess. 5:23). This spirit came from God; it began its existence at conception.

2. When a child's heartbeat first starts, am I right in saying that it's not the rhythmical factors that cause it but it's the Spirit that causes it?

Perhaps the *physical definition or description* of what begins the heart beat of the child could be called "rhythmical action," but biblically we say the heart beat is but one evidence of the life God has placed within the genetic combination provided by the mother and the father. We are not discussing the Holy Spirit but the human spirit (person) in the creation of man in this context. The human spirit sent by God (Who is Spirit) causes the heart to beat.

3. I know that abortion is wrong, but what about birth control?

Birth control is but one of the many decisions man makes as he relates to his life on earth. Any man or woman could choose not to marry and thus prevent birth of children; this would not be wrong. Man is asked to assume the consequences for his choices. If he begins life he should consider himself responsible for the care of that life. He can choose to control or prevent the beginning of life — for this decision he is responsible. This decision is not wrong; he needs to carefully examine his motives for whatever decision he makes as it relates to life — his or his children's.

4. How do we know that the Spirit of God is present at conception? Is the giving of the Spirit at the time of sex what causes pregnancy and not just the biological action?

We are not saying the Holy Spirit is present at conception. (He might be, but I have no Bible reference.) The Holy Spirit is surely present in both the mother and the father if they are Christians. But in the act of procreation we have no reference to the Holy Spirit. The spirit that *is* present is the human spirit. The human spirit which is the likeness or image of God comes from God as a part of Himself who is Spirit (Jn. 4:24; Num. 22:16; Acts 17:28, 29). Yes, pregnancy is caused by the entrance of the spirit (human spirit) into the genetic combination provided by the mother and the father. We can observe the biological action and know biblically what is happening.

APPENDIX - THE NATURE OF MAN

5. Does the spirit enter the body at birth, and is this the gift of the Holy Spirit?

The spirit that enters the body at birth is not the Holy Spirit, but the human spirit. The only reference to the presence of the Holy Spirit in the bodies of men and women in the New Testament is a reference to the presence of the Holy Spirit in Christians.

6. If the soul is formed in the mother's womb, then is a retarded child born with a retarded soul or a normal soul? If his genetic make-up was messed up to form a retarded body and mind, is the soul God gave him like ours?

The soul formed in the mother's womb is but the response of the spirit (human spirit sent from God) to the body (genetic combination). The soul is what happens to the spirit when it enters the body. If the body it enters is abnormal, it cannot function properly. The ability to function is present; but the instrument it enters is imperfect. Therefore the life (soul) expressed is imperfect, abnormal, or retarded.

Questions and Answers About Man's Sensory Capacities

1. If the spirit-soul experiences pain through the body, it seems that it would be possible to destroy the soul in a materialistic sense. It is not clear how the spirit-soul can in a sense "physically" experience pain.

Pain or pleasure are experienced by the spirit-soul through the body. The capacities of joy or anguish are of the spirit-soul but are expressed through the physical body. Peter said, "And I think it right, *as long as I am in this tabernacle,* to stir you up by putting you in remembrance; knowing that *the putting off of my tabernacle* cometh swiftly, even as our Lord Jesus Christ signified unto me" (II Peter 1:13,

14). When the apostle's clay house was put off, he would yet be alive. The spirit-soul is not destroyed or "put off" in the action of death (Cf. II Cor. 5:6-9).

2. You said that there is no pain without the spirit. Are you saying the spirit replaces the nervous system, or are you saying that the spirit feels through the nervous system? Sight will be different without eyes; pain will be different when non-physical. You feel pain because it registers in your brain. The spirit is not burning. The key is not the presence of the spirit but the activity in the brain.

The spirit-soul does not replace the nervous system; it works through such systems. Sight will be the same without eyes; the capacity of seeing is of the spirit-soul through the eyes. When such a capacity no longer uses the eyes, the only difference will be in what is seen in the world to come as contrasted to what is seen in the world that is now. If the pain suffered by the soul-spirit in the world to come is the pain of being burned, and the spirit-soul can through the body suffer the pain of being burned now, I can see no difference. The nervous system registers the pain in the brain. This is but the physical mechanism used by the spirit-soul. Paul said, "For verily in this we groan, longing to be clothed upon with our habitation from heaven" (II Cor. 5:2). Paul as a spirit-soul (person) groaned as a resident in an earthly house. The discomfort was of Paul through the house. When he put off the body as a garment, he did not cease to exist any more than we do when we change our clothes.

3. If it is true that the spirit sees through our eyes and hears through our ears, etc., why, if you poke out your eye or something, can't you still see? Or if you have brain

damage or are born retarded if it is your spirit that does the thinking why can't you still think correctly or function correctly? Does this mean that your spirit is damaged or your spirit is not functioning? Will it be permanently that way? We have answered this question in our earlier answers. We are glad to affirm the fact that there are no blind, dumb, or deaf spirit-souls—only bodies which make the functioning of these capacities impossible because they are imperfect instruments.

4. *If* man's capacities to see, hear, etc. are of the spirit *because* God can and does do all these, what then of animals who *can* also see, hear, feel, and know? Does this mean they have or are spirit? If not, then how do God's abilities prove that man's capacities are *of* the spirit?

Animals can see, hear, and feel, but not in "the image of God," i.e., they do not share the nature of God which is Spirit (Jn. 4:24). Animals are body-soul or body-life beings. The life-soul or animation in animals has instinctive capacities, but such capacities are neither eternal nor intelligent. God is an intelligent Spirit-being; man shares this likeness with God. Animals do not. The ability to reason, judge, evaluate, feel remorse, etc., is the expression of the image of God in man. Such ability is not in an animal. We do have a strong tendency to "read into" the actions of animals human abilities which they do not have. Neither am I prepared to say just what is the extent of the instincts of animals.

Questions and Answers: About Death and After

1. When you are on your death bed and aren't a Christian, but you want to become one and really mean it, and you die before you get baptized, will God accept you?

We have no promise that He will. What did we do with the opportunities God gave us before we came to our death bed? We simply cast ourselves on the mercy of God and know that both love and mercy will be expressed in His decision as to what He will do with us. It is much better to do what God asked us to do when we can than to speculate on what He will do with someone who has not. God will consider the total reason for our inability and will judge us accordingly.

2. Where does the spirit go immediately after death?

The spirit-soul of man goes immediately at death into the unseen world called Hades.

3. Is there immediate judgment right after you die?

John 4:24 says, ". . . He that heareth my word, and believeth him that sent me, hath eternal life, and cometh not into judgment but hath passed out of death into life." The decision is made in this life where we will spend eternity — in heaven, or eternal life, or in condemnation or judgment. At death we will either be "at home with the Lord" (II Cor. 5:8) or "in torment" (Luke 16:23).

4. What kind of life will there be after death before Christ comes.? Where will we be, and in what state, soul or spirit?

We shall be "at home with the Lord" in a place or condition of comfort. Until the resurrection we will not have bodies. But since the body is but the house, the instrument, the clothes we will yet be as conscious in the unseen world to come as we are in this world.

5. What do we know about the after life of mentally retarded people or infants who die? What sort of intelligence do they carry into the eternal life?

APPENDIX - THE NATURE OF MAN

Mental sickness is not of the spirit but of the instrument of the spirit — the brain. All the capacities of the spirit will be released at death. No one will suffer limitations of expression in the world to come, either by injury to the brain or through the immaturity of infancy. When our spirit-souls are given complete unlimited freedom, who can tell to what extent they will exercise such innate abilities? We carry into the next world the total capacity of a spirit which shares the nature of God. That we also sustain our personal identity is to be considered. I am not prepared to say how we shall balance these two facts, but I'm sure we shall not be there long before we all shall know.

6. Can we after death be able to remember sins that we did?

We shall have no recollection of sins in the world to come if we are "at home with the Lord." If we are lost, part of our suffering will be such remembrance (Luke 16:25). Since God has forgotten our sins we should try to do so even in this life. If we could remember sin we would not be happy, and all in the presence of the Lord share the fullness of unallowed happiness.

7. When the spirit leaves the body at death, is there no longer a soul? Is the soul only existent when the spirit is in contact with the body?

It is the spirit-soul who leaves the body. The soul is what happens to the spirit when it enters the body. We are spirit-soul beings. When we die the body is dead; we have moved out. The spirits of all men are alike since they came from the One God, but they enter different bodies, each uniquely different. The difference is provided by the genes of the mother and the father. When the human spirit from God enters that body in the womb of our mother, the human spirit is affected, modified, or changed. Such effect, modification or change is man's soul — *his life* — *his aliveness* — *his soulishness* — *his distinctiveness*. Man is essentially spirit, but each man expresses himself in a different manner. It is the spirit-soul that leaves the body at death. The spirit-soul is eternal because it shares the nature of God who is eternal. It is the proper circulation of the blood of man that keeps the life or soul (and spirit) in the body. "The life or soul is in the blood" (Lev. 17:10-12). When man's blood-pump, his heart, ceases to function his life or spirit-soul leaves his body.

8. Since we do not lose our identity when our bodies die, will we know who has gone to hell?

Whereas we do not lose our identity at death, we will not have any knowledge of the lost. In the record of Luke 16:19-31 the knowledge of Lazarus did not include the condition of the rich man. There would be no happiness in the presence of the Lord if we knew our loved ones were suffering in torment. Since absolute happiness must include an absence of remorse, we believe God simply makes us unable to recall any thought that would cause pain or unhappiness.

9. After the resurrection will we be in heaven as a spiritual being, or will we be reunited with a "perfect" body and once again become a soul?

At the resurrection we are joined again to our new body, our incorruptible, immortal body (I Cor. 15:42ff). Since we are to be given a spiritual body we have no reason to

APPENDIX - THE NATURE OF MAN

believe there will be any change whatsoever at the entrance of our spirit-soul into the new body. We are spirit-souls when we leave the body at death; we are the same spirit-souls when we enter the eternal body at the resurrection. The entrance of the resurrection body will be but reclothing the unclothed spirit-soul. Read II Cor. 5:3, 4.

Questions and Answers: About Body, Soul and Spirit

1. Genesis 2:7 tells us that God "breathed the breath of life" into man. The only thing that happened to man as a result is that he "became a living being." All other creatures "became living beings" also. All animals (except dead ones) have breath and life. I cannot see the implication that the "breath of life" has anything to do with the spirit of God.

Furthermore, Gen. 6:17 and 7:22 both seem to imply that *all* flesh had the breath of life. If only man had the "breath of life," *man* would have been the only creature to die in the flood according to Gen. 6:17.

The "breath of life" in Genesis 2:7 describes the creation of man. Man is a triune being, as seen in the following reference: "And the God of peace himself sanctify you wholly; and may your *spirit and soul and body* be preserved entire, without blame at the coming of our Lord Jesus" (I Thess. 5:23). Therefore the spirit, soul and body of man must have been present at his creation. Man's body was made out of the dust of the ground. Where did the spirit and soul come from? Eccl. 12:7 states the spirit came from God. God as a spirit shared a part of Himself with Adam (Acts 17:28, 29) for He is "the Father of the spirits of all men" (Num. 16:22). "The breath (spirit) of life" is but another way of saying God gave a part of Himself to Adam. When He did, something happened; i.e., there was a result. What was that result? "Adam became a living soul," or as the *Jerusalem Bible* translates it, "and thus man became a living being." The "living being" consisted of body, soul and spirit (I Thess. 5:23).

If the writer of this question is saying that the Spirit of God or the *Holy Spirit* had nothing to do with the description of creation of man in Genesis, we agree. The spirit of man and God as a Spirit were both present; the Holy Spirit is not mentioned.

Genesis 7:16 reads, "all came to Noah in the ark, two by two *of all creatures that had life in them.*" Genesis 6:17 reads, "I intend to bring the waters of the flood over the earth to destroy every *living being* under heaven, everything on earth shall persih." Genesis 7:22 reads, "And so all things of flesh perished that moved on the earth, birds, cattle, wild beasts, everything that swarms on the earth, and every man. *Everything with the breath of life in its nostrils* died, everything on dry land" *(Jerusalem Bible).* God gave life to all living creatures — birds, animals and reptiles, but only man was created in His image. Only with man did God share His nature. All other creatures, like man, have a body and life, or a body and soul or life, but such life (or soul) in animals is not expressed in intelligence as is the spirit-soul of man; for only man is created in the likeness of God. God did not share spirit with animals; only life (soul) with instinctive capacities was given to animals. Man's life (or soul) had the unlimited and at the same time distinctive abilities of God Himself since only man is in His likeness.

APPENDIX - THE NATURE OF MAN

2. Is the spirit one in all men? What of different colored skin of people?

All men are created equal as to the nature of their spirit. All are distinctive as to the expression of their spirits, which are their souls. The body of man is but the house for the person who is the spirit-soul. The size or sex of the body or the color of the skin has no relation to the likeness of God. We have no reference biblically to why there is more pigment in the skin of some persons or why there is less pigment in the skin of others. The area of the world could well be the answer. Perhaps the amount of sunlight relates, or some other explanation. Whatever explanation we offer, it has no reference to the likeness of God. All men are in His image; the house they live in is just that — a house, not the occupant.

3. How do you conclude that the soul is the result of the spirit and the body? What scripture is your basis?

We ask the writer of this question to refer to several answers given earlier. We believe we have answered this several times above.

4. If the soul is the by-product of the entrance of the spirit into the body, are we without a soul before we are baptized?

The "spirit" we are discussing is not the Holy Spirit but the human spirit. All men partake of the image of God — not just Christians. All men are body, soul, and spirit.

5. If the soul is the spirit and body together, how can the terms soul and spirit be used interchangeably? How can we differentiate between the meaning of soul and spirit used in scripture?

The context of any reference to "soul" will indicate its meaning. Please read the grand full discussion of *Spirit and*

WHAT THE BIBLE SAYS ABOUT THE END TIME

Soul by Wilbur Fields.* The essential meaning of "soul" is "life." As brother Fields states, "Soul refers to any and all of the manifestations of life, both human and animal, material, mental, or emotional, both in the body and out of the body." 215 times it refers to a person or the person himself, to the total person as a living being. 195 times soul refers to the aliveness of the person, to the fact that man and animals are living creatures. None of these 410 references should confuse us in our understanding of the specific, technical definition of man's essential being. The life or soul as used to define man's nature is his own distinctive life as expressed by his spirit. All we need to do is ask ourselves: Just what kind of life is involved in the use of the term? 115 times soul refers to the deep inntermost nature of man, i.e., to his unique essential self or spirit. 53 times life or soul refers to the emotional life of man and is translated many times "heart." This is but a very good synonym for man's total inward being, i.e., his spirit-soul.

6. Are spirit and soul the same thing? Does that mean that God does not have a soul?

God does indeed have life — eternal in nature, but God is never referred to as a "soul" being. Soul is limited to this earth as to origin. God is a living Spirit being, but the term soul is inappropriate in reference to the eternal God.

7. Is the spirit-soul *matter* in the scientific sense?

Science cannot isolate the spirit-soul of man in a test tube. We learn of man's true nature by the revelation given us in the Bible. Matter as solid substance has no similarity to the spirit-soul of man. Spirit is not matter; it is eternal, invisible and immortal. We would not characterize matter with these words.

---

* Available from Ozark Bible College Bookstore, Joplin, Mo.

Bibliography

Adams, Jay E. *The Time is at Hand*. Philadelphia: Presbyterian and Reformed, 1970

Allis, Owald T. *Prophecy and the Church*. Philadelphia: Presbyterian and Reformed, 1945

Anderson, Stanley. *Armstrongism Exposed*. Nashville: Christian Growth Publications, 1973

Arndt, William and Gingrich, F. Wilbur, *A Greek-English Lexicon of the New Testament*. Chicago-Cambridge: University Press, 1957

Bales, James D. *Prophecy and Premillennialism*. Searcy, 1972

Barnes, Albert. *Barnes Notes on the New Testament: Matthew and Mark, Luke*. Grand Rapids: Baker (reprint) 1949

Bass, Clarence B. *Backgrounds to Dispensationalism*. Grand Rapids: Eerdmans, 1960

Beckwith, C. A. "Purgatory," *New Schaff-Herzog Encyclopedia of Religious Knowledge,* Vol. IX. (Ed., Samuel Johnson) New York: Funk & Wagnalls, 1909

Bierwolf, Wm. *The Second Coming Bible*. Grand Rapids: Baker, 1972

Boatman, Russell E. *The Big Lie: An Analysis of the Dogma of Original Sin*. St. Louis: (reprint) St. Louis Christian College, 1965

Boettner, Loraine. *The Millennium*. Philadelphia: Presbyterian and Reformed

Bowman, John W. "Dispensationalism" *Interpretation,* pp. 170-87, (April, 1956)

Brown, Francis, Driver, S. R., and Briggs, Chas. A. *A Hebrew and English Lexicon of the Old Testament,* Oxford: Clarendon

Buis, Harry. *The Doctrine of Eternal Punishment*. Philadelphia: Presbyterian and Reformed, 1957

Campbell-Skinner. *Debate on Everlasting Life* (1840) Joplin: College Press (Reprint Library, 1952)
Canwright, D. M. *Seventh Day Adventism Renounced*, New York, Abingdon, 1856
Clarke, Adam, *Clarke's Commentary*, Vols. V., VI. (Reprint) New York, Abingdon
Clouse, Robert G. (Ed.) *The Meaning of the Millennium*. George Eldon Ladd, "Historic Premillennialism"; Herman A. Hoyt, "Dispensational Premillennialism"; Loraine Boettner, "Postmillennialism"; Anthony A. Hoekema, "Amillennialism." Downers Grove: Inter-Varsity, 1977
Cox, William E. *Amillennialism Today*. Philadelphia: Presbyterian and Reformed, 1972
Cox, William E. *Biblical Studies in Final Things*. Philadelphia: Presbyterian and Reformed, 1967
Cox, William E. *An Examination of Dispensationalism*. Philadelphia: Presbyterian and Reformed, 1971
Cruden, Alexander. *Complete Concordance to the Old and New Testaments*, Grand Rapids: Zondervan (Reprint) 1968
Cullman, Oscar. *Immortality of the Soul or Resurrection of the Dead?* New York: Macmillan, 1964
Davidson, A. B. *The Theology of the Old Testament* (Ed. S. D. F. Salmond). Edinburgh: T. & T. Clark, 1904
Davies, W. D., and Daube, D. (Eds.) *The Background of the New Testament and its Eschatology*. Cambridge: University Press, 1956
DeCaro, Louis A. *Israel Today: Fulfillment of Prophecy?* Philadelphia: Presbyterian and Reformed, 1974
DeHaan, M. R. *Coming Events in Prophecy*. Grand Rapids: Zondervan, 1962
Delitzsch, Franz, "Isaiah" (Vol., I, II) *Kiel & Delitzsch - Commentary on the Old Testament*. Grand Rapids: Eerdmans, 1969

Douty, Norman F. *Has Christ's Return Two Stages?* New York: Pageant Press, 1956

Erickson, Millard. *Contemporary Opinions in Eschatology.* Grand Rapids: Baker, 1977

Fairburn, Patrick. *The Typology of Scripture.* 2 vols. New York: Funk & Wagnalls, 1900

Fienberg, Chas. L. *Premillennialism or Amillennialism?* New York: American Board of Missions to the Jews, 1961

Ford, Herschel. W. *Seven Simple Sermons on the Second Coming.* Grand Rapids: Zondervan, 1945

Gatch, Milton. *Death: Meaning and Mortality in Christian Thought and Culture.* New York: Seabury Press, 1969

Grant, T. W. *Facts and Theories as to the Future State,* New York and Glasgow: Holness Publishers, 1894

Grier, William. *The Momentous Event.* Belfast: Evangelical Bookshop, 1945

Gundy, Robt. H. *The Church and the Tribulation.* Grand Rapids: Zondervan, 1973

Hamilton, Floyd E. *Basis of Millennial Faith.* Grand Rapids: Eerdmans, 1942

Hanhart, L. *The Intermediate State of the New Testament.* Franeker: Wever, 1966

Hanna, Ed. J. "Purgatory," *The Catholic Encyclopedia,* Vol. XII., pp. 575-80, New York: Appleton, 1911

Hendricksen, William E. *Israel in Prophecy.* Grand Rapids: Baker, 1974

Hendricksen, William E. *More Than Conquerors.* Grand Rapids: Baker, 1940

Hoekema, Anthony A. *The Bible and The Future.* Grand Rapids: Eerdmans, 1979

Hughes, Philip E. *Interpreting Prophecy.* Grand Rapids: Eerdmans, 1976

Jackson, Paul G. "An Interview with G. Campbell Morgan," pp. 16, 17, *Christianity Today,* August 13, 1959

Johnson, Ashley S. *The Resurrection and the Future Life.* Knoxville: Knoxville Lithographic, 1913

Josephus, Flavius, "Wars of the Jews" *The Works of Flavius Josephus,* (Transl. by William Whiston). Philadelphia: Whiston

Kik, Marcellus. An *Eschatology of Victory.* Philadelphia: Presbyterian and Reformed, 1971

Kittel, G. and Friedrich G. (Eds.) *Theological Dictionary of the New Testament* (10 Vols.). Grand Rapids: Eerdmans, 1964-76

Kromminga, D. H. *The Millennium in the Church.* Grand Rapids: Eerdmans, 1945

Kubler-Ross, Elisabeth. *On Death and Dying.* New York: McMillan, 1959

Ladd, George Eldon. *Commentary on the Revelation of John.* Grand Rapids: Eerdmans, 1972

Ladd, George Eldon. *The Gospel of the Kingdom.* Grand Rapids: Eerdmans, 1978

Ladd, George Eldon. *The Last Things.* Grand Rapids: Eerdmans, 1978

Lindsay, Hal. *The Late Great Planet Earth.* Grand Rapids: Zondervan, 1974

Lenski, R. C. H. *The Interpretation of St. Paul's Epistles.* Columbus: Wartburg, 1937

McPherson, David. *The Unbelievable Pre-trib Origin.* Kansas City: Heart of the American Bible Society, 1973

Marsh, John. *The Fullness of Time.* London: Nisbet, 1952

Meserve, Albert Dallas: *The Olivet Discourse:* A Study of Matthew 24. San Jose: San Jose Bible College, 1970

Miladin, George C. *Is This Really the End?* Cherry Hill: Mack Publ., 1972

Moody, Ray A. *Life After Life.* Atlanta: Mockingbird Books, 1975

BIBLIOGRAPHY

Morris, Leon. *The Biblical Doctrine of Judgment.* Grand Rapids: Eerdmans, 1960

Mounce, Robert H. *The Book of Revelation.* Grand Rapids: Eerdmans, 1977

Perrin, Norman. *The Kingdom of God in the Teaching of Jesus.* Philadelphia: Westminster, 1963

Perry, Ray. *Christian Eschatology and Social Thought.* New York: Abingdon, 1956

Pieters, Albertus. "Chiliasm in the Writings of the Apostles," *Calvin Forum,* August and September, 1938

Pieters, Albertus. *The Seed of Abraham.* Grand Rapids: Zondervan, 1937

Roberts, Oral. *How to Be Personally Prepared for the Second Coming.* Tulsa.

Russell, David S. *The Method and Message of Jewish Apocalyptic.* Philadelphia: Westminster, 1964

Ryrie, Chas. C. *The Basis of Premillennial Faith.* New York: Loizeaux, 1953

Schneidman, Edwin S. "The Enemy," *Psychology Today,* (p. 37), August, 1970

Schofield, C. I. *Schofield Reference Bible.* New York: Oxford

Silvers, Jesse. *The Lord's Return.* London: Fleming H. Revell, 5th Edit.

Smith, Wilbur. *World Crises and the Prophetical Scriptures.* Chicago: Moody, 1951

Summers, Ray. *The Life Beyond.* Nashville: Broadman, 1969

Thomas, Dr. Lewis. "Warts, Brains and Other Astonishments," *Reader's Digest,* pp. 97-100, October, 1979

Torrance, Thomas F. *Kingdom and Church.* Edinburgh: Oliver & Boyd, 1953

Van Impe, Jack. *Israel's Final Holocaust*. New York: Thos. Nelson, 1979

Vine, W. E. *Expository Dictionary of the New Testament*. Westwood: Fleming H. Revell, 1966

Wallace, Foy. *Neal-Wallace Discussion on the Thousand Year Reign of Christ*. Oklahoma City: Foy Wallace Publications, 1953

Walvoord, John F. *Israel in Prophecy*. Findlay: Dunham, 1974

Walvoord, John F. *The Millennial Kingdom*. Findlay: Dunham, 1958

Walvoord, John F. *The Rapture Question*. Findlay: Dunham, 1957

Wilmington, H. L. *The King is Coming*. Wheaton: Tyndale House, 1973

Woodrow, Ralph. *Great Prophecies of the Bible*. Riverside: Ralph Woodrow Evangelistic Association, 1971

Young, Robert. *Analytical Concordance of the Bible*. Grand Rapids: Eerdmans, (Revised Edition)

Zorn, Raymond O. *Church and Kingdom*. Philadelphia: Presbyterian and Reformed, 1962

TOPICAL INDEX TO THE BIBLE'S TEACHING CONCERNING THE END OF TIME

As arranged in *Monser's Topical Index and Digest of the Bible* edited by Harold E. Monser with A. T. Robertson, D. R. Dungan and Others.

ANTICHRIST. I John 2:18, 22; 4:3; II John 7. See Mt. 24:5, 24.
DEATH.—**Metaphorical equivalents of the term death:** "Returning to dust"—Gen. 3:19; Ps. 104:29; Eccl. 3:20; 12:7. Going "to the fathers"—Gen. 15:15. "Gathered to his people"—Gen. 25:8; 49:29. "Giving up the ghost"—Gen. 25:8; 35:29. "To sleep with thy fathers"—Deut. 31:16. "Crushed like the moth."—Job 4:19. "Tent cord pulled up"—Job 4:21. "An exhaled breath"—Job 7:7. "Not to be"—Job 7:8, 21; 27:19. "Cut down like a flower"—Job 14:2. "Not to be found"—Job 20:7, 9; *cf.* Gen. 5:24; Heb. 11:5. "Brought to the king of terrors"—Job 18:14. Devoured by a divine fire—Job 20:26. Lying down in the dust—Job 7:21; 21:26. The spirit going upward—Eccl. 3:21. The spirit returning to God—Eccl. 12:7. Going to his everlasting home—Eccl. 12:5. Sleeping in the dust of the earth—Dan. 12:2. A sleep—Mt. 9:24. Fallen asleep—John 11:11; Acts 7:60; 13:36; I Cor. 15:18, 51; I Thess. 4:14. Clothed with the house not made with hands—II Cor. 5:2. Swallowed up of life—II Cor. 5:4. Absence from the body—II Cor. 5:8. A journey—Phil. 1:23; II Tim. 4:6; II Pet. 1:15, marg. "Putting off the tabernacle"—II Pet. 1:14; *cf.* John 1:14, marg.
Result of sin.—Pr. 2:18; 5:5; 7:27; 8:36; 11:19; 13:13, 14; 14:12; 15:10; 16:25; 21:6; 24:11; Ez. 18:32; 31:14; 33:11; John 5:14; Rom. 5:12-21; 6:16-23; 7:5-8; 8:2-6; I Cor. 15:21; II Cor. 7:10; Jas. 1:15; I John 3:14.

Penalty for sin.—Gen. 2:17; Ex. 10:17; 11:5; Num. 14:35; 16:31-35; 35:30, 31; Deut. 30:15; I Ki. 1:52; II Chr. 24:24; Ezra 7:26; Pr. 10:21; Jer. 9:21; 15:2; 21:8; 31:30; 43:11; Ez. 18:4; Amos 9:10; Mt. 15:4; Mk. 7:10; John 19:7; Rev. 18:8.
Mysterious and terrible.—II Sam. 22:5, 6; Job 3:5; 10:21; 12:22; 16:16; 18:4; 24:17 28:3; 34:22; 38:17; Ps. 13:3; 23:4; 44:19; 55:4; 107:10-14; Is. 9:2; Jer. 2:6; 13:16; Amos 5:8; Mt. 4:16; Lu. 1:79; Heb. 2:15.
End of earthly things.—Ruth 1:17; Job 7:9, 10; 14:12; Ps. 6:5; Eccl. 9:5-10; 12:5-7; Is. 38:18; Rom. 7:2; I Cor. 7:39; Gal. 2:19; Heb. 9:15-27.
Robs of our possessions.—Job 1:21; Ps. 49:17; Lu. 12:16-20.
To be braved in line of duty.—Ju. 5:18; Is. 53:12; Mt. 10:28, 39; 26:35; Mk. 14:31; Lu. 11:50, 51; 12:32, 33; 18:32, 33; 21:16; 22:33; Acts 20:24; 21:13; 25:11; Rom. 5:7; I Cor. 15:31; II Cor. 4:11, 12; 7:3; Phil. 2:8, 30; 3:10, 11; Heb. 2:9-15; 11:35-38; 12:2-4; I Pet. 2:24; Rev. 2:10; 12:11.
Figurative.—As a state of sin—John 5:24, 40; 6:50; 8:21, 24; Rom. 7:9-11; Eph. 2:1, 5; Col. 2:13; I John 3:14; Rev. 3:1. It includes lack of knowledge of God and His Christ—John 17:3. Absence of faith—John 8:21, 24; Heb. 11:5, 6. Dwelling in darkness—Mt. 4:16; John 1:4, 9; 3:19, 20.
Alienation from God and Christ.—Ez. 18:4; John 15:5, 6; Rom. 8:6; Eph. 2:12, 13; 4:18.

WHAT THE BIBLE SAYS ABOUT THE END TIME

Death is not annihilation. — Eccl. 12:5, 7; Mt. 17:3; 22:32; Mk. 9:4; Lu. 9:30, 31; 23:43; Acts 7:55, 56, 59; II Cor. 5:1-8; Phil. 1:20-26; II Tim. 1:10; 4:6-8; II Pet. 1:13-15; Rev. 6:9, 10.

Christ saved by His death. — Is. 53:5, 6; Mt. 20:28; 26:26, 28; Mk. 10:45; 14:22-24; Lu. 22:19, 20; 24:46, 47; John 3:14, 12:32; Acts 3:18; 4:12; Rom. 5:10; 6:3-5; I Cor. 1:22-24; Eph. 2:16; Col. 1:20-22; I Tim. 2:6; Heb. 2:9-15; I Pet. 2:24.

Jesus conquered death. — Mt. 9:23-25; 11:5; 28:1-10; Mk. 5:40-42; 16:1-7; Lu. 7:11-15; 8:49-55; 24:1-6; John 2:19; 10:18; 11:43, 44; 20:1-17; Acts 2:24; 9:36-40; 20:9, 10; Rom. 1:4; 6:23; 7:24, 25; 8:6-10; I Cor. 15:4,20-22, 55-57; Eph. 4:8-10; Col. 2:12; 3:1; II Tim. 1:10; Heb. 2:14, 15.

Jesus' teaching on death. — Mt. 10:28; Lu. 12:20; John 6:49; 8:21, 24; 9:4; 11:4, 11-44; 21:19-23. Sorrowful even unto death — Mt. 26:38; Mk. 14:34. Brother shall deliver brother up to death — Mt. 10:21; Mk. 13:12. Taste of death — Mt. 16:28; Mk. 9:1; Lu. 9:27. He that believeth on Me shall never die — John 3:16; 6:47-51; 8:51; 11:25, 26. Conscious existence: *The Rich Man and Lazarus* — Lu. 16:19-31. *Neither marry nor given in marriage* — Mt. 22:23-30; Mk. 12:18-25; Lu. 20:27-36. Spiritual death eternal — Mt. 23:33; 25:30, 41, 46; John 5:29. See HELL. He foretold His own death, and resurrection the third day — Mt. 12:40; 16:21; 17:9, 12, 22, 23; 20:17-19; 21:33-45; 26:2, 12, 21-28, 32; 27:63; Mk. 8:31; 9:9, 10; 10:33, 34; 14:18-25, 28, 58; Lu. 9:22, 24; 18:32, 33; 22:15, 37; 24:7; John 2:19-21; 3:14; 8:28; 12:32, 33; 13:18-21; Chs. 14-17.

Death of the wicked. — A judgment — Nu. 16:29, 30; I Sam. 25:38; Is. 14:9; Lu. 12:20; Heb. 9:27. Sudden — Job 21:13, 23; Pr. 10:25, 27; 29:1; Is. 17:14; Acts 5:3-10. Feared — Job 18:11-15; 27:19-21. In sin — Ez. 3:19; John 8:21. Illustrated — Lu. 16:23-26.

Death of the righteous. — Release from toil and care — I Ki. 19:4; Job 3:21; 7:15; 14:13; I Cor. 9:15. From evil — II Ki. 22:20; Is. 57:1, 2. To a crown — II Tim. 4:8; Rev. 2:10. To rest — Job 3:13; II Thess. 1:7. To glory — Ps. 73:24-26. To Christ and gain — Phil. 1:21, 23. To new body — II Cor. 5:1, 2. Precious to God — Ps. 116:15; Rev. 14:13.

Entrance upon new state. — Pr. 14:32; Is. 25:8; Mt. 17:2, 3; 22:32; Mk. 12:27; Lu. 16:19-31; 20:35-38; 23:43; John 5:28, 29; 12:24; I Cor. 3:22; II Cor. 5:6-8; Phil. 1:21-23; II Tim. 4:8; Heb. 9:27; Rev. 14:13.

Death chosen. — Num. 23:10; Jer. 8:3; Rev. 9:6.

For the believer. — Christ has abolished death — John 6:47, 50, 51; 8:51, 52; 11:26; Heb. 2:9, 14; II Tim. 1:10.

Death is a separation from the source of life and joy. — (1) Physical: A branch separated from the vine dies — John 15:6. A fish taken from water dies — Is. 50:2. Man cut off from air dies — II Ki. 8:15. (2) Spiritual: Fools die from lack of wisdom — Pr. 10:21. Sin kills —

TOPICAL INDEX

Rom. 7:10, 11, 24. Separates from life and peace—Rom. 8:6. From church and God—5:17, 18; Eph. 2:12; I Tim. 5:6. (3) Eternal, or the second death of the soul is banishment, under a curse, from the kingdom, into the eternal fire and company of wicked angels—Mt. 25:41, 46; II Thess. 1:9. Undying worm—Mk. 9:43-48. A lake of fire —Rev. 2:11; 19:20; 20:6; 21:8.
Death penalty for crime.—Murder— Gen. 9:5, 6; Num. 35:16-21. Adultery—Lev. 20:10; Deut. 22:24. Incest—Lev. 20:11, 12, 14. Sodomy Lev. 18:22; 20:13. Perjury—Zech. 5:4. Kidnapping—Ex. 21:16. Witchcraft—Ex. 22:18. Abusing parents —Ex. 21:15, 17. Blasphemy—Lev. 24:23. Sabbath-breaking—Ex. 35: 2; Num. 15:32-36. False teaching —Deut. 13:1-10. Sacrificing to false gods—Ex. 22:20.
Death a penalty inflicted only on testimony of two or more witnesses.—Nu. 35:30; Deut. 17:6.
Exemplified.—Korah. Num. 16:32. Absalom—II Sam. 18:9, 10.
DESTRUCTION. The flood—Gen. 6:17; 7:11, 23; 8:1-3; Mt. 24:38, 39; Lu. 17:27; II Pet. 2:5.
Destruction of nations.—Pharaoh and host—Ex. 14:27, 28. Amalekites—I Sam. 15:3, 20; I Chr. 4:43. Nameless nations—Deut. 8:20; II Ki. 21:19; Job 12:23.
Destruction of cities.—Ai—Josh. 8:19. Capernaum—Mt. 11:23; Lu. 10:15. Jericho—Josh. 6:24. Sodom and Gomorrah—Gen. 13:10; 19::29; Lu. 17:28, 29. Cities of Midianites—Num. 31:10. Of various nations—Deut. 20:16-18; 31:3; Josh. 11:19, 20. Destruction of Jerusalem—II Ki. 25:8, 9; Jer. 39:8; Dan. 9:2; Mt. 14:15-22; Lu. 21: 20-24.
Vandalism of temple.—Nebuchadrezzar—II Ki. 24:13; Ps. 74:5-8.
Destruction of persons.—Abel— Gen. 4:8; Achan—Josh. 7:25. Agag —I Sam. 15:33. Absalom—II Sam. 18:14. Baal's prophets—I Ki. 18: 40; II Ki. 10:25, 28. Goliath—I Sam. 17:49. James—Acts 12:2. Jezebel—II Ki. 9:33. Job's children —Job 1:15-18. Judas—Mt. 27:5; Acts 1:18. Korah, etc.—Num. 16:31, 32. Nadab, etc.—Num. 3:4. Samson, etc.—Ju. 16:30. Stephen—Acts 7:59, 60. Uriah— II Sam. 11:14-17.
Destruction of armies.—Chedorlaomer, etc.—Gen. Ch. 14. Pharaoh and host—Ex. 14:27, 28. Army of Ai—Josh. 8:22. Sennacherib, etc. —II Ki. 19:35. Syrians—I Ki. 20:28, 29.
Destruction of altars and high places.—Ex. 34:13; Lev. 26:30; Deut. 7:5; Ju. 2:2; II Chr. 14:3; 23:17; 32:12; Hos. 10:2.
Calamities.—Egyptians—Fish—Ex. 7:21. Cattle—Ex. 9:6. First-born children—Ex. 12:29. Fall of tower of Siloam—Lu. 13:4, 5. Fall of Aphek's wall—I Ki. 20:30. Pestilence—II Sam. 24:15-16. Poisonous serpents—Num. 21:8; John 3:14.
Destruction of wicked.—Is. 59:7; Mt. 10:28; 21:14; Mk. 12:9; Lu. 20:16; II Thess. 1:8-9; Rom. 9:22; I Tim. 6:9; I Cor. 10:10; II Pet. 3:16.
Destruction of sin.—I John 3:8; Rom. 6:6, 13; I Cor. 5:5; II Cor. 5:17.

WHAT THE BIBLE SAYS ABOUT THE END TIME

Destruction of church's enemies.—
II Thess. 2:8; Phil. 3:19; Heb. 2:14;
II Pet. 2:1; Rev. 11:18; 20:9-10.
END. Blessing, Of—Gen. 27:30.
Christ both died and lived again to this—Rom. 14:9. Communing, Of—Ex. 31:18. Darkness, To—Job 28:3. Death, Ways of—Pr. 14:12; 16:25. Dividing, Of—Josh. 19:51. Earth, Of—Deut. 33:17; I Sam. 2:10; Ps. 59:13; 67:7; 72:8; 98:3; Pr. 30:4; Is. 45:22; 52:10; Jer. 16:19; Mic. 5:4; Zech. 9:10. Endureth to the—Mt. 10:22; 24:13; Mk. 13:13. Faith, Of—I Pet. 1:9. Full—Jer. 4:27; 5:10, 18; 30:11; 46:28; Ez. 11:13. Hand, Is at—I Pet. 4:7. Heaven, Of—Mt. 24:31. Hope in—Jer. 31:17. I am the beginning and the—Rev. 21:6; 22:13. I am with you alway, Even unto the—Mt. 28:20. Iniquity shall have an—Ez. 21:25, 29; 35:5. Kingdom, Of his—Lu. 1:33. Labor, Of—Eccl. 4:8. Law, Of—Rom. 10:4. Life, Of—Heb. 7:3. Loved unto the—John 13:1. Men, Of all—Eccl. 7:2. Mirth, Of—Pr. 14:13. Perfection, Of all—Ps. 119:96. Praying, Of—I Ki. 8:54. Prophesying, Of—I Sam. 10:13. Sins, Of—Dan. 9:24. Tithing, Of—Deut. 26:12. To this end was I born—John 18:37. Treasures, Of—Is. 2:7. Vain words shall—Job 16:3. War—Ps. 46:9; Dan. 9:26. Wicked, Of the—Ps. 37:38. Wits, At their—Ps. 107:27. World, Of—Mt. 13:39, 40, 49. World without—Is. 45:17. Writing, Of—Deut. 31:24.
Jesus' teaching on the End.—Mt. 10:22; 12:42; Mk. 13:7; Lu. 11:31; John 18:37. End of the world—Mt. 13:39, 40, 49; 24:3; 28:20.

ETERNAL. Is. 60:15; II Cor. 4:18. Comfort—II Thess. 2:16. Destruction—II Thess. 1:9. Fire—Mt. 18:8; 25:41; Jude 7. Glory—II Cor. 4:11; II Tim. 2:10; I Pet. 5:10. God—Deut. 33:27; Rom. 16:26. Gospel—Rev. 14:6. Honor—I Tim. 6:16. Inheritance—Heb. 9:14. Judgment—Heb. 6:2. King—I Tim. 1:17. Kingdom of God—II Pet. 1:11. Life—See LIFE. Mountains—Hab. 3:6. Power—I Tim. 6:16. Punishment—Mt. 25:46. Purpose—Eph. 3:11. Redemption—Heb. 9:2. Salvation—Heb. 5:9. Sin—Mk. 3:29. Spirit—Heb. 9:15.
EVERLASTING. Mic. 5:2; Hab. 1:12. Bonds—Jude 6. Burnings—Is. 33:14. Contempt—Dan. 12:2. Covenant—Gen. 9:16; 17:7, 13, 19; Lev. 24:8; II Sam. 23:5; I Chr. 16:17; Ps. 105:10; Is. 24:5; 55:3; 61:8; Jer. 32:40; Ez. 16:60; 37:26. Dishonor—Jer. 20:11. Everlasting, To—I Chr. 16:36; Neh. 9:5; Ps. 41:13; 90:2; 103:17; 106:48. Father—Is. 9:6. God—Gen. 21:33; Ps. 93:2; Is. 40:28. Joy—Is. 35:10; 51:11; 61:7. King—Jer. 10:10. Kingdom—Ps. 145:13; Dan. 4:3, 34; 7:14, 27. Light—Is. 60:19, 20. Love—Jer. 31:3. Loving kindness—Is. 54:8. Name—Is. 56:5; 63:12. Possession—Gen. 17:8; 48:4. Priesthood—Ex. 40:15; Num. 25:13. Redeemer—Is. 63:16. Remembrance—Ps. 112:6. Reproach—Jer. 23:40. Righteousness—Ps. 119:142; Pr. 10:25; Dan. 9:24. Rock—Is. 26:4. Salvation—Is. 45:17. Sign—Is. 55:13. Statutes—Lev. 16:34. Way—Ps. 139:24.

TOPICAL INDEX

EXPECTATION. Is. 20:5, 6; Lam. 3:18; Zech. 9:5; Rom. 8:19; Phil. 1:20; Heb. 10:13. God, Of—Ps. 62:5. Jesus, Of—Lu. 3:15. Jesus, Of—Acts 12:11. Judgment, Of—Heb. 10:27. Poor, Of—Ps. 9:18. Wicked, Of—Pr. 10:28; 11:7, 23.
FAITHFUL.—Mt. 24:45; 25:20-23; Lu. 12:42-46; 16:10-12.
FALSE CHRISTS.—Mt. 24:5, 24; Mk. 13:22.
FALSE TEACHERS.—Mt. 5:19; 7: 15, 22, 23; 15:9, 13, 14; 23:3, 4, 13; 24:4, 5, 24; Mk. 13:22; Lu. 11:35, 52; John 5:43; 10:1-12.
FEARFUL. Rev. 21:8. Appearance—Heb. 10:21. Expectation of judgment—Heb. 10:27. Let it be—John 14:27. Thing—Heb. 10:31. Why are ye—Mt. 8:26; Mk. 4:40.
FIRE: Used on altar.—Gen. 22:6, 7; Lev. 6:13; 9:24; 22:22; 23:8, 13, 18, 25, 27, 36, 37; 24:7, 9; Ju. 13:20; II Chr. 35:13.
Offerings made with fire.—Ex. 29: 18, 25, 41; 30:20; Lev. 1:7, 8, 9, 13, 17; 2:2, 3, 9, 10, 11, 16; 3:3, 5, 9, 11, 14, 16; 6:17, 18; 7:5, 25; 8:21, 28; 10:12, 13; 16: 12, 13; 21:6-21; 22:27; 23:8, 13, 18, 25, 27, 36, 37; 24:7; Num. 15:3, 10, 13, 14, 25; 18:17; 28:2, 3, 6, 8, 13, 19, 24; 29:6, 13; Deut. 18:1; Josh. 13:14; Ps. 148:8, etc.
Incense must only be burned on the altar fire.—Lev. 6:9, 10, 12, 13; 10:1; 16:12; Num. 15:46.
Used miraculously.—Ps. 18:12, 13. Abraham—Gen. 15:17. Aaron—Lev. 9:24. Gideon—Ju. 6:21. Manoah—Ju. 13:20. David—I Chr. 21:26. Solomon—II Chr. 7:1. Elijah—I Ki. 18:23-25, 38; 19:12; II Ki. 1:10, 12, 14; 2:11.

Coming down from heaven.—Gen. 19:24; Ex. 9:23, 24; I Ki. 18:24, 38; II Chr. 7:1, 3; Job 1:16; Ez. 38:22; Lu. 9:54; 17:29; Rev. 8: 5, 7; 9:18; 13:13; 16:8; 20:9.
Used as a symbol of God's presence.—To Abraham—Gen. 15:17. To children of Israel—Ex. 19:18; Deut. 4:11, 12, 15, 33, 36; Is. 4:5. In burning bush—Ex. 3:2; Acts 7:30. At Sinai—Ex. 19:18; Lev. 10:2; Deut. 5:4, 5, 22, 24, 26; 9:10, 15; 10:4; Heb. 12:18. At Pentecost—Acts 2:3.
Used as a propitiation to Molech.—Lev. 18:21; I Ki. 11:7; II Ki. 16:3; 17:17; 23:10.
Child sacrifice forbidden.—Lev. 18: 21; 20:2-5; Deut. 18:10.
Sons and daughters pass through fire.—II Ki. 17:17, 31; 21:6; 23:10, 11; II Chr. 28:3; 33:6; Jer. 7:31; 19:5; Ez. 16:21; 20:26, 31; 23:37.
Cooking with.—Ex. 12:8, 9; Lev. 10:18; John 21:9.
Burnt with fire.—Ps. 80:16. Remains of offering—Ex. 12:10; 29:14, 34; Lev. 4:12; 7:17, 19; 8:17, 32; 9:11; 16:27; 19:6. Chariots—Josh. 11:6, 9; II Ki. 23:11. Fir-trees—Is. 44:16, 19. Forest—Ps. 83:14; Jer. 21:14; 22:7; Ez. 15:1-8; 20: 46-48; Joel 1:19, 20; Zech. 11:1. Golden calf—Ex. 32:20; Deut. 9:21. Grain—Ex. 22:6; Ju. 15:5; II Sam. 14:30, 31. Gods—Is. 37: 19; Jer. 43:13. Graven images—Deut. 7:5, 25; II Ki. 19:18. Asherim—Deut. 12:3. Hair of Nazirite—Num. 6:18. Rings cast into fire—Ex. 32:24. Weapons—Ez. 39:9, 10. Hires—Mic. 1:7.

WHAT THE BIBLE SAYS ABOUT THE END TIME

Consuming Fire.—Job 31:12; Jer. 48:45. Cities and encampment—Num. 21:28; 31:10; Deut. 13:16; Josh. 6:24; 8:8; Ju. 1:8; 9:49, 52; II Ki. 8:12; Neh. 1:3; 2:3, 13, 17; Ps. 74:7; Is. 1:7; Jer. 21:10; 32:29; 34:2, 22; 37:8, 10; 38:17, 18, 23; 39:8; 49:2, 27; 50:32; 51:31, 32, 58; 52:13; Ez. 5:2; 15:1-8; 23:47; Hos. 8:14; Amos 1:4, 7, 10, 12, 14; 2:2, 5. Adversaries—Job 22:20; Ps. 97:3; Is. 26:11. Sheep and servants—Job 1:16. Tents of bribery—Job 15:34.
Punishment.—Josh. 7:15, 25; Job 31:11; Ps. 11:6; 21:9; 68:2; 89:46; 105:32; 140:10; Is. 9:5, 18, 19; 47:14. Upon Egypt—Ex. 9:23, 24; Ez. 30:8-16. Upon Sodom and Gomorrah—Gen. 19:24, 25; Lu. 17:29; Jude 7. Consumes Korah's followers—Lev. 21:9; Num. 16:35; Ps. 106:18. At Taberah—Num. 11:1-3. Elijah—II Ki. 1:9-12.
Used as a torture.—Lev. 21:9; Deut. 18:10; Jer. 29:22; Dan. 3:6.
Burning of garments for leprosy.—Lev. 13:52, 55, 57.
Fire of vengeance.—Deut. 32:22; Ju. 12:1; 14:15; 15:6; 18:27; 20:48; I Sam. 30:1, 3, 14; I Ki. 9:16; 16:18; II Ki. 25:9; I Chr. 14:12; II Chr. 36:19; Neh. 1:3; Ps. 78:21; Is. 50:11; 66:15, 16, 24; Jer. 4:4; 5:14; 15:14; 17:4, 27; Lam. 1:12, 13; Ez. 16:41; 21:31, 32; 23:25; 24:8-12; 28:18; 39:6; Joel 1:19, 20; 2:3, 5; Amos 1:4, 7, 10, 12, 14; 2:2, 5; 5:6; Ob. 18; Mic. 1:4; Zeph. 1:18; 3:8; Zech. 9:4; Heb. 12:29; Jude 7, 23; Rev. 17:16; 18:8. See HELL.
Used as a war signal.—Ju. 20:38, 40; Jer. 6:1.

A refining process.—Num. 31:23; Ps. 12:6; Is. 48:10; Zech. 13:9; Mal. 3:2; Mt. 3:10-12; Rev. 1:15; 3:18.
Forbidden.—Not to be kindled on the Sabbath—Ex. 35:3. Vain—Mal. 1:10.
Pillar of.—Ex. 13:21-22; 14:24; 40:38; Num. 9:15-16; 14:14; Deut. 1:33; Neh. 9:12, 19; Ps. 78:14; 105:39; Rev. 10:1.
The righteous endure it.—Is. 33:14-16; Dan. 3:24-27.
Strange.—Lev. 10:1; Num. 3:4; 26:61.
Eternal.—Mt. 18:8; 25:41.
Hell of fire.—Mt. 5:22; 13:40-42, 50; 18:9; Mk. 9:43, 45-48; Jas. 3:6; II Pet. 3:7; Jude 7, 23; Rev. 14:10, 11.
Unquenchable.—Mk. 9:43.
Lake of.—Rev. 19:20; 20:10, 14, 15; 21:8.
Salted with.—Mk. 9:49.
Baptism of (fig.).—Mt. 3:11-12; Lu. 3:16-17; 12:49.
References.—Abraham carries fire in his hand—Gen. 22:6. Like as—Pr. 6:27; 26:20, 21; Is. 5:24. Chariots of—II Ki. 6:17. Of jealousy—Ps. 79:5; Song of Sol. 8:6; Ez. 36:5; Zeph. 1:18; 3:8. Heap coals of—Pr. 25:22; Rom. 12:20. Contend by—Amos 7:4. Unsatisfied—Pr. 30:16. Devouring—Ex. 24:17; Deut. 4:24; 9:3; 32:22; Ju. 9:15, 20; Job 20:26; Ps. 18:8; 21:9; 50:3; Is. 29:6; 30:30, 33. See Deut. 18:16; Is. 30:17. Reserved from—Num. 18:9. Stones of—Ez. 28:14, 16; Rev. 18:16. Burnt flax—Ju. 15:14; 16:9. Take fire from the hearth—Is. 30:14. Kindle a—Jer. 7:18; 11:16; 17:27; 21:14; 43:12; 44:27; 50:32; Lam. 4:11; Ez. 20:47;

TOPICAL INDEX

Amos 1:14; Acts 28:2. Flames of —Ps. 29:7; 104:4; Dan. 3:22; Hos. 7:6. Through fire and water—Ps. 66:12; Is. 43:2. In the brazier—Jer. 36:22, 23, 32. Underneath the earth—Job 28:5. Furnace of—Gen. 15:17; Ps. 21:9; Dan. 3:11, 15. Wall of—Zech. 2:5. Quench power of—Heb. 12:18. Brand from the —Zech. 3:2. Pan of—Zech. 12:6. Heavens on—II Pet. 3:7, 12. Falling in—Mt. 17:15; Mk. 9:22. Branches and trees cut down and cast into—Mt. 3:10; 7:19; Lu. 3:9, 17; John 15:6; Rev. 14:18. Peter warming by—Mk. 14:54, 67; Lu. 22:55, 56; John 18:18. Shook off serpent into—Acts 28:2-5. Fuel for —Is. 9:5, 19; Ez. 15:4, 6; 21:32.
Figurative. —II Sam. 22:13; Job 41: 19; Is. 10:16, 17; 65:5; Ez. 1:4, 13, 27; 5:2, 4; 8:2; 10:2, 6, 7; 19:12, 14; Dan. 7:9; 10:6; Hos. 7:6; Joel 2:30; Acts 2:19; Rev. 1:14; 2:18; 4:5; 8:8; 9:17; 11:5. Of Jehovah—II Sam. 22:9; Is. 31:9. Anger—Ps. 39:3; 57:4; 78:21; Is. 42:25; Jer. 4:4; 20:9; 21:12; Lam. 2:3, 4; Ez. 21:31, 32; 22:20-22, 31; 38:19; Nah. 1:6. Thorns burnt in—II Sam. 23:6, 7; Ps. 58:9; 118: 12; Is. 33:12. Breath as—Is. 33:11. Tares burnt—Mt. 13:40-43. Tongue on—Pr. 16:27; Jas. 3:6. Word of Jehovah as—Jer. 5:14; 23:29. Ministers a flame of—Heb. 1:7. Lips as scorching—Pr. 16:27. Sea of glass mingled with—Rev. 15:2. Flesh as—Jas. 5:3. Tested by— I Cor. 3:13-25.
GLORY. Temporal. —Mt. 4:8; Lu. 4:6. Passeth away—Is. 20:5; I Cor. 15:40; II Cor. 5:12; 11:12, 18; I Pet. 1:7, 24. Turned to shame— Hos. 4:7. Of tribulation—Eph. 3:13. Of riches—Esth. 5:11. Cherubim of—Heb. 9:5. Garments of—Ex. 28:2, 40.
Of men — Jer. 9:23, 24; Mt. 6:2; I Cor. 2:7, 8; 3:21; 4:7; 11:7; Gal. 6:13; I Thess. 2:6; Heb. 2:7. Of Jacob— Gen. 31:1. Is. 17:4. Of Joseph— Gen. 45:13. Of Job—Job 19:9; 29: 20. Of David—Ps. 3:3; 4:2; 30:12; 57:8; 62:7; 108:1, Ez. 20:6, 15; 25:9; 26:20. Of young men—Pr. 20:29. Of king of Assyria—Is. 8:7. Of Nebuchadrezzar—Dan. 5:18, 20; 7:14. Of Paul—II Cor. 7:4; 11: 30; 12:1, 5, 6, 9.
Of women. —I Cor. 11:15.
Of children. —Pr. 17:6.
Of nations. —Is. 13:19; 61:6; 66:12; Jer. 4:2; Dan. 11:20; Zech. 2:8; Rev. 21:24, 26. Of Moab—Is. 16: 14. Of Jerusalem—Is. 66:11; Zech. 2:5; 12:7. Of Kedar—Is. 21:16. Of Israel—Ps. 106:20; Is. 17:3; Jer. 2:11; Mic. 1:15; Lu. 2:32. Of Lebanon—Is. 35:2; 60:11-13; Zech. 11:3. Of Judah—Hag. 2:3, 7, 9. Sleep in—Is. 14:18.
Warnings against. — Jer. 9:23; Hab. 2:16; I Cor. 1:29; 9:16; Gal. 5:26; Jas. 3:14; I Pet. 2:20.
Glory used in prophecy. —Chariots of—Is. 22:18, 24. Pride of all—Is. 23:9.
In wisdom. —Jer. 9:23. Of wicked— Is. 5:14; Phil. 3:19. Of Moab—Is. 16:14. Of Babylon—Is. 13:19. Of Zion—Is. 61:6; 66:12.
Of God. —Ex. 24:10; 33:20; 40:34; Deut. 28:58; Num. 14:21; Job 35: 5-7; Ps. 8:1, 9; 18:9-15; 19:1; 24: 7-10; 29:2; 57:5; 72:19; 85:9; 102:15, 16, 21, 22; Is. 5:1, 3; 43: 7; 52:10; 61:1, 2; 63:14; Hab. 2:14; Eph. 1:6, 12; 2:7; 3:21; Phil. 2:11; I Tim. 6:15, 16; Heb. 12:18-21; Jude 25; Rev. 4:11; 15:8; 21:10, 11, 23.

385

WHAT THE BIBLE SAYS ABOUT THE END TIME

Of Jesus. — Mt. 17:2-8; Lu. 9:26, 32; John 1:14; 2:11; 7:39; 12:16, 23; 13:31, 32; 16:14; 17:1-5; 22:24; Rom. 9:5; II Pet. 1:16-18.
Second coming of Jesus in. — Mt. 16:27; 24:27; 30:31; 25:64; Mk. 8:38; 13:26, 27; 14:62; Lu. 21:27.
Teaching of Jesus concerning. — Lu. 14:10; John 8:50; 17:5, 22. Of God — Mt. 16:27; Mk. 8:38; Lu. 9:26; John 7:18; 8:50; 11:4, 40; 17:5, 22. From men — Mt. 6:2, 5, 16; Lu. 6:24; John 5:41. Solomon in all his — Mt. 6:2; Lu. 12:27.
Of the Gospel. — II Cor. 3:9, 10. Joy of believers full of — I Pet. 1:8. Wisdom foreordained unto our — I Cor. 2:7.
Spiritual. — Eternal — Ps. 73:24; Pr. 3:35; Is. 24:16; Dan. 11:39; Rom. 2:7, 10; 8:18; II Cor. 4:17; Eph. 1:18; 3:16, 21; Col. 3:4; II Cor. 4:17; I Thess. 2:20; II Tim. 2:10; Heb. 2:10; I Pet. 5:10. God gives grace and — Ps. 84:11; 85:9.
Celestial. — I Cor. 15:40, 41. Glory in highest — Lu. 19:38. Joy of — Ez. 24:25. Throne of — I Sam. 2:8; Jer. 14:21; Mt. 19:28.
Called to. — II Thess. 2:14.
Raised in. — I Cor. 15:43; Phil. 3:21; Col. 3:4; I Tim. 3:16; Heb. 3:10.
Crown of. — Pr. 16:31; Is. 28:5; Jer. 13:18; Heb. 2:9; I Pet. 5:4.
Of light. — Acts 22:11.
GRAVE,n. No graves in Egypt — Ex. 14:11. Of Rachel — Gen. 35:20. Of Jacob: In Canaan — Gen. 50:5. Of Abner — II Sam. 3:32. Of Barzillai — II Sam. 19:37. Man of God laid in prophet's grave — I Ki. 13:30. Of Asshur — Ez. 32:22, 23. Of Elam — Ez. 32:24, 25. Of Meshech — Ez. 32:26. Of common people — II Ki. 23:6; Jer. 26:23. Shall come to — I Ki. 14:13; Job 5:26; 10:19. Thou shalt be gathered unto — II Ki. 22:20; II Chr. 34:28. Borne to — Job 21:32. Lie in — Ps. 88:5. Declared in — Ps. 88:11. With wicked — Is. 53:9. Make — Nah. 1:14. Find grave — Job 3:22. Strewed upon — II Chr. 34:4. Made ready — Job 17:1. Among — Is. 65:4. Out of — Jer. 8:1; Ez. 37:13.
Law of. — Num. 19:16, 18.
Prophecy concerning. — Ez. 37:12.
Figurative. — Jer. 20:17.
HADES. Heb. Sheol. The underworld, abode of the dead, hence sometimes death. Brought down unto — Lu. 10:15. Cast into lake of fire — Rev. 20:14. Church, Shall not prevail against — Mt. 16:18. Dead, Gave up — Rev. 20:13. Death, Hades followed — Rev. 20:14. Go down unto — Mt. 11:23. Keys of — Rev. 1:18. Rich man in — Lu. 16:23. Soul, Will not leave my soul in — Acts 2:27, 31.
HEAVEN. Physical heavens. — Created by God — Gen. 1:1; Ex. 20:11; II Ki. 19:15; I Chr. 16:26; II Chr. 2:12; Neh. 9:6; Ps. 8:3; 33:6; 148:5-6; Pr. 8:27; Is. 37:16; 42:5; Jer. 10:12; 32:17; 51:15; Acts 4:24; Heb. 1:10; Rev. 10:6; 14:7.
Their function. — To declare God's glory — Ps. 19:1. To declare His righteousness — Ps. 50:6; 97:6. To shew His wonders — Mt. 24:29; Acts 2:19. To contain the lights — Gen. 1:14-19.
Their destruction. — Ps. 102:26; Is. 34:4; 51:6; Mt. 24:35; Heb. 1:11-12; II Pet. 3:10; Rev. 6:12; 20:11.
The new heavens. — Is. 65:17; 66:22; II Pet. 3:13; Rev. 21:1.

TOPICAL INDEX

Heaven, the dwelling-place of God. — Deut. 26:15; I Ki. 8:30, 39, 43, 49; II Chr. 6:21, 27, 30, 33, 35, 39; Neh. 9:37; Ps. 2:4; 11:4; 20:6; 33:13; 102:19; Is. 63:15; 66:1; Mt. 5:34; 6:9; 10:22; 12:50; 16: 17; 18:10; Mk. 11:25; Acts 7:45. Of the Christ—Mt. 24:30; Mk. 14:62; John 3:13, 31; 6:38; 14:2-3; Acts 1:11; I Cor. 15:47; I Thess. 1:10; 4:16; Heb. 1:3; Rev. 22:1. Of the angels—Lu. 2:13-15; Rev. 1:4; 18:1; 20:1. Of the righteous—Mt. 5:12; 25:34, 46; John 12:26; 14:2-3; 17:24; I Thess. 4:17; Phil. 3:20; Rev. 2:7; 3:21; 22:14.
God reigns in heaven. — Over angels —Ps. 103:20; Mt. 6:10; Deut. 4: 35-36; 33:26-27; I Sam. 12:12-15; Ps. 47:8; Jer. 23:23, 24. Over the devil—Job 1:12; 2:6; Lu. 10: 18; II Pet. 2:4; Jude 6; Rev. 20:1-3.
Hears petitions in. — I Ki. 8:30, 32, 34, 36, 39, 54-56; I Chr. 21:26; II Chr. 7:14; Neh. 9:27; Ps. 20:6; Mt. 6:9; 7:7-11.
Sends His judgments from. — Gen. 19:24; I Sam. 2:10; Dan. 4:13-17; Rom. 1:18.
Descriptions of. — The Father's house —John 14:2. A garner—Mt. 3:12. A city—Heb. 11:10, 16. A kingdom —Mt. 25:34; Lu. 12:32; Eph. 5: 5. Paradise—II Cor. 12:4. The holy city—Rev. 21:1-3, 10-27; 22:1-5.
Characteristics of. — No marriages there—Mt. 22:30. No sorrow—Rev. 7:17; 21:4. No curse—Rev. 22:3. No pain—Rev. 7:16; 21:4. No night—Rev. 22:5. No death—Rev. 21:4. No flesh and blood—I Cor. 15:50. No corruption—I Cor. 15:42, 50. Joy there—Ps. 16:11; Lu. 15:7, 10. Treasure in —Mt. 6:20; 19:21. Righteousness in—II Pet. 3:13. Service in—Rev. 7:15.
Conditions of entrance. — Mt. 25:34-36, 46; Lu. 6:47-48; 13:24; John 3:5, 18, 21; 8:24; 11:25-26; 20: 31; Rom. 8:17; 12:1-2; II Pet. 1:5-11; Rev. 2:7, 10-11; 21:7; 22:14.
Conditions which bar entrance. — Mt. 5:29-30; 7:26-27; 10:37-39; 13:41-42; Lu. 13:23-28; I Cor. 6:9-10; Gal. 5:19-20; Eph. 5:5; Jude 14, 15; Rev. 21:8; 22:11, 15.
Signs of the heavens. — Planets and bow originally for signs—Gen. 1:14; 9:13. Nations became dismayed because of them—Jer. 10:2. Astrologers vainly interpreted them—Is. 47:12-14. Pharisees seek signs from heaven—Mt. 12:38; 16:1-3; Mk. 8:11; Lu. 11:16; 12:54-56; I Cor. 1:22. Used as witness for spiritual truth—Ps. 89:36-37; 72:5. Inability to read heavenly signs—Job 37:14-17, 21-22. The signs of the Son of Man—Mt. 24:29-31; Mk. 13:24-27. Visions of John—Rev. 4:1; 7:1-3; 10:1-6; 12:1-3; 15:1; 18:1; 20: 1-3; 21:1-2; 22:1-2.
Jesus' teaching on heaven. — Angels in—Mt. 18:10; 22:30, 24:36; Mk. 13:32; John 1:51. See Mt. 16:27; Mk. 8:38. Ascending and descending—John 1:51; 2:13. Baptism of John the Baptist—From heaven or men?—Mt. 21:25-27; Mk. 30-33; Lu. 20:4-7. Birds of the—Mt. 8:20. Bound in—Mt. 18:18. Bread out of—John 6:32, 33, 50, 51, 58. Clouds of—Mt. 24:30; 26:64; Mk. 13:26; 14:62. Dwelling place of God —Mt. 5:16, 45; 6:9; 7:11; 10:32, 33; 11:25; 12:50; 16:17; 18:10,

WHAT THE BIBLE SAYS ABOUT THE END TIME

14, 19; 23:9; Mk. 11:25; Lu. 10: 21. *God is Lord of*—Mt. 6:10; 11: 25; Lu. 10:21. *Throne of God*—Mt. 5:34; 23:22. *Called Father's house*—John 14:1-3. Dwelling place of Jesus—John 12:26; 14:3; 17:5, 24. *Descended from*—John 3:13, 31-36; 6:38, 39, 62; 8:23. *Came from the Father*—John 3:16; 6:46; 8:42; 13:3; 16:28-30; 17:5, 8, 18. *Ascending into*—Lu. 24:26; John 1:51; 6:62; 7:33; 14:2, 3, 12, 28; 16:5, 7, 10, 28; 17:13; 20:17. *Seated on right hand of God*—Mt. 26:64; Mk. 14:62; Lu. 22:69. *Shall come again from*—Mt. 24:30; Mk. 14:62; Lu. 21:27; John 14:3, 18, 28. Dwelling place of the righteous—Mt. 5:12; 25:34; Lu. 6:23; John 14:1-3; 17:24. End, From one to another—Mt. 24:31; Mk. 13:27; Lu. 17:24. Exalted unto—Mt. 11: 23; Lu. 10:15. Face of, Interpret—Lu. 12:56. See HEAVEN. Fire and brimstone from—Lu. 17:29. Joy in —Mt. 13:43; Lu. 15:7, 10. Lightning out of—Lu. 17:24. Marriage in heaven, No—Mt. 22:30-33; Mk. 12:18-27. Names written in—Lu. 10:20. Opened—John 1:51. Passing away, Heaven and earth—Mt. 5:18; 24:35; Mk. 13:31; Lu. 16: 17; 21:33; 24:35. Powers of heaven shaken—Mt. 24:29; Lu. 21:26. Red—Mt. 16:2, 3. Reward in—Mt. 5:12; 25:34; Lu. 6:23. Satan falling from—Lu. 10:18. Sign of the Son of Man—Mt. 24:30. Sinned against—Lu. 15:21. Stars falling from—Mt. 24:29; Mk. 13:25. Swearing by—Mt. 5:34; 23:22. Terrors and signs from—Lu. 21:11. Throne of God—Mt. 5:34; 23:22. Treasures in—Mt. 6:20; 19:21; Mk. 10:21. Will done on earth as in heaven—Mt. 6:10.

HELL. Gr. *Gehenna*, "Valley of Hinnom." From Heb. *Ge*, "valley," and "Hinnom," name of the owner. (West of Jerusalem, where noxious things were burned up.) Used figuratively as name or place of everlasting punishment. Distinct from Hades which is the place or state of all departed souls, and corresponds to Sheol in Old Testament. The expression "lowest sheol" in Old Testament is indicative of Hell.
References in Old Testament where hell is probably meant.—Deut. 32: 22; Ps. 86:13; Pr. 9:18; 15:24; 23:14; Is. 14:15; 28:18, 19; 30:33; 33:14. Proselytes of—Mt. 23:15; II Pet. 2:10-12.
Danger of.—Mt. 5:22, 29, 30; 10:28; 18:8, 9; Mk. 9:43-48; Lu. 12:5.
The judgment of.—Mt. 23:33; Lu. 16:23, 25, 26; II Pet. 2:4. (*Cf.* Mk. 14:64; II Cor. 1:9.)
Its destructive nature.—Mt. 3:12; 10:28; Lu. 3:17; Jas. 3:6.
The abode of the wicked.—Mt. 13: 41, 42; 25:41-46; Lu. 16:23; Rev. 19:20; 20:14, 15.
Not in O.T. of A.R.V. N.T. usage.
(1) "Hades" translated "hell" ten times in A.V. ("death" once) is translated "hades" in A.R.V. ten times ("death" once). Sometimes "hades" is used in context where it is clear that the abode of the wicked is meant. *Cf.* Lu. 16:23, "in hades," "in torments." Death and hades cast into the lake of fire—Rev. 20:14. English word "hell" is from Anglo-Saxon *helan*, to hide, conceal. Originally the other world, like "hades" the "unseen" world, then confined to the abode of the damned.
(2) **"Tartarus"** used but once, limited to evil angels, is retained in A.R.V. II Peter 2:4.

TOPICAL INDEX

(3) "**Gehenna**" used eleven times by Jesus, once by James and by no others, is translated hell uniformly.
Jesus' teaching on Hell. — Cast into — Mt. 18:9; Mk. 9:43, 45, 47; Lu. 12:5. Body cast into — Mt. 5:29. Body and soul destroyed in — Mt. 10:28. Fire, Of — Mt. 5:22; 13:40, 42, 50; 18:9. *Eternal fire* — Mt. 18:8; 25:41. *Unquenchable fire* — Mk. 9:43, 48. Judgment of — Mt. 23:33. Son of — Mt. 23:15. See Mt. 7:13, 14; 22:13; 25:46.
HOPE: What is it? A union of desire and expectation. — Rom. 8:25.
A reasonable act. — I Pet. 3:15.
One of the three graces. — I Cor. 13:13.
A triumphant fact. — Rom. 8:38, 39.
Its basis. — Job 4:6; I Pet. 1:3; Acts 26:6-8.
Objects of. — Ps. 39:7; 130:6; 131:3; Jer. 17:7, 13; Lam. 3:24; Joel 3:16; Rom. 15:13; I Pet. 1:21. The Christ — I Cor. 15:19; I Tim. 1:1. The promises — Acts 26:6, 7; Tit. 1:2. The word — Ps. 119:81; 130:5. Righteousness — Gal. 5:5. Gladness — Pr. 10:28.
JUDGMENT: The Judge, God. — Gen. 16:5; Ju. 11:27; I Sam. 2:10; 24:12, 15; I Chr. 16:33; Job 21:22; Ps. 26:1, 2; 35:24; 50:4, 6; 58:11; 75:7; 76:8, 9; 82:8; 96:13; 135:14; Pr. 29:26; Eccl. 3:17; 11:9; 12:14; Is. 2:4; 3:13; 28:17; 30:18; 33:22; Dan. 7:10; Mal. 3:5; Acts 17:31; I Cor. 5:13; Heb. 10:30; 12:23; Rev. 11:17, 18; 16:5; 18:8.
Christ. — Mt. 16:27; 25:31-46; John 5:22, 23, 27, 30; Acts 10:42; Rom. 2:16; I Cor. 4:5; II Cor. 5:10; II Tim. 4:1, 8; Rev. 22:12.
The saints. — Mt. 19:28; I Cor. 6:2.

Sentence rendered according to righteousness. — Gen. 4:7; 18:25; I Sam. 26:23; Job 34:11, 12; Ps. 62:12; Acts 10:24, 25; Mt. 16:23; 23:13; Mk. 10:21; John 1:47; 6:70; Acts 10:34, 35.
According to one's deeds. — Pr. 12:14; 24:12; Is. 3:10, 11; 59:18; Jer. 17:10; 32:19; Ez. 7:3; 18:4, 9, 19-32; 33:8-20; Hos. 4:9; 12:2; Zech. 1:6; Lu. 12:47, 48; 19:12-24; John 3:20, 21.
Final judgment. — Mt. 13:30; 25:31-46; Acts 17:31; Heb. 9:27; II Pet. 3:7, 10, 12; Rev. 20:11-13.
Judgment as criticism. — Mt. 7:3-5; Lu. 6:41, 42; Rom. 2:1; I Cor. 5:12.
Unfair judgment forbidden. — Mt. 7:1; Rom. 14:10, 13; Jas. 4:11.
Must not judge by appearances. — John 7:24; 8:15.
Must not usurp judgment. — Rom. 14:10; I Cor. 4:5.
Jesus' teaching on Judgment. — Mt. 16:27; Mk. 8:38; Lu. 12:36; John 3:19; 5:29; 12:31; 16:8, 11. With what judgment ye judge — Mt. 7:1-5; Lu. 6:37-42. All judgment given to the son — John 5:22, 27, 30; 9:39. Righteous — John 5:30; 7:24; 8:16. In danger of the — Mt. 5:21, 22. Day of — Mt. 10:15; 11:22, 24; 12:36, 41, 42; 13:30, 40-43; 22:11-13; 24:29-35; 25:31-46; Lu. 10:14; 11:31, 32. See Mt. 7:22, 23. Cometh not unto — John 5:24. See Lu. 12:47, 48.
KINGDOM OF GOD. — "It is only when we take the fourfold narrative in its entirety that we begin to catch sight of the satisfying and convincing fulness of the idea of the kingdom of heaven. This idea underlies the whole

Gospel of John. In the Synoptic Gospels we have the conditions of entrance into the kingdom, a child-like spirit, faith, repentance, and obedience—Mt. 18:3; 9:22; 5:20; Lu. 13:3. In John we have the spiritual birth by which alone those conditions are made possible—John 3:5. In the Synoptics we have the laws of the kingdom—Mt. 5-7. In John we have the new life in which alone these laws can be fulfilled—John 6:22-65. In the Synoptics we have the parables and pictures of the kingdom—Mt. 13, etc. In John we have the inmost sense of those parables, spoken directly to the soul, in words of which Christ Himself says 'they are spirit, and they are life.' In the Synoptics we have the new order of human society in the imitation by the disciples of Christ's obedience to the will of God—Mt. 12:50. In John we have the organizing principle of that new order in Christ's revelation of Himself to the disciples as the way, the truth, and the life—John 14:6. In the Synoptics we have the supremacy of Christ's example over men's hearts. In John we have the supremacy of Christ's teachings over men's minds."
— HENRY VAN DYKE.

"Put together the Sermon on the Mount, the Charge to the Twelve Apostles, the Parables of the Kingdom, the Discourse in the Supper-room, and the institution of the two great Sacraments, and the plan of our Saviour is before you. And it is enunciated with an accent of calm, unfaltering conviction that it will be realized in human history." —HENRY P. LIDDON

Called: The Kingdom of God—Mt. 21:31; Mk. 1:15; 4:11, 26, 30; 9:1, 47; 10:14, 15, 23-25; 12:34; 14:25; 15:43; Lu. 4:43; 6:20; 7:28; 8:1, 10; 9:2, 11, 27, 60, 62; 10:9, 11; 11:20; 13:20, 28, 29; 14:15; 16:16; 17:20, 21; 18:16, 17, 24, 25, 29; 19:11; 22:16; John 3:3, 5; Acts 1:3; 8:12; 14:22; 19:8; 28:23, 31; Rom. 14:17; I Cor. 6:9, 10; 15:50; Gal. 5:21; Col. 4:11; II Thess. 1:5; Rev. 12:10.
The Kingdom of Heaven—Mt. 3:2; 4:17, 5:19, 20; 7:21; 10:7; 11:11, 12; 13:11, 24, 31, 33, 44, 45, 47, 52; 18:1, 3, 4, 23; 19:12, 14, 23, 24; 20:1; 22:2; 23:13; 25:1.
The Kingdom of Christ and God—Eph. 5:5; Rev. 11:15.
His Kingdom—Mt. 6:33; 13:41; 16:28; 20:21; Lu. 1:33; 12:31; 22:29, 30; John 18:36; I Thess. 2:12; II Tim. 4:1, 18; Heb. 1:8.
Kingdom of their Father—Mt. 13:43.
My Father's Kingdom—Mt. 26:29.
The Kingdom of the Son of His Love —Col. 1:13.
Temporal kingdom, or, Kingdom of this world.—The disciples and Jews thought it was a—Mt. 20:21; Lu. 14:15; 19:11-27; John 6:15; Acts 1:6.
Not of this world.—John 6:15; 18:36. See Mt. 26:52-56; Rom. 14:17; I Cor. 4:20.
Within you.—Lu. 17:20, 21.
Not established before death of Jesus.—Mt. 16:19, 28; Mk. 11:10; 15:43; Lu. 12:32; 17:20; 19:11; 21:31; 23:42, 51; Acts 1:3, 6.
To be established "in the days of these kings."—Dan. 2:31-45. See Is. 9:6, 7.
At hand.—Mt. 3:2; 4:17; 10:7; Mk. 1:15; Lu. 10:9, 11.

TOPICAL INDEX

To come with power. —Mk. 9:1; Acts 1:4-8; 2:1-4.
During the lifetime of the disciples standing near Him. —Mt. 16:28; Mk. 9:1; Lu. 9:27; 21:31; 22:16, 18; Acts 1:6-8.
Prepared for you before the foundation of the world. —Mt. 25:34.
Jews natural heirs, but rejected. — Mt. 8:11-12; 21:43; 23:13.
Suffereth violence. —Mt. 11:12; Lu. 16:16.
Kingdom in heaven. —Mt. 8:11, 12; 13:37-42; 19:28; 25:31-46; Lu. 13:28, 29; 22:29, 30; I Cor. 15:50; Rev. 11:15.
Who may enter. —He that is but little, is greater than John the Baptist— Mt. 11:11; Lu. 7:28.
Seek first the kingdom—Mt. 6:33; Lu. 12:31.
Those who do the will of God—Mt. 5:19; 7:21-27.
Righteous—Mt. 5:20; I Cor. 6:9-11; Gal. 5:19-24; Eph. 5:3-6; II Thess. 1:5.
Repentance a condition—Mt. 3:2; 4:17.
Poor in spirit—Mt. 5:3; Lu. 6:20.
Publicans and harlots enter before the pharisees—Mt. 21:31; Lu. 7:29-50.
Hard for the rich to enter—Mt. 19:23, 24; Mk. 10:23-27; Lu. 18:24, 25, 29.
Those who do not look back—Lu. 9:62.
Must become as little children—Mt. 18:1-4; 19:14; Mk. 10:14, 15; Lu. 18:15-17.
Those who are born anew of water and the Spirit—John 3:3-5.
Those who endure tribulations—Mk. 9:47; Lu. 18:29; Acts 14:22; II Thess. 1:5.

Everlasting kingdom. —II Sam. 7: 12, 13; Ps. 45:6, 7 (Heb. 1:8, 9); 89:3, 4, 29-37; Dan. 2:44, 45; 7: 14; Mic. 4:7; Lu. 1:33.
Righteous. —Ps. 45:6; Is. 9:7; 11:1-10; 62:1, 2; Jer. 23:5; 33:15; Zech. 9:9; Heb. 1:8, 9.
Universal. —Ps. 2:8; Is. 2:2-4; 11:9; 42:4, 10-13; 62:1, 2; Jer. 31:34; Dan. 2:44, 45; Zech. 14:9; Mt. 24: 14; 28:18, 19; Mk. 16:15, 16; Lu. 24:46, 47; Acts 1:8; Rom. 10:18; Phil. 2:10; Col. 1:6, 23; Rev. 11: 15.
Gospel of kingdom. —Mt. 4:23; 9: 35; Lu. 4:43; 8:1; 9:2, 60; Acts 1:3.
To be preached in the whole world —Mt. 24:14; 28:18, 19; Mk. 16: 15, 16; Lu. 24:46, 47; Acts 1:8.
Word of the kingdom. —Mt. 13:19; Acts 8:12; 19:8; 20:25; 28:23-31.
Keys of. —Is. 22:22; Mt. 16:19; Rev. 3:7.
Mysteries of. —Mk. 4:11; Lu. 8:10.
Parables of. —The growth of the kingdom by addition from without: *The Sower*—Mt. 13:3-8, 18-23; Mk. 4:3-8, 13-20; Lu. 8:5-8, 11-15. *The Tares*—Mt. 13:24-30, 36-43; Mk. 4:26-29. *The Mustard Seed*— Mt. 13:31, 32; Mk. 4:30-32; Lu. 13:18, 19. *The Net*—Mt. 13:47-50. Influence upon the world: *The Leaven*—Mt. 13:33; Lu. 13:20, 21. Growth from within: *The Blade, the Ear, and the Full Grain in the Ear*—Mk. 4:26-29. *The Vine*— John 15:1-8.
Kingdom of God the supreme good: *The Hidden Treasure*—Mt. 13:44. *The Pearl*—Mt. 13:45, 46.
Rebuke to Phariseeism, Parables of grace: *The Lost Sheep*—Mt. 18:12, 13; Lu. 15:4-6. *The Lost Piece of*

391

WHAT THE BIBLE SAYS ABOUT THE END TIME

Silver—Lu. 15:8-10. *The Prodigal Son*—Lu. 15:11-32. *Pharisee and Publican*—Lu. 18:9-14. *Two Debtors*—Lu. 7:36-50. *Strife for First Places at Feasts*—Lu. 14:7-11. *The Great Supper*—Mt. 22:1-14; Lu. 14:16-24. *The Good Samaritan*—Lu. 10:30-37. *The Unjust Steward*—Lu. 16:1-12. *The Rich Man and Lazarus*—Lu. 16:19-31. *The Judgment*—*Children in the Marketplace*—Lu. 7:31-35. *The Barren Fig-tree*—Lu. 13:6-9. *The Wicked Husbandman*—Mt. 21:33-41; Mk. 12:1-9; Lu. 20:9-17. *The Wedding Feast and the Wedding Robe*—Mt. 22:1-14. *The Unfaithful Servant*—Mt. 24:45-51. *The Ten Virgins*—Mt. 25:1-13. Service in the kingdom: *The Laborers*—Mt. 20:1-16. *The Hours, the Talents, and the Pounds*—Mt. 20:1-16; 25:14-30; Lu. 19:12-27.

The right use of worldly possessions: *The Unjust Steward*—Lu. 16:1-12. *Rich Man and Lazarus*—Lu. 16:19-31.

High priest, after the order of Melchizedek.—Ps. 110:4; Is. 53:12; Zech. 6:13; Rom. 8:34; Eph. 2:13, 18; I Tim. 2:5; Heb. 2:17, 18; 3:1; 4:14; 5:5-10; 6:20; 7:1-28; 8:1-6; 9:11-28; 10:1-21; I John 2:1.

Head of the Church.—Rom. 8:29; I Cor. 11:3; Eph. 1:10, 22, 23; 4:15; 5:23, 24; Col. 1:18; 2:10, 19; Heb. 3:3, 6; Rev. 3:7.

The head of the corner—Ps. 118:22; Is. 28:16; Mt. 21:42; Lu. 20:17; Acts 4:11; Eph. 2:20; I Pet. 2:6, 7.

Eternity of.—Mt. 18:20; 28:20 (Acts 18:10); John 1:1-4, 15; 6:62; 8:23, 58; 17:5; II Cor. 8:9; Eph. 4:10; Col. 1:17; Heb. 1:8-12; 6:20; 7:16, 24, 25; 13:8; Rev. 1:8, 17, 18; 21:6; 22:13.

Exaltation.—Ps. 68:18; Mt. 28:18; Lu. 24:26; John 7:39; 12:23; 14:2, 3; Acts 1:2, 11; 3:13, 20, 21; Rom. 6:4; 8:17; I Cor. 15:25-28; Eph. 4:8-10; Phil. 2:6-11; Heb. 2:9; 5:9; 9:12, 24; I Pet. 1:21; II Pet. 1:16.

Glory of.—Mt. 17:2-8; Lu. 9:26, 32; John 1:14; 2:11; 7:39; 12:16, 23; 13:31, 32; 16:14; 17:1-5, 22, 24; Rom. 9:5; II Pet. 1:16-18.

He came in fulfillment of the scriptures.—Mt. 5:17; 26:52-56; Lu. 24:25-27, 44-47; John 5:39, 45, 46; Acts 8:32-35; 13:27-40; 17:2, 3; 18:28; Gal. 4:4. The prophet who was to come—Deut. 18:15 (John 1:21, 25; Acts 3:22; 7:37). The Only Begotten Son—Ps. 2:7 (Acts 13:33; Heb. 1:5-8; 5:5). The Crowned Son of David—Ps. 110:1 (Mt. 22:41-46; Mk. 12:35-37; Lu. 20:41-44; Acts 2:34-36; Heb. 1:13; Rev. 8:5). The stone which the builders rejected—Ps. 118:22 (Mt. 21:42; Mk. 12:10, 11; Lu. 20:17; Acts 4:11; Eph. 2:20; I Pet. 2:7, 8). Born of a virgin—Is. 7:14 (Mt. 1:23; Lu. 1:26-38). A light to the Gentiles—Is. 9:1, 2 (Mt. 4:14-16). The Spirit of the Lord upon Him—Is. 11:1, 2; 35:5; 42:1; 61:1, 2 (Mt. 11:5; Lu. 2:28-32; Acts 2:2-4, 16-21, 33).

His miracles a proof of His divinity.—Mt. 11:20-24; Mk. 2:5-12; John 2:11, 23; 3:2, 11; 4:48-53; 9:4; 10:37, 38; 11:45, 46; 14:11, 12; 15:24; 20:30, 31; Acts 2:22.

He foretold His own death, burial, and resurrection on the third day.—Mt. 12:40; 16:21; 17:9, 12, 22, 23; 20:17-19; 21:33-45; 26:2, 12, 21-28, 32; 27:63; Mk. 8:31; 9:9, 10; 10:33, 34; 14:18-25, 28, 58; Lu. 9:22, 44; 18:32, 33; 22:15,

37; 24:7; John 2:19-21; 3:14; 8: 28; 12:32, 33; 13:18-21; Chs. 14-17.

His resurrection a proof of His divinity. — Acts 2:22-32; 3:15; 5:29-32; 10:39-42; 13:30-37; 17:31; Rom. 10:9; I Cor. 15:1-19; I Pet. 1:21.

He knew the thoughts and purposes of men. — Mt. 9:4; 12:25; Lu. 6:8; 7:39, 40; 9:47; John 1:42, 47-50; 2:24, 25; 6:61, 64; 13:11; 16:30.

His sinlessness. — John 8:46; II Cor. 5:21; Heb. 4:15; 7:26-28; I Pet. 2:21-23; I John 3:5.

He is the sufficer of all needs. — Mt. 11:28-30; John 4:14; 6:35, 48-58; 8:31-36, 51.

He will send the Holy Spirit. — John 14:26; 15:26; Acts 2:33.

He commanded to baptize in the name of Father, Son, and Holy Spirit. — Mt. 28:19.

Baptism was "in His name." — Acts 2:38; 8:12, 16; 10:48; 19:5.

Kingdom of heaven. — Mt. 13:52. At hand — Mt. 4:17; Lu. 10:9, 11. Belongs to children — Mt. 19:14; Mk. 10:15. Belongs to the poor — Mt. 5:3. Entrance into — Mt. 5:20; 7:21; 8:11; 18:3, 4; 19:14, 23; 25:34-46. Great in the kingdom of heaven — Mt. 5:19; 11:11. Keys of — Mt. 16:19. Least in — Mt. 5:19; 11:11. Mysteries of — Mt. 13:11. Parables of — Sake of, For the — Mt. 19:21. Shut by pharisees — Mt. 23:13. See Lu. 11:52.

LIFE: Temporal. — Lu. 6:9; 8:14; 21:34; John 13:38. Value of life — Mt. 16:25, 26; 18:8, 9; Mk. 8:36, 37; Lu. 12:22, 23. Life consisteth not in the abundance of the things which a man hath — Mt. 6:25-34; Mk. 8:35-38; Lu. 12:15-21. He that findeth his life shall lose it — Mt. 10:37-39; Mk. 8:35-38; Lu. 9:24-26; 14:25-27; 17:33; John 12:25. Lifetime — Lu. 16:25. Living or subsistence — Mk. 12:44; Lu. 8:43; 15:12, 30; 21:4.

Spiritual. — John 5:21, 40; 6:33, 51, 53-57. We must be born again — John 3:3-5. We must be begotten through the gospel — Mt. 13:19, 23; Lu. 8:11, 12. We must become as little children — Mt. 18:3; 19:14; Mk. 10:15; Lu. 18:17; John 13:33.

Eternal. — Mt. 25:46; John 4:14, 36; 5:29, 39; 6:27, 35, 48, 54, 63, 68; 8:12; 10:28; 12:50. This is life eternal — To know God — John 17:2, 3. Jesus the resurrection and the life — John 5:26; 11:25; 14:6. Jesus lays down His life for the sheep — Mt. 20:28; Mk. 10:45; John 10:15, 17, 18; 15:13. Eternal life conditioned on faith — John 3:15, 16, 36; 5:24; 6:40, 47. Life more abundantly — John 10:10. Those who have left houses and lands shall inherit eternal life — Mt. 19:29; Mk. 10:29, 30; Lu. 18:29, 30. The narrow gate — Mt. 7:14. See Mt. 18:8, 9; Mk. 9:41, 45.The rich young ruler — Mt. 19:16-22; Mk. 10:17-22; Lu. 18:24.

MAN: Is created by God. — Gen. 2:7; Deut. 4:32; Job 4:17; 10:3, 8; 14:15; 31:15; 32:22; 23:4; 34:19; 35:10; 36:3; Ps. 95:6; 100:3; 119:73; 138:8; 139:15, 16; Pr. 14:31; 22:2; Eccl. 7:29; Is. 17:7; 45:12; Jer. 27:5; Hos. 8:14.

Man made in the image of God. — Gen. 1:26, 27; 5:1, 2; 9:6; I Cor. 11:7; Jas. 3:9.

WHAT THE BIBLE SAYS ABOUT THE END TIME

Man formed from the dust of the earth. — Gen. 2:7; 3:19; Job 4:19; 10:9; 33:6; Is. 29:16; 45:9; 64:8; Jer. 18:6; Rom. 9:20, 21; II Cor. 4:7.
God gives to man the breath of life — The Father of his spirit — Gen. 2:7; Num. 16:22; 27:16; Job 12:10; 27:3; 33:4; 34:14; Is. 42:5; 57:16; Dan. 5:23; Ez. 37:5, 6, 9, 10; Zech. 12:1; Acts 17:25; Heb. 12:9; Rev. 22:6.
Man consists of body (*Heb.* Basar. *Gr.* Soma). — **Soul** (*Heb.* Nephesh. *Gr.* Psuche). **Spirit** (*Heb.* Ruach, Neshama. *Gr.* Pneuma). See SPIRIT; Gen. 2:7; Job 32:8, 18; 34:14; Ps. 31:9; Is. 10:18; Mt. 10:28; II Cor. 5:6, 8; I Thess. 5:23; Heb. 4:12.
Man is the completion of creation. — Gen. 1:28; 2:4-7; Ps. 8:4-8; Heb. 2:6-8.
Made but a little lower than God. — Ps. 8:5. **Than angels.** — Heb. 2:7.
Granted dominion over the earth. — Gen. 1:26, 28; Ps. 8:6-8; 49:14; 72:8.
Wonderfully made. — Job 10:8-11; Ps. 149:14-16; Eccl. 11:5. A puzzled saint — Job 12:4-6; Rom. 7:15-24. Thwarted plans — Ps. 33:10-19.
Differs from everything else living. — I Cor. 15:39.
Male and female represented in. — Gen. 1:26-28; 5:2; Mt. 19:4; Mk. 10:6.
Endowed with intellect. — Job 13:3, 15; Is. 1:18; 41:1, 21; 43:26; Jer. 12:1; Mt. 11:25; 16:7.
Endowed with affections. — Gen. 3:16; Lev. 19:18; Deut. 18:6; I Chr. 29:3; Mt. 19:19; John 13:34; Rom. 12:10; 13:9, 10; Col. 3:12; I Thess. 4:9; Heb. 13:1; I Pet. 1:22; I John 3:14.

Man made to toil. — Gen. 1:28; 2:5, 15; 3:19; 31:42; Ex. 31:16; Ps. 104:23; Pr. 13:11; 14:23.
Full liberty granted with but one restriction. — Gen. 2:16, 17; 8:2, 3.
Fall of. — Gen. 3:1-8; Eccl. 7:27-29; Rom. 5:12-19; I Cor. 15:21, 22.
Enticed by the tempter. — Gen. 3:4, 5, 13; Pr. 1:10-19; 12:26; 16:29; John 8:44; II Cor. 11:3; I Tim. 2:14; I Thess. 3:5; I Tim. 2:14; Jas. 1:13-15; I John 2:16, 17; Rev. 12:9, 13.
Sinfulness of. — Gen. 6:5, 6, 12; 8:21; I Ki. 8:46; Job 15:14-16; Ps. 14:1-3; 51:5; Pr. 20:9; Eccl. 7:20; 9:3; Is. 53:6; Jer. 17:9; Mk. 7:21-23; John 3:19; 7:7; Rom. 3:9-18; 7:18; Gal. 5:17; Jas. 1:13-15; I John 1:8.
Imperfection and weakness of. — Job 4:17-21; Ps. 39:5-13; Is. 41:21-24; Mt. 6:27; Rom. 9:16; II Cor. 3:5; Gal. 6:3.
Man subject to suffering. — Gen. 3:17-19; Job 5:7; 14:1, 2; Rom. 8:22, 23.
Man rebuked for perversity. — Is. 59:1-15; John 8:21-24, 38-48.
Vanity of man's life. — Job 7:7-10, 16; Ps. 103:14-16; Eccl. Chs. 1; 2; 7:15; 12:1-8; I Pet. 1:24.
Equality of. — I Sam. 2:7; Job 21:23-26; Ps. 49:6-14; Pr. 22:2; 29:13; Acts 10:34-35; Gal. 3:28; Eph. 6:5-9; Jas. 2:1-9.
The shortness of his life. — Job 14:1-22; Ps. 39:5; 49:6-14; 89:48; 90:5-10; Eccl. 1:4; 12:1-8; Heb. 9:27.
Man is great, though in ruins. — Lu. 15:17-24; 19:7-10; Rom. 5:7-8.
Man honored in the assumption of humanity by Jesus. — I Cor. 15:45-49; Eph. 1:19-23; Phil. 2:5-9; Col. 1:12-20; Heb. 2:5-18.

TOPICAL INDEX

Man's salvation provided for from the beginning. — Gen. 3:15; 12:3; Is. 53:1-12; Mt. 25:34; Rom. 16:25; Eph. 1:3-14; 3:1-11; II Thess. 2:13, 14; II Tim. 1:9, 10; Tit. 1:2, 3; II Pet. 1:10-12, 18-20; Rev. 13:8.

Man at his best when following Christ. — Mt. 4:19; 19:28, 29; II Cor. 3:18; 5:17; Eph. 2:4-7, 10; 4:11-13.

Man's individuality respected. — Lu. 12:57; John 8:15; 12:47; 15:14-16; Rev. 3:20, 21.

Man obtains enlargement of life. — John 1:4; 5:21-26; 6:33-35; 10:10; 17:2, 3; 20:31; I John 3:1-3.

Endowed with will. — John 7:17; Rom. 7:18; I Cor. 9:17; Phil. 2:13; Rev. 22:17.

Value of. — Mt. 10:31; 12:12; 16:26; Mk. 2:27; John 3:16; I Cor. 11:7.

Whole duty of. — Deut. 10:12; Eccl. 12:13; Mic. 6:8; I John 3:18-22.

Man proposes, but God disposes. — I Sam. 17:47; II Chr. 20:15; Eccl. 9:11; Is. 10:11; 47:1-15; Jer. 9:23, 24; Amos 2:14-16; Lu. 12:16-21.

Obtains an advocate in time of trouble. — Rom. 8:34; I Tim. 2:5, 6; Heb. 7:25; 9:24-28; I John 2:1, 2.

Man the partaker of the divine nature. — John 1:16; Eph. 3:19; 4:13, 24; Heb. 3:1, 14; 6:4; 12:10; II Pet. 1:4; I John 3:2.

He shall be recompensed according to his works. — Deut. Chs. 27; 28; Job 34:1, 12, 25; Ps. 62:12; Pr. 12:14; 24:12; Is. 3:10, 11; Jer. 32:19; Mt. 7:15-27; 16:27; John 5:29; Rom. 2:5, 6; 6:20-23; 14:12; I Cor. 3:8; II Cor. 5:10; Eph. 6:8; Col. 3:25; Rev. 2:23-27; 20:12, 13; 21:7, 8; 22:12.

PROPHECY: Nature of prophecy. It is one person's speaking for another. — Illustrated by Aaron speaking for Moses — Ex. 7:1, 2; *cf.* 4:16. Especially it is man's speaking for God — Deut. 18:18; II Chr. 36:15, 16; Is. 45:21; Jer. 20:7-9; 23:22; Ez. 3:17-19; Dan. 9:22; Amos 3:7, 8; Jonah 1:2; Hag. 1:13.

Source of prophecy. — Not the prophet's private interpretation of the times, but given of God — Num. 12:6; I Ki. 22:14; Jer. 19:14; Amos 3:8; 7:15; Lu. 1:67; II Pet. 1:20, 21.

Delivery of prophecy. — To the masses — Jer. 19:14; Ez. 33:31; Amos 5:1; 7:10; Hag. 2:2-4. To individuals — I Ki. 20:13, 22, 39-42; Amos 7:14-17; Hag. 2:21-23. Committed to writing — Ex. 17:14; Is. 8:1, 2, 16; 30:8; Jer. 30:2; 36:1-4, 17, 18, 32; 45:1; 51:60; Dan. 12:4, 9; Rev. 1:11, 19; 21:5.

Material of prophecy. — Prediction — Gen. 41:25; 49:1; Deut. 18:22; Num. 24:16, 17; I Ki. 11:29, 39; Is. 42:9; Jer. 28:9; Dan. 2:45; Rev. 1:1, 19; 22:6. Warnings — Ex. 3:18; Deut. 18:19; Is. 58:1; Jer. 1:16, 17; 26:2-6; Ez. 33:7-9. Religious instruction — Deut. 31:19, 21, 22; Is. 1:18; 2:3; Jer. 32:33. Moral exhortation — Is. 1:2-6, 16, 17; 3:10, 11; Jer. 25:4-6; Hos. 4:1-14; 6:5. Political or practical advice — II Sam. 7:5; 2:25; I Ki. 1:11-14; II Ki. 6:12, 21, 22; 14:25; Is. 7:3, 4; 37:21, 33; Jer. 27:1-15. Promotion of an enterprise — Ez. 6:14; Hag. 1:2-11. Interpretation of current events — Joel 1:2; 2:27; Hag. 1:5, 6, 9-11; 2:15-19. Revealing hidden things — Gen. 40:8; II Ki. 6:12; 7:1, 2; Is. 48:6; Dan. 2:19,

22, 23; 8:16-25; Mt. 26:68. Blessings—Gen. 9:26, 27; 27:27-29, 40; 49:3-27; Num. 23:9, 20-24; 24:7-9, 17-19; Lu. 2:29-32. Promises—II Sam. 7:8-17; Is. 2:2-4; Jer. 2:1, 2, 4; Hos. 4:1; Joel 2:31, 32; 3:18-21; Amos 3:1; Hag. 2:6-9; Zech. 13:1; Mal. 3:1. Threats and judgment—I Ki. 13:21, 22; II Sam. 12:10-12; Is. 1:20, 24-31. Doom of cities and nations: *Babylon*—Is. 13:1-22; 21:1-10; Jer. 25:12-14. *Assyria*—Is. 14:24-27. *Damascus*—Is. 17:1; Jer. 49:23-27; Amos 1:3-5; Zech. 9:1. *Philistia*—Is. 14: 29-31; Jer. 47:1-7. *Arabia*—Is. 21: 13-17. *Egypt*—Is. 19:1-22; 20:3, 4; Jer. 46:13-26; Ex. 29:1-16, 19, 20; 30:4, 6; 32:32. *Moab*—Is. 15: 1; 16:14; Jer. 48:1-42. *Ammon*—Jer. 49:1-6; Ez. 21:28-32; 25:2-11; Amos 1:13-15; Zeph. 2:8, 9. *Edom*—Is. 21:11, 12; Jer. 49:7-22; Ez. 25:12-14; 35:1-15; *Amos* 1:11, 12; Ob. 1-21. *Tyre*—Is. 23:1-18; Jer. 25:22; 47:4; Ez. 26:2; 28:24; Amos 1:9, 10; Zech. 9:2-4. *Jerusalem*—Is. 22:1-14; Jer. 26:18; 9: 11; Mic. 3:12. *Judah*—Jer. 1:15- 18; 4:16; 7:30-34; 13:9-14, 19; 20:4, 5; 21:4-10; Ez. 8:17, 18; Hos. 5:10; 6:4; Amos 2:4-5.

Characteristics of prophecy.—Usually fragmentary or limited in scope—I Cor. 13:9; Heb. 1:1. Connected with the times of utterance—e.g., Gen. 3:14-19; I Sam. 13:13, 14; Is. 7:10-17; and very often. Usually conditional, expressed—Is. 55:6, 7. Or unexpressed—e.g., Jonah 3:5-10. For general principle, see Jer. 18:1-12. Conditions based on Jehovah's character—Joel 2:12- 14; Jonah 4:2, 11. Some are unconditional, mostly messianic utterances—e.g., II Sam. 7:14-16; Is. 55:3; Acts 13:34. Often for posterity—Deut. 18:18, 19; 31:19, 24-29; I Cor. 10:11; I Pet. 1:10-12. Rarely dates future events—e.g., II Chr. 36:21; Jer. 25:11; 29:10; cf. Dan. 9:2. Exceeds other gifts in value—I Cor. 14:1-5.

Form of prophecy.—Public addresses—I Sam. 12:6-17; Is. 1:4-20; Jonah 3:4. Object lessons—I Ki. 18:38; Is. 8:1-4; Jer. 27:1-8; Ez. 37:15- 23; Hos. 3:1-5. (See prophet's use of emblems). Historical illustrations—Ju. 6:7-10; Ez. 17:11-16; Hos. 11:1-4; Nah. 3:8; Hag. 2:5; Zech. 1:5, 6; Mt. 24:37, 38; II Pet. 2:5. Poetry (the following and many other prophecies have poetic form in the original language)—Gen. 9: 25-27; 49:2-27; Ps. 2:7-9; 110:4- 7; Is. 52:13-53:12; 61:1-9. Dramatic composition—e.g., Ps. 24:7- 10; 91:1-16; Is. 21:6-11; 63:1-6. Allegory or parable—e.g., Is. 5:1- 7; Ez. 17:1-24; 20:49; 24:3-14; Zech. 1:8-11, 18, 21; 2:1-5; 3:1-5; 4:2-14; Gal. 4:21-31.

Fulfilment of prophecy.—Many fulfilled in short time—Gen. 40:12- 14, 18-22; 41:25-36, 47-56; Josh. 6:26; I Sam. 13:32; I Ki. 16:34; 20:13-21; II Ki. 2:10-14; 14:25; 15:12; 23:16; Acts 11:28; 21:11, 27-36. Many fulfilled in Christ. Some to be fulfilled after Christ's ascension—Acts 3:21. Others to be fulfilled at the end of the world—Dan. 12: 2; Mt. 24:30, 31, 40, 41; 25:31- 46; Jas. 5:28, 29; I Cor. 15:22-25; I Thess. 4:14-17; II Thess. 1:9, 10; II Pet. 3:10-13; Rev. 20:11. Fulfilments a confirmation of prophecy—I Sam. 2:34; cf. 4:11; I Ki. 13: 3-6; 18:37-38; II Ki. 7:1-18; 19:32- 37; Jer. 28:15-17.

Christ in prophecy.—As seed of the woman—Gen. 3:15. As Abraham's Seed—Gen. 22:17; Gal. 3:8, 16. As David's Seed—II Sam. 7:12-16; Ps. 89:35-37; Mt. 22:42-45. As King—I Chr. 17:12, 14; Ps. 2:6; 45:6; 110:1, 2; Is. 9:7; 16:5; 55: 3, 4; Jer. 30:9; Ez. 37:24; Dan. 7:14. As Priest—Ps. 110:4; Ez. 21:26, 27; Zech. 3:5, 8; 6:12, 13. As Prophet—Deut. 18:15-19. As Shepherd—Is. 40:11; Ez. 24:23, 24; 37:24. As Judge—Is. 11:3, 4; 16:5; Ps. 110:6; Mic. 4:3. As Servant of Jehovah—Is. 52:13; 49:5, 6; 53:11. As a Sufferer—Is. 52:14, 15; 53:3-12; Zech. 13:7. As Son of God—II Sam. 7:14; Ps. 2:7. As a Redeemer—Job 19:25; Is. 59:20. As the Anointed—Ps. 2:2; Is. 61:1. As the Branch—Is. 11:1-5; Jer. 23:5; 33:15; Zech. 3:8; 6:12, 13.

Man in prophecy.—Gen. 1:26-30; Job 8:20; Ps. 8:4-8; 144:3, 4; Heb. 2:5-18.

Church in prophecy.—As Jehovah's people—Ps. 47:9; 87:5, 6; 110:3; Jer. 31:33, 34; Dan. 7:27; Hos. 2: 23; Mic. 4:2-5; Zech. 13:9; 2:11. As a kingdom—Ps. 145:13; Is. 9:7; Dan. 2:45; 4:3; 7:27. As the redeemed—Ps. 107:2; Is. 35:9, 10; 62:12; 51:11.

World in prophecy.—Nations in unity under Jehovah—Ps. 22:27; 67:7; 82:8; Is. 19:23; 2:2-4; 56:6-8; Mic. 4:1-2. World's blessing—Gen. 22: 18; Is. 11:9; Jer. 3:19; 4:21; Acts 3:25; Gal. 3:8, 16, 29. World's conquest—Ps. 2:8, 9; 65:2; 110: 5, 6; Is. 66:18, 19; Jer. 3:17; 16: 19. World judged—Ps. 58:11; 82: 8; 110:6; Is. 66:23, 24; Jer. 25:31; Joel 3:2, 12-15; Mic. 4:3; Mt. 25: 31, 32. World's salvation—Is. 45: 22; 49:6; 52:10. New heavens and new earth—Is. 65:17; 66:22; Rom. 8:21, 22; II Pet. 3:13; Rev. 21:1, 2.

PROPHETS: Are God's messengers.—I Sam. 8:7-9; I Ki. 13:1, 3, 9; II Ki. 17:13, 23; 20:4, 5; II Chr. 36:15-21; Is. 6:8-11; 48:16; Jer. 7:13, 25; 11:7; 25:3, 4; 26:5; 32:33; Ez. 2:4; 3:4-11, 17-21, 27; Dan. 9:1, 6-10; Hos. 12:10; Amos 7:14, 15; Zech. 7:12; Heb. 1:1; Rev. 10:11.

Are inspired by Jehovah.—I Sam. 9:6; II Ki. 3:12; Is. 50:4, 5; Jer. 20:9; Amos 3:7, 8; Zech. 7:7; Lu. 1:70; Acts 3:18; Rom. 1:1, 2; Jas. 5:10; I Pet. 1:10, 11; II Pet. 1:21; Rev. 4:1; 10:7; 22:6.

Methods of Jehovah in communication to them: By voice.—To Moses—Ex. 6:13, 29; 7:2; 19:3-5; 25: 22; 33:11; Lev. 1:1; Num. 1:1; 7: 89; 9:8; 12:8; Deut. 5:5, 31; 18: 18; 34:9, 10; Josh. 3:7. To Joshua—Josh. 3:7; 4:14. To Balaam—Num. 22:18-20, 38; 23:5-12, 16, 20, 26; 24:15, 16. To Samuel—I Sam. 3:4-14, 21; 9:15; 15:16, 19-21. To David—II Sam. 23:2. To Elijah—I Ki. 22:14, 28. To Isaiah—Is. 6:8, 9; 51:15, 16. To Jeremiah—II Chr. 36:12, 15; Jer. 1:1-10; 13:1-3; 16:1; 18:1; 24:4-10; 26:1, 2; 27:1, 2; 29:30; 33:1, 2; 34:1, 2; 42:4, 7; Dan. 9:2. To Ezekiel—Ez. 3:10, 11, 22, 27.

By dreams and visions—Gen. 41:15-40; Num. 12:6; I Chr. 17:15; II Chr. 26:5; Job 4:12-16; 33:14-17; Is. 6:1-9; Ez. Chs. 1-3, 8-10; Dan. 2:19; 7:13, 15; 8:1, 15-27; 10:7-9; Hos. 12:10; Joel 2:28.

By angels.—To Moses—Gal. 3:19; Heb. 2:2. See Heb. 3:2-5. To Balaam—Num. 22:35. To Gad—I Chr. 21:18, 20, 30. To Daniel—

WHAT THE BIBLE SAYS ABOUT THE END TIME

Dan. 7:13-28; 8:15-19. To John —Rev. 1:1; 17:1; 19:9, 10; 21:9; 22:1-9, 16.

By the Holy Spirit.—Neh. 9:20, 30; Joel 2:28; Zech. 7:12; Mt. 22:43; Acts 7:51, 52; Heb. 3:7-11; 10:15-17; I Pet. 1:10, 11; II Pet. 1:21; Rev. 1:10.

Instances of inspiration of the Holy Spirit.—Noah—I Pet. 3:18-20. Joseph—Gen. 41:38. Bezalel—Ex. 31:2, 3; 35:31. Seventy elders—Num. 11:16, 17, 25, 26-29. Balaam Num. 24:2. The judges: Othniel—Ju. 3:10. Gideon—Ju. 6:34. Jephthah—Ju. 11:29. Samson—Ju. 13:25; 14:6, 19; 15:14; 16:28. Saul—I Sam. 10:6, 13; 11:6; 16: 13, 14; 19:23, 24. Messengers of Saul—I Sam. 19:20, 21. David—I Sam. 16:13; II Sam. 23:2; I Chr. 28:11, 12; Mk. 12:36; Acts 1:16. Azariah—II Chr. 15:1. Ezekiel—Ez. 2:1-4; 11:5, 24. Micaiah—I Ki. 22:14, 23, 28; II Chr. 18:23, 27. Jahaziel—II Chr. 20:14. Zechariah —II Chr. 24:20. Micah—Mic. 3:8. Isaiah—Acts 28:25. Elizabeth—Lu. 1:41. John the Baptist—Lu. 1:15. Zacharias—Lu. 1:67. Simeon—Lu. 2:25-27. Apostles—Mt. 10:20; Mk. 13:11; John 20:22; Acts 2:4; 4:8; 9:17; Rev. 1:10, 11. Agabus—Acts 11:28; 21:10, 11. Stephen—Acts 7:55. Disciples at Tyre—Acts 21:4.

By the gift of knowledge and wisdom. —I Chr. 28:19; Job 32:8; Jer. 11: 18; Dan. 1:17-20; 2:21, 23; 4:8, 9; 5:11-14; 9:22. See I Ki. 3:12, 28.

By permission of the divine name. —Ex. 3:13, 14; Deut. 18:18, 19; II Chr. 33:18; Ez. 3:11; Jas. 5:10.

Christ came in fulfilment of prophecy. —II Sam. 7:12; Mic. 5:2 (Mt. 2:5; John 7:42); Lu. 1:70.

Christ appealed to Moses and the prophets as if they were inspired to show that He came to fulfil their predictions.—Lu. 24:27, 44, 45; John 1:45; 5:45, 46. See John 13: 18; 17:12.

The apostles appealed to Moses and the prophets as if they were inspired.—Acts 1:16, 20; 2:25-35; 3:18, 22, 23; 7:37 (Deut. 18:15); 8:28-35; 10:43; 13:29, 33-41; 17: 2, 3; 24:14, 15; 26:22, 23; 28:23-27; Rom. 1:1-4; 3:21; 15:8; 16: 25, 26.

Prophets worked miracles as their endorsement.—Moses—Ex. 4:1-9; 7:9; 8:16-19; Num. 16:28-33. Elijah—I Ki. 18:30-39. Elisha—II Ki. 5:3, 8, 14. Daniel—Dan. 3:19-28; 4:2.

They taught the people through emblems.—Is. 20:2-4; Jer. 19:1, 10, 11; 27:1-11; 43:8-10; 51:63; Ez. 4:1-13; 5:1-4; 7:23; 9:4-6; 12:3-7; 21:6, 7; 24:1-24; Hos. 1:2-9.

Wickedness destroys prophetic vision.—I Sam. 28:6; Lam. 2:9; Ez. 7:26-27.

Must deliver God's message faithfully.—Num. 22:8, 18, 19, 38; 23: 5, 11, 12, 17, 26; 24:12, 13; I Sam. 3:16, 17; II Sam. 7:17; I Ki. 22:13-14; Is. 21:10; Jer. 6:27; 23: 28; 26:2, 12; Ez. 3:10-21; 11:25; 13:10-14; Mic. 2:6, 7.

Jehovah supports His faithful prophets.—Ex. 4:10-12; Jer. 1:6-19; 15:19-21; Ez. 2:6; 3:8-9.

False prophets described and denounced.—Deut. 18:20; I Ki. 13: 11-25; Is. 9:15; Jer. 6:13-15; 14: 13-16; 23:9-40; 27:14-18; 28:15-

17; 29:8-9; Lam. 2:14; Ez. 13:4-7, 22; 21:29; 22:25-28; Mic. 2:11; Mt. 24:11; Lu. 6:26; II Pet. 2:1; I John 4:1. Adulterous—Jer. 23: 14; 29:21-23. Covetous—Mic. 3: 11. Drunken—Is. 28:7.
The people are warned against them. —Deut. 13:1-3; Jer. 23:16; 27:14-17; 29:8; Mt. 7:15; 24:5, 23-26; Mk. 13:6,21-23; Lu. 21:8.
Punishment of false prophets.—Deut. 18:20; I Ki. 13:11-25; 18:22-40; 22:24-25; Jer. 13:13-14; 14:15; 20:6; 23:13, 15, 30-32; 28:15-17; 29:15-32; Ez. 13:2, 3, 8, 9; Mic. 3:5-7; Zech. 13:3-6. Punishment of their followers—Jer. 14:16; Ez. 13:15-16; 14:10-11.
Maltreatment of God's prophets.— I Ki. 19:10; II Chr. 36:16; Neh. 9: 26; Jer. 2:30; Mt. 5:12; 23:29-38; Lu. 11:47-51; Rom. 11:3; I Thess. 2:14-16; Rev. 18:24. God avenges wrongs done to His prophets—Deut. 32:43; II Ki. 9:7; I Chr. 16:21-22; Mt. 23:35-38; Lu. 11:47-51.
List of prophets in their order according to Old Testament.—Enoch— Gen. 5:21-24; Jude 14, 15. Noah— Gen. 9:25-27; II Pet. 2:5 (see marginal note). Jacob—Gen. 49:1. Moses—Deut. 18:18; Acts 3:22; 7:37. Aaron—Ex. 7:1. Balaam— Num. 22:20, 38; II Pet. 2:16. The prophet sent to Israel—Ju. 6:8, 9. The prophet sent to Eli—I Sam. 2:27. Samuel—I Sam. 3:20-21; Acts 3:24; 13:20; Heb. 11:32-34. David—Ps. 22:1, 16, 18; Acts 1: 16; 2:25-31; 4:25, 26. Nathan— II Sam. 7:2-3; 12:1-7. Gad—II Sam. 24:11-14. Ahijah—I Ki. 11: 29-32. The prophet of Judah—I Ki. 13:1-10. Iddo—II Chr.9:29. Shemaiah—I Ki. 12:21-24; II Chr. 12:5. Azariah—II Chr. 15:2-7. Hanani—II Chr. 16:7-10. Jehu— I Ki. 16:1, 7, 12. Elijah—I Ki. 17: 1; 18:1-2; 19:1-8; Rom. 11:2-4. Elisha—I Ki. 19:16, 19-21; II Ki. 5:1-14; Lu. 4:27. Micaiah—I Ki. 22:7-9. Joel—Joel 1:1. Jonah—II Ki. 14:25; Mt. 12:39-41. Amos— Amos 1:1; 7:14, 15. Hosea—Hos. 1:1. Isaiah—II Ki. 19:2; Lu. 4:17. Micah—Mic. 1:1. Nahum—Nah. 1:1. Zephaniah—Zeph. 1:1. Jeremiah—Jer. 1:1-2. Habakkuk—Hab. 1:1. Obadiah—Ob. 1, 2. Ezekiel —Ez. 1:3. Daniel—Dan. 2:14-16. Haggai—Ezra 5:1; Hag. 1:1. Zechariah—Ezra 5:1; Zech. 1:1. Malachi —Mal. 1:1.
New Testament prophets.—Zacharias —Lu. 1:67-79. John the Baptist— John 1:6, 29-31. Jesus—Mt. 6:14-21. (See His prophecies throughout the gospels.) Agabus—Acts 11: 28; 21:10. Paul—I Tim. 4:1. Peter —II Pet. 1:1-2; 3:3. John—Rev. 1:1-3.
Customs and habits.—Were anointed —I Ki. 19:16. Attached to king's household—II Sam. 24:11; II Chr. 29:25; 35:15. Had servants—I Ki. 19:3; II Ki. 3:11; 4:12. Presents offered—I Sam. 9:7, 8; I Ki. 14:3; II Ki. 4:42. Presents refused—Num. 22:18; II Ki. 5:5, 16. Frequently married men—II Ki. 4:1; Ez. 24: 18; Hos. 1:2, 3. Often led a wandering life—I Ki. 18:10-12; 19:3, 8, 15; II Ki. 4:10. Wore coarse mantle —Zech. 13:4; Mt. 3:4.
Were sent to reprove and to call to repentance.—II Ki. 17:13; II Chr. 24:18, 19; Is. 62:6; Jer. 6:17; 7:3-7, 25; 11:7; 18:11; 25:4, 5; Ez. 3:17-21; 18:30-32; 33:7-9. To denounce the weakness of kings:

WHAT THE BIBLE SAYS ABOUT THE END TIME

Samuel to Saul—I Sam. 15:10-23. Nathan to David—II Sam. 12:7-14. Elijah to Ahab and Jezebel—I Ki. 18:17, 18; 21:17-29. To predict the downfall of nations—Is. Chs. 13-23; Jer. Chas. 46-51. To foretell the coming of the Messiah.

PUNISHMENT. Gen. 3:13-24; 4:13, 14; Chs. 6 and 7; Lev. 24:10-23; 26:14-45; Num. 32:23; Deut. 11: 26-29; 24:16; Chs. 27 and 28; 30: 15-19; I Sam. 3:10-14; I Ki. 21:17-29; I Chr. 10:13, 14; Esth. 7:1-10; 9:14; Is. 26:21; Jer. 16:18; 30:14; 48:44; Lam. 3:39; 4:22; Ez. Chs. 7-9, 21-35; Hos. Chs. 8-10; 13:16-21; Amos 1:3; Mic. Ch. 6; Nah. 1: 12; Hab. 3:12; Zeph. 1:12; 3:8.

Discussed by Job and his friends.—Job 4:7-9; 5:3-7; 8:20; 10:14; 11: 20; 15:20-35; 18:1-21; 19:29; 20: 1-29; 21:1-34; 27:13-23; 31:3.

Design of: To check crime—Gen. 9: 5-6; Lev. 24:18:22; Deut. 24:7; 25:2-3; I Ki. 2:36-38. To correct the life—II Sam. 7:14-15; Job 5:17-20; 23:10; Ps. 94:12-13; Pr. 13: 24; 19:18; 22:15; 23:13-14; Mal. 3:2-3; John 15:2; Eph. 6:4; Heb. 12:5-11; I Pet. 2:20. To warn others —Num. 15:1-21, 40; Deut. 13:11; 17:13; 19:20.

Kinds of capital punishment.—Burning—Gen. 38:24; Lev. 20:14; 21:9; Dan. 3:6. Hanging—Gen. 40:22; 41:13; Num. 25:4; Deut. 21:22-23; Josh 8:29; II Sam. 21:9; Esth.

THE PROPHETS AND THEIR BOOKS IN THEIR ORDER

Name	Place of Ministry	Date B.C.	Historical Connection
Joel	Israel and Nineveh	About 830-810	In reign of Joash of Judah.
Jonah	Judah	About 800	In reign of Jehoahash of Israel.
Amos	Israel	About 760	In reign of Jeroboam II.
Hosea	Israel	About 750-725	From reign of Jeroboam II to that of Hezekiah.
Isaiah	Jerusalem	About 740-695	From death of Uzziah to reign of Manasseh.
Micah	Judah	About 735-700	From reign of Jotham to that of Hezekiah.
Nahum	Probably Judah	About 640-610	In reign of Assurbanipal or later.
Zephaniah	Judah	About 630	In reign of Josiah.
Jeremiah	Judah and Egypt	About 628-585	From reign of Josiah till after the commencement of Babylon exile.
Habakkuk	Judah	About 609-600	In reign of Jehoiakim.
Obadiah	Judah or Babylonia	About 585 (?)	Shortly after destruction of Jerusalem.
Daniel	Babylon and Persia	About 602-534	During the exile.
Ezekiel	Chaldea	About 593-571	Among Jewish exiles.
Haggai	Judea	About 520	In reign of Darius Hystaspes.
Zechariah	Judea	About 520-480	During rebuilding of temple and afterwards.
Malachi	Judea	About 433	Contemporary with Nehemiah.

TOPICAL INDEX

2:23; 7:9-10. Crucifixion—Mt. 20: 19; 27:35; Mk. 15:24-25; Lu.23: 33. Beheading—Gen. 40:19; II Ki. 6:31; 10:7; Mt. 14:10; Mk. 6:16, 27. Stoning—Ex. 19:13; Lev. 20: 2, 27; 24:14; Num. 15:35-36; Deut. 13:10; 17:5; 22:21-24; Josh. 7: 25; I Ki. 21:10, 13; Ez. 16:40; John 8:5, 59; Acts 7:58-59; 14:19; II Cor. 11:25; Heb. 11:37. Slaying with sword—Ex. 32:27-28; I Sam. 15:8, 33; Acts 12:2. Cut in pieces —Dan. 2:5. Exposing to wild beasts —Dan. 6:16, 24; I Cor. 15:32.

Punishment of lesser degree.—Imprisonment—Ezra 7:26; Mt. 5:25. Confinement in stocks—Jer. 20:2; Acts 16:24. In dungeon—Jer. 38:6; Zech. 9:11. Binding with fetters—Ps. 105:18. Restitution—Ex. 21: 36; 21:1-4, 6, 11; Lev. 6:4-5; 24: 18; Num. 5:6. Retaliation—Ex. 21: 23-36; Lev. 24:17-22; Deut. 19: 21. Scourging—Lev. 19:20; Deut. 25:1-3; Mt. 20:19; 23:34; 27:26; Mk. 10:34; Lu. 18:33; John 19:1; Acts 22:24, 25; II Cor. 11:24; Heb. 11:36. Beating with rods—Pr. 23: 14; Acts 16:22. Selling the criminal —Mt. 18:25. Banishment—Ezra 7:26; Rev. 1:9. Confiscating property—Ezra 7:26.

Torturing.—By putting out eyes—Ju. 16:21; I Sam. 11:2. Cutting off nose and ears—Ez. 23:25. Hanging by hands—Lam. 5:12. Plucking out hair—Neh. 13:25; Is. 50:6. Fining —Ex. 21:22, 32; 22:1-4, 7-9, 16, 17; Deut. 22:18, 19, 28, 29.

General—Mt. 18:34; 26:67; Acts 23:2.

Future punishment.—Mt. 3:10-12; 5:21, 22, 27-30; 7:18-23; 10:28; 18:5-9; 21:41-44; Chs. 23-25; Mk. 9:43-48; Lu. 6:49; 12:5; 16:19-31; 19:27; 20:16-18; Acts 1:25; I Cor. 3:17; 6:9, 10; Eph. 5:3-6; Heb. 10: 31; II Pet. 2:4-21; Rev. 21:27; 22: 14, 15.

RESURRECTION. Anticipation in Old Testament.—Ps. 16:10; 110: 1; Is. 26:19; Dan. 12:2, 13; Hos. 13:14; Heb. 11:35.

Apostles testified concerning it.—Lu. 24:45-48; Acts 1:8, 22; 2:24-32; 4:10, 33; 5:31, 32; 10:39-42; 17:3, 31; 26:22, 23; I Cor. 15:1-4; II Cor. 4:13, 14; Col. 3:1-4; I Thess. 4:13-17.

The foundation of Christianity.—John 11:25; Rom. 1:3, 4; 6:4-11; 8:11, 19-23; I Cor. 3:10, 11; 15:3, 4; Eph. 2:4-7; Col. 2:12; 3:1.

Jesus staked his claim upon his resurrection on the third day.—Mt. 16:21; 17:22, 23; 20:18, 19; John 5:21, 25-29; 6:39, 40, 54; 11:23-27.

The sign Jesus gave of His Messiahship: Jonah—Mt. 12:39, 40. The Temple—John 2:18-22.

Scripture proofs of credibility.—Mt. 22:29-32; Mk. 12:35, 36; Lu. 20: 34-38; Acts 26:6-8; Rom. 8:28-34; I Cor. Ch. 15.

Paul's proof drawn from heaven.—Acts 9:3-5; 22:7, 8; 26:14-19; Gal. 1:15-17.

Appearances of Jesus: Mary Magdalene—Mk. 16:9; John 20:18. The women—Mt. 28:9. Peter—Lu. 24: 34. Two Disciples—Lu. 24:13-31. Apostles and others, except Thomas —Mk. 16:14; Lu. 24:33-43; John 20:19-24. Apostles with Thomas —John 20:26. Apostles at sea of Galilee—John 21:1ff. Apostles in Galilee ("Above 500 brethren in all")—Mt. 28:16, 17; I Cor. 15:6. James—I Cor. 15:7. All the apostles

(Ascension)—Lu. 24:51; Acts 1:9; I Cor. 15:7. Stephen—Acts 7:55f. Paul—I Cor. 15:8. John—Rev. 1:18.
Raised by the power of God.—Mt. 26:64; John 10:18; Rom. 1:4; 8:11; I Cor. 6:14; 15:43; II Cor. 5:1; 13:4; Eph. 1:19-21; Phil. 3:9-11; II Tim. 1:8-10.
The power of God produces hope.—Acts 23:6; Phil. 3:10, 11; I Pet. 1:3, 21; 3:21, 22.
Jesus' resurrection the earnest of ours.—Rom. 8:19-25, 32-34; I Cor. 15:54, 57; Phil. 3:10-14; II Tim. 2:11, 12.
The resurrection body,—Lu. 24:39; John 20:27; I Cor. 15:42-54; II Cor. 5:1-4; Phil. 3:21.
The order of the resurrection.—John 5:29; Acts 24:15; I Cor. 15:20-23; I Thess. 4:15ff.; Rev. 20:12, 13.
Form of baptism illustrates the resurrection.—Rom. 6:3-11; Col. 2:11-13.
Resurrection of Jesus commemorated on the first day of the week.—John 20:19-23, 26; Acts 20:7; Rev. 1-10.
Typified by: Isaac—Gen. 22:13, with Heb. 11:19. Jonah 2:10, with Mt. 12:40.
Instances cited (but not resurrections strictly in the class with Jesus): The ruler's daughter—Mt. 9:18-26. Saints at crucifixion—Mt. 27:53. Son of widow at Nain—Lu. 7:4. Lazarus—John 11:44. Dorcas—Acts 9:40. Eutychus—Acts 20:9-12. Old Testament worthies—Heb. 11:35. The Shunammite's son—II Ki. 4:32-37. Man thrown into Elisha's sepulchre—II Ki. 13:20-21.
Resurrection of Jesus not understood by disciples at first.—Mt. 16:21, 22; Mk. 8:31-33; 9:9, 10; 16:14; Lu. 18:31-34; 24:36-43. Afterwards emboldened—Acts 2:14-32; 4:19, 20, 31-33; 26:8-19.
A stumbling block to the Greeks.—Acts 17:32; I Cor. 1:22, 23.
Resurrection of man.—Believed in by the Pharisees—Acts 23:5-8; 24:15; 26:6-8. By the Jews—John 11:24. Denied by the Sadducees—Mt. 22:23-28; Acts 23:6-8.
Errors concerning the resurrection.—I Cor. 15:12-19, 35-42; II Tim. 2:16-18.
REVEAL. Deut. 29:29; I Sam. 2:27; Mt. 10:26; 11:27. Cause, My—Jer. 11:20. Flesh and blood hath not—Mt. 16:17. Gates of death—Job 18:2. Glory—Rom. 8:18; I Pet. 4:13; 5:1. Heart—Pr. 18:2. Iniquity—Job 20:27. Lawless one—II Thess. 2:8. Ready to be—I Pet. 1:5. Righteousness—Is. 56:1; Rom. 1:17. Secrets—Dan. 2:19, 22-29, 27. Thoughts—Lu. 2:35. Wrath, Of—Rom. 1:18.
REVELATION: The disclosure of heavenly knowledge.—Ps. 119:19, 130; Eph. 1:17-20. Revelation is the self-manifestation of God as the God of a gracious purpose—Eph. 1:9, 10. Inspiration is that divine influence which imparts this manifestation to the human mind—John 16:13. Revelation has to do with the content—II Tim. 3:11-17. Inspiration with the mode of delivery—II Pet. 1:21.
Revelation of God in Christ.—Is. 7:14; Mt. 1:23; John 1:14; 3:16; 14:9, 10; I Cor. 1:24, 30; Eph. 1:9, 10; Rev. 1:1.
Revelation of Christ's glory.—John 17:4, 5; Rom. 8:18; I Pet. 4:13, 14; 5:1.

TOPICAL INDEX

Revelaton of the Lord Jesus. — II Cor. 12:1-4; II Thess. 1:7. Of the Son of Man — Lu. 17:30.
How revelation came. — Through the prophets — Is. 9:6, 7; Rom. 16:25, 26; I Pet. 1:12. Through the Holy Spirit — Lu. 12:12; John 14:26; 15: 26; 16:13; I Cor. 2:10; Eph. 3:5. Through Jesus Christ — John 8:26; 17:8; Rom. 10:17; I Cor. 1:7, 24; 15:1-4; Gal. 3:22-26. Through the apostles — Mt. 28:19, 20; Mk. 16: 15, 16; Lu. 12:11, 12; 24:45-49; John 15:27; I Cor. 2:6-16; 14:6; II Cor. 5:19, 20. Through the gospel — Rom. 1:16, 17.
What revelation does. — Brings to nought human wisdom — I Cor. 1: 20-29. Pierces the sinful heart — Acts 2:37. Giveth light — Ps. 119: 130. Giveth knowledge of duty — Gal. 2:2. Reveals inheritance of God in Christ — Eph. 1:11-20. Brings truth to babes — Lu. 10:21; I Cor. 1:26-29.
Other revelations. — Of secrets — Deut. 29:29; Pr. 11:13; 20:19; Dan. 1: 22, 28, 29, 47; Amos 3:7.
Of judgment. — John 3:18, 19; 8:21-24; 16:7-11; Rom. 2:5. Of wrath — Rom. 1:18; II Thess. 1:7-10.
Man of sin. — II Thess. 2:3-10.
REWARD: Dispensing of. — God prepares it — Gen. 15:1; Mt. 25:34; I Cor. 2:9; Heb. 11:10, 16.
God and Christ give it. — Is. 40:10; 62:11; Mt. 25:31-46; Lu. 12:32; Rev. 22:12.
Ground of. — Dependent on character — Ez. Ch. 18; Mk. 16:16; Rev. 22: 12. The righteous — II Sam. 22:21; Ps. 18:20; 58:11; Mt. 25:34-36, 46; Lu. 6:22, 23, 35; Jas. 1:12; Rev. 2:10. The wicked — Gen. 2: 17; 4:6, 7; II Sam. 3:39; Ps. 9:17; Mt. 6:1, 2, 5; 25:41-46; Rom. 2: 8; Heb. 2:2, 3; 10:26; I Pet. 4:18; Rev. 22:15.
Reasons for reward. — Boldness — Heb. 10:35. Deeds — Ps. 31:23; Lu. 23:41. Desire for service — I Cor. 9:17, 18; Heb. 11:6. Faithfulness — I Cor. 4:1-4. Faith — Rom. 4:4, 5, 16; Heb. 11:6. Humility — Lu. 14:10, 11. Kindness — Lu. 6:35. Ministering to others — Mt. 25:34-36. Obedience — Ps. 19:11; Pr. 13: 13. Patience — Rom. 2:7. Wisdom — Pr. 24:14.
Spiritual reward to be sought for. — Is. 55:6, 7; II John 8. Promise of — Joel 2:28, 29; Mt. 10:42; Mk. 9: 41; Acts 2:17-21.
When spiritual rewards are given. — In present life — Mt. 5:4-7; 19:29; Mk. 10:30; Lu. 17:30; John 6:40; 17:2, 3; Rom. 6:23; Heb. 12:28; I John 5:11, 13; Rev. 2:26, 27. In the future life — Mt. 5:8; 16:27; 19: 21; Lu. 12:33;14:13, 14; 18:30; Rom. 2:7, 8; I Cor. 9:25; II Cor. 11:18; 5:1; Jas. 1:12; Rev. 2:7, 10, 17; 3:12, 21; 22:12.
Reward of the worker. — II Chr. 15: 7; Jer. 31:16; Dan. 2:6; Rom. 4:4; I Cor. 3:8, 14. A prophet's — Mt. 10:40f. A disciple's — Mt. 10:42.
No reward for iniquity. — Num. 14: 20-23; Ps. 103:10; Pr. 24:20. For the dead — Eccl. 9:5.
Temporal. — To Abraham — Gen. 15: 1. To Levites — Num. 18:31. Israel — Lev. 20:22-24. Caleb — Num. 14: 24. Ruth — Ruth 2:12. Mordecai — Esth. 6:1-10. David — II Sam. 7:11, 12; Solomon — I Ki. 3:11-13. Disciples — Mt. 5:5.

WHAT THE BIBLE SAYS ABOUT THE END TIME

Features of future.—Glory—Ps. 73: 24; Rom. 8:17, 18; II Cor. 4:17; Phil. 3:21; Col. 3:4; I Pet. 5:4. Inheritance—Mt. 5:12; John 14:3; Acts 20:32; 26:18; Rom. 8:17; Col. 1:12; 3:24; Heb. 9:15; I Pet. 1:4; Rev. 21:7. Life—Dan. 12:2; Mt. 19:29; Mk. 10:30; Lu. 17:33; 18: 30; John 6:40; I Cor. 15:51. Rest—Heb. 4:9, 10; Rev. 14:13. Eternal life gift of God—Rom. 6:23.

Rewards as bribes.—God declines them—Deut. 10:17. Men decline them—Abraham—Gen. 14:22, 23. Moses—Heb. 11:26. Samuel—I Sam. 12:3. Daniel—Dan. 5:17. Some desire bribes—Judas—Mt. 26:14-16; Mk. 14:10, 11; Lu. 22: 3-6; Acts 1:18. See also Ps. 15:5; 26:10; Is. 33:15; 45:13; Amos 5: 12. Wages of sin—Rom. 6:23.

Rewards of men.—Just—II Sam. 19: 36-38; Mt. 6:3, 5; Lu. 23:41. Evil for good—Gen. 44:4; II Chr. 20: 11; Ps. 35:12; Pr. 17:13. Good for evil—I Sam. 24:19; Pr. 25:22; Rom. 12:20, 21.

SATAN.—**Names:** Abaddon—Rev. 9:11. Accuser of Saints—Rev. 12: 10. Adversary—Job Chs. 1, 2; Zech. 3:1; I Pet. 5:8. Angel of the Abyss—Rev. 9:11. Apollyon (Destroyer)—Rev. 9:11. Beelzebub—Mt. 12: 24; Mk. 3:22; Lu. 11:15. Belial—II Cor. 6:5. Deceiver—Rev. 12:9; 20:3, 8, 10. Devil—Mt. 4:1: Thirty-five times only in the New Testament. Dragon—Rev. 12:3, 7, 9. Enemy—Mt. 13:39. Evil One—Mt. 13:19, 38; I John 2:13, 14; 3:12; 5:18. Father of lies and liars—John 8:44. God of this world—II Cor. 4: 4. Murderer—John 8:44. Prince of powers of air—Eph. 2:2. Prince of demons—Mt. 2:24; Mk. 3:22; Lu. 11:15. Prince of this world—John 12:31; 14:30; 16:11. Satan—I Chr. 21:1. Serpent—II Cor. 11:3; Rev. 12:9; 20:2. Tempter—Mt. 4:3; I Thess. 3:5.

His nature and origin.—An angel—Job 1:6; 2:1; II Cor. 11:14. Fell from heaven—Lu. 10:18. Because of sin—II Pet. 2:4; Jude 6. Ruler of demons—Mt. 12:24, 26-28; Mk. 3:22, 23; Lu. 11:15, 18. Ruler of the unsaved—II Cor. 4:4; I John 5:19. Adversary of man—I Pet. 5:8.

His character.—Murderer—John 8: 44. Liar and deceitful—John 8:44; II Thess. 2:9, 10; II Cor. 11:14. Sinner—I John 3:8. Tempter—Mt. 4:3; I Thess. 3:5. Enemy of righteousness—Acts 13:10. Cunning—II Cor. 2:11; Eph. 6:11, 12.

His works.—Author of all sin and suffering—Rom. 5:12; Rev. 12:9. Cause of sickness—Lu. 13:16; Acts 10:38. Has the power of death—Heb. 2:14. Tempts to evil: David—I Chr. 21:1. Jesus—Mt. 4:1, 11; Mk. 1:13; Lu. 4:2, 13. Judas—Lu. 22:3. Peter—Lu. 22:31. Ananias—Acts 5:3. Paul—II Cor. 12:7. Adversary of Joshua—Zech. 3:1, 2. Robs of the truth—Mt. 13:19; Mk. 4:15; Lu. 8:12; Mt. 13:17. Blinds to the glory of God—Mt. 13:17; John 8:54, 55; 9:39-41; 12:39, 40; II Cor. 4:4. Makes deaf—John 8: 43, 45-47. Destroys the word of Christ—Mt. 13:37-39; John 8:41-44. Hinders Christ's cause—Mt. 13: 39; I Thess. 2:17, 18.

Overruled for good.—To prove the righteous—Mt. 4:10; Lu. 22:31, 32; I Tim. 3:6, 7. To check undue exaltation—II Cor. 12:7. To destroy the dominion of the flesh—I Cor.

TOPICAL INDEX

5:7; II Cor. 2:5-11. To teach men not to blaspheme—I Tim. 1:20. To bring victory out of persecution—Rev. 2:10.
He counterfeits the spiritual universe. —False God—I Thess. 1:9; II Thess. 2:3, 4, 9-12. False Christs—Mt. 24:24; Mk. 13:22. False angels—II Cor. 11:14; Rev. 9:11; 12:7, 9. False prophets—Mt. 7:15; 24:11, 24; Lu. 6:26; Acts 13:6; II Pet. 2:1; I John 4:1; Rev. 16:13; 19:20; 20:10.
False teachers.—I Tim. 4:1, 2; 6:3-5; II Tim. 4:3, 4; Tit. 1:10; II Pet. 2:1. False apostles—II Cor. 11:13; Rev. 2:2.
False churches.—Rev. 2:9; 3:16; 18:4. Brethren—Acts 15:1, 24; II Cor. 11:26; Gal. 2:4.
Our duty.—Watch and pray—Mt. 26:41; Mk. 14:38; Lu. 21:36; I Pet. 4:7; 5:8, 9. Put on the whole armor of God—Eph. 6:11. Resist—Eph. 4:27; Jas. 4:7; I John 2:13, 14, 18.
His overthrow.—In fact, bound by the truth—John 8:31-36; Rom. 8:2; Rev. 20:1-3. To be destroyed—I John 3:8. Under man—Gen. 3:15; Rom. 16:20. Safety of the believer—Lu. 10:19; John 10:27-30. Reserved for eternal fire—Mt. 25:41; Rev. 20:10.
SECOND COMING. Mt. 16:27; 24:36-39; 25:1-46; Mk. 8:38; 13:32-37; Lu. 9:26; 18:7-8; 19:11-27; John 14:1-3, 28; 21:22, 23; Acts 1:9-11; 2:34, 35; 3:20, 21; Rom. 2:16; I Cor. 1:7, 8; 4:5; 11:26; 15:23-25; Phil. 3:20; Col. 3:4; I Thess. 4:16, 17; 5:1-3, 23; II Thess. 1:7-10; 2:1-4; II Tim. 4:1-8; Tit. 2:13; Heb. 9:28; Jas. 5:7-9; I Pet. 5:4; II Pet. 3:7-11; I John 2:28; Jude 14-15; Rev. 1:7; 11:15; 22:10-12.

Time known only to God—Mt. 24:36-39; Mk. 13:32.
Long deferred—Mt. 25:19; Mk. 13:35, 36; Lu. 18:7, 8; 19:11-15; John 21:22, 23; Acts 2:34, 35; 3:21; I Cor. 15:23-25; II Thess. 2:1-4; II Pet. 3:3-11; Rev. 11:15.
Disciples looked for immediate—Lu. 19:11; II Thess. 2:1, 2; Jas. 5:7, 8; I John 2:28.
In glory—Mt. 16:27; 24:36-39; 25:31, 32; Mk. 8:38; Lu. 9:26; Col. 3:4; I Thess. 4:16, 17; II Thess. 1:10; Tit. 2:13; I Pet. 5:4.
With power—Acts 2:34, 35; Phil. 3:20; I Thess. 4:16, 17; II Thess. 1:7, 8; Jude 14-15; Rev. 1:7.
Without warning—Mt. 24:36-39; 25:1-13; Mk. 13:32-37; I Thess. 5:1-3; II Pet. 3:10.
To judge the world—Mt. 16:27; 25:31-46; Lu. 19:11-27; Rom. 2:16; I Cor. 1:7, 8; 4:5; II Thess. 1:7-10; II Tim. 4:1-8; Rev. 22:10-12.
SHEOL (Gr. *Hades*). **Described.**—Land of Darkness—Job 10:22; Lam. 3:6; Ps. 143:3. Place of silence—Ps. 31:17. Work and wisdom absent—Eccl. 9:10. Cruel—Song of Sol. 8:6. Never satisfied—Pr. 27:20; 30:16; Hab. 2:5. Painful—Ps. 116:3. All beauty consumed by—Ps. 49:14. Sinner consumed by—Ps. 49:14. Memory gone—Ps. 6:5. Praise and thanks unknown in—Is. 38:18; Ps. 6:5.
Death is the entrance to.—The Grave is the mouth of—Ps. 141:7. The Grave is the gate of—Is. 38:10. Sickness brings near to—Ps. 30:3; 88:3. Soul delivered from—Ps. 86:13. Figuratively—Jonah 2:2.
An underworld of departed persons. —Beneath—Pr. 15:24. Go down

to—I Ki. 2:6, 9; Job 7:9; 21-13; Ps. 55:15; Pr. 5:5; Is. 5:14; 14:15; Ez. 31:15, 16, 17; 32:27. Has depths—Deut. 32:22; Pr. 9:18; Ez. 32:21; Amos 9:2.
Visible to God.—His anger burns to lowest depth of—Deut. 32:22. Naked before God—Job 26:6.
Knowledge of God is deeper than.—Job 11:8.
Compared with heaven equally open—Ps. 139:8; Amos 9:2. Before Jehovah—Pr. 15:11.
The wicked journey toward.—By sin —Pr. 7:27; Is. 14:11; Ps. 9:17; 49:14. Man cannot deliver from power of—Ps. 89:48.
The righteous to be delivered from. —Soul redeemed from power of—Ps. 49:15. Soul not to be left in—Ps. 16:10. By living wisely depart from—Pr. 15:24.
Is evil.—Wicked make covenant with —Is. 28:15, 18. Wicked debase themselves into—Is. 57:9.
God brings down to.—I Sam 2:6.
God brings back from.—I Sam. 2:6; II Sam. 22:6, 7; Ps. 18:5, 6.
SPIRIT. *Heb.* Neshamah; *Gr.* Pneuma.
Used in reference to God.—Gen. 41:38; Ex. 31:3; 35:31; Num. 24:2; Job 26:13; 27:3; 33:4; Ps. 104:30; 139:7; 143:10; Is. 30:1; 34:16; 40:13; 48:16; 63:14; Ez. 36:27; 37:14; Mic. 2:7; 3:8; Hag. 2:5; Zech. 4:6; John 4:24; II Cor. 3:17, 18.
An entity (real being).—Job 10:12; 14:10; 32:8, 18; 34:14; Pr. 20:27; Is. 38:16; 42:5; 57:16; Zech. 12:1; Mt. 27:50; Lu. 24:37; Acts 23:8, 9; I Cor. 2:11-15; 14:14-16, 32; Heb. 12:23; Jas. 4:5. See Ez. 1:12, 20; 10:17; Mt. 14:26; Mk. 6:49.

Came forth from God—Job 26:4; I Cor. 2:12.
Returns to God—Ps. 31:5; Eccl. 12:7; Lu. 23:46; Acts 7:59. Spirit came again (*seems to mean* animation)—Ju. 15:19. Lu. 8:55.
Contrast between flesh and spirit.—Is. 31:3; Lu. 24:39; John 3:6; I Cor. 5:3-5; 7:34; 15:44, 45; II Cor. 5:1-8; 7:1; Col. 2:5; I Thess. 5:23; Jas. 2:26; I Pet. 3:18; 4:6.
Spirits of all flesh—Num. 16:22; 27:16.
Soul and spirit—I Thess. 5:23; Heb. 4:12.
Equivalent to person.—Gen. 41:8; Job 10:12; Ps. 77:3, 6; 106:33; Gal. 6:18; II Tim. 4:22; I John 4:1, 3.
Seat of emotion—Intellect—Heart. —Gen. 41:8; 45:27; Num. 14:24; Deut. 2:30; Josh. 5:1; I Ki. 21:5; I Chr. 5:25, 26; II Chr. 9:4; 21:16; Ezra 1:1, 5; Job 6:4; 15:13; 17:1; 20:3; 34:14; Ps. 32:2; 76:12; 77:3, 6; 78:8; 142:3; 143:4, 7; Pr. 14:29; 16:2, 32; 25:28; Eccl. 7:9; 10:4; Is. 29:9; Jer. 51:11; Ez. 13:3; Hag. 1:14; Zech. 6:8; Mal. 2:15, 16; Lu. 1:47; Rom. 1:9; II Cor. 2:13; 7:1, 13; 16:18; II Thess. 2:2.
Anguish of—Ex. 6:9; Job 7:11. Bound in—Acts 20:22; Broken—Ps. 51:17; Pr. 15:4, 13; 17:22; 18:14. Contrite—Ps. 34:18; 57:15; Is. 66:2. Cool—Pr. 17:27. Excellent—Dan. 5:12; 6:3. Fainting—Ez. 21:7. Fearfulness—II Tim. 1:7. Fervent in—Acts 18:25; Rom. 12:1. Gentle —I Cor. 4:21; Gal. 6:1. Grieved in—Is. 54:6; Dan. 7:15. Groaned in—John 11:33. Haughty—Pr. 16:18. Humble—Is. 57:15. Meek —I Pet. 3:4. New—Ez. 11:19; 18:31; 36:26; Rom. 7:6; Eph. 4:23.

TOPICAL INDEX

Patient—Eccl. 7:8. Poor in—Mt. 5:3. Proud—Eccl. 7:8. Provoked in—Acts 17:16. Purposed in—Acts 19:16. Quiet—I Pet. 3:4. Sighed in His—Mk. 8:12. Sorrowful—I Sam. 1:15; I Ki. 21:5. Strong in—Lu. 1:80. Troubled in—Dan. 2:1, 3; John 13:21. Willing—Ps. 51:12. *Offerings for tabernacle*—Ex. 35: 21-29. *Disciples of Jesus*—Mt. 26: 41; Mk. 14:38. *Paul*—Rom. 7:14-25.
Evil spirits.—Acts 19:15, 16; Eph. 2:2. Sent from God—Ju. 9:23; I Sam. 16:14-16, 23; 18:10; 19:9; I Ki. 22:21-24; II Chr. 18:20-23.
Error, Of—Is. 29:24; I John 4:6.
Falsehood—Mic. 2:11.
Familiar—Lev. 19:31; 20:27; Is. 29: 4. *The Necromancer of En-dor*—I Sam. 28:7-9. *Saul punished for consulting*—I Chr. 10:13. *Manasseh punished for associating with*—II Chr. 33:6-13.
Greed—Pr. 28:25.
Hasty—Pr. 14:29; Eccl. 7:9.
Jealousy—Num. 5:30.
Lying—I Ki. 22:22.
Perverse—Is. 19:14.
Seducing—I Tim. 4:1.
Unclean—Zech. 13:2; Mt. 8:16; 12: 43-45; Mk. 1:23-27; 3:11, 12, 20; 5:2-16; 6:7; 7:25-30; 9:17-27; Lu. 4:33-36; 6:18; 7:21; 8:26-36; 9: 38-43; 11:24-26; Acts 5:16; 8:7; 19:13-16; Rev. 16:13, 14.
Whoredom, Of—Hos. 4:12; 5:4.
Miscellaneous uses of the word "spirit": Adoption, Of—Rom. 8: 15. Antichrist, Of—I John 4:3. Bondage, Of—Rom. 8:15. Burning, Of—Is. 4:4. Different—II Cor. 11:4; I John 4:1, 3. Divination, Of—Acts 16:16-18. Egypt, Of—Is. 19:3. Excellent—Dan. 5:12; 6:3. Faith, Of—Pr. 11:13; II Cor. 4:13. Grace, Of—Zech. 12:10. Holiness, Of—Rom. 1:4. Infirmity, Of—Lu. 13:11. Just men, Of—Heb. 12:23. Justice, Of—Is. 4:4; 28:6. Letter and spirit—Rom. 2:2. Life giving—John 6:63; I Cor. 15:45; II Cor. 3:6. See Is. 38:16; Rom. 8:2-11; Gal. 6:8; I Pet. 3:18; 4:6. Ministering—Heb. 1:14. Prophecy, Of—Rev. 19:10. Prophets, Of—I Cor. 14:32. Seven spirits of God—Rev. 1:4; 3:1; 4:5; 5:6. Sleep, Of—Is. 29:10. Stupor, Of—Rom. 11:8. Supplication, Of—Zech. 12:10. Truth, Of—John 14:17; 15:26; 16:13; I John 4:6. *In spirit and in truth*—John 4:23. Unity of—Eph. 4:1-6; Phil. 1:27. See Acts 4:32; I Cor. 1:10-13; 6:17; II Cor. 12:18. Vexation of—Is. 65:14. Walking in—II Cor. 12:18. Wisdom, Of—Pr. 1:23. *Workmen under Moses*—Ex. 28:3. Joshua—Deut. 34:9. See Num. 27:18, 23. *Jesus*—Is. 11:2. *Ephesians*—Eph. 1:17. World, Of—I Cor. 2:12.
TRIBULATION. Deut. 4:30. Anguish, And—Rom. 2:9. Come out of—Rev. 7:14. Deliver you up—I Sam. 26:24; Mt. 24:9. Faint at—Eph. 3:13. Flesh, In—I Cor. 7:28. Great—Mt. 24:21, 29; Mk. 13:24; 7:14; Rev. 2:22. Know thy—Rev. 2:9. Many—Acts 14:22. Partaker in—Rev. 2:10. Patient in—Rom. 12:12. Rejoice in—Rom. 5:3. Separate us from Christ—Rom. 8:35. Stedfastness, Worketh—Rom. 5:3. Stephen, About—Acts 11:19. Suffer—I Thess. 3:4. Ten days—Rev. 2:10. Word, Because of—Mt. 13:21; Mk. 4:17. World, In the—John 15:33.

WHAT THE BIBLE SAYS ABOUT THE END TIME

WATCHFULNESS. Pr. 8:34; Mt. 24: 42-51; 25:13; Mk. 13:35; Lu. 12: 35-48; Acts 20:31; I Cor. 10:12; Eph. 6:18; Col. 4:2; I Thess. 5:6; I Pet. 5:8; Rev. 3:2; 16:15.

WICKED: Source of wickedness in the heart. — Set to do evil — Eccl. 8:11; 9:3. Wash thy heart — Jer. 4: 14; Jas. 4:8. Soul of wicked desireth — Ps. 36:4; 52:3; Pr. 2:14; 10:23; 15:21; 21:10; Hos. 4:18. Out of the heart proceeds evil — Mt. 12:34, 35; 15:18, 19; Mk. 7:21-23; Lu. 6:45. Loving darkness rather than light — John 3:19. Evil heart of unbelief — Ps. 34:14; Heb. 3:12.

God's attitude toward. — Will not justify them — Ex. 23:7; Deut. 10:17. See Is. 5:23. Withdrawn Spirit — Gen. 6:3; Hos. 4:17; Rom. 1:24, 26, 28. Angry with them — Ps. 7:11; 11:5, 6; 78:49-51; Is. 13:9; 62:10; Jer. 4:4; 5:9; 21:5; Ez. 5:13; Rom. 2:5; Col. 3:6; Rev. 21:8; 22:18. Shall be turned back to Sheol — Ps. 9:17; 49:14. He shall judge them — Ps. 75:2-4; Eccl. 3:17. Will punish the wicked — Ps. 50:22; 68: 2; 119:119; 129:4; 146:9; 147: 6; Pr. 3:33; 10:3; 11:8; Is. 1:20; 5:24; 13:11; 14:5; 24:6; 26:21; 47:14; 50:11; Jer. 8:12; 12:3; 30: 14; Ez. 3:19; 21:32; Amos 1:3-15; 2:1-16; Mic. 6:3. Punishment for sin — Gen. 3:6. Hell — Mk. 9: 43. The Judgment — II Pet. 2:4. Their light put out — Job 18:5; 21: 17; Pr. 13:9; 20:20; 24:20; Is. 8:22. Their seed cut off — Ps. 21: 10; 37:9, 28; Pr. 2:22; 10:30. Stripped and banished — Ps. 92;7; 104:35; Ez. 22:15; Mt. 25:26-30. Shall be condemned — Ps. 91:8; 145:20; Pr. 12:2; 16:4; Eccl. 8:13; Is. 28:21, 22; Jer. 14:12; Ez. 18: 4. Given over to reprobate mind — Rom. 1:24-28. Have part in lake of fire — Mt. 5:22, 29, 30; 13:42, 50; Rev. 19:20; 21:8.

Description of. — Children in whom there is no faithfulness — Deut. 32: 20. Children of transgression — Is. 57:4. Children of disobedience — Eph. 2:2; 5:6; Col. 3:6. Children of the devil — Mt. 13:38; John 8:44; Acts 13:10; I John 3:10. Children of the flesh — Rom. 9:8. Children who will not hear the law of the Lord — Is. 30:9. Rebellious children — Is. 1:2; 30:1. See Is. 65:2. Lying children — Is. 30:9. Servants of sin — John 8:34; Rom. 6:20. Servants of corruption — II Pet. 2:19. Unprofitable servants — Mt. 25:30. Seed of falsehood — Is. 57:4. Seed of the wicked — Ps. 37:28; Mt. 13:38. Seed of evil-doers — Is. 1:4; 14:20. Lovers of darkness — John 3:19-20. Despisers of God — Job 21:14. Dead in trespasses and sins — Eph. 2:1-3.

Results of wickedness. — Reap as they sow — Job 4:8; Pr. 22:8; Hos. 10: 13; Gal. 6:7-8. Eat fruit of their deeds — Pr. 1:31; Jer. 6:19. Fall by their own wickedness — Pr. 5: 22, 23; 11:5, 19. Wrath responds to expectation — Pr. 11:23. Overthrown by; wickedness — Ps. 27:2; Pr. 13:6, 21. Driven out of power — Ez. 31:11. No peace — Is. 57:20, 21. Indignation and wrath their lot — Rom. 2:8. Wages of sin is death — Rom. 6:23. Disinherited — I Cor. 6:9, 10; Gal. 5:19-21; Eph. 5:5. Everlasting destruction — II Thess. 1:9. Brings many sorrows — Ps. 16: 4; 32:10; Is. 47:11. Chaff — Job 21:18; Ps. 1:4; Mt. 3:12. Tares — Mt. 13:38-41. Autumn trees without fruit—Jude 12. Clouds without water—II Pet. 2:17. Springs without water—II Pet. 2:17. Fools building on sand—Mt. 7:26, 27; Lu. 6:49. Whited sepulchres—Mt. 23:27. Raging waves of the sea—Jude 13. Wandering stars—Jude 13. Goats—Mt. 25:32-33. Swine—Mt. 7:6; II Pet. 2:22. Blind—Zeph. 1:17; Mt. 15:14; 23:16-24. Bad fish—Mt. 13:48. Corrupt trees—Mt. 7:17, 18; Lu. 6:43.

Index of Scriptures

Old Testament

Genesis
1:1 222
1:26 351
2:7 . . . . 322,351,354, 361,369
2:8 282
2:9,16,17 282,321
2:17 86,321
3:3 282,283
3:15 69,70,209
3:19 353
3:22-24 287,321
3:24 282
4:1 285
4:1-7 285
5:4,5 86
5:24 186
6:11 82
6:17 369,370
7:16 370
7:22 369,370
8:22 96
10:1 263
12:1-3 27,56
12:2,3 96
17:1,2 227
17:7,8 225,227
18:10 235
18:25 306
21:12 235
37:7,8 144
37:9 144
37:11 144
46:27 85
49:1 120

Exodus
1:5 356
7:1 2
12:14,17 227
12:40,41 229
13:16 91
31:16,17 227
32:32 320
34:6 319
40:15 271

Leviticus
16:34 227
17:10-12 368
23:11,41 227
24:8,9 227

Numbers
2:33 243
14:34 113,177,181
16:22 352,369
22:16 362
16:30,33 304
24:20 120

Deuteronomy
4:8 31
4:30 120,247
13:1-5 28
17:16 118,193
18:15-19 55,105,109
23:2 227
31:16 300

WHAT THE BIBLE SAYS ABOUT THE END TIME

31:29 120
32:21 238
32:22 306
32:29 238

Joshua
8:28 227
17:16 93

Judges
6:33 93
10:14 247

Ruth
4:12-22 347

I Samuel
18:18 247
26:24 247
28:11-19 302,328
28:15 302

II Samuel
12:33 302,316

I Kings
11:43 301
14:20,31 301
15:8,24 301
16:6,28 301
19:14-18 238

II Kings
2:11 186
5:27 227
8:24 301
10:35 301
13:9,13 301
14:16,22,29 301
15:7,22,38 301
16:20 301
20:21 301
21:18 301
24:6 301

I Chronicles
Chs.1-9 263
1:5 263
5:5 263

II Chronicles
2:4 227

Job
1:12 78
2:6 78
14:12 300
14:21 301
14:21,22 300
17:6 304
27:3 361
32:8 351
38:4 361

Psalms
Ps. 2 52,56,105
2:8 50,105
6:5 300
Ps. 16 100
16:8-11 56
Ps. 23 302
23:4 272
23:4,6 304
Ps. 24 212,213
50:10 54
51:5 332,346
63:18 300
88:10 300
88:12 300
90:4 54,74,204
103:9 319
110:1 56,100,105
. . . . 118,138
115:17 300
139:13ff 356
139:13-17 361
146:4 300

Ecclesiastes
9:4-10 301
9:5 267,270
12:7 322,361,369
12:12 327
12:13,14 326

INDEX OF SCRIPTURES

Isaiah
2:2	120
2:2,3	56
9:6-8	37
11:4	170
11:6-9	280
13:1-22	142
13:1,9,10,13	142
13:9,10	218
14:9-11	300,327
14:14	171
28:16,17	56,237
34:1-4	143
34:4,5,9,10	143
38:2	92
40:22	90
45:18	96
53:1	237
59:2	343
65:1,2	237
65:17	96,222
65:25	280

Jeremiah
12:4	120
15:9	144
23:5-7	119
23:20	119
30:3	111
30:5-17	247,248
30:24	120
31:27	119
31:29	347,348
31:29,30	331,332
31:31	11,114,119
31:33	120,329
31:31-34	348
31:34	286
31:38	119
48:47	120
49:39	120

Ezekiel
Chs. 1-6	70
4:6	13,177,181
18:1-4,19,20	331
18:2	332,347
18:3	348
18:4	357
18:4,20	325,348
18:20	325,348
32:7,8	143
32:21	328
32:31	327
Chs. 38-45	261,262
38:2	92,264
38:3	263
38:5	70
38:6	92
38:15	264
38:16	120,261,263
Ch. 39	261
39:1	263
39:4	261
39:6	263
Ch. 40	261
Chs. 40-48	21
40:38-43	261
40:46	261
Ch. 43	261
43:18-27	261
43:19	261
43:20-28	261
44:15-31	57
44:23,24	261
45:17	144,261
45:22,23	261
45:24,25	261
46:2	57,114
46:2-5	261
46:4	261
46:12	261
47:12	31

Daniel
Ch. 2	46,52,110,116
2:28	120
2:31-35	110
2:34-45	110
2:36-45	110
2:44	14,41
7:22	91
7:25	154,170,177
8:19	125
8:25	154,174
Ch. 9	46,52,116
9:24-27	110,112,181
9:25	113
10:14	120
11:31	248
11:36	154,174
12:1	247
12:2	301
12:11	247

Hosea
3:5	120

Joel
2:1-3	247
2:10,30,31	144
2:28-31	11,85,105, 120,146,147,218
3:15	144

Amos
9:11-14	56

Obadiah
4	174
15,16	218

Jonah
2:6	227

Micah
3:6	120,144
4:1,2	56,120

Zephaniah
1:14-3:8	218
3:19	31

Zechariah
Ch. 14	114
14:6	114
14:12-17	114

Malachi
3:1	219
4:1	324,325
4:1-3	346
4:5	219

New Testament

Matthew
1:2-6	347
1:17	259
2:2-9	107
3:16,17	113
5:12	324
10:28	304,322
10:41,42	324
11:7-14	219
11:12	187
11:16	259
11:23	174,304
11:25	74
12:22-24	79
12:22-32	79
12:29	79
12:33	37,62
12:39,41,42,45	259
12:45	9
13:4	187
13:19	187
13:24-33	183,197,208
13:28-30	197
13:30	25,184
13:30-43	163
13:33	92

INDEX OF SCRIPTURES

13:37-43 197	24:3-25:46. 208
13:39-42. 25,198	24:3-51 134
13:41 37,183	24:6. 150
13:47-50 37,198,208	24:7 150,151
16:4. 259	24:14 199,200
16:6. 334	24:15 138,248
16:11. 259	24:15-18 136
16:13-18 37	24:16-28 141
16:13-28 57	24:21. 247,249,251
16:18,19 140,187,306	22:22. 252
16:27. 218	24:23-27 195
16:27,28 218	24:23,24 252
16:28 108,140,146,	24:29. 141,144,145
218,258	24:29-31 141
17:1-3 302	24:30,31 146,147,247
17:17. 256	24:32,33 147,255,256
18:9. 309	24:34 132,133,139,
18:10. 316	141,146,259
18:14. 319	24:35. 141
18:16. 118	24:35-51 211
19:14. 316	24:36 111,139,141,152
19:30. 9	24:37-39. 136,218
21:1-11. 108,137	24:38-40 136
21:12-16 137	24:39. 136
21:18 254,256	24:40,41 36
21:19. 256	24:41. 36
21:27. 137	24:43. 195
21:28-32 137	24:43,44 136
21:33-45 137	24:44. 152
21:46. 137	25:1-13 208
22:1-14 137	25:14-30 324
22:14. 137	25:31-46 222
22:16-32 137	27:20. 314
22:32. 89	27:64. 10
22:41-45 138	**Mark**
23:1-12 138	3:23-30 79
23:13-36 138	9:1 108,258
23:15,23 138	9:35. 9
23:36. 259	9:43,45,47. 304
23:37-39 138	11:1-10 107
Ch. 24 35,145,152,260	Ch. 13 35
24:2 139,150	13:3-37. 134,208
24:3 139,248	13:14. 248

13:28,29 255
13:29 256
13:30 258
15:12-14 221
16:16 285,333

Luke

1:3 255
2:9-11,13,14 211
4:14 80
4:18,19 81
4:21 81
6:23 324
9:27 108,140,258
9:30,31 302
10:15 304
10:17-19 80
11:14-23 79
11:20 80
12:5 304
12:10 79
12:35-38 126,202
12:42-46 202,215
12:45,46 126
12:47,48 325
13:3 257
13:6-9 256
14:9,10 9
15:13 290
15:24 290
15:32 279
16:19-31 300,302,327,
357,368
16:22,23 306,322
16:23 304,366
16:24-28 300,302
16:25 367
16:25-27 300,302
16:26 302
19:11-27 324
Ch. 21 35
21:6-35 134
21:8-36 208
21:20 146,248,249,260
21:21-28 249

21:23,24 250
21:29 257
21:31 257
21:32 258
23:37-43 107
23:43 306,307
24:21 311
24:39 295
24:47 242
24:50 212
24:51 182

John

1:3 351
1:10,11 221
1:29 113
1:33 113
2:19 120,139
2:19-22 138
3:3-5 334
3:18 309,310
4:22 242
4:24 352,362,365,366
5:23ff 353
5:28,29 51,55,85,184,
199,222,322,345
6:14,15 48
6:15 109,187
6:39 10,120
6:40 10,120
6:44 10,120
6:54 10,120
6:66 48,109
7:35 . . . . 10,ß137
8:9 9
8:44 349
10:12 187
10:28,29 188
10:34 358
11:4-14 301
11:24 10,120
12:12-19 107
12:16 59,124
12:48 10,120
13:33-37 57
14:1-3 211
14:1-6 189

INDEX OF SCRIPTURES

14:2	328
14:3	182,202,203, 218,312
14:23	201,208
14:26	252
16:33	71,247,252
17:4	59
17:21	81
18:33,38	107
18:36,37	48,49
19:14,15	221
19:33-37	57
20:1-7	307
20:23	108
20:30,31	295

Acts

1:8	9,50,105,242
1:9-11	182,212
1:11	218,219
2:4	100,122
2:5	242
2:14	242
2:16	11,56
2:16-21	120,146
2:16-35	55
2:17	10,120,122
2:22	242
2:22-32	56
2:23	56,237
2:27,31	304
2:29	109
2:29-37	56,101,118
2:30-36	56
2:36-38	239
2:38	285,333
2:39	242
2:41	239
3:1,2	241
3:19-24	56,219
3:20,21	312
3:21	220
3:24	11,56,105
4:21-31	56
4:23-28	52,105
6:1-7	239
7:56	182
7:59	322
7:60	301
8:39	188
10:12	241
10:19	240
10:37,38	80
10:38	113
11:28	151
12:21-23	174
13:33	52,56,105
13:41	9
14:22	247
15:7-9	242
15:7-11	245
15:14-18	51
17:11	125,224
17:24	174
17:28	321,323,354
17:28,29	362,369
20:21	242
20:29,30	173
23:10	188
26:17,20	252

Romans

1:5	237,339
1:10	242
2:28,29	50,56,117,244
3:1,2	241,242
3:4	1,220
4:11	50,56,118
5:3	247
5:12	280
5:12-21	290,320,342,345
5:12ff	352,353
5:14	270
Ch. 6	55,237
6:1-11	50,321
6:3-5	289
6:4	280
6:12-18	237
6:16-18	325,339

6:23 322,324,326	**I Corinthians**
8:12,13 352	3:8-15 324
8:18-23 207	3:16,17 174
8:35-39 89,247,254	6:2 91
Chs. 9-11 234	6:17-19 353
9:4 242	6:19 174
9:6-8 244,245	10:6,11 37
9:8,9 235	14:33 310
9:9-12 235	Ch. 15 312
9:11 235	15:6,18,51 301
9:14-16 236	15:8 9
9:19-24 236	15:20-26 290
9:24-32 236	15:22 10,286,353
9:29 236	15:20-26 290
10:1 236	15:20-28 320
10:4 237	15:20-55 321
10:8 17,237	15:21,22 342,344,345
10:9-13 237	15:22 10,286,353
10:11-13 237	15:24,25 95
10:11-21 237	15:26 9,95
10:12 237,241,245	15:27,28 52,95
10:16,20,21 239	15:35-38 295,329
10:17 339	15:42-44 353
10:19 228	15:42ff 368
Ch. 11 238	15:44 329
11:1 238	15:50-58 184,270
11:2,3 238	15:51,52 189,199,296
11:4 106	15:53,54 321,322,325,328
11:5 238	15:54-58 329
11:6 238	15:55 304
11:7 239,240	**II Corinthians**
11:11,12,15 223	1:4 247
11:11-15 240	5:1ff 352
11:12 243	5:2 364
11:16-24 248	5:3,4 369
11:18 242	5:6-9 309,364
11:22-36 223	5:8 366
11:25 239,240,243	5:8,9 88,309,327
11:26 243,245,246	5:10 270,271,309,
12:12 247	322,326,327
14:11,12 319	5:17 278
15:26 237	7:4 247
16:26 325,339	8:16 174
	12:1-4 278
	12:2 188
	12:3,4 186,188
	12:4 306
	13:1 118,193

INDEX OF SCRIPTURES

Galatians
1:6,7 252
2:20 12
3:1 252
3:6-9 50,56,118,244
3:26-29 50,56,58,118,241
3:27 285,321
4:4 243
4:25,26 226
4:26 144,182,221
5:1 262
5:2 262
5:4 262
5:7 262
6:14 212
6:14-16 50
6:16 56,70,118,244

Ephesians
1:20-22 83
Ch. 2 55
2:1 87
2:1-3 87
2:1-8 321
2:1-9 50
2:2,5 343
2:4-6 87
2:7,8 88,325
2:11-22 50,56,118,240
2:5-10 222
2:21 174
3:1-13 240
3:4-9 240
3:13 247
4:8 308
6:10-18 51
6:12 70

Philippians
1:21 1
2:6,7 312
2:12-16 215
3:2-4 243
3:2-11 236
3:21 353

3:3 50,56,118
3:4-11 238
3:20 99
3:20,21 85,220

Colossians
1:23 200
2:12,13 50,295,321
2:15 308
3:3,4 55
3:11 56,118

I Thessalonians
1:9,10 210
1:10 125
2:19 125,210
3:4 247
3:13 125,310
4:13-17 4,125,160,181,183,
187,188,210,221,312,313
4:13,14 301
4:14 310,327
4:16,17 125,220
4:17 184,220
5:1-4 196
5:2 199
5:23 125,210,352,361,
369,370

II Thessalonians
1:6 247,249
1:7-10 183
1:9,10 322,325
1:11,12 32
Ch. 2 160,165,171
2:1-3 125,161
2:1-12 33,168
2:3,4 125,154,168,
173,174
2:5 125
2:8 154,161,168,
170,179
2:9 168
2:10 168

I Timothy
1:13 241
2:11 169
2:14 342
4:1-3 172,174
4:3,4 283
4:10 221
6:16 321,325

II Timothy
2:19 327
3:1 10,120
3:1-5 172
3:6 122
3:13 35
3:16 6,122
4:3,4 172

Titus
2:13 209
3:5 335

Hebrews
1:1 122
1:2 10,11,120
1:3 201,221
1:10 11
2:7ff 353
5:1-10 263
6:13-20 263
Ch. 7 57
7:11-17 .57
7:11-28 263
7:26-28 57
8:1-5 263
8:4 57
8:6-13 263
8:8-11 11,58,119,120
8:8-13 348
8:13 114,145,157
9:1-10 263
9:6-10 263
9:11-28 263
9:22 263
9:24-28 57,287
9:27 8,270,271,327
9:27,28 184,209
9:28 218
10:1-11 263
10:1-25 263
10:10-14 113
10:19-22 57
11:5 186
11:7 136
11:9 228
11:11-16 328
12:1 89
12:9 352
12:18-20 226
12:19 263
12:22-24 56,223

James
1:2 247
2:26 354,358
3:6 304
5:3 10,120
5:7,8 210

I Peter
1:5 10
1:5,20 220
1:11 221
1:18-20 120
2:1-6 57
2:9 54,57,118
3:19 302,315
3:19,20 307
3:21 285
4:12,13 247

II Peter
1:13,14 363,364
1:20,21 2,101
2:1-3 173
2:4 304,306
2:5 136
2:20 9
3:3 10,120
3:4 267,301
3:5-13 52

INDEX OF SCRIPTURES

3:8 54,74,204,209
3:9 316,320
3:10 163,195
3:10-13 97,209,222

I John
2:18 10,120,155
2:18-22 154,168
2:19 159,168
2:20,21 168
2:24-28 168
3:3 208
3:2,3 217
4:1-3 295
4:1-6 158,168
4:3 154
4:4-6 168
4:8,16 319

II John
7 154,158,168,295

Jude
6 322
13 322
14,15 191
18 10,120
18:21 210
23 188

Revelation
Ch. 1 62
1:3 72
1:6 184
1:7 220
1:9 71,77
1:18 304
1:19 62,71
Chs. 2,3 53
2:7 282,306,328
Chs. 4-7 63

4:8 77
5:2 79
5:9,10 64,214
5:10 184
5:12,13 214
6:8 304
6:9 89
6:9-11 300,327
6:10,11 89,328
6:16 223
7:2 79
7:4-8 245
7:9,10 64
7:11 65
7:13 65
7:14 247,249
7:14-17 65,239
Chs. 8-11 65
9:11 79
9:12 264
10:1 79
11:2 177
11:15 33,66
11:17 67
Chs. 12-19 66
12:5 188
12:6 177
13:1-10 112
13:5 154
14:9-11 13
14:13 89,327
15:3 79
16:7 77
16:13-16 4,93
16:14 77
16:16 51
17:10,11 177
18:1 79
19:6,15 77
19:11-16 67
19:15 95
Chs. 20-22 67
Ch. 20 29,51,54,65,67,145
20:1 81

20:1-10 4,77,93	20:12,13 85,86,271,321,322,
20:2 67,82	325,326,327,328
20:2-7 75,85,89	20:13 222,312
20:3 82,329	20:13,14 304
20:4 22,184	20:14 86,329,343
20:4-6 74,85,89	20:15 305
20:5,6 321	Ch. 21 65
20:5-15 76	21:3 329
20:6 184	21:4 329
20:6,14,15 279	21:6 90
20:8 92,163	21:22 67,77
20:9,10 79,82,226	Ch. 22 65,67
20:10 325,328	22:2,14,19 282,328
20:11-15 15,179,222,299,	22:3 90,223,329
309,322	22:4 329
20:11-22:5 222	22:5 85,329

Index of Subjects

Abomination of desolation 148, 248, 260
Abraham's bosom 303, 306, 308
Amillennialism 24, 25, 35, 53-60 (See *Millennialism*)
Annihilationism (Nihilism) 291, 323, 324
Antichrist 7, 40, 41, 42, 43, 154-158, 161, 164-168, 170-172, 206
Apocalyptic language 72-74, 135, 142-147
Armstrongism 112, 141, 182, 191, 227, 234, 262, 324
Astrology 11, 14, 15
Battle of Armageddon 4, 7, 34, 35, 43, 69, 70, 90, 206
Beasts (mark) 66, 76, 91
Binding, loosing of Satan 38, 41, 44, 50, 71, 74, 75, (71-85), 318
Daniel's 70 week vision 46, 112-118, 181

Darby-Schofield Hypothesis 42, 43, 103, 140, 252, 253, 257, 258
Date setting fiascos 125-130
Days of Noah 7, 36, 136, 164
Death and Dying 256-290
  After death experiences 276-278
  Metaphysical representations 87, 279, 120
  Origin of Death 280-290
  Physical death 85-88, 256-283, 287-290
  Second death 86, 279
Destruction of Jerusalem 14, 114, 145, 148-152, 199, 200, 248, 250-252, 260, 262
Dispensationalism 45-48, 103-108
Eschatology 7-22
  Defined 8-11
  Demythologized 13-22
  Scope 12, 95, 96

INDEX OF SUBJECTS

Eternal-Everlasting
  Age-lasting: "for ever" 227
  Endless: "for ever and ever" 74, 287, 319, 329, 330
Equitable punishment 322, 323, 324-326
Fig tree 254-260
Fullness of Israel, etc. 243-246
Gap hypothesis 42, 46, 103, 104, 108, 109, 140, 206, 258
Gog and Magog 76, 92, 93, 226, 261-265
Gnosticism 155-158, 295
Grace redemption 322-334
Great tribulation 7, 40, 41, 177, 181, 246-253
Hades-Sheol 302-312
  Compartmentalized View 302, 305, 327
  Limbo-purgatory 313-318
  Semi-intermediate state 308-313
Hell-Gehenna 51, 304-306, 313, 316, 317, 322
Immortality 296, 321, 322, 326-330
  Conditional 321, 323
  Innate 295, 296
Intermediate state 293-330
Israel in prophecy 95-97, 99, 225-245, 262
Jehovah's Witnesses 27, 28, 34, 35, 98, 130-133, 182, 245, 323, 324
Judgment 308-310, 324, 325
Kingdom 95-118
  Church and Kingdom 49, 55, 99-101, 103-118
  Messiah's Kingdom 50, 95-118
  Parables of Kingdom 36, 37, 190, 197-199
Latter (last) days 119-135
Limbo-purgatory 313-317
Man of Sin 154, 159-179
Mark of the beast 75, 91
Martyred saints 91, 92

Millennialism 4, 15-22, 23-37, 38-60, 61-94
  Definitions 23-25
  General theory 38, 39
  History in Christian era 23-27
  Pedigree (origin) 15-22
  Millennium of Revelation Twenty 54, 74-94
Millennial Theories 23-37, 38-60
  Amillennialism 24, 25, 35, 53-60
  Postmillennialism 24, 32, 33, 48-53, 60
  Premillennialism 23, 32, 33, 40-47, 60, 81
  Simple historical premillennialism 23, 32, 33, 40, 41, 46, 47
  Tribulational premillennialism 42-44, 181
  Ultradipsensational premillennialism 45-47, 60, 246
Nebuchadnezzar's image-vision 46, 110-112, 116
Olivet Discourse 36, 134-153, 199, 211, 248, 259
Original sin 283-287, 320 See also: *Appendix: Excursus on Original Sin: "The Big Lie"*
Paradise 36, 143-145, 307, 308, 312
Pre and Post Millennialism; See: *Millennial Theories*
Purgatory-Limbo 313-317
Rapture 3, 38, 41, 42, 43, 51, 55, 180-201, 206, 310-312
Regathering of Israel 225-245
Reincarnation 297-299
Resurrection 296, 312
  First and Second 55, 76, 85-89
  General 312
  Saints 311, 312, 321
  Wicked 313

Revelation, Book of: 61-71
  Chapter Twenty 18, 29, 54, 74-94
  Diagram 68
  Format 61, 62
  Overview 61-71
Schofield 42, 45, 57, 97, 103, 116, 140, 150, 252, 255, 256, 257, 258
Scare tactics 27, 131-133
Second Coming 23, 38, 40, 43, 51, 202-233
  Certainty 207-213
  Manner 189-195, 218, 219
Purpose 51, 219-223
Time 214-217
Signs of the times 119-153
Sheol-Hades — See:
  Intermediate State
Soul Sleeping 299-302, 209, 311
Tartarus 303, 304, 306
Transmigration of souls 296-298
Universalism 256, 257, 318-320
Ultradispensationalism — See:
  Millennial theories
Usher chronology 13, 14, 22
Zionism 206, 231, 232, 256